D0357697

Discover
Italy

Experience the
best of Italy

This edition written and researched by

Abigail Blasi,
Cristian Bonetto, Kerry Christiani, Gregor Clark, Duncan
Garwood, Paula Hardy, Virginia Maxwell, Brendan Sainsbury,
Helena Smith, Donna Wheeler

Contents

Plan Your Trip

Discover

Contents

Discover Italy

In Focus

Survival Guide

This Is Italy

Italy positively overflows with charm and brilliance. It's endlessly amazing, ebullient and highly strung, like any bona fide genius.

This is a country that's blessed with natural splendour.
Italy effortlessly combines knife-edge mountains, glimmering beaches, hilltop towns and the royal-blue Mediterranean. It's packed with artistic masterpieces: Leonardo, Michelangelo, Raphael, Verdi and Puccini have all left their mark. It's full of Unesco World Heritage Sites (49 at last count), with the evocative remains of lost empires ready to be explored. There are the exquisite cities: Florence, Venice and Rome, to name a few, and beautiful towns and villages, such as Lucca, Positano, Ravello, and Orvieto.

Italians themselves are full of warmth and wit, and often notably handsome.
The nation might sometimes feel more like a collection of regions, but there's a shared love of celebration, particularly if food's involved. Festivals take place all year round; you don't have to wait for Venice's Carnevale or yet another World Cup victory to party in the streets.

And oh, the food and wine...
Most locals would argue, with good reason, that their cuisine is the best in the world. Thanks to ancient volcanoes and an unusually sunny disposition, there's always some seasonal speciality bursting with flavour, and it will be delivered to you atop the best pasta or risotto you will eat in this lifetime. City-state turf battles long fought by armies are now waged by *pizzaioli* (pizza makers) over the correct thickness of a crust – best not to get the Neapolitans and Romans started. Just eat and smile, which should be easy.

Italy wears its millennia of turbulent history extraordinarily well.
Roman towns such as Pompeii, Herculaneum and Ostia Antica were stunningly preserved by their better-than-botox masks of mud and volcanic ash. And there are glimpses into the future, too, with myriad cutting-edge design showcases and some dazzling new contemporary art museums.

66
Italy overflows with charm and brilliance
99

Gondolas, Venice (p170)
JEAN-PIERRE LESCOURRET/GETTY IMAGES ©

25

Top Highlights

1. Historic Rome
2. Basilica di San Marco, Venice
3. Amalfi Coast
4. Pompeii
5. Florence
6. Piedmont's Slow Food
7. Lago di Como
8. St Peter's Basilica, Rome
9. Duomo, Milan
10. Rome's Museums
11. Grotta Azzura, Capri
12. Mt Etna
13. Turin
14. Lecce
15. Aeolian Islands
16. Bologna
17. Da Vinci's Last Supper, Milan
18. Italian Riviera
19. Matera
20. Grand Canal, Venice
21. Naples
22. San Gimignano
23. The Dolomites
24. Basilica di San Francesco, Assisi
25. Positano

25 Italy's Top Highlights

Historic Rome

Once *caput mundi* (capital of the world), Rome was spawned by a wolf-suckled wild boy (according to legend), grew to be Western Europe's first superpower, became the spiritual centrepiece of the Christian world, and is now the repository of more than 2500 years worth of European art and architecture. From the Pantheon (p75) and the Colosseum (p70) to Michelangelo's Sistine Chapel (p85) and controversial Caravaggios, there's simply too much for one visit. So toss a coin into the Trevi Fountain (p77) and promise to return. Below: Colosseum

Basilica di San Marco, Venice

Stepping through the portals of Basilica di San Marco (p175), try to imagine what it might have been like for an medieval peasant glimpsing those shimmering gold mosaic domes for the first time. It's not such a stretch – once you see the millions of tiny gilt tesserae cohere into a singular heavenly vision, every leap of human imagination since the 12th century seems comparatively minor.

Amalfi Coast

With its scented lemon groves, flower-strewn cliff-sides, tumbling sherbet-hued towns and bobbing fishing boats, the Amalfi Coast (p306) still claims the crown as the prettiest coast on the peninsula. Hollywood divas and starry-eyed day-trippers alike insist that the stretch from Sorrento to Positano is the least developed and most beautiful. Below: Ravello (p309)

The Best...
Underground Sights

CATACOMBE DI SAN CALLISTO
Rome's subterranean city of the dead, from popes to paupers. (p83)

MATERA
A town of cave-dwellings carved out along a ravine, complete with cave hotels and churches. (p347)

ST PETER'S BASILICA
Book ahead to enter a tunnel to the tomb of St Peter under the basilica. (p86)

NAPOLI SOTTERANEA
Naples' ancient labyrinth of aqueducts, passages and cisterns. (p301)

Ruins of Pompeii

Nothing piques human curiosity quite like a catastrophe, and little beats the ruins of Pompeii (p302), a once thriving Roma town frozen for all time in its 2000-year-old death throes. Wander Roman streets, the grassy, column-lined forum, the city brothel, the 5000-seat theatre and the frescoed Villa dei Misteri, and ponder Pliny the Younger's terrifying account of the tragedy: 'Darkness came on again, again ashes, thick and heavy. We got up repeatedly to shake these off; otherwise we would have been buried and crushed by the weight.'

The Best...
Shopping Destinations

MILAN
Street fashion competes with Fashion Week runways to define Italian style. (p131)

FLORENCE
Exquisite stationery, butter-soft leather goods, rare wines and heavenly scented candles. (p241)

VENICE
Modern artisan-made statement pieces, from marble-paper cocktail rings to Murano glass chandeliers. (p197)

ROME
Backstreet artisans create bespoke wares from handbags to marble carvings. (p104)

5

Renaissance Florence

The heart of Italy's most romanticised region, Florence is tailor-made for aesthetes. From Brunelleschi's Duomo (p228) to Masaccio's Cappella Brancacci (p235) frescoes, Florence, according to Unesco, contains 'the greatest concentration of universally renowned works of art in the world'. Not only this, but beyond Florence's blockbuster museums and flawless Renaissance streetscapes sprawls an undulating wonderland of regional delights.

Above: Duomo

Piedmont's Slow Food

Piedmont offers a staggering menu. Compare the size of the human stomach to the scale of Eataly (p151), the Turin factory converted into a showcase for Slow Food specialities, and you might despair of ever making it through the gauntlet of tasting counters. For a mellower gastronomic experience, take a day trip to the small Piedmont town of Bra, the home of Slow Food.

Lago di Como

Formed at the end of the last Ice Age, dazzling Lago di Como (p135), nestled in the shadow of the Rhaetian Alps, is the most spectacular of the Lombard lakes, and its grand Liberty-style villas are home to movie moguls and Arab sheikhs. Surrounded on all sides by luxurian' greenery, among the lake's siren calls are the landscaped gardens of Villa Serbelloni, Villa Carlotta and Villa Balbianello, which blush pink with camellias, azaleas and rhododendrons in April and May. Above: Bellagio (p139)

St Peter's Basilica, Rome

Many a Renaissance genius was defeated by the puzzle: how do you build a suitable shrine for apostle and church founder St Peter, while making room for all humanity within its portals? Michelangelo topped everyone with a novel solution. Instead of resting the dome of St Peter's Basilica (p86) squarely on angular supports, Michelangelo lifted it high above a rippling colonnade that allows light to flood the vast basilica interiors. The basilica remains grounded over St Peter's tomb, but the dome adds boundless glory.

The Best...
Unbelievable Architecture

ALBEROBELLO
Pugliese stone cottages that look like cupcakes with white icing, or homes for gnomes. (p346)

VENICE BIENNALE
In even-numbered years, Venice's ancient Arsenale shipyards become a launching platform for avant-garde architecture. (p187)

FIERA MILANO
Massimiliano Fuksas upstages Italy's biggest design fair with pavilions that resemble billowing glass sails. (p131)

LEANING TOWER
Tilted climbs up Pisa's Leaning Tower are even giddier on moonlit summer nights. (p244)

Duomo, Milan

Six centuries in the making, Milan's Duomo (p121) is the gran
finale of International Gothic and a monument to Milanese
determination. Candoglia marble had to be hauled from
suburban docks via a canal system, aided by Leonardo da
Vinci–designed hydraulic locks. By the time the cathedral too
shape, Renaissance had replaced Gothic as a favoured global
style. But Milan continued its singular monument.

The Best...
Modern Art Museums

PUNTA DELLA DOGANA
Provocative art fills ancient
Venetian warehouses re-
vamped by architect Tadao
Ando. (p183)

**MUSEO D'ARTE
CONTEMPORANEA**
Art innovations in Turin,
from Arte Povera found-
material sculpture to site-
specific video art. (p150)

MADRE
From Jeff Koons'
uberkitsch *Wild Boy and
Puppy* to Rebecca Horn's
Neapolitan-esque *Spirits*
in Naples. (p286)

**GALLERIA NAZIONALE
D'ARTE MODERNA**
Great Italian and inter-
national modern art dis-
played in a belle epoque
building. (p87)

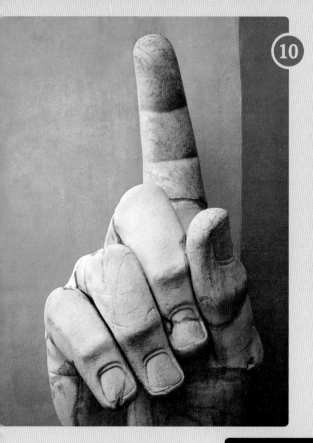

10 Rome's Museums

A browse through your art-history textbook will highlight the names of seminal movements such as classical, Renaissance, mannerist, baroque, futurist and metaphysical – all of which were forged in Italy by a pantheon of artists including Giotto, da Vinci, Michelangelo, Botticelli, Bernini, Caravaggio, Carracci, Boccioni, Balla and de Chirico. Find the best of them in Rome's Vatican Musuems (p85), Museo e Galleria Borghese (p88), Capitoline Museums (p68) and Galleria Nazionale d'Arte Antica (p77). Left: Hand of statue of Emperor Constantine II, Capitoline Museums

Capri's Grotta Azzurra

Some Italian place names embellish the facts, but the water in this sea cave on the isle of Capri really does glow an ethereal blue. Squeeze through the mouth of the cave in a rowboat and experience an optical effect no amusement park ride with artificial lighting can capture. No wonder Romans built a shrine to appease the local water sprite: the Blue Grotto (p297) casts a spell on all who enter.

HAUKE DRESSLER/GETTY IMAGES ©

Mt Etna

Known to the Greeks as the 'column that holds up the sky', Mt Etna (p336) is Europe's largest volcano and one of the world's most active. The ancients believed the giant Tifone (Typhoon) lived in its crater and lit up the sky with regular, spectacular pyrotechnics. At 3323m, it towers above Sicily's Ionian Coast, and since 1987 its slopes have been part of the Parco Naturale dell'Etna, an area that encompasses both Alpine forests and Etna's forbiddingly black summit.

Turin's Savoy Splendour

Like the Medicis in Florence and the Borgheses in Rome, Turin's Savoy princes had a penchant for extravagant royal palaces. The Reggia di Venaria Reale (p147), a hunting lodge of Duke Carlo Emanuele II, is one of the largest royal residences in Europe. The mammoth €200-million-odd restoration of this Unesco-certified building involved the preservation of 1.5 million sq ft of stucco and plasterwork and 11,000 sq ft of frescoes.

Left: Ceiling of Reggia di Venaria Reale

Baroque Lecce

The extravagant architectural character of many Puglian towns is due to the local style of *barocco Leccese*, which features carved sandstone facades with swirling vines, gargoyles and strange zoomorphic figures. Lecce's Basilica di Santa Croce (p348) is the high point of a style that was so outrageously busy, the Marchese Grimaldi said it made him think a lunatic was having a nightmare.

Below: Basilica di Santa Croce

The Best...
Natural Wonders

MT ETNA
Scale the slopes of Europe's most vocal volcano. (p336)

CINQUE TERRE
Secluded coves, rocky bluffs, turquoise waters, tiered vineyards and terraced lemon groves. (p156)

VILLA CARLOTTA
Orange-blossom bowers and camellias perfume a Prussian princess' garden along Largo di Como. (p140)

VULCANO
Black-sand beaches, thermal mud baths and bubbling hot springs beneath an island volcano. (p332)

The Best...
Hill Towns

RAVELLO
Artists' retreats are interrupted by romantic cliff-top sunsets. (p309)

ORVIETO
Truffles, ceramics, white wines and apocalyptic omens inside a pretty pink cathedral. (p265)

MONTALCINO
Medieval town perched atop vineyards, with Brunello wine tastings in the town castle's cellar. (p255)

URBINO
The ideal Renaissance city on a hill, from gracious palaces to glorious frescoes. (p260)

Aeolian Islands

These furiously beautiful volcanic islands (p332) off the coast of Sicily punch far above their weight. With pale white beaches lapped by azure, balmy Mediterranean, set against frozen-lava landscapes, the islands of Lipari, Vulcano, Salina, Panarea, Stromboli, Alicudi and Filicudi well deserve their Unesco-listed World Heritage recognition.

LEFT: NICHOLAS DEVORE/GETTY IMAGES ©; TOP RIGHT: MAREMAGNUM/GETTY IMAGES ©

Parmesan & Prosciutto in Bologna

They don't call Bologna *la grassa* (the fat one) for nothing. Many of Italy's belt-busting classics call this city home, from *mortadella* (pork cold cut) and meat-stuffed tortellini to its trademark *tagliatelle al ragù*. Shop for regional produce in the deli-packed Quadrilatero (p208), including Modena's world-famous aged balsamic vinegar, and Parma's *parmigiano reggiano* cheese and incomparable *prosciutto di Parma*.

Da Vinci's Last Supper

In da Vinci's *The Last Supper* (p124), apostles leap out of their chairs in shock as Jesus calmly reports that one of them will betray him. For his dynamic mural, da Vinci used a trick that street artists now take for granted: he applied wet paint onto a dry wall, instead of the medieval wet-on-wet fresco technique. The experimental mix proved unstable, but even badly faded, this Renaissance breakthrough shows indelible genius.

Italian Riviera

For the sinful inhabitants of the five Cinque Terre villages (p156) – Monterosso, Vernazza, Corniglia, Manarola and Riomaggiore – penance involved a lengthy and arduous hike up the vertiginous cliff side to the local village sanctuary to appeal for forgiveness. Scale the same trails today, through terraced vineyards and hillsides smothered in *macchia* (shrubbery) and, as the heavenly views unfurl, it's hard to think of a more benign punishment.

Below: Riomaggiore (p159)

The Best...
Food & Wine Spots

BOLOGNA
Italy's gastronomic Holy Grail, home to *prosciutto di Parma, parmigiano reggiano* and balsamic vinegar. (p212)

PIEDMONT
Truffles, gorgonzola, chocolate and Barolo beckon in the home of Slow Food. (p150)

NAPLES & SURROUNDS
Real-deal pizza and *mozzarella di bufala* (buffalo mozzarella) meet crispy *sfogliatelle* (ricotta-filled pastries). (p291)

SICILY
Cuisine with a kick and Arabic undertones, from wild-caught tuna and *arancini Siciliani* (risotto balls) to marzipan and ricotta-stuffed *cannoli*. (p322)

Cave Town Matera

19

In the moonscape hills of Basilicata, the town of Matera (p347) clusters around the edge of a gaping gorge, its terraces of buildings arranged higgeldy-piggeldy across the rocky land like an overgrown *presepe* (Nativity scene). It comes as no surprise that Mel Gibson chose this as the setting for his film of the Passion; it's an epic scene. The houses are built above the caves that pock the cliffs, and many hotels offer rooms in caves, which are some of Italy's most dramatic places to stay.

MARTIN CHILD/GETTY IMAGES ©

![stars icon]

The Best...
Street Markets

MERCATO DI BALLARÒ
A Sicilian market with the flavours and colourful characters of a Middle Eastern souk. (p324)

PORTA PORTESE
Rome's flea market stretches for blocks: sunglasses, comics and even kitchen sinks. (p106)

MERCATO DI PORTA NOLANA
Market vendors peddle pastries and buffalo-milk mozzarella with a chorus of sing-song chants. (p283)

Grand Canal, Venice

20

Venice's Grand Canal (p176) makes all other byways seem downright pedestrian. Drifting is the only way to cover this shimmering stretch of the imagination, from the controversial modern fish-tail Calatrava Bridge to the lacy pink Palazzo Ducale. Grand buildings lining the waterway span centuries and architectural styles, from medieval Moorish Gothic to 21st-century postmodern baroque. Gondolas tied to striped mooring poles bob in waves, as though bowing at passing dignitaries in their sleek teak taxi-boats.

RICHARD I'ANSON/GETTY IMAGES ©

Street Life, Naples

There's nothing like waking up to the sound of the Porta Nolana (p283) market. What a feast for the senses! It's as similar to a North African bazaar as to a European market: fruit vendors raucously hawking their wares in Neapolitan dialect; swordfish heads casting sidelong glances across heaps of silvery sardines on ice; the irresistible perfume of lemons and oranges; and the warm, just-baked aroma of *sfogliatella* pastries.

Right: *Sfogliatelle*

San Gimignano

Medieval hill towns dot the Tuscan hillside, but this one's more of an exclamation mark. Eleven medieval skyscrapers loom over tiny San Gimignano (p254), where neighbourly competition for status fuelled a 14th-century tower-building boom. Centuries later, the town's towering ambitions have paid off: San Gimignano is now a Unesco World Heritage Site and one of Tuscany's premier attractions.

The Dolomites

Scour the globe and you'll find plenty of bigger and more geologically volatile mountains, but few can match the romance of the pink-hued, granite Dolomites (p197). Their jagged summits dress themselves in vibrant skirts of wildflowers in spring and skiers zigzag their valleys in winter. This tiny pocket of northern Italy has drawn some of the most daring mountaineers on the planet.

23

The Best...
Opera Performances

TEATRO ALLA SCALA
Verdi premieres set high standards for opera's toughest crowds, who've made grown tenors cry. (p125)

ROMAN ARENA, VERONA
Roman games seem tame compared to epic productions in this open-air Roman amphitheatre. (p203)

LA FENICE
From Rossini to Stravinsky, this gilded jewel-box theatre has lured the world's best to Venice. (p196)

TEATRO SAN CARLO
Italy's largest opera house makes Naples sing. (p293)

Giotto in Assisi

During the grim days of the Black Death, Giotto di Bondone brought living colour to his daring naturalistic frescoes for the Basilica di San Francesco (p262) in Assisi. He revealed a human side to spiritual figures that sparked a renaissance. The frescoes inspire such devotion that after being shattered by a 1997 earthquake they were painstakingly reconstructed from thousands of fragments.

The Best...
Beaches

24

25

Positano

Draped steeply over a coastal cliff, Positano (p307) is the most glamorous and gorgeous resort on the Amalfi Coast. The sugar-bright buildings gleam in the sun, overlooking sparkling Mediterranean and a bijou beach. It's heart-rendingly pretty, and also a place to see and be seen against a backdrop of colours that reflect off every surface, from the bobbing fishing boats to Santa Maria Assunta's ceramic dome.

Italy's Top Itineraries

Florence to Rome World Heritage Wonders

5 DAYS

Italy is home to an astounding 49 Unesco World Heritage Sites, with 40 more on the short list for confirmation. Cover some of Italy's most celebrated sites on this brief trip – and see how many make your own list of all-time favourite destinations.

Adriatic Sea

FLORENCE ①

SAN MARINO

② SAN GIMIGNANO

③ SIENA

④ ASSISI

Tyrrhenian Sea

⑤ ROME

① Florence (p224)

Florence's Unesco World Heritage historic centre is full of treasures: the **Duomo** and its **Battistero**, the **Basilica di Santa Maria Novella** and the **Palazzo Vecchio** make Renaissance razzle-dazzle hard to miss. Circle the monuments, devote an afternoon to the **Uffizi** and the next morning to the **Galleria dell'Accademia**.

FLORENCE ❍ SAN GIMIGNANO

🚌 **1¼ hours** 14 buses daily. 🚗 **One hour** SP1 to Poggibonsi, then SR2 to RA3.

② San Gimignano (p254)

In the afternoon of day two, head to San Gimignano, famous for its medieval towers. Step into the town's **Collegiata** for 14th-century frescoes, including di Bartolo's hungry devil, then sate your own hunger at **La Mandragola.**

SAN GIMIGNANO ❍ SIENA

🚌 **One to 1½ hours** 10 daily Monday to Saturday. 🚗 **One to 1½ hours** Take RA3 (Siena–Florence *superstrada*).

③ Siena (p248)

Kick off day three with cappuccino in **Piazza del Campo** (Il Campo). Admire **Palazzo Pubblico**, see the stunning inlaid marble floors of the **Duomo**, then view its exterior from your room at **Campo Regio Relais**.

SIENA ❍ ASSISI

🚌 **2½ to three hours** Daily bus to Perugia, then hourly Perugia–Assisi train. 🚗 **One to 1½ hours** SS326 to Perugia, then SS75 (Ospedalicchio exit).

④ Assisi (p261)

Pause for reflection on day four in the Unesco heralded home of St Francis. His life unfolds in glowing colour in Giotto's **Basilica di San Francesco** frescoes. Head to Rome late afternoon.

ASSISI ❍ ROME

🚌 **Two to 2½ hours** Hourly trains leave for Rome via Foligno. 🚗 **2½ to three hours** Take SS75 to Perugia, then A1 to Rome.

⑤ Rome (p60)

Explore ancient Rome, wandering from the **Pantheon** to **Piazza Navona**, and the **Colosseum** to the **Vatican**.

Spanish Steps (p74), Rome
RICHARD I'ANSON/GETTY IMAGES ©

5 DAYS

Rome to Pompeii
Ancient Rome's Greatest Hits

Ancient Rome didn't just fall – it was smothered in volcanic ash, buried in mudslides and stomped underfoot. But in Italy, millennia-old Roman artefacts have been found remarkably intact, from temple altars to brothel menus. See the relics of Italy's late, great civilisation.

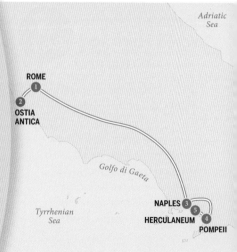

❶ Rome (p60)

Experience the city as ancient Romans did. Swing by the **Roman Forum** to hear news; pray to the gods for peace, marriage and success in politics; and don't miss imagining the roar of the crowds at the **Colosseum**. Also explore the *centro storico* (historic centre): the theatricality of **Piazza Navona**, the awe-inspiring **Pantheon** and works of art in every neighbourhood church.

ROME ➔ OSTIA ANTICA

🚆 **25 minutes** From Stazione Porta San Polo, catch Ostia–Lido train. 🚘 **30 minutes** Take A12 toward Fiumicino; take the Scavi exit.

❷ Ostia Antica (p104)

On day two, follow ancient Romans fed up with chariot traffic, and take a day trip down to Ostia Antica. Traces of this 2300-year-old resort town were buried during medieval floods, but archaeologists have recently uncovered spa complexes with wrestling rings, restaurants with frescoed menus and even ancient door-less latrines.

ROME ➔ NAPLES

🚆 **1¼ to 1¾ hours** 42 Rome–Naples trains daily, including Frecciarossa (High Velocity). 🚘 **Two to three hours** Take A1 south.

❸ Naples (p282)

Head to Naples on day three, where ancient Rome lurks around every corner. A city of the dead can be found in **catacombs** under Naples' vibrant streets, and palatial **Museo Archeologico Nazionale** is littered with looted antiquities, from Pompeii mosaics to vividly illustrated menus for Roman brothels. On day four, explore Roman secret passages by candlelight with **Napoli Sotterranea**, emerging for dinner at legendary **Pizzeria Gino Sorbillo**.

NAPLES ➔ POMPEII

🚆 **35 minutes** Frequent, fast service. 🚆 **30 minutes** Every half hour. 🚘 **45 minutes** Take A3 south.

❹ Pompeii (p302)

Day five leads you to remarkable ruins. Talk about unlucky: Pompeii was recovering from an AD 63 earthquake when Mt Vesuvius erupted, burying the town. Today, the preservation allows visitors to see how citizens died – plaster casts of adult victims trying to shelter children are especially poignant – but also how ancient Romans lived, between wars and disasters.

POMPEII ➔ HERCULANEUM

🚆 **25 minutes** Frequent service from Pompeii to Ercolano-Scavi station and Naples. 🚘 **30 minutes** Take A3 north.

❺ Herculaneum (p301)

A short trip away from Pompeii, continue your exploration into the past. The eruption that buried Pompeii caused mudslides in Herculaneum, and this Roman city is arguably even better preserved. Looters were lax here, leaving fossilised home decor, gorgeous mosaics and a statue of Hercules urinating.

Ruins of Pompeii (p302)
GREG ELMS/GETTY IMAGES ©

Rome to Barolo
Gourmet Grand Tour

Earn the ultimate gourmet bragging rights on an Italian adventure that leads you by the tastebuds from cappuccino in Rome to decadent deli in Bologna, red wine in Verona, chocolate in Turin, Slow Food feasts in Bra, truffles in Alba, and ending with a world-class nightcap in Barolo.

① Rome (p60)

Spend your first three days in Rome. After experiencing Michelangelo's **Sistine Chapel**, summit the dome of **St Peter's**, then hit **Pizzarium** for gourmet pizza. Sightseeing in **centro storico** is a fine excuse for gelato at **Il Gelato** and drinks in **Campo de' Fiori**.

ROME ⟶ BOLOGNA

🚊 **2¼ to four hours** Frequent Rome–Naples trains daily, including Frecciarossa (High Velocity).
🚗 **3¾ hours** Take A1 north.

② Bologna (p205)

On day four, head to Bologna. Browse the **Quadrilatero**, where medieval porticos shelter mouth-watering deli displays; climb one of Bologna's russet-red towers to overlook it all; and dine deliciously at simple yet sublime **Osteria dell'Orsa**.

BOLOGNA ⟶ VERONA

🚊 **1½ hours** Hourly departures. 🚗 **1½ hours** Take A22 north.

③ Verona (p200)

Fair Verona is where Shakespeare set his scene for *Romeo and Juliet,* and romance is aided by Veneto's famed wines at **Piazza delle Erbe**. On day five, catch a summer outdoor opera at Verona's ancient **Roman Arena**.

VERONA ⟶ TURIN

🚊 **Three to four hours** Several trains daily; change in Milan. 🚗 **Three to 3½ hours** Take the A21 via Piacenza to avoid Milan traffic.

Barolo (p151)
PHILIP AND KAREN SMITH/GETTY IMAGES ©

④ Turin (p146)

Devote two days to Turin's excellent **museums**, with frequent fuel stops at **historic cafes**. Stay the night in converted car factory **Le Meridien Art + Tech**, before diving into **Eataly**, where tastings and culinary workshops double as meals.

TURIN ⟶ BRA

🚊 **45 minutes** Frequent commuter trains.
🚗 **One hour** Take A6 south to Marene; exit to SS231 east to Bra.

⑤ Bra (p151)

Next day, make your way to Bra, the home of Slow Food, where artisans make chocolates, cheeses and cured meats from historic recipes. Dine upstairs from Slow Food HQ at **Osteria del Boccondivino**.

BRA ⟶ ALBA

🚊 **15 to 30 minutes** Frequent commuter trains.
🚗 **30 minutes** Take E74 east.

⑥ Alba (p151)

On day nine, head to the source of Italy's truffles and celebrated red wine. Browse the local stores and markets, and undergo an edible education with **cooking classes, winery tours** and **truffle-foraging** excursions.

ALBA ⟶ BAROLO

🚊 **20 minutes** Trains every hour.
🚗 **20 minutes** Take SP3 south.

⑦ Barolo (p151)

End your tour with a day in this tiny village. It makes Italy's most prized food-friendly wines, and offers bargain **Enoteca Regionale** tastings in a castle dungeon. The town's namesake red is stunning with the local truffle-laced cuisine.

10 DAYS

Naples to the Aeolian Islands
Seaside Splendours

Vertiginous cliffs, pastel-hued fishing villages, sun-drenched Mediterranean flavours: this trip takes in seriously stunning coasts. Peak beach season is late summer, so book July and August accommodation well ahead.

1 NAPLES
CAPRI **2**
3 POSITANO
Golfo di Salerno
Golfo di Taranto
Tyrrhenian Sea
Ionian Sea
5 AEOLIAN ISLANDS
4 TAORMINA

① Naples (p282)

Begin your seaside getaway in hyperactive Naples. The city's *centro storico* is home to baroque splendour galore, from the **Duomo** to the **Certosa di San Martino** (aloof above the city, with stunning views), the unparalleled **Museo Archeologico Nazionale**, and the ultrahip **MADRE** museum of contemporary art. Take a trip to **Mt Vesuvius** and wonder at the preservation of **Pompeii**. In between exploration, graze at myriad delicious restaurants, and decide whether Neapolitan pizza is the best in the world at **Pizzeria Gino Sorbillo**.

NAPLES ➡ CAPRI

⚓ **40 to 50 minutes** Ferries leave from Molo Beverello; some hydrofoils depart Mergellina.

② Capri (p296)

On day four, catch a ferry from Naples to dazzling Capri. Take a boat trip into the famed, incandescent **Grotta Azzurra** (Blue Grotto) and indulge in *la dolce vita* on **Piazza Umberto I**. Day five options include taking a **diving course**, riding the **seggiovia** to the top of Monte Solaro for panoramas, or exploring imperial ruins at **Villa Jovis**.

CAPRI ➡ POSITANO

⚓ **30 to 40 minutes** Direct hydrofoil service in summer; via Sorrento autumn to spring.

③ Positano (p307)

The Amalfi Coast's most photogenic town is short on sights but big on charm – a fine excuse to explore boutique-lined streets or soak up the sun on **Spiaggia Grande** for a day or two.

POSITANO ➡ TAORMINA

⚓ **10½ hours** Overnight ferry from Naples. ✈ **One hour** Fly from Naples to Messina or Catania; connect to Taormina by train. 🚆 **6½ hours** Train from Naples to Taormina, with ferry between Villa San Giovanni and Messina.

④ Taormina (p337)

Unwind in Sicily's jet-set-favourite Taormina. Take a rowboat to **Isola Bella** for lazy beachside lounging or stroll its medieval streets that sell local ceramics. In summer, don't miss concerts in Taormina's iconic amphitheatre, **Teatro Greco**.

TAORMINA ➡ AEOLIAN ISLANDS

⚓ **Three hours** Take the train to Milazzo, where frequent summer ferries depart for the Aeolian Islands.

⑤ Aeolian Islands (p332)

Spend a couple of days on the stunning Aeolian Islands, surrounded by crystal-clear waters. **Lipari** has an impressive citadel museum; **Vulcano** offers therapeutic hot springs and black-sand beaches; and verdant, flower-strewn **Salina** sprinkles pasta with island-grown capers.

Vulcano, Aeolian Islands (p332)
HOLGER LEUE/GETTY IMAGES ©

Rome to Milan Classic Cities

While Italy's riches could easily take a lifetime to explore, two weeks will allow you a respectable taste of its astounding architectural, artistic, culinary and geographic diversity. The focus here is on the big-hitters, with a speedy side trip thrown in.

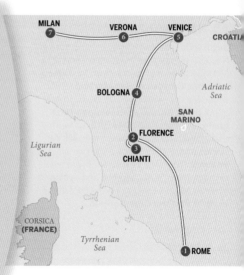

1 Rome (p60)

Spend your first day exploring ancient must-see sights such as the **Imperial Forums** and the **Capitoline Museums**, before *aperitivo* hour at **Salotto 42**. The following day, take in the cultural riches of the **Vatican** before a rustic Roman feast in **Trastevere**. On day three, meet masterpieces at **Museo e Galleria Borghese** and flip a coin into the **Trevi Fountain** to ensure a return visit.

ROME ➔ FLORENCE

🚆 **1½ to four hours** Two to three trains per hour.
🚗 **Three hours** Take A1 north.

2 Florence (p224)

Head to the Renaissance jewel of Florence. Take in the whole of the city from the top of the **Duomo** before spending the afternoon at the **Uffizi**. Save the next morning to say *'ciao'* to *David* at the **Galleria dell'Accademia**, see luminous works by Fra' Angelico at the **Museo di San Marco**, and watch the sun set behind the **Ponte Vecchio**.

FLORENCE ➔ CHIANTI

🚌 **One hour** Buses depart hourly for Greve in Chianti. 🚗 **40 minutes to one hour** Take SR222 south.

3 Chianti (p253)

Take a break from Italy's urban intensity with a bike tour to the vine-draped hills of Chianti. Indulge in a little wine tasting, soak up the sun-blessed Tuscan countryside and pedal back to Florence in time for a dinner at **L'Osteria di Giovanni**.

FLORENCE ➔ BOLOGNA

🚆 **35 minutes to 1 hour** Two to three trains hourly.
🚗 **1½ hours** Take A1 north.

4 Bologna (p205)

The following morning it is time to travel north to food-obsessed **Bologna**. Take in art and medieval architecture on **Piazza Maggiore** before diving into the delectable delis of the **Quadrilatero**. Finally, whet your appetite for dinner by climbing **Torre degli Asinelli**.

Chianti (p253), Tuscany
GLENN VAN DER KNIJFF/GETTY IMAGES ©

6 **Verona** (p200)

On day 12 travel west to **Verona**, the setting of Shakespeare's *Romeo and Juliet*. Fall head over heels for the city's beautiful churches *palazzi* (palaces) and monuments, including Romanesque **Basilica di San Zeno Maggiore** and the pink marble Roman amphitheatre. If you're visiting between July and September, don't miss opera at the **Roman Arena**.

VERONA ⟩ MILAN

🚆 **1½ to two hours** Trains every half hour.
🚗 **1¾ to two hours** Take A4 west.

7 **Milan** (p120)

Complete your adventure in high-octane Milan, home of the outlandishly Gothic **Duomo**, high-fashion **Galleria Vittorio Emanuele II** and legendary opera house **Teatro alla Scala** (La Scala). Make sure you're booked to see Leonardo da Vinci's **The Last Supper**. If you miss out, get your cultural fix at the **Pinacoteca di Brera** before a wardrobe overhaul in the fashionista heartland **Quadrilatero d'Oro**.

BOLOGNA ⟩ VENICE

🚆 **1¼ to 2¼ hours** Frequent trains, some via Mestre. 🚗 **20 minutes** Take A13 north; park at Tronchetto, Venice's parking garage.

5 **Venice** (p170)

Arriving in Venice on day eight, allow the wonder to sink in over a few days. Bask in the architectural glories of **Piazza San Marco**, stroll winding streets to the **Rialto Bridge**, and sample rare Veneto vintages at **I Rusteghi**. Discover modern art at **Peggy Guggenheim Collection** and **Punta della Dogana**, and follow masterpieces at **I Frari** and **Scuola Grande di San Rocco** with a glass of prosecco in **Campo San Giacomo dell'Orio**. Explore the outer lagoon islands to find glass on Murano, colour-blocked houses on Burano, and perhaps overnight in Ernest Hemingway's writer's retreat on Torcello.

VENICE ⟩ VERONA

🚆 **1¼ to 2¼ hours** At least three trains hourly.
🚗 **1¾ hours** Take A4 west.

Month by Month

Top Events

🌀 **Settimana Santa**,
March/April

🌀 **La Biennale di Venezia**,
June–October

🌀 **Estate Romana**,
June–September

🌀 **Il Palio di Siena**,
July & August

🍴 **Truffle Season**, November

January

🌀 **Regata della Befana**
Venice celebrates Epiphany on 6 January with the Regatta of the Witches, complete with a fleet of brawny men dressed in their finest *befana* (witch) drag.

February

🌀 **Carnevale**
In the period leading up to Ash Wednesday, many Italian towns stage pre-Lenten carnivals, with whimsical costumes, confetti and special festive treats.

🍴 **Mostra Mercato del Tartufo Nero**
An early-spring taste of truffles from the gastronomic Umbrian town of Norcia. Thousands of visitors sift through booths tasting all things truffle alongside other speciality produce.

March

🍴 **Taste**
Foodies flock to Florence for Taste (www. pittimmagine.com), a bustling food fair held inside industrial-chic Stazione Leopolda.

🌀 **Settimana Santa**
On Good Friday, the Pope leads a candlelit procession to the Colosseum and on Easter Sunday he gives his blessing in St Peter's Square, while in Florence, a cartful of fireworks explodes in Piazza del Duomo. Other notable processions take place in Procida and Sorrento in Campania, Taranto (Puglia) and Trapani (Sicily).

Left: February Carnevale, Venice
RUTH EASTHAM & MAX PAOLI/GETTY IMAGES ©

April

◉ Salone Internazionale del Mobile

Held annually in Milan, the world's most prestigious furniture fair (www.cosmit. it) is joined in alternate years by lighting, accessories, office, kitchen and bathroom shows, too.

◉ Settimana del Tulipano

The tulips are spectacular during the Week of the Tulip, held at Lake Maggiore's Villa Taranto; the dahlia path and dogwood are also in bloom, in what is considered one of Europe's finest botanical gardens.

⊕ VinItaly

Sandwiched between the Valpolicella and Soave wine regions, Verona hosts the world's largest wine fair, VinItaly. During four days 4000 international exhibitors give wine tastings, lectures and seminars.

May

✷ Processione dei Serpari

Possibly Italy's most peculiar patron-saint day is held on 1 May in Cocullo, Abruzzo. The event sees a statue of St Dominic draped with live snakes and carried in the Snake Charmers' Procession.

✷ Festa di San Gennaro

Naples' Festa di San Gennaro has a lot riding on it: securing the city from volcanic and other disasters. The faithful gather in the cathedral to see their patron saint's blood liquefy. If it does, the city is safe. Repeat performances take place on 19 September and 16 December.

✷ Ciclo di Rappresentazioni Classiche

Classical intrigue in an evocative setting, the Festival of Greek Theatre (www.inda

fondazione.org), held from mid-May to mid-June, brings Syracuse's 5th-century-BC amphitheatre to life with performances from Italy's acting greats.

June

✷ Napoli Teatro Festival

For three weeks in June, Naples celebrates all things performative with the Napoli Teatro Festival (www.napoliteatrofestival. it). Using both conventional and unconventional venues, the program ranges from classic works to specially commissioned pieces from both local and international acts.

✷ La Biennale di Venezia

Held in odd-numbered years, the Venice Biennale (p187) is one of the art world's most prestigious events. Exhibitions are held in venues around the city from June to October.

✷ Ravello Festival

Perched high above the Amalfi Coast, Ravello draws world-renowned artists during its summer-long Ravello Festival (p310), covering everything from music and dance to film and art exhibitions. Several events take place in the exquisite Villa Rufolo gardens, June to mid-September.

✷ Spoleto Festival dei Due Mondi

Held in the Umbrian hill town of Spoleto from late June to mid-July, the Spoleto Festival (p264) is an international arts event, featuring music, theatre, dance and art.

✷ Estate Romana

Between June and the end of September, the Estate Romana (p87) puts on a summer calendar of events that turns Rome into an outdoor stage.

even before Christianity the Romans honoured their gods on Feriae Augusti. Naples celebrates with particular fervour.

Mostra Internazionale d'Arte Cinematografica

The Venice International Film Festival (www.labiennale.org/en/cinema) is one of the world's most prestigious silver-screen events, with red-carpet premieres and paparazzi glamour.

September

Regata Storica

On the first Sunday in September, gondoliers in period dress work those biceps in Venice's Historic Regatta. Period boats are followed by gondola and other boat races along the Grand Canal.

Festival delle Sagre

On the second Sunday in September more than 40 communes in the province of Asti put their wines and local gastronomic products on display at this festival (www.festivaldellesagre.it).

Couscous Fest

The Sicilian town of St Vito celebrates multiculturalism and its famous fish couscous at this six-day event in late September (www.couscousfest.it). Highlights include an international couscous cook-off, tastings and live world-music gigs.

July

Il Palio di Siena

Daredevils in tights thrill the crowds with this chaotic bareback horse race around the piazza in Siena. Preceding the race is a dashing medieval-costume parade. Held on 2 July and 16 August.

Taormina Arte

Ancient ruins and languid summer nights set a seductive scene for Taormina Arte (www.taormina-arte.com), a major arts festival held in July and August.

August

Ferragosto

After Christmas and Easter, Ferragosto, on 15 August, is Italy's biggest holiday. It marks the Feast of the Assumption, but

October

Romaeuropa Festival

From late September to November, top international artists take to the stage for Rome's premier festival of theatre, opera and dance (www.romaeuropa.net).

Salone Internazionale del Gusto

Hosted by the home-grown Slow Food Movement, this biennial food expo (www.salonedelgusto.it) takes place in Turin in even-numbered years.

November

Ognissanti

Celebrated all over Italy as a national holiday, All Saints' Day on 1 November commemorates the Saint Martyrs, while All Souls' Day, on 2 November, is set aside to honour the deceased.

Truffle Season

From the Piedmontese towns of Alba (www.fieradeltartufo.org) and Asti, to Tuscany's San Miniato, and Le Marche's Acqualagna, November is prime truffle time, with local fairs, events and music.

Opera Season

Italy is home to four of the world's great opera houses: Teatro alla Scala (p125) (La Scala) in Milan, La Fenice (p196) in Venice, Teatro San Carlo (p293) in Naples and Teatro Massimo (p328) in Palermo. The season traditionally runs from mid-October to March.

December

Natale

The weeks preceding Christmas are studded with religious events. Churches set up *presepi* nativity scenes and there's a month-long Christmas market in Rome's Piazza Navona. On Christmas Eve the Pope serves midnight mass in St Peter's Square.

Far left: July Il Palio di Siena
Left: September Regata Storica, Venice

What's New

For this new edition of Discover Italy, our authors hunted down the fresh, the transformed, the hot and the happening. Here are a few of our favourites. For up-to-the-minute recommendations, see lonelyplanet.com/italy.

1 MUSEUMS IN BOLOGNA
Bologna delivers a trio of new museums under the of umbrella 'Genus Bononiae: Museums in the City', a loose itinerary designed to protect and promote the city's heritage. Top billing goes to the amazing Museo della Storia di Bologna. Set in a medieval *palazzo* redesigned by architect Mario Bellini, its high-tech, interactive galleries recount Bologna's action-packed back story. (p205)

2 PALAZZETTO BRU ZANE, VENICE
Refreshed and restored, the 17th-century Palazzetto Bru Zane is doing what it does best: delighting pleasure seekers with concerts of romantic music by Europe's leading talents. (p196)

3 MUSEO NAZIONALE DELL'AUTOMOBILE, TURIN
This museum is back after a major makeover. Drool over 200 vehicles, among them an 1892 Peugeot and a 1980 Ferrari 308. (p150)

4 EATALY, ROME
Turin-based food emporium Eataly has opened its biggest outlet yet. The multilevel eating, drinking and food shopping complex reflects Rome's growing trend for all-day dining. (p100)

5 TUNNEL BORBONICO, NAPLES
Revisit the Naples of paranoid royals and WWII bombings at the lovingly restored Bourbon Tunnel. Guided tours of this subterranean labyrinth range from standard saunters to speleological adventures. (p289)

6 VENICE DAY TRIPS, VENETO
Dig deeper into Veneto life with this boutique tour outfit. Options include art, food wine or shopping tours in Venice and Padua, and wonderful wine and food tours of the Veneto countryside. (p186)

7 PALAZZO MARGHERITA, BERNALDA
Hollywood meets Italy's deep south at filmmaker Francis Ford Coppola's boutique hotel in Basilicata. The luxe 19th-century villa has bedded some red-carpet names, including Justin Timberlake. (☎0835 54 90 60; www.coppolaresorts.com/palazzomargherita; Corso Umberto 64; ste incl breakfast & cooking lessons from €360-€1800, 2-night minimum stay)

8 VILLA ROMANA DEL CASALE
Sparkling from a multiyear renovation, this Roman villa's stunning floor mosaics are back on the A-list of Italy's greatest ancient assets. (p335)

Get Inspired

📖 Books

- **Christ Stopped at Eboli** (1947) Carlo Levi's bitter-sweet tale of an exiled dissident doctor.

- **History** (1974) War, sexual violence and a mother's struggles define Elsa Morante's controversial novel.

- **The Baron in the Trees** (1957) Italo Calvino's tragicomic fable is a metaphor for Italy's postwar reinvention.

- **The Name of the Rose** (1980) A medieval murder mystery from literary heavyweight Umberto Eco.

- **The Snack Thief** (2000) A maverick cop on his toes in Andrea Camilleri's whodunit.

🎞 Films

- **La Dolce Vita** (1960) Federico Fellini's tale of hedonism, celebrity and suicide in 1950s Rome.

- **Il Postino** (1994) Massimo Troisi plays Italy's most adorable postman.

- **Gomorra** (2008) In-your-face mafia exposé based on Roberto Saviano's best seller.

- **Videocracy** (2009) Chilling documentary about Italy's celebrity and television-infused culture.

- **La Grande Bellezza** (2013) Set in Rome, Paolo Sorrentino's wonderful Fellini-esque peer into modern Italy's psyche.

🎵 Music

- **Crêuza de mä** (Fabrizio de André) Bob Dylan–style poetry in Genovese dialect.

- **Mina** (Mina) Best-selling album from Italy's foremost female rocker.

- **Stato di Necessità** (Carmen Consoli) Guitar riffs and soulful lyrics from Sicily's favourite singer/songwriter.

- **Suburb** ('A67) Neapolitan rock-crossover group 'A67 collaborate with anti-Mafia activists.

🐟 Websites

- **Delicious Italy** (www.deliciousitaly.com) Research cooking courses, food and wine.

- **Ente Nazionale Italiano per il Turismo** (www.enit.it) Italian national tourist board's website.

- **Life in Italy** (www.lifeinitaly.com) Italian news in English, from current affairs to fashion.

- **Lonely Planet** (www.lonelyplanet.com) Info, forums and articles.

Short on time?

This list will give you an instant insight into Italy.

Read *The Leopard* (1958) Giuseppe di Lampedusa's epic tale of Sicily's Independence upheavals is Italy's all-time best seller.

Watch *Bicycle Thieves* (1958) Vittorio di Sica's poignant tale of an honest man trying to provide for his son in postwar Rome.

Listen *La Traviata* (1955) Diva Maria Callas embodies Verdi's fallen woman in La Scala's production by film-maker Luchino Visconti.

Log on www.tweetaly.com offers Italian updates on the arts, festivals, recipes and more.

Need to Know

●●●

Currency
Euro (€)

Language
Italian

Visas
Generally not required for stays under 90 days (or for most EU nationals; exceptions include the UK and Ireland).

Money
ATMs readily available; Visa and MasterCard widely accepted.

Mobile Phones
Italy uses GSM 900/1800, compatible with Europe and Australia. Use a local SIM for cheaper local calls.

Wi-Fi
Wi-fi hot spots are irregular and often require payment. Larger towns have cafes or bars offering free wi-fi, the easiest way to log on.

Internet Access
Bring ID for internet cafes. Standard rates range between €2 and €6 per hour.

Tipping
Optional 10% for good service.

When to Go

Dry climate
Warm to hot summer, mild winter
Warm to hot summer, cold winter
Mild summer, cold winter
Cold climate

Milan
GO Dec–Mar (skiing) & Sep

Venice
GO Feb–Mar & Sep–Nov

Rome
GO Apr–May, Jul & Nov–Dec

Naples
GO May–Jun & Sep

Palermo
GO Sep–Oct

High Season
(Jul & Aug)
○ Queues at big sights and on the road; festival season.

○ Prices also skyrocket for Christmas, New Year and Easter.

○ Late December to March is high season in the Alps and Dolomites.

Shoulder Season
(Apr–Jun, Sep & Oct)
○ Good deals on accommodation, especially in the south.

○ Spring for flowers and local produce.

○ Autumn for warm weather and grape harvest.

Low Season
(Nov–Mar)
○ Prices at their lowest – up to 30% lower than high season.

○ Many sights and hotels closed in coastal and mountainous areas.

○ Good for cultural events in large cities.

Advance Planning

○ **Three months before** Shop for flight deals, book accommodation if travelling during peak times, and research classes.

○ **One month before** Scan local websites for special events or festivals on during your stay, and book tickets where possible.

○ **One week before** If taking prescription medications, ask your physician for a signed and dated letter describing your condition and medication. Scan or photocopy all important documents (passport, drivers licence), reconfirm accommodation bookings and make key restaurant reservations.

Daily Costs

Budget Less than €100
- Dorm bed: €15-25
- Double room in a budget hotel: €50-110
- Pizza and pasta: €6-12

Midrange €100-250
- Double room in a hotel: €110-200
- Lunch and dinner in local restaurants: €25-50

Top end Over €250
- Double room in four- or five-star hotel: €200-450
- Top restaurant dinner: €50-150

Exchange Rates

Australia	A$1	€0.69
Canada	C$1	€0.69
Japan	¥100	€0.74
NZ	NZ$1	€0.60
UK	UK£1	€1.16
USA	US$1	€0.72

For current exchange rates, see www.xe.com

What to Bring

- **Clothing** Smart casual clothes – T-shirts, shorts and dusty sandals don't cut it in bars and restaurants in fashion-conscious Italy.
- **ID** Passport or Italian ID card obligatory for hotel check-in and internet cafes. Valid licence and car documents required if driving.
- **Insurance** Comprehensive coverage for theft, cancellations and medical expenses, and car insurance if driving.

Be Forewarned

- **Appropriate attire** Cover torsos, shoulders and upper legs when visiting religious sites.
- **Petty theft** Be mindful of personal possessions, especially in crowded public areas.
- **Public holidays** Many restaurants and shops close for at least part of August.

Arriving in Italy

- **Aeroporto Leonardo Da Vinci-Fiumicino (Rome)**

Train To Rome centre every 30 minutes from 6.38am to 11.38pm (€14)

Night bus Runs hourly from 12.30am to 5am (€5 to €7)

Taxis €48 set fare; 45 minutes

- **Aeroporto Milano Malpensa (Milan)**

Malpensa Express To Milan centre every 30 minutes from 5.25am to 10.40pm

Malpensa Shuttle Every 20 minutes from Milan centre to airport from 3.45am to 12.30am (€7)

Taxis €90 set fare; 50 minutes

- **Aeroporto Capodichino (Naples)**

Airport shuttle To Naples centre every 20 minutes from 6.30am to 11.40pm (€3)

Taxis €15 to €23 set fares to central locations; 30-40 minutes

Getting Around

- **Air** Best for travellers on tight schedules.
- **Boat** Frequent ferries and hydrofoils connect Italy's islands to mainland ports.
- **Bus** Handy for smaller towns, Italy's extensive bus network spans local to intercity routes.
- **Car** Rental is limited to persons aged 25 years or over.
- **Train** Extensive and affordable train network spans high-speed intercity to slower regional services.

Sleeping

- **Agriturismi** Farmstays range from few-frills rustic to pool-side chic.
- **B&Bs** Affordable and popular, from a room in a family home to self-contained studio apartments.
- **Convents and monasteries** Tranquillity and an early curfew define Italy's more spiritually inclined slumbering options.
- **Hotels** An extensive range of options spanning cheap dosshouses to uberluxe retreats.
- **Pensioni** Modest, smaller-scale hotels, usually family run.
- **Villa rentals** Self-contained accommodation in picturesque rural dwellings.

Rome & the Vatican

When high culture meets street culture, it's pure Roman romance. Rome has impressive credentials: it ran an empire for a millennium, starred in dozens of classic films, created more than enough artistic masterpieces to fill its many palaces, and maintains a close (if complicated) relationship with the pope.

Seeing this city in action marks the beginning of an epic crush. Priests in designer shades march through the Vatican while chatting on mobile phones; politicians toss silk ties over their shoulders to gorge on gelato in baroque piazzas; safety-helmeted fashionistas throw farewell kisses as they roar down ancient cobblestone lanes on their scooters. With a packed calendar of arts festivals, alternative underground events and reservations at legendary trattorias, Romans are usually running late for some fabulous date. Join them, and discover for yourself why all roads lead to Rome.

Trevi Fountain (p77)

St Peter's Basilica (p86)

Rome & the Vatican

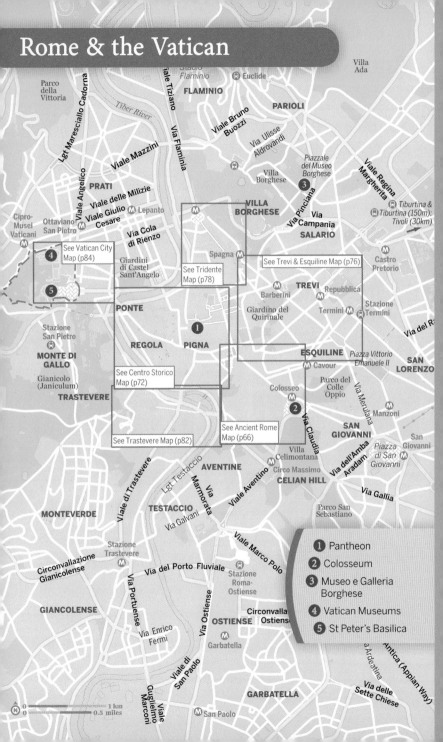

Parco della Vittoria

Stadio Flaminio

Ⓜ Euclide

Villa Ada

FLAMINIO

PARIOLI

Tiber River

Viale Tiziano

Viale Bruno Buozzi

Via Ulisse Aldrovandi

Lgt Maresciallo Cadorna

Viale Mazzini

Via Flaminia

Viale Regina Margherita

Piazzale del Museo Borghese

Tiburtina & Tiburtina (150m); Tivoli (30km)

Viale Angelico

PRATI

Viale delle Milizie

Viale Giulio Cesare

Ⓜ Lepanto

Villa Borghese

❸

Via Pinciana

VILLA BORGHESE

Via Campania

SALARIO

Ottaviano San Pietro

Via Cola di Rienzo

Cipro- Musei Vaticani

Ⓜ

Giardini di Castel Sant'Angelo

Spagna Ⓜ

See Vatican City Map (p84)

❹

See Tridente Map (p78)

See Trevi & Esquiline Map (p76)

Castro Pretorio Ⓜ

❺

Barberini

TREVI

Repubblica

Stazione San Pietro Ⓡ

PONTE

Giardino del Quirinale

Termini Ⓜ Ⓜ

Stazione Termini Ⓡ

MONTE DI GALLO

❶

Via del Ra

REGOLA

PIGNA

ESQUILINE

Piazza Vittorio Emanuele II

SAN LORENZO

Gianicolo (Janiculum)

See Centro Storico Map (p72)

Ⓜ Cavour

Parco del Colle Oppio

Via Merulana

Ⓜ Manzoni

TRASTEVERE

Colosseo

❷

Via Claudia

SAN GIOVANNI

San Giovanni Ⓜ

See Trastevere Map (p82)

See Ancient Rome Map (p66)

Villa Celimontana

Piazza di San Giovanni

Viale di Trastevere

Lgt Testaccio

Via Marmorata

AVENTINE

Viale Aventino

Circo Massimo

CELIAN HILL

Via dell'Amba Aradam

Via Gallia

MONTEVERDE

TESTACCIO

Via Galvani

Parco San Sebastiano

Circonvallazione Gianicolense

Ⓜ Stazione Trastevere

Viale Marco Polo

Stazione Roma- Ostiense Ⓡ

GIANCOLENSE

Via del Porto Fluviale

Via Portuense

Via Ostiense

Circonvalla Ostiens

OSTIENSE

Via Enrico Fermi

Viale di San Paolo

Garbatella

Via Ardeatina

Antica (Appian Way)

GARBATELLA

Viale Guglielmo Marconi

Ⓡ San Paolo

Via delle Sette Chiese

Ⓝ

0 ——— 1 km
0 ——— 0.5 miles

❶ Pantheon

❷ Colosseum

❸ Museo e Galleria Borghese

❹ Vatican Museums

❺ St Peter's Basilica

Rome & the Vatican Highlights

Pantheon

More than 2000 years old, this Roman temple has been incredibly well preserved, saved from plunder by its consecration in 608. Visiting the Pantheon (p75) gives you the opportunity to walk into an ancient Roman building. Its enormous, unsupported dome is still the largest such in the world. Most audacious of all is the oculus in the roof that opens to the heavens.

Colosseum

Even before stepping foot in the ancient stadium, you'll find the Colosseum (p70) is an astounding sight, set amid the bustle of the modern city. Not only is this Roman arena impressive for its size and endurance, but its well-preserved condition makes for an evocative insight into ancient life.

Museo e Galleria Borghese

3

What makes the Museo e Galleria Borghese (p88) so special is that there are so many important artworks in a relatively compact space. The result is a journey with less museum fatigue that takes you from the Roman period to golden-age masters such as Caravaggio, Bernini, Borromini, Titian and Canova...to name just a few!

Right: *David* by Gian Lorenzo Bernini

4

Vatican Museums

Modesty may be a cardinal virtue, but it doesn't apply when discussing the pope's palace, which is also home to the glorious Vatican Museums (p85). The highlight is the Sistine Chapel, with Michelangelo's iconic ceiling of God bringing Adam to life with a touch, but don't miss the Raphael rooms and priceless Renaissance paintings.

5

St Peter's Basilica

The Vatican City may be the world's smallest independent state, but it has a landmark befitting one of the grandest. St Peter's (p86) was built by a brain trust of Renaissance architects and capped by Michelangelo's dome (p86), which offers views over Bernini's colonnade-framed piazza. Inside there's Michelangelo's moving *Pietá*, priceless papal jewels, Bernini's gilded altar and serene light streaming from every angle.

Rome & the Vatican's Best...

Freebies

○ **Pantheon** Walking into a rain shower inside. (p75)

○ **Spanish Steps** Watching Rome's street fashionistas parade past. (p74)

○ **Vatican Museums** Viewing priceless treasures for free on the last Sunday of the month. (p85)

○ **St Peter's Square** Receiving papal blessings on Sundays at noon. (p87)

Sweeping Views

○ **St Peter's Basilica Dome** Thank Michelangelo for dizzying views over Rome and the pope's backyard. (p86)

○ **Caffè Capitolino** Watch flocks of starlings form storm clouds over Rome's domes. (p101)

○ **Gianicolo** See church spires catch Rome's golden late-afternoon light. (p83)

○ **Palatino** Scan the Roman Forum from the city's ancient Beverly Hills. (p63)

○ **Il Vittoriano** Take the elevator for Roman panoramas. (p68)

Local Drink Orders

○ **CaffèTazza d'Oro** The ultimate summer pick-me-up: *granita di caffè* (shaved-ice coffee). (p101)

○ **Cavour 313** Your choice of 1200 wines, including sentimental local favourite white Est! Est!! Est!!! (p101)

○ **Caffè Sant'Eustachio** Frothy, sweet *gran caffè* espresso. (p102)

○ **Bar San Calisto** *Cioccolato caldo con panna* (cocoa with whipped cream). (p103)

Modern Classics

◦ **Galleria Nazionale d'Arte Moderna** Twentieth-century masterpieces, both Italian and international. (p87)

◦ **Auditorium Parco della Musica** New interpretations of classical symphonies in the Renzo Piano–designed auditorium. (p104)

◦ **Officina Profumo Farmaceutica di Santa Maria Novella** Organic cosmetics made to ancient recipes. (p105)

◦ **Museo dell'Ara Pacis** Augustus' monument to peace inside Richard Meier's controversial museum. (p76)

Left: Ponte Sant'Angelo (p84);
Above: St Peter's Square
(LEFT) WIBOWO RUSLI/GETTY IMAGES ©;
(ABOVE) WITOLD SKRYPCZAK/GETTY IMAGES ©

VITAL STATISTICS

◦ **Population** 2.61 million

ADVANCE PLANNING

◦ **One month before** Book a tour of the Tomb of St Peter. Scan the Auditorium Parco della Musica website (www. auditorium.com) for upcoming events.

◦ **Two weeks before** Reserve a table at the Glass Hostaria and book visits to view Palazzo Farnese frescoes.

◦ **One week before** Purchase tickets online to the Vatican Museums and Museo e Galleria Borghese, and reserve guided tours of the Colosseum.

◦ **Two days before** Reserve tables at L'Asino d'Oro.

RESOURCES

◦ **Roma Turismo** (www. turismoroma.it) Official Rome Tourist Board site; also has an airport office near arrivals.

◦ **Enjoy Rome** (www. enjoyrome.com) Private tourist office that runs tours and publishes the free, useful *Enjoy Rome* city guide.

◦ **Coopculture** (www. coopculture.it) Cultural events calendar and online tickets for major sights and exhibitions.

◦ **In Rome Now** (www. inromenow.com) Handy entertainment listings, though advertising-heavy.

GETTING AROUND

◦ **Air** Major airlines fly to/ from Leonardo da Vinci (Fiumicino). Low-cost carriers use Ciampino.

◦ **Bus** Handy connections between Roma Termini station and centro storico.

◦ **Metro** Useful for ancient Rome and Vatican City.

◦ **Train** To/from Fiumicino airport and Ostia Antica.

◦ **Tram** Handy for Auditorium Parco della Musica and Trastevere.

◦ **Walk** Perfect to explore Rome's distinct neighbourhoods.

BE FOREWARNED

◦ **Museums** Most close on Mondays.

◦ **Restaurants** Many stay open late in summer, and close in August.

◦ **Pickpockets** Operate on transport and at tourist sites.

Rome Walk

Cover two thousand years of history and a dozen priceless masterpieces with a stroll around Rome's historical centre – perfect for a lazy morning, or to fill the pausa (downtime) between lunch and when shops re-open in the afternoon.

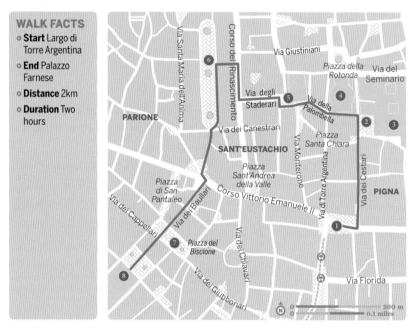

WALK FACTS

- **Start** Largo di Torre Argentina
- **End** Palazzo Farnese
- **Distance** 2km
- **Duration** Two hours

① Largo di Torre Argentina

At the centre of Rome's transit hub is a fenced-off archaeological site, where stray cats stalk the ruins of four Republic-era temples and nap peacefully on the site of Julius Caesar's assassination in 44 BC. From here, walk a couple blocks up Via dei Cestari.

② Elefantino

If getting your luggage home seems like a tricky prospect after shopping in Rome, consider Bernini's hapless elephant (p69), who's stuck carrying a 6th century BC Egyptian obelisk while balancing on a pedestal. Elefan-

tino's long trunk is reaching toward his back, as though trying to scratch an itch under the obelisk – like most Romans, Bernini finds poignant humour in absurd situations.

③ Chiesa di Santa Maria Sopra Minerva

Behind the sympathetic Elefantino is another beloved local landmark: Rome's only Gothic church (p69), built atop a Roman temple to the goddess Minerva. Inside, soaring, vaulted ceilings are frescoed with starry skies, and Filippino Lippi captured sunshine in his luminous 1488–92 Carafa Chapel frescoes.

④ Pantheon

Around the corner awaits an ancient Roman marvel. Built in 27 BC, the dome of the Pantheon (p75) remains the largest unreinforced concrete dome ever built. For the full effect, stand in the centre of the floor, and look up at the open skylight in the centre of the dome. The coffered poured-concrete sides seem to swirl as they soar upwards in a dizzying, uplifting optical effect. Consecrated as a Christian church in 608, the Pantheon houses the tombs of Raphael and Victor Emmanuel II.

⑤ Caffè Sant'Eustachio

From the Pantheon, follow signs towards Piazza Navona, stopping off for the signature foamy, sweet *gran caffè* espresso at Caffè Sant'Eustachio (p102), which many Romans claim is the city's best cafe.

⑥ Piazza Navona

Welcome to Rome's showplace, where street artists, touts and pigeons compete for attention with Bernini, creator of the Fontana dei Quattro Fiumi, and Borromini, responsible for the Chiesa di Sant'Agnese in Agone. From the 17th to 19th century, the square (p69) was flooded on weekends so that mock naval battles and other entertainment could be staged here.

⑦ Campo de' Fiori

Across Corso Vittorio Emanuele II, the Campo de' Fiori (p69) is a colourful Roman street market by day and a foreign-student party scene by night, with nonstop international flirting.

⑧ Palazzo Farnese

Beyond the campo is this stately Renaissance palazzo (p74). Romans still bemoan that this Michelangelo-refurbished palace was rented to the French Embassy, limiting access to superb frescoes by Annibale Carracci (book visits in advance) – but according to 17th century records, Palazzo Farnese's worst tenant was scandalous Queen Christina of Sweden, whose staff burned painted doors for kindling.

Rome in...

TWO DAYS

On day one, follow the walking tour in the morning. Afterwards, wander the boutique-lined streets around **Piazza Navona** and the **Pantheon** until lunchtime. Fuel up with espresso at **Tazza d'Oro** before taking on ancient Rome: the **Colosseum**, the **Roman Forum** and **Palatino** (Palatine Hill). Explore the **Capitoline Museums**, and then go on to spend the evening in Trastevere. On day two, hit the Vatican, marvelling at **St Peter's Basilica** and the Sistine Chapel in the **Vatican Museums.**

FOUR DAYS

On day three, check out the **Trevi Fountain**, the **Spanish Steps** and the **Museo e Galleria Borghese**. At night, head to **Campo de' Fiori** for a drink, and find some thin-crust Roman pizza. Next day, visit the **Museo Nazionale Romano: Palazzo Massimo alle Terme** before exploring the **Jewish Ghetto** and backstreets such as Via del Governo Vecchio. Round off your visit with drinks and dining in the charming district of Monti.

Foot of statue of Emperor Constantine, Capitoline Museums (p68)
JEAN-PIERRE LESCOURRET/GETTY IMAGES ©

Discover Rome & the Vatican

Basilica di San Giovanni in Laterano (p80)
RUSSELL MOUNTFORD/GETTY IMAGES ©

History

According to myth, Rome was founded on the Palatino (Palatine Hill) by Romulus, the twin brother of Remus. Historians proffer a more prosaic version of events, involving Romulus becoming the first king of Rome on 21 April 753 BC. At that time, the city comprised Etruscan, Latin and Sabine settlements on the Palatino, Esquiline and Quirinale hills.

RISE AND FALL OF THE ROMAN EMPIRE

Following the fall of Tarquin the Proud, the last of Rome's seven Etruscan kings, the Roman Republic was founded in 509 BC. From modest beginnings, it spread to become the dominant Western superpower until internal rivalries led to civil war. Julius Caesar, the last of the Republic's consuls, was assassinated in 44 BC, leaving Mark Antony and Octavian to fight for the top job. Octavian prevailed and, with the blessing of the Senate, became Augustus, the first Roman emperor. Augustus ruled well, and the city enjoyed a period of political stability and unparalleled artistic achievement – a golden age for which the Romans yearned as they endured the depravities of Augustus' successors Tiberius, Caligula and Nero. A huge fire reduced Rome to ashes in AD 64 but the city bounced back and by AD 100 it had a population of 1.5 million and was the undisputed *caput mundi* (capital of the world). It couldn't last, though, and when Constantine moved his power base to Byzantium in 330, Rome's glory days were numbered.

THE MIDDLE AGES

By the 6th century, Rome was in a bad way and in desperate need of a leader. Into the breach stepped the Church. Christianity had been spreading since the 1st century AD thanks to the underground efforts of apostles Peter and Paul, and under Constantine it received official recognition. In the late 6th century Pope Gregory I did much to strengthen the Church's grip over the city, laying the foundations for its later role as capital of the Catholic world.

The medieval period was a dark age, marked by almost continuous fighting. The city was reduced to a semi-deserted battlefield as the powerful Colonna and Orsini families battled for supremacy and the bedraggled population trembled in the face of plague, famine and flooding (the Tiber regularly broke its banks).

HISTORIC MAKEOVERS

But out of the ruins of the Middle Ages grew Renaissance Rome. At the behest of the city's great papal dynasties – the Barberini, Farnese and Pamphilj, among others – the leading artists of the 15th and 16th centuries were summoned to work on projects such as the Sistine Chapel and St Peter's Basilica. But the enemy was never far away, and in 1527 the Spanish forces of Holy Roman Emperor Charles V ransacked Rome.

Another rebuild was in order, and it was to the 17th-century baroque masters Bernini and Borromini that Rome's patrons turned. Exuberant churches, fountains and *palazzi* (palaces) sprouted all over the city, as these two bitter rivals competed to produce ever-more virtuosic masterpieces.

The next makeover followed the unification of Italy and the declaration of Rome as its capital. Mussolini, believing himself a modern-day Augustus, also left an indelible stamp, bulldozing new imperial roads and commissioning ambitious building projects such as the construction of the monumental suburb of EUR.

MODERN STYLING

Post-fascism, the 1950s and '60s saw a glittering era of *la dolce vita* and hasty urban expansion, resulting in Rome's sometimes wretched suburbs. A clean-up in 2000 had the city in its best shape for decades, and in recent years some

Roman Forum (p63)

WIBOWO RUSLI/GETTY IMAGES ©

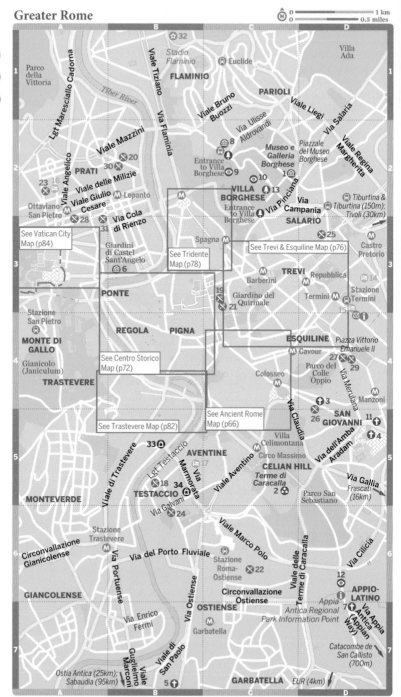

0 ———————————— 1 km
0 ———————————— 0.5 miles

Parco della Vittoria

Villa Ada

⭐ 32

Stadio Flaminio

🚉 Euclide

FLAMINIO

PARIOLI

Viale Liegi

Viale Tiziano

Viale Bruno Buozzi

Viale Flaminia

Via Ulisse Aldrovandi

Via Salaria

Viale Regina Margherita

Viale Mazzini

⊗ 20

🏛 8

🎭

Museo e Galleria Borghese

Piazzale del Museo Borghese

PRATI

30 ⊗

Viale delle Milizie

Entrance to Villa Borghese ⓐ 9

⊙ 10

🏛 1

23 ⊗ 16

Viale Angelico

Viale Giulio Cesare

Ⓜ Lepanto

VILLA BORGHESE

ⓐ 13

Via Pinciana

Tiburtina & Tiburtina (150m); Tivoli (30km)

Ottaviano-San Pietro

28 ⊗

31 ⊗

Via Cola di Rienzo

Entrance to Villa Borghese ⓐ

Via Campania

SALARIO

Castro Pretorio Ⓜ

See Vatican City Map (p84)

Giardini di Castel Sant'Angelo

🏛 6

Ⓜ Spagna

See Tridente Map (p78)

⊗ 25

See Trevi & Esquiline Map (p76)

PONTE

Stazione San Pietro 🚉

MONTE DI GALLO

Ⓜ Barberini

TREVI

Repubblica Ⓜ

🏛 14

Stazione Termini

REGOLA

PIGNA

19 ⊗ 21

Giardino del Quirinale

Termini Ⓜ

15 ✉ ❶

Gianicolo (Janicolum)

See Centro Storico Map (p72)

ESQUILINE

Piazza Vittorio Emanuele II

TRASTEVERE

Ⓜ Cavour

27 ⊗ 29

Via Merulana

Colosseo

Parco del Colle Oppio

Ⓜ Manzoni

Colosseo Ⓜ

ⓐ 3

SAN GIOVANNI

11 🅿

See Ancient Rome Map (p66)

26 ⊗

Via Claudia

ⓐ 4

See Trastevere Map (p82)

33 ⓐ

Lgt Testaccio

AVENTINE

Villa Celimontana

Via dell'Amba Aradam

Viale di Trastevere

🏛 17

Via Marmorata

Circo Massimo

CELIAN HILL

Via Gallia

Frascati (16km)

18 ⊗ 34

TESTACCIO

Viale Aventino

Terme di Caracalla

2 ⓐ

MONTEVERDE

⊗ 24

Via Galvani

Parco San Sebastiano

Viale Marco Polo

Via delle Terme di Caracalla

Via Cilicia

Circonvallazione Gianicolense

Ⓜ

Via del Porto Fluviale

Stazione Trastevere Ⓜ

Stazione Roma-Ostiense

⊗ 22

Via Portuense

Circonvallazione Ostiense

12 ⊙

APPIO-LATINO

GIANCOLENSE

Via Enrico Fermi

OSTIENSE

Ⓜ Garbatella

Appia Antica Regional Park Information Point

Appia Antica (Appian Way)

❶

Ostia Antica (25km); Sabaudia (95km)

Viale Guglielmo Marconi

Viale di San Paolo

5 ❶

GARBATELLA

EUR (4km)

Catacombe de San Callisto (700m)

Greater Rome

dramatic modernist building projects have given the Eternal City some edge, such as Richard Meier's Museo dell'Ara Pacis and Massimiliano Fuksas' Nuvola building in EUR.

◉ Sights

They say that a lifetime's not enough for Rome (Roma, non basta una vita!). There's simply too much to see. So the best plan is to choose selectively, and leave the rest for next time.

Note that many of Rome's major museums and monuments, including the Capitoline Museums and all four seats of the Museo Nazionale Romano, host regular exhibitions. When these are on, ticket prices are increased slightly, typically by about €3.

ANCIENT ROME

Arco di Costantino   Monument
(Map p66; [M]Colosseo) On the western side of the Colosseum, this triumphal arch was built in 312 to honour the emperor Constantine's victory over rival Maxentius at the battle of Ponte Milvio (Milvian Bridge).

Palatino (Palatine Hill)   Ruins
(Palatine Hill; Map p66; [☎]06 3996 7700; www.coopculture.it; Via di San Gregorio 30; adult/child incl Colosseum & Roman Forum €12/7.50; [⏱]8.30am-1hr before sunset; [M]Colosseo) Sandwiched between the Roman Forum and the Circo Massimo, the Palatino (Palatine Hill) is a gorgeous, atmospheric area of towering pine trees, majestic ruins and memorable views. According to legend, this is where Romulus and Remus were saved by a wolf and Romulus founded Rome in 753 BC. Archaeological evidence has dated human habitation here to the 8th century BC.

Roman Forum   Ruins
(Foro Romano; Map p66; [☎]06 3996 7700; www.coopculture.it; Largo della Salara Vecchia; adult/child incl Colosseum & Palatino €12/7.50; [⏱]8.30am-1hr before sunset; [☐]Via dei Fori Imperiali) Today an impressive, if rather confusing sprawl of ruins, the Roman Forum (Foro Romano) was once the beating heart of the ancient world, a grandiose district of marble-clad temples, basilicas and vibrant public spaces.

Roman Forum

In ancient times, a forum was a market place, civic centre and religious complex all rolled into one, and the greatest of all was the Roman Forum (Foro Romano). Situated between the Palatino (Palatine Hill), ancient Rome's most exclusive neighbourhood, and the Campidoglio (Capitoline Hill), it was the city's busy, bustling centre. On any given day it teemed with activity. Senators debated affairs of state in the **Curia ❶** shoppers thronged the squares and traffic-free streets, crowds gathered under the **Colonna di Foca ❷**, to listen to politicians holding forth from the **Rostrum ❸**. Elsewhere, lawyers worked the courts in basilicas including the **Basilica di Massenzio ❸**, while the Vestal Virgins quietly went about their business in the **Casa delle Vestali ❹**.

Special occasions were also celebrated in the Forum: religious holidays were marked with ceremonies at temples such as the **Tempio di Saturno ❺** and the Tempio di **Castore e Polluce ❻**, and military victories were honoured with dramatic processions up Via Sacra and the building of monumental arches like the Arco di **Settimio Severo ❼** and the **Arco di Tito ❽**.

The ruins you see today are impressive but they can be confusing without a clear picture of what the Forum once looked like. This spread shows the Forum in its heyday, complete with temples, civic buildings and towering monuments to heroes of the Roman Empire.

TOP TIPS

» Get grandstand views of the Forum from the Palatino and Campidoglio.

» Visit first thing in the morning or late afternoon; crowds are worst between 11am and 2pm.

» In summer it gets hot in the Forum and there's little shade, so take a hat and plenty of water.

Colonna di Foca & Rostrum

The free-standing, 13.5m-high Column of Phocus is the Forum's youngest monument, dating to AD 608. Behind it, the Rostrum provided a suitably grandiose platform for pontificating public speakers.

Campidoglio (Capitoline Hill)

ADMISSION

Although valid for two days, admission tickets only allow for one entry into the Forum, Colosseum and Palatino.

Tempio di Saturno

Ancient Rome's Fort Knox, the Temple of Saturn was the city treasury. In Caesar's day it housed 13 tonnes of gold, 114 tonnes of silver and 30 million sestertii worth of silver coins.

JONATHAN SMITH/GETTY IMAGES ©

LONELY PLANET/GETTY IMAGES ©

Tempio di Castore e Polluce

Only three columns of the Temple of Castor and Pollux remain. The temple was dedicated to the Heavenly Twins after they supposedly led the Romans to victory over the Etruscans.

Arco di Settimio Severo
One of the Forum's signature monuments, this imposing triumphal arch commemorates the military victories of Septimius Severus. Relief panels depict his campaigns against the Parthians.

Curia
This big barnlike building was the official seat of the Roman Senate. Most of what you see is a reconstruction, but the interior marble floor dates to the 3rd-century reign of Diocletian.

Basilica di Massenzio
Marvel at the scale of this vast 4th-century basilica. In its original form the central hall was divided into enormous naves; now only part of the northern nave survives.

JULIUS CASEAR
Julius Caesar was cremated on the site where the Tempio di Giulio Cesare now stands.

Via Sacra

Tempio di Giulio Cesare

Casa delle Vestali
White statues line the grassy atrium of what was once the luxurious 50-room home of the Vestal Virgins. The virgins played an important role in Roman religion, serving the goddess Vesta.

Arco di Tito
Said to be the inspiration for the Arc de Triomphe in Paris, the well-preserved Arch of Titus was built by the emperor Domitian to honour his elder brother Titus.

ROME & THE VATICAN

Ancient Rome

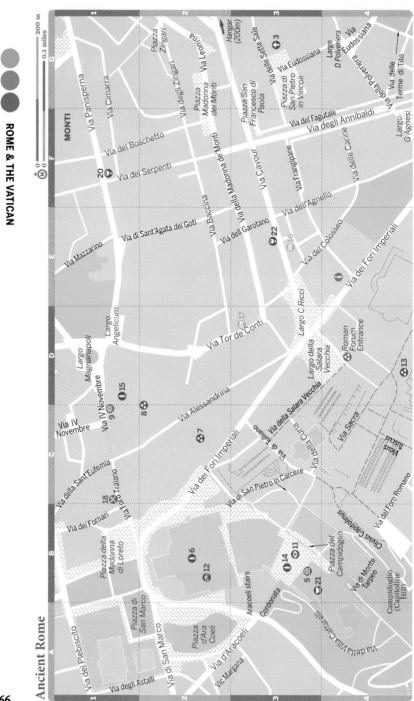

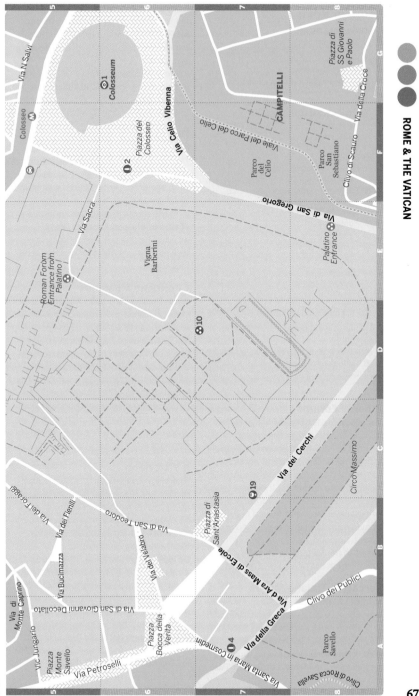

Via N Salvi

Colosseo Ⓜ

Ⓜ

🔵1
Colosseum

Via Celio Vibenna

Piazza del
Colosseo

🔵2

Via Sacra

Via di San Gregorio

Piazza di
SS Giovanni
e Paolo

Via della Croce

CAMPITELLI

Viale del Parco del Celio

Parco
del
Celio

Parco
San
Sebastiano

Clivo di Scauro

Vigna
Barberini

Palatino
Entrance

Roman Forum
Entrance from
Palatino

🔵10

Via dei Cerchi

Via dei Foraggi

Via dei Fienili

Via Bucimazza

Via del Velabro

Via di San Teodoro

Piazza di
Sant'Anastasia

🔵19

Via di
Monte Caprino

Vic Jungario

Via di San Giovanni Decollato

Piazza
Monte
Savello

Via Petroselli

Piazza
Bocca della
Verità

Via Santa Maria in Cosmedin

Via della Greca

🔵4

Via di Ara Mass di Ercole

Clivo dei Publici

Circo Massimo

Parco
Savello

Clivo di Rocca Savella

Ancient Rome

Imperial Forums   Ruins

(Map p66; Via dei Fori Imperiali; 🚇Via dei Fori Imperiali) The ruins over the road from the Roman Forum are known collectively as the Imperial Forums (Fori Imperiali). Constructed between 42 BC and AD 112 by successive emperors, they were largely buried when Mussolini bulldozed Via dei Fori Imperiali through the area in 1933. Excavations have since unearthed much of them but work continues and visits are limited to the Mercati di Traiano, accessible through the Museo dei Fori Imperiali.

Mercati di Traiano Museo dei Fori Imperiali   Museum

(Map p66; 🖉06 06 08; www.mercatiditraiano.it; Via IV Novembre 94; adult/reduced €9.50/7.50; ⊙9am-7pm Tue-Sun, last admission 6pm; 🚇Via IV Novembre) This striking museum brings to life the **Mercati di Traiano (Map p66)**, emperor Trajan's great 2nd-century

market complex, while also providing a fascinating introduction to the **Imperial Forums** with detailed explanatory panels and a smattering of archaeological artefacts.

From the main hallway, a lift whisks you up to the **Torre delle Milizie (Map p66)** (Militia Tower), a 13th-century red-brick tower, and the upper levels of the Mercati.

Piazza del Campidoglio   Piazza

(Map p66; 🚇Piazza Venezia) Designed by Michelangelo in 1538, this elegant piazza sits atop the Campidoglio (Capitoline Hill), one of the seven hills on which Rome was founded.

In the centre, the bronze equestrian **statue of Marcus Aurelius (Map p66)** is a copy. The original, which dates from the 2nd century AD, is in the Capitoline Museums.

Capitoline Museums   Museum

(Musei Capitolini; Map p66; 🖉06 06 08; www.museicapitolini.org; Piazza del Campidoglio 1; adult/reduced €9.50/7.50; ⊙9am-8pm Tue-Sun, last admission 7pm; 🚇Piazza Venezia) The world's oldest national museums, the Capitoline Museums occupy two *palazzi* on Piazza del Campidoglio. Their origins date to 1471, when Pope Sixtus IV donated a number of bronze statues to the city, forming the nucleus of what is now one of Italy's finest collections of classical art.

Il Vittoriano   Monument

(Map p66; Piazza Venezia; ⊙9.30am-5.30pm summer, to 4.30pm winter; 🚇Piazza Venezia) **FREE** Love it or loathe it (as most locals do), you can't ignore the massive mountain of white marble that towers over Piazza Venezia. Known also as the Altare della Patria (Altar of the Fatherland), it was begun in 1885 to commemorate Italian unification and honour Victor Emmanuel II, Italy's first king and the subject of its vast equestrian statue.

For Rome's best 360-degree views, take the **Roma dal Cielo (Map p66; adult/reduced €7/3.50; ⊙9.30am-6.30pm Mon-Thur, to 7.30pm Fri-Sun)** lift up to the top.

Bocca della Verità   Monument

(Map p66; Piazza Bocca della Verità 18; donation €0.50; ⏱9.30am-4.50pm winter, to 5.50pm summer; 🚌Piazza Bocca della Verità) A round piece of marble that was once part of an ancient fountain, or possibly an ancient manhole cover, the *Bocca della Verità* (Mouth of Truth) is one of Rome's most popular curiosities. Legend has it that if you put your hand in the carved mouth and tell a lie, it will bite your hand off.

The mouth lives in the portico of the **Chiesa di Santa Maria in Cosmedin** (Map p66), one of Rome's most beautiful medieval churches.

CENTRO STORICO

Chiesa di Santa Maria Sopra Minerva   Church

(Map p72; Piazza della Minerva; ⏱8am-7pm Mon-Fri, 8am-1pm & 3.30-7pm Sat & Sun; 🚌Largo di Torre Argentina) Bernini's much-loved **Elefantino** (Map p72; Piazza della Minerva; 🚌Largo di Torre Argentina) sculpture trumpets the presence of the Dominican Chiesa di Santa Maria Sopra Minerva, Rome's only Gothic church. Built on the site of an ancient temple to Minerva, it has been much altered over the centuries and little remains of its original 13th-century form.

Piazza Navona   Piazza

(Map p72; 🚌Corso del Rinascimento) With its ornate fountains, baroque *palazzi*, cafes and colourful circus of street performers, hawkers, artists and tourists, Piazza Navona is Rome's most iconic public square. Laid out on the ruins of a 1st-century arena built by the emperor Domitian – the name Navona is a corruption of the Greek word *agon*, meaning public games – it was paved over in the 15th century and for almost 300 years hosted the city's main market.

Campo de' Fiori   Piazza

(Map p72; 🚌Corso Vittorio Emanuele II) Noisy, colourful 'Il Campo' is a major focus of Roman life: by day it hosts a much-loved market, while at night it morphs into a raucous open-air pub. Towering over the

❤ **If You Like...**
Ancient Rome

If you're fascinated by Ancient Rome, seek out these sights that will illuminate imperial life.

1 AREA ARCHEOLOGICA DEL TEATRO DI MARCELLO E DEL PORTICO D'OTTAVIA
(Map p72; entrances Via del Teatro di Marcello 44 & Via Portico d'Ottavia 29; ⏱9am-7pm summer, 9am-6pm winter; 🚌Via del Teatro di Marcello) Rising like a mini-Colosseum, the **Teatro di Marcello** (Map p72; Theatre of Marcellus) is the star of this dusty archaeological area. The 20,000-seat theatre was planned by Julius Caesar and completed in 11 BC by Augustus who named it after a favourite nephew, Marcellus.

2 MUSEO NAZIONALE ROMANO: TERME DI DIOCLEZIANO
(Map p76; ✆06 3996 7700; www.coopculture.it; Viale Enrico de Nicola 78; adult/reduced €7/3.50; ⏱9am-7.30pm Tue-Sun; Ⓜ Termini) The 3rd-century Terme di Diocleziano was ancient Rome's largest bath complex, covering 13 hectares and accommodating up to 3000 people. Today its ruins house part of the Museo Nazionale Romano. The collection of memorial inscriptions and ancient artefacts provides a fascinating insight into the structure of Roman society, with exhibits relating to cults and the development of Christianity and Judaism.

3 MUSEO NAZIONALE ROMANO: PALAZZO ALTEMPS
(Map p72; ✆06 3996 7700; http://archeoroma.beniculturali.it/en/museums/national-roman-museum-palazzo-altemps; Piazza Sant'Apollinare 44; adult/reduced €7/3.50; ⏱9am-7.45pm Tue-Sun; 🚌Corso del Rinascimento) This gem of a museum houses the best of the Museo Nazionale Romano's formidable collection of classical sculpture.

square is a sinister statue of Giordano Bruno, a philosopher monk who was burned at the stake for heresy in 1600.

Colosseum

Rome's great gladiatorial arena is the most thrilling of the city's ancient sights. Originally known as the Flavian Amphitheatre, the 50,000-seat Colosseum (Colosseo) was inaugurated in AD 80 and used to stage spectacular gladiatorial games in front of baying, bloodthirsty crowds. Two thousand years on and it's Italy's top tourist attraction, drawing up to five million visitors a year.

Map p66

☎ 06 3996 7700

www.coopculture.it

Piazza del Colosseo

adult/reduced incl Roman Forum & Palatino €12/7.50

🕙 8.30am-1hr before sunset

Ⓜ Colosseo

History

When the amphitheatre opened, Vespasian's son and successor Titus (r 79–81) held games that lasted 100 days and nights, during which some 5000 animals were slaughtered. Although it was Rome's most fearful arena, it wasn't the biggest; the name Colosseum, when introduced in medieval times, was not a reference to its size but to the Colosso di Nerone, a giant statue of Nero that stood nearby.

The Structure

The external walls were originally covered in travertine, and marble statues once filled the niches on the 2nd and 3rd storeys. The upper level, punctuated with windows and slender Corinthian pilasters, had supports for 240 masts that held a canvas awning over the arena, shielding the spectators from sun and rain. The 80 entrance arches, known as *vomitoria*, allowed the spectators to enter and be seated in a matter of minutes.
The Colosseum's interior was divided into three parts: the arena, *cavea* and podium. Trapdoors led down to the underground chambers and passageways beneath the arena floor – the *hypogeum*. Animals in cages and sets for the various battles were hoisted onto the arena by a complicated system of pulleys. The top tier and *hypogeum* are open to the public by guided tour only. Visits, which cost €8 on top of the normal Colosseum ticket, require advance booking.

Withstanding Time

With the fall of the empire in the 6th century, the Colosseum was abandoned. In the Middle Ages, it became a fortress occupied by two of the city's warrior families: the Frangipani and the Annibaldi. Damaged several times by earthquakes, it was later used as a quarry for travertine and marble for Palazzo Venezia, Palazzo Barberini and Palazzo Cancelleria among other buildings. Pollution and vibrations caused by traffic and the metro in modern times have also taken their toll.

Local Knowledge

Colosseum

RECOMMENDATIONS FROM ROSSELLA REA, DIRECTOR OF THE COLOSSEUM; ARCHAEOLOGISTS MARIA LAURA CAFINI AND VALENTINA MASTRODONATO.

1 THE AFTERNOON LIGHT
Especially as the days get longer, the afternoon is an extraordinary time to visit. Choose a queue-free entrance at around 4 or 5pm. You will still have two more hours to visit the building, and can enjoy the light of the approaching sunset.

2 THE ANTIQUARIUM
On the first floor, this displays the beautiful portico capitals, barriers, balustrades, inscriptions on the senators' reserved seats, and drawings of gladiators and hunting. Don't miss the models showing the Colosseum's underground 'backstage'.

3 TRANSFORMATION
In the western part, where the protagonists of the games used to enter, there are particularly interesting displays illustrating the building's transformation from a place of entertainment to a devotional setting. Looking up, you can see a 16th-century fresco, depicting the symbolic plant of Jerusalem, whose famous treasures were used to fund the amphitheatre's construction.

4 VALADIER & STERN
On the ground floor, there's a magnificent buttress constructed by the architect Valadier in 1827, which mirrors that to the east by Stern (1805–07). Both support the northern side, which remains standing despite the systematic destruction of the southern part. It's worth walking along the southern side to see how the building became an open quarry for use by papal authorities.

5 MR GERONTI, I PRESUME
Count 14 arches right from the visitors' exit. On the pillar to the right, 3m up, is the inscription *Geronti V(ir) S (pectabilis)*. This probably referred to a relative of a senator who lived between the 5th and 6th centuries, and ascribes responsibility for dismantling part of the building's outer ring.

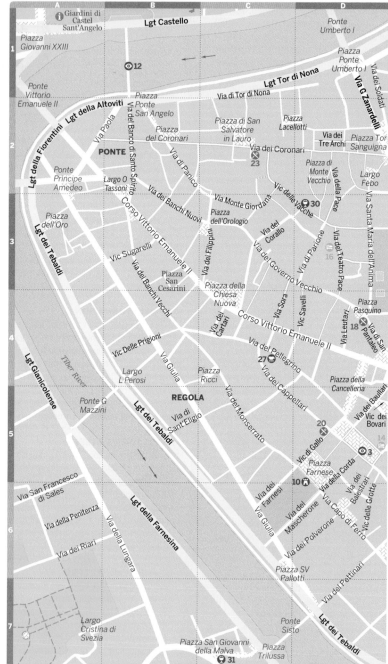

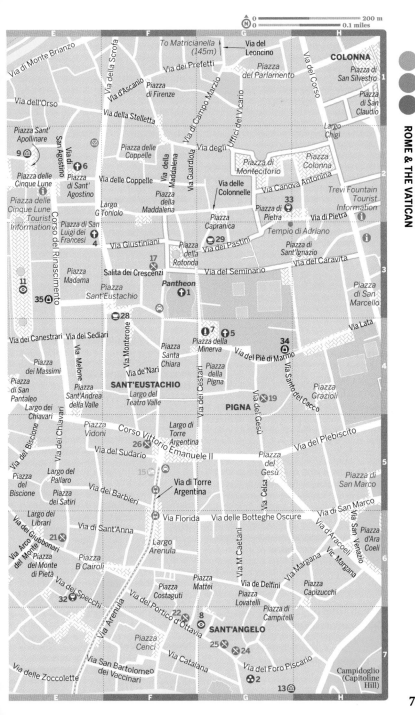

Via di Monte Brianzo

Via della Scrofa

To Matricianella (145m)

Via del Leoncino

Via dei Prefetti

COLONNA

Piazza del Parlamento

Piazza di San Silvestro

Via dei Prefetti

Via d'Ascanio

Piazza di Firenze

Via dell'Orso

Via della Stelletta

Via di Campo Marzio

Uffici del Vicario

Piazza di San Claudio

Via del Corso

Piazza Sant' Apollinare

9 🏛

Via di Sant'Agostino

Piazza delle Coppelle

Via degli

Via della Maddalena

Via Guardiola

Largo Chigi

Piazza di Montecitorio

Piazza Colonna

Piazza delle Cinque Lune

🏛 **6**

Piazza di Sant' Agostino

Via delle Coppelle

Via delle Colonnelle

33 🏛

Piazza di Pietra

Trevi Fountain Tourist Information 🏛

Piazza delle Cinque Lune Tourist Information

Corso del Rinascimento

Piazza di San Luigi dei Francesi

4 🏛

Largo G Toniolo

Piazza della Maddalena

Via Canova Antonina

Via di Pietra

Piazza Capranica

Tempio di Adriano 🏛

Via Giustiniani

29 🏛

Via dei Pastini

Piazza di Sant'Ignazio

11 ◉

Piazza Madama

17 🏛

Salita dei Crescenzi

Piazza della Rotonda

Via del Caravita

35 🏛

Piazza Sant'Eustachio

Pantheon

🏛 **1**

Via del Seminario

Piazza di San Marcello

Via dei Canestrari

Via dei Sediari

28 🏛

Via Monterone

🏛 **7** 🏛 **5**

Piazza della Minerva

Via del Piè di Marmo

34 🏛

Via Lata

Piazza dei Massimi

Piazza Santa Chiara

Via dei Cestari

Piazza della Pigna

Piazza di San Pantaleo

Via de'Nari

Piazza Graziali

Largo dei Chiavari

Piazza Sant'Andrea della Valle

SANT'EUSTACHIO

Largo del Teatro Valle

PIGNA

Via del Gesù

Via Santo del Cacco

Via del Biscione

Via dei Chiavari

Piazza Vidoni

Corso Vittorio Emanuele II

Largo di Torre Argentina

19 ✕

Piazza del Biscione

Largo del Pallaro

26 ✕

Via del Sudario

Piazza del Gesù

Via del Plebiscito

Piazza dei Satiri

Via dei Barbieri

15 🏛

Via di Torre Argentina

Piazza di San Marco

Largo dei Librari

Via di Sant'Anna

Via Florida

Via delle Botteghe Oscure

Via di San Marco

Via dei Giubbonari

21 ✕

Largo Arenula

Via d'Aracoeli

Via San Venazio

Piazza d'Ara Coeli

Via Arco del Monte

Piazza del Monte di Pietà

Via dei Specchi

32 ✕

Via Arenula

Via del Portico d'Ottavia

Largo Arenula

Piazza B Cairoli

Piazza Costaguti

Piazza Mattei

Via de Delfini

Piazza Capizucchi

Vic Margana

Via Margana

Piazza Lovatelli

Piazza di Campitelli

22 ✕

8 ◉

SANT'ANGELO

Piazza Cenci

Via Catalana

25 ✕ **24** ✕

Via San Bartolomeo dei Vaccinari

Via del Foro Piscario

Via delle Zoccolette

2 🏛

Campidoglio (Capitoline Hill)

13 🏛

200 m

0.1 miles

Centro Storico

Palazzo Farnese   Palace
(Map p72; www.inventerrome.com; Piazza Farnese; admission €5; ⊙guided tours 3pm, 4pm, 5pm Mon, Wed & Fri; ⊒Corso Vittorio Emanuele II) One of Rome's greatest Renaissance *palazzi*, Palazzo Farnese was started in 1514 by Antonio da Sangallo the Younger, continued by Michelangelo, and finished by Giacomo della Porta. Nowadays, it's home to the French Embassy, and open only to visitors who've booked a guided tour – see the website for details. Visits, for which you'll need to book at least a week in advance, take in the Galleria dei Carracci, home to a cycle of frescoes by Annibale Carracci that are said to rival those of the Sistine Chapel.

The twin fountains in the square are enormous granite baths taken from the Terme di Caracalla.

Jewish Ghetto   Neighbourhood
(Map p72; ⊒Lungotevere de' Cenci) Centred on lively Via del Portico d'Ottavia, the Jewish Ghetto is a wonderfully atmospheric area studded with artisans' studios, vintage clothes shops, kosher bakeries and popular trattorias.

TRIDENTE, TREVI & THE QUIRINALE

Piazza di Spagna & the Spanish Steps   Piazza
(Map p78; Ⓜ Spagna) A magnet for visitors since the 18th century, the Piazza di Spagna and the Spanish Steps (Scalinata della Trinità dei Monti) provide perfect people-watching perches and you'll almost certainly find yourself taking stock here at some point.

Piazza di Spagna was named after the Spanish Embassy to the Holy See, although the staircase, designed by the Italian Francesco de Sanctis and built in 1725 with a legacy from the French, leads to the French Chiesa della Trinità dei Monti.

At the foot of the steps, the Barcaccia (the 'sinking boat' fountain) is believed to be by Pietro Bernini, father of the more famous Gian Lorenzo.

Keats–Shelley House   Museum
(Map p78; ☎06 678 42 35; www.keats-shelley-house.org; Piazza di Spagna 26; adult/reduced €4.50/3.50; ⊙10am-1pm & 2-6pm Mon-Fri, 11am-2pm & 3-6pm Sat; Ⓜ Spagna) Overlooking the

SVARIOPHOTO/GETTY IMAGES ©

⭐ Don't Miss
Pantheon

A striking 2000-year-old temple, now church, the Pantheon is the city's best-preserved ancient monument and one of the most influential buildings in the Western world. The greying, pock-marked exterior might look its age, but inside it's a different story, and it's an exhilarating experience to pass through the towering bronze doors and have your vision directed upwards to the largest unreinforced concrete dome ever built.

NEED TO KNOW

Map p72; Piazza della Rotonda; ⏱8.30am-7.30pm Mon-Sat, 9am-6pm Sun; 🚌Largo di Torre Argentina

Spanish Steps, this is where the 25-year-old Romantic poet John Keats died of TB in February 1821. The house is now a small museum crammed with memorabilia relating to the ill-fated poet and his fellow scribes Byron, Mary Shelley and Percy Bysshe Shelley, who drowned off the Tuscan coast in 1822 and is buried with Keats in Rome's non-Catholic cemetery.

Piazza del Popolo   Piazza
(Map p78; Ⓜ Flaminio) For centuries the site of gruesome public executions, this

dazzling piazza was originally laid out in 1538 to provide a grandiose entrance to what was then Rome's main northern gateway. It has been remodelled several times since, most recently by Giuseppe Valadier in 1823.

Guarding its southern entry are Carlo Rainaldi's twin 17th-century baroque churches, Chiesa di Santa Maria dei Miracoli and Chiesa di Santa Maria in Montesanto, while over on the northern flank is the Porta del Popolo, created by Bernini in 1655 to celebrate Queen

75

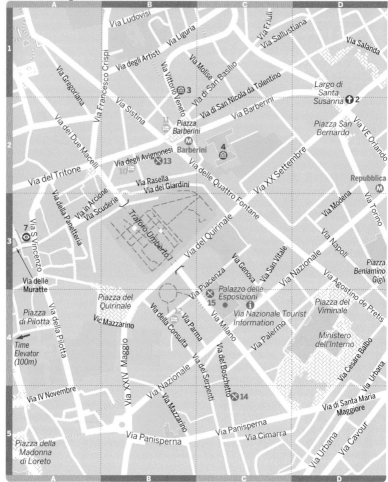

Christina of Sweden's defection to Catholicism. In the centre, the 36m-high obelisk was brought by Augustus from Heliopolis, in ancient Egypt, and originally stood in the Circo Massimo.

Museo dell'Ara Pacis Museum
(Map p78; ☎ 06 06 08; http://en.arapacis.it; Lungotevere in Augusta; adult/reduced €8.50/6.50; ⏰ 9am-7pm Tue-Sun, last admission 6pm; Ⓜ Flaminio) The first modern construction in Rome's historic centre since WWII,

Richard Meier's controversial, and widely detested, glass-and-marble pavilion houses the Ara Pacis Augustae (Altar of Peace), Augustus' great monument to peace. One of the most important works of ancient Roman sculpture, the vast marble altar – it measures 11.6m by 10.6m by 3.6m – was completed in 13 BC and positioned near Piazza San Lorenzo in Lucina, slightly to the southeast of its current site.

Trevi & Esquiline

two seahorses – one wild, one docile – representing the moods of the sea.

Galleria Nazionale d'Arte Antica: Palazzo Barberini   Gallery
(Map p76; ☎ 06 3 28 10; www.gebart.it; Via delle Quattro Fontane 13; adult/reduced €7/3.50, incl Palazzo Corsini €9/4.50; ⊙8.30am-7pm Tue-Sun; Ⓜ Barberini) Commissioned to celebrate the Barberini family's rise to papal power, Palazzo Barberini is a sumptuous baroque palace that impresses even before you go inside and start on the breathtaking art. Many high-profile architects worked on it, including rivals Bernini and Borromini: the former contributed a large squared staircase, the latter a helicoidal one.

Amid the masterpieces, don't miss Pietro da Cortona's *Il Trionfo della Divina Provvidenza* (Triumph of Divine Providence; 1632–39), the most spectacular of the palazzo's ceiling frescoes in the 1st-floor main salon.

Trevi Fountain   Fountain
(Fontana di Trevi; Map p76; Piazza di Trevi; Ⓜ Barberini) The Fontana di Trevi, scene of Anita Ekberg's dip in *La Dolce Vita*, is Rome's largest and most famous fountain. A flamboyant baroque ensemble of mythical figures, wild horses and cascading rock falls, it takes up the entire side of the 17th-century Palazzo Poli.

The design, the work of Nicola Salvi in 1732, depicts Neptune in a shell-shaped chariot being led by Tritons and

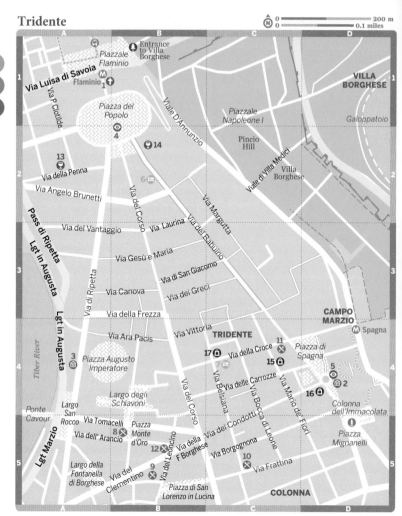

Tridente

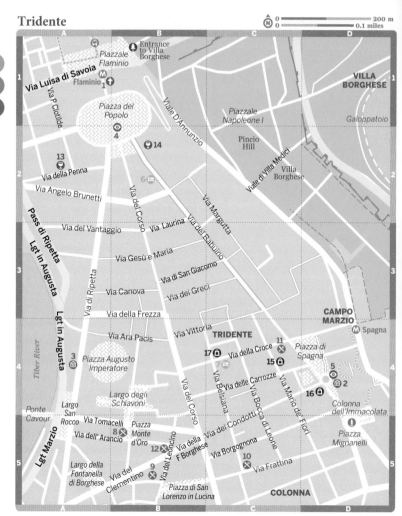

Entrance to Villa Borghese

Tridente

◎ Sights

1 Chiesa di Santa Maria del Popolo	A1
2 Keats–Shelley House	D4
3 Museo dell'Ara Pacis	A4
4 Piazza del Popolo	B2
5 Piazza di Spagna & Spanish Steps	D4

◎ Sleeping

6 Babuino 181	B2
7 Hotel Panda	C4

✖ Eating

8 Il Gelato	B5
9 Matricianella	B5
10 Palatium	C5
11 Pastificio	C4
12 Pizzeria al Leoncino	B5

◎ Drinking & Nightlife

13 La Scena	A2
14 Stravinskij Bar – Hotel de Russie	B2

◎ Shopping

15 C.U.C.I.N.A.	C4
16 Sermoneta	D4
17 Vertecchi Art	C4

ROME & THE VATICAN SIGHTS

78

Other must-sees include Hans Holbein's famous portrait of a pugnacious Henry VIII (c 1540), Filippo Lippi's luminous *Annunciazione e due devoti* (Annunciation with two Kneeling Donors) and Raphael's *La Fornarina* (The Baker's Girl), a portrait of his mistress who worked in a bakery in Trastevere.

Convento dei Cappuccini   Museum
(Map p76; [📞]06 487 11 85; Via Vittorio Veneto 27; adult/reduced €6/4; [🕐]9am-7pm daily; [Ⓜ]Barberini) This church and convent complex has an interesting multimedia museum telling the story of the Capuchin order of monks. The main attraction, however, is the extraordinary **Capuchin Cemetery** that lies below, where everything from the picture frames to the light fittings is made of human bones.

MONTI, ESQUILINE & SAN LORENZO

Chiesa di Santa Maria della Vittoria   Church
(Map p76; Via XX Settembre 17; [🕐]7am-noon & 3.30-7pm; [Ⓜ]Repubblica) This modest church is an unlikely setting for an extraordinary work of art – Bernini's *Santa Teresa trafitta dall'amore di Dio* (Ecstasy of St Teresa). This sexually charged sculpture depicts Teresa, engulfed in the folds of a flowing cloak, floating in ecstasy on a cloud while a teasing angel pierces her repeatedly with a golden arrow.

Basilica di Santa Maria Maggiore   Basilica
(Map p76; Piazza Santa Maria Maggiore; basilica free, museum €3, loggia €2; [🕐]7am-7pm, museum & loggia 9.30am-6.30pm; [🚍]Piazza Santa Maria Maggiore) One of Rome's four patriarchal basilicas, this monumental church stands on the summit of the Esquiline hill, on the spot where snow is said to have miraculously fallen in the summer of AD 358. In its earliest form it dates to the 5th century but it has been much altered over the centuries.

Outside, the exterior is decorated with glimmering 13th-century mosaics, protected by Ferdinand Fuga's 1741 baroque facade. Rising behind is a 14th-century Romanesque **belfry**, which, at 75m, is the highest in Rome.

Basilica di San Pietro in Vincoli   Basilica
(Map p66; Piazza di San Pietro in Vincoli 4a; [🕐]8am-12.30pm & 3-7pm Apr-Sep, to 6pm Oct-Mar; [Ⓜ]Cavour) Pilgrims and art lovers flock to this 5th-century church for two reasons: to marvel at Michelangelo's macho Moses sculpture and to see the chains that bound St Peter when he was imprisoned in the Carcere Mamertino.

Crypt in the Capuchin Cemetery
RICHARD ROSS/GETTY IMAGES ©

If You Like...
Controversial Caravaggios

Caravaggio painted some of the most dramatic and influential artworks in Rome in the 17th century.

1 CHIESA DI SAN LUIGI DEI FRANCESI
(Map p72; Piazza di San Luigi dei Francesi; ☺10am-12.30pm & 3-7pm, closed Thu afternoon; 🚊Corso del Rinascimento) This art-rich baroque bonanza boasts no less than three canvases by Caravaggio: *La Vocazione di San Matteo* (The Calling of Saint Matthew), *Il Martiro di San Matteo* (The Martyrdom of Saint Matthew) and *San Matteo e l'Angelo* (Saint Matthew and the Angel), together known as the St Matthew cycle.

2 CHIESA DI SANT'AGOSTINO
(Map p72; Piazza di Sant'Agostino 80; ☺7.30am-12.30pm & 4-6.30pm; 🚊Corso del Rinascimento) This 15th-century early Renaissance church contains Caravaggio's *Madonna dei Pellegrini* (Madonna of the Pilgrims), which caused uproar when it was unveiled in 1604, due to its depiction of Mary as barefoot and her two devoted pilgrims as filthy beggars.

3 CHIESA DI SANTA MARIA DEL POPOLO
(Map p78; Piazza del Popolo; ☺7.30am-noon & 4-7pm; Ⓜ Flaminio) A magnificent repository of art, this is one of Rome's earliest and richest Renaissance churches. The dazzling highlight is the Cappella Cerasi with its two Caravaggio masterpieces: the *Conversione di San Paolo* (Conversion of St Paul) and the *Crocifissione di San Pietro* (Crucifixion of St Peter).

Museo Nazionale Romano: Palazzo Massimo alle Terme   Museum
(Map p76; 🕿06 3996 7700; www.coopculture.it; Largo di Villa Peretti 1; adult/reduced €7/3.50; ☺9am-7.45pm Tue-Sun; Ⓜ Termini) One of Rome's great unsung heroes, this fabulous museum is a treasure trove of classical art and sculpture. The first two floors are devoted to sculpture, with some breathtaking pieces. These include the 2nd-century BC Greek bronze, the *Pugile* (Boxer), a crouching Aphrodite from Villa Adriana, the graceful 2nd-century BC *Ermafrodite dormiente* (Sleeping Hermaphrodite), and the idealised *Il discobolo* (Discus Thrower). However, it's the rich, vivid frescoes on the 2nd floor that are the undoubted highlight. Particularly breathtaking are the frescoes (dating from 30 BC to 20 BC) from Villa Livia, one of the homes of Augustus' wife Livia Drusilla.

CELIAN HILL & SAN GIOVANNI

Basilica di San Clemente   Basilica
(Map p62; www.basilicasanclemente.com; Via di San Giovanni in Laterano; church/excavations free/€5; ☺9am-12.30pm & 3-6pm Mon-Sat, noon-6pm Sun; Ⓜ Colosseo) This fascinating basilica provides a vivid glimpse into Rome's multilayered past: a 12th-century basilica built over a 4th-century church, which, in turn, stands over a 2nd-century pagan temple and 1st-century Roman house. Beneath everything are foundations dating from the Roman Republic.

Basilica di San Giovanni in Laterano   Basilica
(Map p62; Piazza di San Giovanni in Laterano 4; basilica free, cloister €3; ☺7am-6.30pm, cloister 9am-6pm; Ⓜ San Giovanni) For a thousand years this monumental cathedral was the most important church in Christendom. Commissioned by the Emperor Constantine and consecrated in AD 324, it was the first Christian basilica built in the city and, until the late 14th century, was the pope's main place of worship. It is still Rome's official cathedral and the pope's seat as the bishop of Rome.

Scala Santa & Sancta Sanctorum   Chapel
(Map p62; Piazza di San Giovanni in Laterano 14; Scala/Sancta free/€3.50; ☺Scala 6.15am-noon & 3.30-6.30pm summer, 6.15am-noon & 3-6pm winter, Sancta Sanctorum 9.30am-noon & 3-5pm, closed Wed am & Sun year-round; Ⓜ San Giovanni) Brought to Rome by St Helena in the 4th century, the Scala Santa is said to be the

DORLING KINDERSLEY/GETTY IMAGES ©

★ Don't Miss
Terme di Caracalla

The remnants of Emperor Caracalla's vast baths complex, Terme di Caracalla are among Rome's most awe-inspiring ruins. Inaugurated in 216, the 10-hectare complex comprised baths, gymnasiums, libraries, shops and gardens, and was used by up to 8000 people every day. Underground, slaves sweated in 9.5km of tunnels, tending to the plumbing systems.

NEED TO KNOW
Map p62; 📞 06 3996 7700; www.coopculture.it; Viale delle Terme di Caracalla 52; adult/reduced €7/4; ⏱ 9am-1hr before sunset Tue-Sun, 9am-2pm Mon ; 🚇 Viale delle Terme di Caracalla

staircase that Jesus walked up in Pontius Pilate's palace in Jerusalem. Pilgrims consider it sacred and climb it on their knees, saying a prayer on each of the 28 steps.

SOUTHERN ROME
Basilica di San Paolo
Fuori le Mura   Basilica
(Map p62; www.abbaziasanpaolo.net; Via Ostiense 190; cloisters €4; ⏱ 7am-6.30pm; 🚇 San Paolo) The largest church in Rome after St Peter's (and therefore the world's third-largest), this magnificent basilica stands on the site where St Paul was buried after being decapitated in AD 67.

Built by Constantine in the 4th century, it was largely destroyed by fire in 1823 and much of what you see is a 19th-century reconstruction.

Via Appia Antica   Historic Site
(Appian Way; Map p62; 📞 06 513 53 16; www.parcoappiaantica.it; 🚇 Via Appia Antica) Named after consul Appius Claudius Caecus who laid the first 90km section in 312 BC, ancient Rome's *regina viarum* (queen of roads) was extended in 190 BC to reach Brindisi on Italy's Adriatic coast. Nowadays, Via Appia Antica is one of Rome's most exclusive addresses, a beautiful cobbled

81

Trastevere

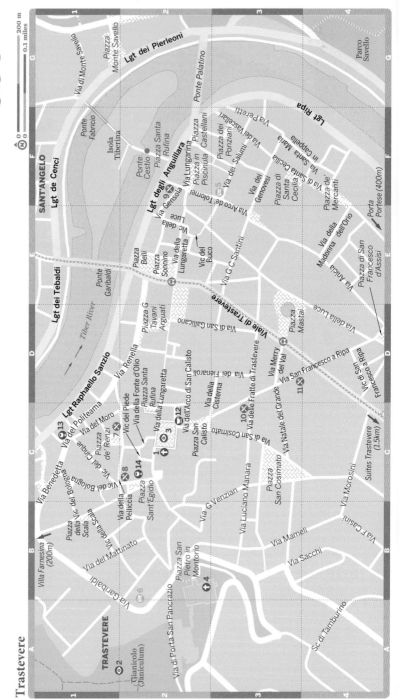

Ê 0
N 0 ⊙

200 m
0.1 miles

TRASTEVERE

SANT'ANGELO

thoroughfare flanked by grassy fields, ancient ruins and towering pine trees.

The **Appia Antica Regional Park Information Point** (Map p62; ☎ 06 513 53 16; www.parcoappiaantica.it; Via Appia Antica 58-60; ⊗9.30am-1pm & 2-5.30pm Mon-Fri, 9.30am-6.30pm Sat & Sun, to 5pm winter) sells maps of the park and hires bikes (per hour/day €3/15) and electric bikes (€6/20). To get to Via Appia Antica, catch bus 218 from Piazza di San Giovanni in Laterano, bus 660 from the Colli Albani stop on metro A, or bus 118 from the Piramide stop on metro B. From Termini, the hop-on, hop-off **Archeobus** (Map p76; ☎ 800 281281; www.trambusopen.com; family/adult €40/12; ⊗half-hourly 9am-12.30pm & 1.30-4.30pm) serves Via Appia Antica, stopping at points of archaeological interest along the way.

Chiesa del Domine Quo Vadis?
Church

(Map p62; Via Appia Antica 51; ⊗8am-6.30pm Mon-Fri, 8.15am-6.45pm Sat & Sun winter, to 7.30pm summer; 🚍Via Appia Antica) This pint-sized church marks the spot where St Peter, fleeing Rome, met a vision of Jesus going the other way. When Peter asked: '*Domine, quo vadis?*' (Lord, where are you going?), Jesus replied, '*Venio Roman iterum crucifigi*' (I am coming to Rome to be crucified again). Reluctantly deciding to join him, Peter tramped back into town where he was arrested and executed.

Catacombe di San Callisto
Catacomb

(☎ 06 513 01 51; www.catacombe.roma.it; Via Appia Antica 110 & 126; adult/reduced €8/5; ⊗9am-noon & 2-5pm, closed Wed mid-Jan–mid-Feb; 🚍Via Appia Antica) These are the largest and busiest of Rome's catacombs. Founded at the end of the 2nd century and named after Pope Calixtus I, they became the official cemetery of the newly established Roman Church. In the 20km of tunnels explored to date, archaeologists have found the tombs of 500,000 people and seven popes who were martyred in the 3rd century.

TRASTEVERE & GIANICOLO

Standing atop **Gianicolo** (Map p82; Via del Gianicolo; 🚍Via del Gianicolo) hill, you'll experience the city's best views, the closest you can get to soaring like a bird.

Piazza Santa Maria in Trastevere
Piazza

(Map p82; 🚍Viale di Trastevere, 🚊Viale di Trastevere) Trastevere's square is a prime people-watching spot. By day it's full of mums with strollers, chatting locals and guidebook-toting tourists; by night it's the domain of both foreign students and young Romans, all out for a good time. The fountain in the centre is of Roman origin and was restored by Carlo Fontana in 1692.

Basilica di Santa Maria in Trastevere
Basilica

(Map p82; Piazza Santa Maria in Trastevere; ⊗7.30am-9pm; 🚍Viale di Trastevere, 🚊Viale di Trastevere) This glittering basilica is said to be the oldest church in Rome dedicated to the Virgin Mary. Dating to the early 3rd century, it stands on the spot where, according to legend, a fountain of oil miraculously sprang from the ground. Its current form is the result of a major overhaul in 1138 that saw the addition of a Romanesque belltower and glittering facade. The portico came later, added by Carlo Fontana in 1702.

Vatican City

Map legend:

PRATI

Entrance to Vatican Museums

Pizzarium (500m)

Viale Vaticano

Viale della Zitella

Via Vespasiano

Piazza del Risorgimento

Via Cola di Rienzo

Via Silla

Via Terenzio

Via Tibullo

Via Properzio

Via Crescenzio

2 Vatican Museums

Via Leto

Via S Porcari

Borgo Angelico

Via S Porcari

Via Alberico II

Piazza Amerigo Capponi

Via della Posta

Via del Pellegrino

Via di Porta Angelica

VATICAN CITY

Via del Belvedere

Borgo Vittorio

Via Plauto

Borgo Pio

Via Ombrellari

BORGO

Vatican Gardens

Largo San Martino

Piazza della Città Leonina

Via dei Corridori

Borgo Sant'Angelo

3 Entrance to St Peter's Dome

St Peter's Square (Piazza San Pietro)

Largo Colonnato

Via Erba

Piazza Giovanni XXIII

St Peter's Basilica 1

4

Piazza Pio XII

Via della Conciliazione

Piazza dei P Romani

Centro Servizi Pellegrini e Turisti

Borgo Santo Spirito

Largo I Gregore

Piazza Santa Marta

Via del Sant'Uffizio — Via Paolo VI

Gianicolo (Janiculum)

Vatican City

Don't Miss Sights
1 St Peter's Basilica B3
2 Vatican Museums A1

Sights
3 Sistine Chapel B3
4 St Peter's Square B3

Sleeping
5 Hotel Bramante C2

Tempietto di Bramante & Chiesa di San Pietro in Montorio   Church

(Map p82; www.sanpietroinmontorio.it; Piazza San Pietro in Montorio 2; ☾Chiesa 8.30am-noon & 3-4pm Mon-Fri, Tempietto 9.30am-12.30pm & 2-4.30pm Tue-Sun; ☒Via Garibaldi) Considered the first great building of the High Renaissance, Bramante's sublime Tempietto (Little Temple; 1508) stands in the courtyard of the Chiesa di San Pietro in Montorio, on the spot where St Peter is said to have been crucified.

VATICAN CITY, BORGO & PRATI

Castel Sant'Angelo   Museum

(Map p62; ☏06 681 91 11; Lungotevere Castello 50; adult/reduced €8.50/6; ☾9am-7.30pm Tue-Sun, last admission 6.30pm ; ☒Piazza Pia) With its chunky round keep, this castle is an instantly recognisable landmark. Built as a mausoleum for the emperor Hadrian, it was converted into a papal fortress in the 6th century and named after an angelic vision that Pope Gregory the Great had in 590.

Thanks to a secret 13th-century passageway to the Vatican palaces (the Passetto di Borgo), it provided sanctuary to many popes in times of danger.

Ponte Sant'Angelo   Bridge

(Map p72; ☒Piazza Pia) The emperor Hadrian built Ponte Sant'Angelo in 136 to provide an approach to his mausoleum (now Castel Sant'Angelo), but it was Bernini who brought it to life with his angel sculptures in the 17th century.

★ Don't Miss
Vatican Museums

Founded by Pope Julius II in the early 16th century, the Vatican Museums contain one of the world's greatest art collections. Exhibits range from Egyptian mummies and Etruscan bronzes to Old Masters and modern paintings, but the main drawcards are the spectacular classical statuary and Michelangelo's frescoes in the Sistine Chapel.

Often overlooked by visitors, the **Pinacoteca** boasts Raphael's last work, *La Trasfigurazione* (Transfiguration; 1517–20), and paintings by Giotto, Bellini, Caravaggio, Fra Angelico, Filippo Lippi, Guido Reni, Van Dyck, Pietro da Cortona and Leonardo da Vinci, whose *San Gerolamo* (St Jerome; c 1480) was never finished.

The stunning **Museo Pio-Clementino** contains some of the Vatican Museums' finest classical statuary, including the peerless *Apollo Belvedere* and the 1st-century *Laocoön*, both in the **Cortile Ottagono** (Octagonal Courtyard).

The four frescoed **Stanze di Raffaello** (Raphael Rooms) were part of Pope Julius II's private apartments. Raphael himself painted the Stanza della Segnatura (1508–11) and the Stanza d'Eliodoro (1512–14), while the Stanza dell'Incendio (1514–17) and Sala di Costantino (1517–24) were decorated by students following his designs.

The 15th-century **Sistine Chapel** (Capella Sistina; Map p84; ☎06 69 88 43 41; www.vatican. va/museums; Viale del Vaticano; adult/concession/child €13/8/free; ☺hours vary; 🚌to Piazza del Risorgimento, ⓂOttaviano, Cipro-Musei Vatican) can attract up to 20,000 people a day. It's home to two of the world's most famous works of art – Michelangelo's ceiling frescoes and the *Giudizio Universale* (Last Judgment).

NEED TO KNOW

Musei Vaticani; Map p84; ☎06 6988 4676; http://mv.vatican.va; Viale Vaticano; adult/concession €16/8, admission free last Sun of month; ☺9am-6pm Mon-Sat, last admission 4pm, 9am-2pm last Sun of month, last admission 12.30pm; ⓂOttaviano–San Pietro

JEAN-PIERRE LESCOURRET/GETTY IMAGES ©

⭐ Don't Miss
St Peter's Basilica

In a city of outstanding churches, none holds a candle to St Peter's Basilica (Basilica di San Pietro), Italy's largest, richest and most spectacular church. It's also one of Rome's busiest tourist attractions, drawing up to 20,000 people on a busy day.

The original basilica was commissioned by Emperor Constantine and built around 349 on the site where St Peter is said to have been buried between AD 64 and 67. But like many medieval churches, it eventually fell into disrepair and it wasn't until the mid-15th century that efforts were made to restore it.

Built between 1608 and 1612, the immense facade by Carlo Maderno is 48m high and 118.6m wide. Eight 27m columns support the upper attic on which 13 statues stand representing Christ the Redeemer, St John the Baptist and the 11 apostles.

The cavernous 187m-long interior covers more than 15,000 sq metres and contains spectacular works of art, including Michelangelo's hauntingly beautiful *Pietà* at the head of the right nave. To climb the **dome** (with/without lift €7/5; ⊙8am-6pm Apr-Sep, 8am-5pm Oct-Mar), enter to the right of the basilica. A lift takes you halfway, but it's still a long climb to the top (320 steps).

Beneath the basilica, the **Vatican Grottoes** (admission free; ⊙8am-6pm Apr-Sep, 8am-5.30pm Oct-Mar) were created as a burial place for popes. You'll see tombs and sarcophagi, as well as several huge columns from the original 4th-century basilica. Excavations have also uncovered what the Vatican believes is the **Tomb of St Peter** (admission €13, over 15s only; ⊙by reservation only). Excavation visits are by 90-minute guided tour; email Ufficio Scavi (scavi@fsp.va).

NEED TO KNOW
Map p84; www.vatican.va; St Peter's Square; ⊙7am-7pm Apr-Sep, to 6.30pm Oct-Mar;
Ⓜ Ottaviano–San Pietro

Villa Borghese
Park

(Map p62; Entrances at Piazzale San Paolo del Brasile, Piazzale Flaminio, Via Pinciana, Largo Pablo Picasso; ☺dawn-dusk; ☐Porta Pinciana) Locals, lovers, tourists, joggers – no one can resist the lure of Rome's most celebrated park. Originally the estate of Cardinal Scipione Borghese's 17th-century residence, it covers about 80 hectares and boasts several museums and galleries, as well as the **Giardino del Lago** (Map p62) and **Piazza di Siena** (Map p62), an amphitheatre used for Rome's top equestrian event in May.

Galleria Nazionale d'Arte Moderna
Art Gallery

(Map p62; ☎06 3229 8221; www.gnam.beniculturali.it; Viale delle Belle Arti 131, disabled entrance Via Gramsci 71; adult/reduced €8/4; ☺8.30am-7.30pm Tue-Sun; ☐Piazza Thorvaldsen) Housed in a vast belle époque palace, this impressive but oft-overlooked gallery showcases works by the most important exponents of modern Italian art. There are canvasses by the *macchiaioli* (the Italian Impressionists) and futurists Boccioni and Balla, as well as sculptures by Canova and major paintings by Modigliani and de Chirico.

👉 Tours

A Friend in Rome
Walking Tour

(☎340 501 92 01; www.afriendinrome.it) Silvia Prosperi organises private tailor-made tours (on foot, by bike or scooter). She covers the Vatican and main historic centre as well as areas outside the capital. Rates are €40 to €50 per hour, with a minimum of three hours for most tours.

Trambus 110open
Bus Tour

(Map p76; ☎800 281281; www.trambusopen.com; family/adult/reduced €50/20/18; ☺every 15min 8.30am-7pm) A hop-on hop-off bus tour. It departs from Piazza dei Cinquecento outside Termini and stops at the Colosseum, Bocca della Verità, Piazza Venezia, St Peter's, Ara Pacis and Trevi Fountain. Tickets are valid for 48 hours and are available on board, from author-

ised dealers, and from kiosks on Piazza dei Cinquecento and at the Colosseum.

Papal Audiences

At 11am every Wednesday, the pope addresses his flock at the Vatican (in July and August in Castel Gandolfo near Rome). For details of how to apply for free tickets, see the **Vatican website** (www.vatican.va/various/prefettura/index_en.html).

When he is in Rome, the pope blesses the crowd in **St Peter's Square** (Piazza San Pietro; Map p84; ⓂOttaviano-San Pietro) on Sunday at noon. No tickets are required.

✸ Festivals & Events

Carnevale Romano
Carnival

(www.carnevale.roma.it) Rome goes to town for *carnevale* with horse shows on Piazza del Popolo, costumed parades down Via del Corso and crowds of kids in fancy dress.

Easter
Religious

On Good Friday, the pope leads a candlelit procession around the Colosseum. At noon on Easter Sunday he blesses the crowds in St Peter's Square.

Mostra delle Azalee
Culture

From mid-April to early May, the Spanish Steps are emblazoned with 600 vases of blooming, brightly coloured azaleas.

Natale di Roma
Culture

Rome celebrates its birthday on 21 April with music, historical recreations, fireworks and free entry to many museums. Action is centred on the Campidoglio and Circo Massimo.

Estate Romana
Culture

(www.estateromana.comune.roma.it) From June to September Rome's big summer festival stages hundreds of cultural events and activities across the capital.

Don't Miss
Museo e Galleria Borghese

If you only have time (or inclination) for one art gallery in Rome, make it this one. Housing the 'queen of all private art collections', it boasts paintings by Caravaggio, Botticelli and Raphael, as well as some spectacular sculptures by Gian Lorenzo Bernini. To limit numbers, visitors are admitted at two-hourly intervals, so you'll need to call to book.

Map p62

☎ 06 3 28 10

www.galleriaborghese.it

Piazzale del Museo Borghese 5

adult/reduced €9/4.50, plus €2 booking fee and possible exhibition supplement

🕓 9am-7pm Tue-Sun, pre-booking necessary

🚌 Via Pinciana

Downstairs

Cardinal Scipione Borghese (1579–1633) was the most knowledgeable and ruthless art collector of his day. His collection is housed in the Casino Borghese, whose neoclassical look is the result of a 17th-century revamp of Scipione's original villa. Things get off to a cracking start in the entrance hall, decorated with 4th-century floor mosaics of fighting gladiators and a gravity-defying bas-relief of a horse and rider falling into the void by Pietro Bernini (Gian Lorenzo's father).

Sala I is centred on Antonio Canova's daring depiction of Napoleon's sister, Paolina Bonaparte Borghese, as *Venere vincitrice* (Venus Victorious; 1805–08). Yet Gian Lorenzo Bernini's spectacular sculptures – flamboyant depictions of pagan myths –steal the show. Just look at Daphne's hands morphing into leaves in *Apollo e Dafne* (1622–25) in Sala III.

Caravaggio dominates Sala VIII. There's the strangely beautiful *La Madonna dei Palafenieri* (Madonna with Serpent; 1605–06) and *San Giovanni Battista* (St John the Baptist; 1609–10), probably Caravaggio's last work. Then there's the *Ragazzo col Canestro di Frutta* (Boy with a Basket of Fruit; 1593–95) and the dramatic *Davide con la Testa di Golia* (David with the Head of Goliath; 1609–10) – Goliath's severed head is said to be a self-portrait.

Upstairs

Upstairs, the Pinacoteca offers a wonderful snapshot of European Renaissance art. Don't miss Raphael's *La Deposizione di Cristo* (The Deposition; 1507) in Sala IX, and his *Dama con Liocorno* (Lady with a Unicorn; 1506). In the same room is the superb *Adorazione del Bambino* (Adoration of the Christ Child; 1495) by Fra Bartolomeo and Perugino's *Madonna con Bambino* (Madonna and Child; 16th century).

Other highlights include Correggio's *Danae* (1530–31) in Sala X, Bernini's self-portraits in Sala XIV and Titian's *Amor Sacro e Amor Profano* (Sacred and Profane Love; 1514) in Sala XX.

Museo e Galleria Borghese

RECOMMENDATIONS FROM ALESSIO ZITO, TOUR GUIDE

1 VENERE VINCITRICE
Antonio Canova's depiction of Napoleon's sister, Paolina Borghese, as Venere Vincitrice (Venus Victorious) is sublime. You could spend hours marvelling at how Canova managed to make the figure 'sink' into the cushions.

2 RATTO DI PROSERPINA
Gian Lorenzo Bernini's sculpture *The Rape of Proserpina* (1621–2) is incredible in that its twisting composition allows the simultaneous depiction of Pluto's abduction of Proserpina, their arrival in the underworld and her praying for release. To experience the narrative, start from the left, move to the front, and then view it from the right.

3 RITRATTO DI GIOVANE DONNA CON UNICORNO
Raphael's portrait *Lady with a Unicorn* (c 1506) was inspired by da Vinci's *The Lady with an Ermine* (1490). The painting originally depicted a woman holding a dog, a symbol of fidelity. But when the marriage did not take place, scholars believe, Raphael replaced the dog with a unicorn, a symbol of chastity or virginity.

4 SATIRE SU DELFINO
In Sala VII, the 'Egyptian Room', you'll find the *Satyr on a Dolphin*, dating from the 2nd century and probably intended for a fountain. The piece is believed to have inspired Raphael's design for the figure of *Jonah and the Whale* in the Chigi Chapel inside the Chiesa di Santa Maria del Popolo.

5 BACCHINO MALATO
Of the many Caravaggio paintings, *Sick Bacchus* (1592–5) is particularly intriguing for its portrayal of the god of heady pleasures as a pale, tired-looking youth. Scholars believe the self-portrait was executed when Caravaggio was suffering from malaria.

Lungo il Tevere
Arts

(www.lungoiltevereroma.it) Stalls, clubs, bars, restaurants and dance floors line the banks of the Tiber for this summer-long jamboree.

Festa dei Santi Pietro e Paolo
Religious

Romans celebrate patron saints Peter and Paul on 29 June. Festivities are centred on St Peter's Basilica and Via Ostiense.

Festa de'Noantri
Culture

Trastevere celebrates its roots with a raucous street party in the last two weeks of July. Expect much feasting, drinking, dancing and praying.

RomaEuropa
Performing Arts

(http://romaeuropa.net) From late September to November, top international artists take to the stage for Rome's premier festival of theatre, opera and dance.

Sleeping

Rome doesn't really have a low season as such but most hotels drop prices from November to March (excluding Christmas and New Year) and from mid-July through August.

Always try to book ahead. If you arrive without a reservation, there's a **hotel reservation service** (Map p62; ☎06 699 10 00; booking fee €3; ◷7am-10pm) next to the tourist office at Stazione Termini.

Everyone overnighting in Rome has to pay a room occupancy tax on top of the regular accommodation bill. This amounts to: €2 per person per night for a maximum of 10 days in *agriturismi* (farm-stay accommodation), B&Bs, guesthouses, convents, monasteries and one-, two- and three-star hotels; €3 per person per night for a maximum of 10 days in four- and five-star hotels.

Left: Piazza Navona (p69)
Below: Bocca della Verità (p69)
(LEFT) LES AND DAVE JACOBS/GETTY IMAGES ©; (BELOW) MARTIN MOOS/GETTY IMAGES ©

ANCIENT ROME

Residenza Maritti
Guesthouse €

(Map p66; ☎06 678 82 33; www.residenzamaritti.com; Via Tor de' Conti 17; s €50-90, d €80-130, tr €110-150; ❄@📶; Ⓜ Cavour) Boasting stunning views – from the terrace you can marvel at 360-degrees of ruins and rooftops – this hidden gem is housed in an 18th-century *palazzo* behind the Foro di Augusto. Its rooms, spread over two apartments, are decorated in a simple, cosy style with antiques and family furniture. Each apartment also has a fully equipped kitchen.

Caesar House
Hotel €€

(Map p66; ☎06 679 26 74; www.caesarhouse.com; Via Cavour 310; s €150-200, d €160-260; ❄📶; Ⓜ Cavour) Quiet and friendly, yet in the thick of it on Via Cavour, this is a small hotel in a renovated apartment. Its public areas are polished and modern, while the six guest rooms feature tiled floors, soothing colours and four-poster beds.

CENTRO STORICO

Hotel Pensione Barrett
Pension €€

(Map p72; ☎06 686 84 81; www.pensionebarrett.com; Largo di Torre Argentina 47; s €115, d €135, tr €160; ❄📶; 🚌 Largo di Torre Argentina) A charming Aladdin's cave of a pension on Largo di Torre Argentina. The sheer exuberance of the decor is extraordinary, with everything from pot plants and antiques to busts, statues and stucco. Rooms are cosy and come with a range of thoughtful extras including foot spas and fully-stocked fridges.

Teatropace 33
Hotel €€

(Map p72; ☎06 687 90 75; www.hotelteatropace.com; Via del Teatro Pace 33; s €80-150, d €130-270; ❄📶; 🚌 Corso del Rinascimento) Near Piazza Navona, this welcoming three-star is a class choice with 23 beautifully appointed rooms decorated with parquet, damask curtains and exposed wood beams. There's no lift, just a monumental 17th-century stone staircase and a porter to carry your bags.

Hotel Campo de' Fiori
Boutique Hotel €€€

(Map p72; ☑ 06 687 48 86; www.hotelcampo-defiori.com; Via del Biscione 6; r & apt €90-600; ✴@☎; 🚍Corso Vittorio Emanuele II) This rakish four-star has got the lot – sexy decor, an enviable location, professional staff and a panoramic roof terrace. Rooms are individually decorated and they all feel delightfully decadent with boldly coloured walls, low wooden ceilings, gilt mirrors and restored bric-a-brac. The hotel also has 13 apartments, ideal for families.

TRIDENTE, TREVI & THE QUIRINALE

Hotel Panda
Pension €

(Map p78; ☑ 06 678 01 79; www.hotelpanda.it; Via della Croce 35; s €65-80, d €85-108, tr €120-140, q €180; ✴☎; MSpagna) Only 50m from the Spanish Steps, in an area where a bargain is a Bulgari watch bought in the sales, the friendly, efficient Panda is an anomaly: a budget pension and a splendid one. The clean rooms are smallish but nicely furnished, and there are several triples with a bed on a cosy mezzanine. Air-con costs €6 per night. Book well ahead.

Daphne B&B
B&B €€

(☑06 8745 0086; www.daphne-rome.com; Via di San Basilio 55; d €140-235, without bathroom €100-150; ✴@☎; MBarberini) Boutique B&B Daphne is a gem. Run by an American-Italian couple, it has sleek, comfortable rooms, helpful English-speaking staff, top-notch breakfasts and the loan of a mobile phone for your stay. There are rooms in two locations – the one off Via Veneto is the pick, but there's a second at **Via degli Avignonesi 20** (Map p76). Book months ahead.

Hotel Barocco
Hotel €€

(Map p76; ☑ 06 487 20 01; www.hotelbarocco.com; Piazza Barberini 9; d €170-290; ✴@☎; MBarberini) Very central, this well-run, welcoming hotel overlooking Piazza

Barberini (the pricier rooms have views) has a classic feel, with rooms featuring oil paintings, spotless linen, gentle colour schemes and fabric-covered walls. Breakfast is ample and served in a wood-panelled room.

Villa Spalletti Trivelli
Hotel €€€

(Map p76; ☑ 06 4890 7934; www.villaspalletti.it; Via Piacenza 4; r €450-530; P✴@☎; MSpagna) With 12 rooms in a glorious mansion, Villa Spalletti Trivelli has upped the ante for luxurious stays in the capital. Rooms are soberly and elegantly decorated, overlooking the gardens of the Quirinale or the estate's Italian garden. The overall feel is that of staying in the stately home of some aristocratic friends.

Babuino 181
Boutique Hotel €€€

(Map p78; ☑ 06 3229 5295; www.romeluxurysuites.com/babuino; Via del Babuino 181; r €180-780; ✴☎; MFlaminio) A beautifully renovated old *palazzo*, Babuino offers discreet luxury, with great attention to detail, a sleek roof terrace and modern, chic rooms with touches such as a Nespresso machine and fluffy bathrobes.

MONTI, ESQUILINE & SAN LORENZO

Blue Hostel
Hostel €

(Map p76; ☑ 340 9258503; www.bluehostel.it; Via Carlo Alberto 13; d €45-100, tr & q €60-120; P✴☎; MVittorio Emanuele) A hostel in name only, this pearl of a place offers hotel-standard rooms sleeping from two to four, each with its own en-suite bathroom and decorated in a tasteful low-key style – think beamed ceilings, wooden floors, French windows, and black-and-white framed photos.

Beehive
Hostel €

(Map p62; ☑ 06 4470 4553; www.the-beehive.com; Via Marghera 8; dm €25-30, s €50-60, d €90-100, without bathroom s €40-50, d €80-90, tr €95-105; ✴☎; MTermini) ✿ More boutique chic than backpacker crash pad, the Beehive is one of the best hostels in town. Run by a southern-Californian couple, it's an oasis of style with original artworks on the walls, funky modular furniture and a vegetarian cafe (prices don't include breakfast).

Beds are in a spotless, eight-person mixed dorm or in one of six private double rooms, all with fans. Private rooms also have air-con (€10 per night). Book ahead.

AVENTINE & TESTACCIO

Hotel Sant'Anselmo   Hotel €€€
(Map p62; 06 57 00 57; www.aventinohotels. com; Piazza Sant'Anselmo 2; s €130-265, d €150-290; ❄ @; Via Marmarata) A ravishing romantic hideaway set amid the terracotta villas and umbrella pines of the elegant Aventine district. Its rooms are not the biggest but they are stylish, marrying four-poster beds, polished marble and dripping chandeliers with modern touches and contemporary colours.

TRASTEVERE & GIANICOLO

Arco del Lauro   B&B €€
(Map p82; 9am-2pm 06 9784 0350, mobile 346 2443212; www.arcodellauro.it; Via Arco de' Tolomei 27; s €75-125, d €95-145; ❄ @ ; Viale di Trastevere, Viale di Trastevere) Through a large stone arch and on a narrow cobbled street, this fab six-room B&B in an ancient *palazzo* is a find, offering gleaming white rooms that combine rustic charm with minimalist simplicity. The largest room has a high wood-beamed ceiling. Beds are comfortable, showers are powerful and the owners are eager to please. Book well ahead.

Donna Camilla Savelli   Hotel €€€
(Map p82; 06 58 88 61; www.hoteldonna camillasavelli.com; Via Garibaldi 27; d €180-345; P ❄ @ ; Viale di Trastevere, Viale di Trastevere) If you have the cash, stay here, in this converted convent that was designed by baroque genius Borromini. It's been beautifully updated – muted colours complement the serene concave and convex curves of the architecture – and the service is excellent.

VATICAN CITY, BORGO & PRATI

Hotel San Pietrino   Hotel €
(Map p62; 06 370 01 32; www.sanpietrino.it; Via Bettolo 43; s €45-75, d €55-112, without bathroom s €35-55, d €45-85; ❄ @ ; M Ottaviano–San-Pietro) Within easy walking distance of St Peter's, San Pietrino is an excellent budget choice. Its cosy rooms are characterful and prettily decorated with terracotta tiled floors and the occasional statue. There's no breakfast but a drinks machine can supply emergency coffee.

Arco di Costantino (p63)

Hotel Bramante
Hotel €€

(Map p84; ☎ 06 6880 6426; www.hotelbramante. com; Vicolo delle Palline 24-25; s €100-160, d €140-240, tr €170-250, q €175-260; ❄🔊; 🚇Piazza del Risorgimento) Tucked away in an alleyway under the Vatican walls, the Bramante exudes country-house charm with its cosy internal courtyard and quietly elegant rooms – think rugs, wood-beamed ceilings and antiques. It's housed in the 16th-century building where architect Domenico Fontana once lived.

✖ Eating

Rome teems with trattorias, *ristoranti*, pizzerias, *enoteche* (wine bars serving food) and gelaterie. Excellent places dot the *centro storico*, Trastevere, Prati, Testaccio and San Lorenzo. Be warned that the area around Termini has quite a few substandard restaurants, as does the Vatican, which is packed with tourist traps.

Many restaurants close for several weeks during the traditional summer holiday month of August.

ANCIENT ROME
Enoteca Provincia Romana
Regional Cuisine €€

(Map p66; ☎ 06 6994 0273; Via Foro Traiano 82-4; meals €35, aperitifs from €5; ⏰11am-11pm Mon-Sat; 🚇Via dei Fori Imperiali) The best option in the touristy Forum area, this stylish wine bar-cum-restaurant showcases food from the surrounding Lazio region. There's a full daily menu of pastas and mains, as well as finger foods, wine by the glass and evening aperitifs. Lunchtime is busy but it quietens down in the evening.

CENTRO STORICO
Forno Roscioli
Pizza by Slice, Bakery €

(Map p72; Via dei Chiavari 34; pizza slices from €2, snacks from €1.50; ⏰7.30am-8pm Mon-Fri, 7.30am-2.30pm Sat; 🚇Via Arenula) Join the lunchtime crowds at this renowned bakery for a slice of pizza (the *pizza bianca* is legendary), fresh-from-the-oven pastries and hunger-sating *supplì* (fried rice croquettes). There's also a counter serving hot pastas and vegetable side dishes.

Pizza al taglio (pizza by the slice)

Top 5 Gelato

Gelato is as much a part of Roman life as traffic jams, and the city has some superb *gelaterie artigianale* (artisanal ice-cream shops). To gauge the quality, check out the pistachio flavour: if it's pale olive green it's good; if it's bright green, go elsewhere. Our road-tested top five *gelaterie*:

Fatamorgana (Map p62; www.gelateriafatamorgana.it; Via Bettolo 7; cones & tubs from €2; ⊙noon-11pm; MOttaviano–San Pietro) Try the mouthwatering *agrumi* (citrus fruit) and *basilico, miele e noci* (basil, honey and hazelnuts).

Il Gelato (Map p78; Piazza Monte d'Oro 91; from €2; ☐Via del Corso) Tuck into creative flavours made by Rome's gelato king, Claudio Torcè.

Gelateria del Teatro (Map p72; Via di San Simone 70; cones & tubs from €2; ⊙11am-11.30pm; ☐Corso del Rinascimento) Does a great turn in Sicilian *pistacchio* (pistachio) and *mandorle* (almonds).

Vice (Map p72; www.viceitalia.it; Corso Vittorio Emanuele II 96; cones & tubs from €2; ⊙11am-1am; ☐Largo di Torre Argentina) A contemporary outfit serving traditional and modern flavours such as blueberry cheesecake.

Il Caruso (Map p62; Via Collina 15; ⊙noon-9pm; MRepubblica) Top your gelato with *zabaglione* (egg and marsala custard) mixed with *panna* (whipped cream).

Forno di Campo de' Fiori
Pizza by Slice, Bakery €

(Map p72; Campo de' Fiori 22; pizza slices about €3; ⊙7.30am-2.30pm & 4.45-8pm Mon-Sat; ☐Corso Vittorio Emanuele II) On Campo de' Fiori, this is one of Rome's best takeaways, serving bread, *panini* (sandwiches) and delicious *pizza al taglio* (pizza by the slice). Aficionados swear by the pizza *bianca* ('white' pizza with olive oil, rosemary and salt), but the *panini* and pizza *rossa* ('red' pizza, with olive oil, tomato and oregano) are just as good.

Enoteca Corsi
Osteria €

(Map p72; ☎06 679 08 21; www.enotecacorsi.com; Via del Gesù 87; meals €25; ⊙lunch Mon-Sat; ☐Largo di Torre Argentina) Merrily the worse for wear, family-run Corsi is a genuine old-style Roman eatery. The look is rustic – bare wooden tables, paper tablecloths, wine bottles – and the atmosphere one of controlled mayhem. The menu, chalked up on a blackboard, offers no surprises, just honest, homey fare like *melanzane parmigiana* or roast chicken with potatoes.

Armando al Pantheon
Trattoria €€

(Map p72; ☎06 6880 3034; www.armandoalpantheon.it; Salita dei Crescenzi 31; meals €40; ⊙closed Sat dinner, Sun & Aug; ☐Largo di Torre Argentina, ☐Largo di Torre Argentina) An institution in these parts, wood-panelled Armando is a rare find – a genuine family-run trattoria in the touristy Pantheon area. It's been on the go for more than 50 years and has served its fair share of celebs – philosopher Jean-Paul Sartre and Brazilian footballer Pelé have both eaten here – but the focus remains on traditional Roman food. Reservations recommended.

Cul de Sac
Wine Bar, Trattoria €€

(Map p72; ☎06 6880 1094; www.enotecac-uldesac.com; Piazza Pasquino 73; meals €30; ⊙noon-4pm & 6pm-12.30am; ☐Corso Vittorio Emanuele II) A popular little wine bar, just off Piazza Navona, with an always-busy terrace and narrow, bottle-lined interior. Choose from the encyclopedic wine list and ample menu of Gallic-inspired cold cuts, pâtés, cheeses and main courses. Book for dinner.

Kosher Rome

If you want to eat kosher head to Via del Portico d'Ottavia, the main strip on the Jewish Ghetto. Lined with trattorias and restaurants specialising in kosher food and Roman-Jewish cuisine, it's a lively hang-out, especially on hot summer nights when diners crowd the many sidewalk tables. For a taste of typical Ghetto cooking, try the landmark **Giggetto al Portico d'Ottavia** (Map p72; ✆ 06 686 11 05; www.giggettoalportico.it; Via del Portico d'Ottavia 21a; meals €40; ⊙Tue-Sun; 🚊Via Arenula), or, at No 16, **Nonna Betta** (Map p72; ✆ 06 6880 6263; www.nonnabetta.it; Via del Portico d'Ottavia 16; meals €30-35; ⊙noon-4pm & 6-11pm, closed Fri dinner & Sat lunch; 🚊Via Arenula), a small tunnel of a trattoria serving local staples such as *carciofi alla giudia* (crisp fried artichokes). Further down the road, the unmarked **gelateria** (Map p72; Via del Portico d'Ottavia 1b; tubs €2-5, cones from €3; ⊙9am-10pm Sun-Fri, to midnight summer; 🚊Via Arenula) at No 1b has a small but tasty selection of kosher ice cream.

TRIDENTE, TREVI & THE QUIRINALE

Da Michele
Pizza by Slice €

(Map p62; ✆ 349 2525347; Via dell'Umiltà 31; pizza slice from €3; ⊙8am-5pm Mon-Fri, to 8pm summer; 🚊Via del Corso) A handy address near the Trevi Fountain. Buy your fresh, light and crispy *pizza al taglio*, and you'll have a delicious fast lunch. It's all kosher, so meat and cheese is not mixed.

Pizzeria al Leoncino
Pizzeria €

(Map p78; ✆ 06 686 77 57; Via del Leoncino 28; pizzas from €6; ⊙closed Wed & lunch Sat & Sun; 🚊Via del Corso) Some places just never change and this boisterous neighbourhood pizzeria is one of them. A bastion of budget eating in an otherwise expensive area, it has a wood-fired oven, two small rooms and gruff waiters who efficiently serve bruschettas, excellent Roman-style pizza and ice-cold beer. Cash only.

Colline Emiliane
Emilia-Romagna €€

(Map p76; ✆ 06 481 75 38; Via degli Avignonesi 22; meals €45; ⊙12.45-2.45pm Tue-Sun & 7.30-10.45pm Tue-Sat, closed Aug; Ⓜ Barberini) This welcoming restaurant just off Piazza Barberini flies the flag for Emilia-Romagna, the well-fed Italian region that has blessed the world with Parmesan, balsamic vinegar, bolognese sauce and Parma ham.

Pastificio
Fast Food €

(Map p78; Via della Croce 8; pasta dish €4; ⊙lunch 1-3pm Mon-Sat; Ⓜ Spagna) For most of the day Pastificio goes about its business as a fresh pasta shop, but at lunch time it turns itself into the neighbourhood's budget diner. Locals pile in to fill up on the daily pasta dishes (there's a choice of two) eaten out of plastic bowls wherever there's room.

Palatium
Wine Bar €€

(Map p78; ✆ 06 69 20 21 32; Via Frattina 94; meals €45; ⊙11am-11pm Mon-Sat, closed Aug; 🚊Via del Corso) A rich showcase of regional bounty, run by the Lazio Regional Food Authority, this sleek, ground-breaking wine bar serves excellent local specialities, such as *porchetta* (pork roasted with herbs), artisanal cheese and delicious salami, as well as an impressive array of local wines.

Matricianella
Trattoria €€

(Map p78; ✆ 06 683 21 00; www.matricianella.it; Via del Leone 2/4; meals €40; ⊙Mon-Sat; 🚊Via del Corso) With its gingham tablecloths, chintzy murals and fading prints, this model trattoria is loved for its traditional Roman cuisine. You'll find all the usual menu stalwarts as well as some great Roman-Jewish dishes. Romans go crazy for the fried antipasti, the artichoke *alla giudia* (fried, Jewish style) and the meatballs. Booking is essential.

Baccano
Brasserie €€

(Map p62; www.baccanoroma.com; Via delle Muratte 23; meals €45; ⏰8.30am-2am; 🚇Via del Corso) This is one of a new breed of restaurant–cafe-bars that are open all day. It serves breakfasts (eggs Benedict etc), then lunch, dinner, burgers, club sandwiches, cocktails, *aperitivi* – you name it, they've got it covered. The look is vintage Parisian glamour combined with 1990s New York City chic.

MONTI, ESQUILINE & SAN LORENZO

Panella l'Arte del Pane
Bakery, Cafe €

(Map p62; ☎06 487 24 35; Via Merulana 54; pizza slices around €3; ⏰noon-midnight Mon-Sat, 10am-4pm Sun Mar-Oct; 🚇Vittorio Emanuele) With a sumptuous array of *pizza al taglio, supplì*, focaccia and fried croquettes, this is a sublime lunch stop, where you can sip a glass of chilled *prosecco* while eyeing up gastronomic souvenirs from the deli.

Roscioli
Pizza by Slice, Bakery €

(Map p62; Via Buonarroti 48; pizza slices €3; ⏰7.30am-8pm Mon-Thu, to 9pm Fri & Sat; 🚇Vittorio Emanuele) Off-the-track branch of this splendid deli-bakery-pizzeria, with delish *pizza al taglio*, pasta dishes and other goodies that make it ideal for a swift lunch or picnic stock-up. It's on a road leading off Piazza Vittorio Emanuele II.

L'Asino d'Oro
Modern Italian €€

(Map p76; ☎06 4891 3832; Via del Boschetto 73; meals €45; ⏰Tue-Sat; 🚇Cavour) This fabulous restaurant has been transplanted from Orvieto and its Umbrian origins resonate in Lucio Sforza's exceptional cooking. It's unfussy yet innovative, with dishes featuring lots of flavourful contrasts, such as slow-roasted rabbit in a rich berry sauce and desserts that linger long after that last crumb. For such excellent food, this intimate, informal yet classy place is one of Rome's best deals, especially for the set lunch.

Trattoria Monti
Ristorante €€

(Map p76; ☎06 446 65 73; Via di San Vito 13a; meals €45; ⏰12.45-2.45pm Tue-Sun, 7.45-11pm Tue-Sat, closed Aug; 🚇Vittorio Emanuele) This elegant brick-arched place offers top-notch traditional cooking from the Marches region. There are wonderful *fritti* (fried things), delicate pastas and ingredients such as *pecorino di fossa* (sheep's cheese aged in caves), goose, swordfish and truffles. Try the egg-yolk *tortelli* pasta. Desserts are delectable, including apple pie with *zabaglione*. Book ahead.

Open Colonna
Modern Italian €€€

(Map p76; ☎06 4782 2641; www.antonellocolonna.it; Via Milano 9a; meals €20-80; ⏰noon-midnight Tue-Sat, lunch Sun; 🚇Via Nazionale) Spectacularly set at the back of the Palazzo delle Esposizioni, superchef

Gelati
MATTES RENÀ ©/GETTY IMAGES ©

Right: Piazza della Rotonda

(LEFT) CARLO A/GETTY IMAGES ©; (RIGHT) VISIONS OF OUR LAND/GETTY IMAGES ©

Antonello Colonna's superb restaurant is tucked onto a mezzanine floor under an extraordinary glass roof. The cuisine is new Roman: innovative takes on traditional dishes, cooked with wit and flair. Best of all, there's a more basic but still delectable fixed two-course lunch for €16, and Saturday and Sunday brunch is €30.

CELIAN HILL & SAN GIOVANNI

Li Rioni   Pizzeria €
(Map p62; ☎06 7045 0605; Via dei SS Quattro Coronati 24; pizzas €8; ⏱Thu-Tue, closed Aug; ⓂColosseo) Locals swear by Li Rioni, arriving for the second sitting around 9pm after the tourists have left. A classic neighbourhood pizzeria, it buzzes most nights as diners squeeze into the cosy interior – cheerfully set up as a Roman street scene – and tuck into wood-fired thin-crust pizzas and crispy *supplì*.

AVENTINE & TESTACCIO

00100 Pizza   Pizza by Slice €
(Map p62; www.00100pizza.com; Via G Branca 88; pizza slices from €3, trapizzini from €3.50; ⏱noon-11pm; ⎚Via Marmorata) This pocket-sized pizzeria is one of a select group of Roman takeaways with culinary ambitions. As well as pizzas topped with unusual combos such as potato, sausage and beer, you can snack on *supplì* and *trapizzini*, small cones of pizza stuffed with fillers like *polpette al sugo* (meatballs in tomato sauce) or *seppie con i piselli* (cuttlefish with peas).

Flavio al Velavevodetto Trattoria €€
(Map p62; ☎06 574 41 94; www.flavioalvelavevo detto.it; Via di Monte Testaccio 97-99; meals €30-35; ⏱closed Sat lunch & Sun summer; ⎚Via Marmorata) This welcoming eatery is the sort of place that gives Roman trattorias a good name. Housed in a rustic Pompeian-red villa, it specialises in earthy, no-nonsense Italian food, prepared with skill and served in mountainous portions.

TRASTEVERE & GIANICOLO

Sisini
Pizza by Slice €

(Map p82; Via di San Francesco a Ripa 137; pizza & pasta from €2, supplì €1.10; ☉9am-10.30pm Mon-Sat, closed Aug; 🚃Viale di Trastevere, 🚃Viale di Trastevere) Locals love this fast-food takeaway joint (the sign outside says 'Supplì') serving up fresh *pizza al taglio* and various pasta and risotto dishes. It's also worth sampling the *supplì* and roast chicken.

Da Augusto
Trattoria €

(Map p82; ☎06 580 37 98; Piazza de' Renzi 15; meals €25; ☉lunch & dinner; 🚃Viale di Trastevere, 🚃Viale di Trastevere) For a Trastevere feast, plonk yourself at one of Augusto's rickety tables, either inside or out on the small piazza, and prepare to enjoy some mamma-style cooking. The gruff waiters dish out hearty platefuls of *rigatoni all'amatriciana* (pasta tubes with pancetta, chilli and tomato sauce) and *stracciatella* (clear broth with egg and Parmesan) among a host of Roman classics. Be prepared to queue. Cash only.

Pizzeria Ivo
Pizzeria €

(Map p82; ☎06 581 70 82; Via di San Francesco a Ripa 158; pizzas around €7; ☉Wed-Mon; 🚃Viale di Trastevere, 🚃Viale di Trastevere) One of Trastevere's most famous pizzerias, Ivo's has been slinging pizzas for some 40 years, and still the hungry come. With the TV on in the corner and the tables full (a few outside on the cobbled street), it's a noisy, vibrant place, and the waiters fit the gruff-and-fast stereotype.

La Gensola
Sicilian €€

(Map p82; ☎06 581 63 12; Piazza della Gensola 15; meals €45; ☉closed Sun; 🚃Viale di Trastevere, 🚃Viale di Trastevere) This classy yet unpretentious trattoria thrills gourmets with delicious food that has a Sicilian slant and emphasis on seafood, including an excellent tuna tartare, linguine with fresh anchovies and divine *zuccherini* (tiny fish) with fresh mint. The set menu costs €41.

Eataly

Housed in a renovated rail terminal in trendy Ostiense, **Eataly** (Map p62; [J] 06 9027 9201; www.roma. eataly.it; Air Terminal Ostiense, Piazzale XII Ottobre 1492; ⊙shop 10am-midnight, restaurants noon-11.30pm; [M]Piramide) is an enormous, mall-like complex devoted to Italian food. As well as shops selling foodstuffs from all over the country, books and kitchenware, it's also home to 19 cafes and restaurants, including a *panini* (sandwich) bar, a gelateria, *friggitoria* (traditional Roman fried food), a restaurant specialising in Lazio-sourced vegetables, a *rosticceria* (for roasted meats) and a fine-dining restaurant. There's also an excellent pizza and pasta restaurant, and a microbrewery serving craft beers. The complex is a 10-minute walk from Piramide metro station.

Glass Hostaria Modern Italian €€€
(Map p82; [J] 06 5833 5903; Vicolo del Cinque 58; meals €80; ⊙from 8pm Tue-Sun; [Q]Piazza Trilussa) Trastevere's foremost foodie address, the Glass is a modernist-styled, sophisticated restaurant with cooking to match. Chef Cristina Bowerman creates inventive, delicate dishes that combine fresh ingredients and traditional elements to delight and surprise the palate. There are tasting menus at €70 and €90.

VATICAN CITY, BORGO & PRATI

Pizzarium Pizza by Slice €
(Via della Meloria 43; pizza slices from €3; ⊙11am-9pm Mon-Sat; [M]Cipro–Musei Vaticani) A gourmet revelation masquerading as an unassuming takeaway, hard-to-find Pizzarium dishes up some of Rome's best sliced pizza. Served on a wooden chopping board, its fluffy dough and perfect crust are topped with original, intensely flavoured ingredients. There's also a daily selection of *supplì*, juices and chilled beers.

Cacio e Pepe Trattoria €
(Map p62; [J] 06 321 72 68; Via Avezzana 11; meals €25; ⊙closed Sat dinner & Sun; [Q]Piazza Giuseppe Mazzini) A local institution, this humble trattoria is as authentic as it gets with a menu of traditional Roman dishes, a spartan interior and no-frills service. If you can find a free seat at one of the gingham-clad tables splayed across the pavement, keep it simple with *cacio e pepe* followed by *pollo alla cacciatora* ('hunter's chicken').

Romeo Pizzeria, Ristorante €€
(Map p62; [J] 06 3211 0120; www.romeo.roma.it; Via Silla 26a; pizza slices €3.50, meals €35-40; ⊙9am-midnight Mon-Sat; [M]Ottaviano–San Pietro) One of Rome's new breed of multi-purpose gastro outfits, Romeo serves everything from freshly prepared *panini* to fabulous *pizza al taglio* and full restaurant meals. The look is contemporary chic with black walls and sprouting tubular lights; the food is a mix of classic Italian fare and forward-looking international creations.

Velavevodetto Ai Quiriti Traditional Italian €€
(Map p62; [J] 06 3600 0009; www.ristorantevela vevodetto.it; Piazza dei Quiriti 5; meals €35; ⊙Mon-Sun; [M]Lepanto) Since it opened in spring 2012, this Prati newcomer has won over local diners with its unpretentious earthy food, honest prices and welcoming service. The menu reads like a directory of Roman staples, and while it's all pretty good, standout choices include *polpette di bollito* (fried meat balls) and *carciofi fritti* (fried artichokes).

Osteria dell'Angelo Trattoria €€
(Map p62; [J] 06 372 94 70; Via Bettolo 24; set menu €25; ⊙lunch & dinner Tue-Fri, dinner Mon & Sat; [M]Ottaviano–San Pietro) Laid-back and informal, this hugely popular neighbourhood trattoria (reservations are a must) is a great place to try genuine local cuisine. The set menu features a mixed antipasti, a robust Roman-style pasta and a choice

of hearty mains with a side dish. To finish off, you're offered lightly spiced biscuits to dunk in sweet dessert wine.

Settembrini
Modern Italian €€€

(Map p62; 📞 06 323 26 17; www.viasettembrini.it; cafe Via Settembrini 21, restaurant Via Settembrini 25; aperitif €8, restaurant meals €60; ⏰ cafe 7am-1am daily, restaurant lunch & dinner Mon-Fri, dinner Sat; 🚌 Piazza Giuseppe Mazzini) All labels, suits and lipstick, this fashionable watering hole is a hot foodie fixture. Join the sharply dressed darlings for bar snacks, a light lunch or evening *aperitivo* at the cafe, or make an occasion of it and dine on creative Italian cuisine at the smart restaurant next door.

🍷 Drinking & Nightlife

Rome has plenty of drinking venues, ranging from the ubiquitous traditional *enoteche* (wine bars) and streetside cafes to dressy lounge bars, pubs (trendy by virtue of their novelty) and counter-culture hang-outs.

ANCIENT ROME

Cavour 313
Wine Bar

(Map p66; 📞 06 678 54 96; www.cavour313.it; Via Cavour 313; ⏰ 12.30pm-2.45pm & 7.30pm-12.30am, closed Sun summer; Ⓜ Cavour) Close to the Forum, wood-panelled Cavour 313 attracts everyone from tourists to actors and politicians. Sink into its pub-like cosiness and while away hours over sensational wine (more than 1200 labels) accompanied by cold cuts and cheese (€8 to €12) or a plate of pasta.

Caffè Capitolino
Cafe

(Map p66; Piazzale Caffarelli 4; ⏰ 9am-7.30pm Tue-Sun; 🚌 Piazza Venezia) The charming rooftop cafe of the Capitoline

Museums is a good place to relax over a drink or light snack (*panini,* salads and pizza). Although part of the museum complex, you don't need a ticket to drink here as it's accessible via an independent entrance on Piazzale Caffarelli.

0,75
Bar

(Map p66; www.075roma.com; Via dei Cerchi 65; ⏰ 11am-1.30am; 📶; 🚌 Via dei Cerchi) This funky bar on the Circo Massimo is good for a lingering drink, weekend brunch (€15; 11am to 3pm), *aperitivo* (6.30pm onwards) or light lunch (pastas €7 to €8.50, salads €5.50 to €7.50). It's a friendly place with a laid-back vibe, attractive exposed-brick look and cool tunes. Free wi-fi.

CENTRO STORICO

Caffè Tazza d'Oro
Cafe

(Map p72; www.tazzadorocoffeeshop.com; Via degli Orfani 84; ⏰ 7am-8pm ; 🚌 Via del Corso) A busy, stand-up bar with polished wood and brass fittings, this is one of Rome's best coffee houses. Its espresso hits the

Market, Campo de'Fiori (p69)
MAREMAGNUM/GETTY IMAGES ©

mark perfectly and there's a range of delicious coffee concoctions, including a refreshing *granita di caffè* (a crushed-ice coffee drink served with whipped cream).

Caffè Sant'Eustachio
Cafe

(Map p72; Piazza Sant'Eustachio 82; ⏰8.30am-1am Sun-Thu, to 1.30am Fri, to 2am Sat; 🚊Corso del Rinascimento) This small, unassuming cafe, generally three deep at the bar, is famous for its *gran caffè*, said by many to be the best coffee in town. Created by beating the first drops of espresso and several teaspoons of sugar into a frothy paste, then adding the rest of the coffee, it's superbly smooth and guaranteed to put some zing into your sightseeing.

Barnum Cafe
Cafe

(Map p72; www.barnumcafe.com; Via del Pellegrino 87; ⏰9.30am-2am Tue-Sat, to 9pm Mon; 🚊Corso Vittorio Emanuele II) A relaxed, friendly spot to check your email over a freshly squeezed orange juice or spend a pleasant hour reading a newspaper on one of the tatty old armchairs in the white bare-brick interior. If you like tunes with your drinks, stop by on Tuesday evening

for the DJ-accompanied Sounds Good aperitif (from 7pm).

Etablì
Bar, Ristorante

(Map p72; 📞06 9761 6694; www.etabli.it; Vicolo delle Vacche 9a; ⏰6.30pm-1am Mon-Wed, to 2am Thu-Sat; 🚊Corso del Rinascimento) Housed in a lofty 17th-century *palazzo*, Etablì is a rustic-chic lounge bar and restaurant where Roman beauties drop by to chat over cocktails, snack on tapas and indulge in *aperitivo*. It's laid-back and good-looking, with occasional jam sessions and original French country decor – think wrought-iron fittings, comfy armchairs and a crackling fireplace.

Open Baladin
Bar

(Map p72; www.openbaladinroma.it; Via degli Specchi 6; ⏰12pm-2am; 🚊Via Arenula) A cool lounge bar near Campo de' Fiori, Open Baladin is a leading light in Rome's thriving beer scene. With more than 40 beers on tap and up to 100 bottled brews, many produced by artisanal microbreweries, it's a great place for buffs of the brown stuff. There's also a decent food menu with *panini*, burgers and daily specials.

Trastevere

GLENN BEANLAND/GETTY IMAGES ©

Salotto 42 Bar

(Map p72; www.salotto42.it; Piazza di Pietra 42; ☺10am-2am Tue-Sat, to midnight Sun & Mon; 🚇Via del Corso) On a picturesque piazza, facing the columns of the Tempio di Adriano, this is a glamorous lounge bar, complete with vintage armchairs, suede sofas and a collection of two-tonne design books. Come for the daily lunch buffet or to hang out with the beautiful people over an aperitif.

TRIDENTE, TREVI & THE QUIRINALE

La Scena Bar

(Map p78; Via della Penna 22; ☺noon-3am; 🚇Flaminio) Part of the art deco Hotel Locarno, this bar has a lovely, faded Agatha Christie–era feel, with a greenery-shaded outdoor terrace bedecked in wrought-iron furniture. A refreshing glass of *prosecco* costs from €5.

Stravinskij Bar – Hotel de Russie Bar

(Map p78; ☎06 328 88 70; Via del Babuino 9; ☺9am-1am; 🚇Flaminio) Can't afford to stay at the celeb-magnet Hotel de Russie? Then splash out on a drink at its swish bar. There are sofas inside, but best is a sunny drink in the courtyard overlooked by terraced gardens. Impossibly romantic, it's perfect for a cocktail (€20) and posh snacks.

MONTI, ESQUILINE & SAN LORENZO

Circolo degli Artisti Club, Live Music

(☎06 7030 5684; www.circoloartisti.it; Via Casilina Vecchia 42; ☺7pm-2am Tue-Thu, to 4.30am Fri-Sun; 🚇Ponte Casilino) East of the Pigneto district, the Circolo offers one of Rome's best nights out with top gigs and DJ sets. Friday night cracks open electronica and house for gay night – Omogenic – and Saturday sees the fun-packed Screamadelica (punk-funk, ska and new wave), usually also featuring a live band. There's a cool garden bar and admission is either free or a snip.

Ai Tre Scalini Wine Bar

(Map p66; Via Panisperna 251; ☺12.30pm-1am Mon-Fri, 6pm-1am Sat & Sun; 🚇Cavour) The Three Steps is always packed, with crowds spilling onto the street. As well as a tasty choice of wines, it sells the damn fine Menabrea beer, brewed in northern Italy. You can also tuck into a heart-warming array of cheeses, salami and dishes such as *polpette al sugo* (meatballs with sauce).

TRASTEVERE & GIANICOLO

Ma Che Siete Venuti a Fà Pub

(Map p72; Via Benedetta 25; ☺11am-2am; 🚇Piazza Trilussa) This pint-sized pub – whose name, a football chant, translates politely as 'What did you come here for?'– is a beer-buff's paradise, packing a huge number of on-tap craft beers and obscure bottled tipples into its tiny interior.

Bar San Calisto Cafe

(Map p82; ☎06 589 56 78; Piazza San Calisto 3-5; ☺6am-2am Mon-Sat; 🚇Viale di Trastevere, 🚇Viale di Trastevere) Those in the know head to the down-at-heel 'Sanca' for its basic, stuck-in-time atmosphere and cheap prices. It's famous for its chocolate – drunk hot with cream in winter, eaten as ice cream in summer.

Freni e Frizioni Bar

(Map p82; ☎06 5833 4210; www.freniefrizioni. com; Via del Politeama 4-6; ☺6.30pm-2am; 🚇Piazza Trilussa) The hipsters favourite cool Trastevere bar, this was a garage in a former life, hence its name ('brakes and clutches'). The arty crowd flocks here to slurp well-priced drinks (especially mojitos), feast on the good-value *aperitivo* (7pm to 10pm) and spill into the piazza out the front.

Ombre Rosse Bar

(Map p82; ☎06 588 41 55; Piazza Sant'Egidio 12; ☺8am-2am Mon-Sat, 11am-2am Sun; 🚇Piazza Trilussa) A seminal Trastevere hang-out; grab a table on the terrace and watch the world go by amid a clientele ranging from elderly Italian wide boys to wide-eyed tourists. Tunes are slinky and there's live music (jazz, blues, world) on Thursday evenings from September to April.

Detour:
Ostia Antica

Scavi Archeologici di Ostia Antica (📞 06 5635 2830; www.ostiaantica.net; Viale dei Romagnoli 717; adult/reduced €6.50/3.75; ⏰ 8.30am-7.15pm Tue-Sun Apr-Oct, to 6pm Mar, to 5pm Nov-Feb, last admission 1hr before closing) is the site of the remains of an ancient Roman port. Here you get the evocative sense of a working Roman town. The ruins are spread out and you'll need a few hours to do them justice.

From the **Porta Romana** near the ticket office, the **Decumanus Maximus**, the city's main strip, runs over 1km to **Porta Marina**, a gate which originally led out to the sea.

On the Decumanus, the **Terme di Nettuno** is one of the site's highlights. Next to the Terme is a good-sized **teatro** (amphitheatre), built by Agrippa and later enlarged to hold 4000 people. Nearby is another must-see: the **Thermopolium**, an ancient cafe.

From Rome, take the Ostia Lido train from Stazione Porta San Paolo (next to Piramide metro station), getting off at Ostia Antica. Trains leave half-hourly and the trip, which is covered by standard public-transport tickets, takes approximately 25 minutes.

⭐ Entertainment

Entertainment in Rome can be simply parking yourself at a streetside table and watching the world go by. But the city has a thriving cultural scene with a year-round calendar of concerts, performances and festivals.

An abundance of spectacular settings makes Rome a superb place to catch a classical music concert. The city's cultural and musical hub is the Auditorium Parco della Musica, but free concerts are often held in churches, especially at Easter, Christmas and New Year. Seats are available on a first-come, first-served basis and the programs are generally excellent. Check newspapers and listings for programs.

Auditorium Parco della Musica — Concert Venue
(Map p62; 📞 06 8024 1281; www.auditorium.com; Viale Pietro de Coubertin 30; 🚌 shuttle bus M from Stazione Termini, 🚌 Viale Tiziano) Rome's main concert venue, this state-of-the-art complex combines architectural innovation with perfect acoustics. Designed by Renzo Piano, its three concert halls and 3000-seat open-air arena host everything from classical music concerts to tango exhibitions, book readings and film screenings.

The auditorium is also home to Rome's top orchestra, the world-class **Orchestra dell' Accademia Nazionale di Santa Cecilia** (www.santacecilia.it).

🔒 Shopping

CENTRO STORICO

Confetteria Moriondo & Gariglio — Chocolate
(Map p72; Via del Piè di Marmo 21-22; ⏰ 9am-7.30pm Mon-Sat; 🚌 Via del Corso) Roman poet Trilussa was so smitten with this historic chocolate shop – established by the Torinese confectioners to the royal house of Savoy – that he dedicated several sonnets in its honour. Many of the handmade chocolates and bonbons, laid out in ceremonial splendour in glass cabinets set against dark crimson walls, are still made to 19th-century recipes.

Officina Profumo Farmaceutica di Santa Maria Novella Cosmetics

(Map p72; Corso del Rinascimento 47; ⊙10am-7.30pm Mon-Sat; 🚌Corso del Rinascimento) The Roman branch of one of Italy's oldest pharmacies, this bewitching, aromatic shop stocks natural perfumes and cosmetics as well as herbal infusions, teas and pot pourri, all carefully shelved in wooden cabinets under a giant Murano-glass chandelier. The original pharmacy was founded in Florence in 1612 by the Dominican monks of Santa Maria Novella, and many of its cosmetics are based on 17th-century herbal recipes.

TRIDENTE, TREVI & THE QUIRINALE

Vertecchi Art Art

(Map p78; Via della Croce 70; ⊙3.30-7.30pm Mon, 10am-7.30pm Tue-Sat; Ⓜ Spagna) Ideal for last-minute gift buying, this large paperware and art shop has beautiful printed paper, cards and envelopes that will inspire you to bring back the art of letter writing, plus an amazing choice of notebooks, art stuff and trinkets.

C.U.C.I.N.A. Homewares

(Map p78; 📞06 679 12 75; Via Mario de' Fiori 65; ⊙3.30-7.30pm Mon, 10am-7.30pm Tue- Fri, 10.30am-7.30pm Sat; Ⓜ Spagna) If you're into cooking as much for the gear as the food, you'll enjoy this cool kitchenware shop. A branch of the capital's C.U.C.I.N.A chain, it stocks all sorts of sexy pots and pans, designer cutlery, gourmet gadgets, wine glasses and a range of fashionable cooking apparel.

Sermoneta Accessories

(Map p78; 📞06 679 19 60; www.sermoneta-gloves.com; Piazza di Spagna 61; ⊙9.30am-8pm Mon-Sat, 10am-7pm Sun; Ⓜ Spagna) Buying leather gloves in Rome is a rite of passage for some, and its most famous glove-seller is the place to do it. Choose from a kaleidoscopic range of quality leather and suede gloves lined with silk and cashmere. An expert assistant will size up your hand in a glance. Just don't expect them to smile.

Auditorium Parco della Musica, designed by Renzo Piano

Right: Via della Pace, Centro Storico
(LEFT) ROMAOSLO/GETTY IMAGES ©; (RIGHT) MICHELE FALZONE/GETTY IMAGES ©

AVENTINE & TESTACCIO

Volpetti Food & Drink
(Map p62; www.volpetti.com; Via Marmorata 47; ⊙8am-2pm & 5-8.15pm Mon-Sat; 🚌Via Marmorata) This superstocked deli, considered by many the best in town, is an Aladdin's cave of gourmet treasures. Helpful staff will guide you through the extensive selection of cheeses, pastas, olive oils, vinegars, cured meats, veggie pies, wines and grappas. You can also order online.

TRASTEVERE & GIANICOLO

Porta Portese Flea Market Market
(Map p62; Piazza Porta Portese; ⊙7am-1pm Sun; 🚌Viale di Trastevere, 🚌Viale di Trastevere) To see another side of Rome, head to this mammoth flea market. With thousands of stalls selling everything from rare books and dodgy bikes to Peruvian shawls and MP3 players, it's crazily busy and a lot of fun. Keep your valuables safe and wear your haggling hat.

ℹ Information

Medical Services

For problems that don't require hospital treatment, call the Guardia Medica Turistica (🕾06 7730 6650; Via Emilio Morosini 30).

You can also call a private doctor to come to your hotel or apartment; try Roma Medica (🕾338 6224832; call-out/treatment charge €150; ⊙24hr). The call-out/treatment fee will probably be around €150, but it's worth it if you have insurance. For emergency treatment, go to the *pronto soccorso* (casualty) section of an *ospedale* (hospital).

Money

ATMs are liberally scattered around the city. There are money-exchange booths at Stazione Termini and Fiumicino and Ciampino airports. In the centre, there are numerous bureaux de change, including the American Express (🕾06 6 76 41; Piazza di Spagna 38; ⊙9am-5.30pm Mon-Fri, 9am-12.30pm Sat) office.

Tourist Information

For phone enquiries, the Comune di Roma runs a free multilingual tourist information line (☏06 06 08; www.060608.it; ⊙9am-9pm).

There are tourist information points at Rome's two international airports – Fiumicino (Terminal 3, International Arrivals; ⊙8am-7.30pm) and Ciampino (International Arrivals, baggage reclaim area; ⊙9am-6.30pm) – and at the following locations across the city:

Castel Sant'Angelo Tourist Information (Map p72; Piazza Pia; ⊙9.30am-7pm)

Piazza delle Cinque Lune Tourist Information (Map p72; Piazza delle Cinque Lune; ⊙9.30am-7pm) Near Piazza Navona.

Stazione Termini Tourist Information (Map p62; ⊙8am-8.30pm) In the hall that runs parallel to platform 24.

Fori Imperiali Tourist Information (Map p66; Via dei Fori Imperiali; ⊙9.30am-7pm; 🚇Via dei Fori Imperiali)

Trevi Fountain Tourist Information (Map p72; Via Marco Minghetti; ⊙9.30am-7pm) Near the Trevi Fountain.

Via Nazionale Tourist Information (Map p76; Via Nazionale; ⊙9.30am-7pm)

Centro Servizi Pellegrini e Turisti (Map p84; ☏06 6988 1662; St Peter's Sq; ⊙8.30am-6pm Mon-Sat). For information about the Vatican.

ⓘ Getting There & Away

Air

Rome's main international airport Leonardo da Vinci (☏06 6 59 51; www.adr.it/fiumicino), better known as Fiumicino, is on the coast 30km west of the city.

The much smaller Ciampino Airport (☏06 6 59 51; www.adr.it/ciampino), 15km southeast of the city centre, is the hub for European low-cost carrier Ryanair.

Train

Almost all trains serve Stazione Termini (Piazza dei Cinquecento), Rome's main train station and principal transport hub. There are regular connections to other European countries, all major Italian cities and many smaller towns.

Watch Your Valuables

Rome is a relatively safe city, but petty crime is rife. Pickpockets follow the tourists, so watch out around the Colosseum, Piazza di Spagna, St Peter's Square and Stazione Termini. Be particularly vigilant around the bus stops on Via Marsala, where thieves prey on disoriented travellers fresh in from Ciampino Airport. Crowded public transport is another hot spot – the 64 Vatican bus is notorious. If travelling on the metro, try to use the end carriages, which are usually less crowded.

Getting Around

To/From the Airport

Fiumicino

The easiest way to get to/from Fiumicino is by train, but there are also buses and private shuttle services.

By taxi, the set fare to/from the city centre is €48, which is valid for up to four passengers with luggage. Note that taxis registered in Fiumicino charge more, so make sure you catch a Comune di Roma taxi – they are white with the words *Roma capitale* on the side along with the driver's ID number.

Leonardo Express (adult/child under 4 €14/free) Runs to/from Stazione Termini. Departures from the airport every 30 minutes between 6.38am and 11.38pm; from Termini between 5.52am and 10.52pm. Journey time is 30 minutes.

FR1 Train (€8) Connects to Trastevere, Ostiense and Tiburtina stations, but not Stazione Termini. Departures from the airport every 15 minutes (hourly on Sunday and public holidays) between 5.58am and 11.28pm; from Tiburtina every 15 minutes between 5.47am and 7.32pm, then half-hourly to 10.02 pm Monday to Saturday, half-hourly between 6.02am and 10.02pm Sunday.

Airport Shuttle (📞06 4201 3469; www.airportshuttle.it) Transfers to/from your hotel for €25 for one person, then €6 for each additional passenger up to a maximum of eight.

Cotral (www.cotralspa.it; one way €5, if bought on bus €7) Runs to/from Stazione Tiburtina via Stazione Termini. Eight daily departures including night services from the airport at 1.15am, 2.15am, 3.30am and 5am, and from Tiburtina at 12.30am, 1.15am, 2.30am and 3.45am. Journey time is one hour.

Ciampino

To get into town, the best bet is to take one of the dedicated bus services. You can also take a bus to Ciampino station and pick up a train to Stazione Termini. By taxi, the set fare to/from the airport is €30.

Terravision (www.terravision.eu; one way €4) Twice hourly departures to/from Via Marsala outside Stazione Termini. From the airport services are between 8.15am and 12.15am; from Via Marsala between 4.30am and 9.20pm. Journey time is 40 minutes.

SIT (www.sitbusshuttle.com; from airport €4, to airport €6) Buses run from Ciampino between 7.45am and 11.30am to Via Marsala outside StazioneTermini; from Termini between 4.30am and 9.30pm. Get tickets on board.

Cotral (www.cotralspa.it; one way €3.90) Runs 17 daily services to/from Via Giolitti near Stazione Termini.

Public Transport

Tickets

Public-transport tickets are valid on all Rome's bus, tram and metro lines, except for routes to Fiumicino airport. They come in various forms:

BIT (*biglietto integrato a tempo*, a single ticket valid for 100 minutes and one metro ride) €1.50

BIG (*biglietto integrato giornaliero*, a daily ticket) €6

BTI (*biglietto turistico integrato*, a three-day ticket) €16.50

CIS (*carta integrata settimanale*, a weekly ticket) €24

Abbonamento mensile (a monthly pass) €35

Buy tickets at *tabacchi*, newsstands and from vending machines at main bus stops and metro stations. They must be purchased before you start your journey and validated in the machines on buses, at the entrance gates to the metro or at train stations. Ticketless riders risk an on-the-spot €50 fine. Children under 10 travel free.

The Roma Pass (www.romapass.it; 3 days €34) comes with a three-day travel pass valid within the city boundaries.

Metro

Rome has two main metro lines, A (orange) and B (blue), which cross at Stazione Termini, the only point at which you can change from one line to the other. A third line 'B1' branches off line B and serves the northern suburbs, but you're unlikely to need it.

Trains run between 5.30am and 11.30pm (to 1.30am on Friday and Saturday).

Bus & Tram

Rome's buses and trams are run by ATAC (☎06 5 70 03; www.atac.roma.it). The main bus station (Map p76; Piazza dei Cinquecento) is in front of Stazione Termini on Piazza dei Cinquecento, where there's an information booth (Map p76; ⏰7.30am-8pm). Other important hubs are at Largo di Torre Argentina and Piazza Venezia.

Buses generally run from about 5.30am until midnight, with limited services running throughout the night.

Taxi

Official licensed taxis are white with an ID number and *Roma capitale* written on the sides.

Always go with the metered fare, never an arranged price (the set fares to and from the airports are exceptions).

In town (within the ring road) flag fall is €3 between 6am and 10pm on weekdays, €4.50 on Sundays and holidays, and €6.50 between 10pm and 7am. Then it's €1.10 per kilometre. Official rates are posted in taxis and on www. viviromaintaxi.eu.

You can hail a taxi, but it's often easier to wait at a rank or phone for one. There are taxi ranks at the airports, Stazione Termini, the Colosseum, Largo di Torre Argentina, Piazza San Silvestro, Piazza della Repubblica, Piazza Belli in Trastevere and in the Vatican at Piazza del Pio XII and Piazza del Risorgimento.

You can book a taxi by phoning the Comune di Roma's automated taxi line on ☎06 06 09, or calling a taxi company direct.

Note that when you call for a cab, the meter is switched on immediately and you pay for the cost of the journey from wherever the driver receives the call.

La Capitale (☎06 49 94)

Pronto Taxi (☎06 66 45)

Castel & Ponte Sant'Angelo (p84)

RAINER MIRAU/GETTY IMAGES ©

Milan, the Lakes & Piedmont

Never mind its age, northwest Italy thoroughly enjoys modern living. Sure, the region is known for gilded Bellagio villas, palatial museums, and the ultimate faded glory: Leonardo da Vinci's *Last Supper*. But far from being overshadowed by this rich heritage, northwest Italy puts it to work with fashion photo shoots, avant-garde art collections and digital-image technology. With its obsessive attention to well-designed detail, Milan carries off work and play with equal flair: watch and learn how to eat (happy-hour buffets), where to relax (the Lakes) and when to work that runway (Fashion Week or Saturdays at the club). Turin has grand Napoleonic boulevards criss-crossing its centre, but its defined by its industrial-chic, arty edge. Turin's picturesque Piedmont and Cinque Terre hinterlands are also absurdly delicious. In the home of Slow Food, entire Piedmontese towns seem topped with gooey fontina cheese, lavished with truffles and awash in Barolo.

Piazza del Duomo (p121)
GARY YEOWELL/GETTY IMAGES ©

Milan, the Lakes & Piedmont

SWITZERLAND

Locarno
Ascona
Isole di
Brissago
Domodossola
Cannobio
Riserva Naturale
del Sacro Monte
della SS Trinità
Luino
Monte Rosa
(4633m)
Verbania
Laveno
Mer de
Glace
Courmayeur
Stresa
Varese
Aosta
Lago
d'Orta
Lago
Maggiore
Pila
Gallarate
Cogne
Busto
Arsizio
Magenta
Novara
Vigevano
Lac
de Mont
Cénis
Parco
Regionale
la Mandria
PIEDMONT
Bardonecchia
Susa
Parco Regional
di Gran Bosco
di Salbertrand
Turin
Sestriere
Cesana Torinese
Parco
Regionale
Val Troncea
Pinerolo
FRANCE
Carmagnola
Asti
Saluzzo
Savigliano
Alba
Acqui
Terme
Fossano
Cuneo
Mondovì
Genoa
Varazze
Limone
Piemonte
Parco Naturale
dell'Alta Valle
Pésio e Tanaro
Savona
Golfo di
Genova
Parco Naturale
delle Alpi
Marittime
Arroscia
MONTE
CARLO
Imperia
San Remo
Mediterranean Sea
Nice
Ventimiglia

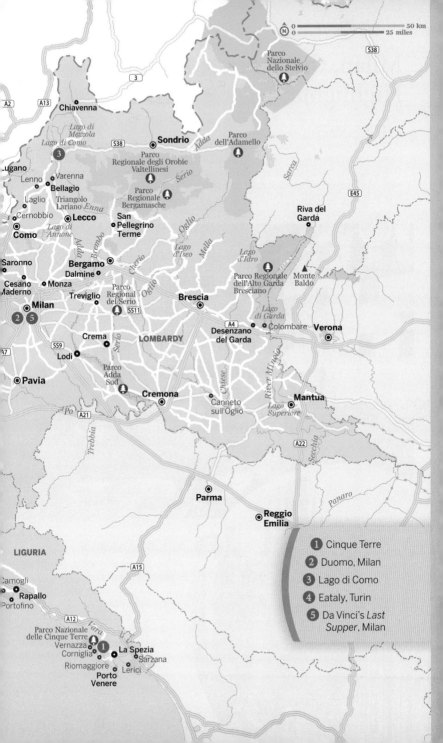

Milan, the Lakes & Piedmont Highlights

Cinque Terre

In Italy's firmament of beautiful places, Cinque Terre (p156) is a dazzling star. This soul-stirring coastal landscape is home to five picturesque medieval villages that seem to cling to the cliff. The steeply terraced hills are bisected by a complicated system of fields and gardens that have been hacked, chiselled, shaped and layered over the course of nearly two millennia.

Below: Riomaggiore (p159)

Milan's Duomo

Milan's Duomo (p121) is the ultimate example of International Gothic; with its teetering spires, the Duomo represents 135 pinnacles of the style. Topping those spires are 3200 statue of saints; previously, no one but the bell-ringer could appreciate them, bu the roof is now open to visitors so tha anyone can take a closer look.

Lago di Como

3

Lago di Como (p135) is the most spectacular of Italy's northern lakes. The surrounding mountains plunge straight into the water, which is edged with lots of small, characterful villages where you can always find a little peace and quiet.

4

Turin's Eataly

To sample Italy's best artisanal cheeses, you could spend a year grazing across the country, or you could spend an afternoon at Eataly (p151), Turin's Slow Food emporium. This gourmet wonderland features tastings and culinary workshops, in addition to Italy's largest selection of regional-specialty pastas, cured meats and wines – plus Willy Wonka–worthy quantities of chocolate.

5

Da Vinci's Last Supper

You have to wonder whether it's worth reserving weeks ahead to glimpse a mural. But, even faded, Leonardo da Vinci's Last Supper (p124) makes the entire Renaissance clear. Da Vinci shows medieval saints leaping from their chairs, shocked at Jesus' news that one of them will betray him. Damaged as they are, their humanity remains indelible.

Milan, the Lakes & Piedmont's Best...

Designer Dreams

○ **Spazio Rossana Orlandi**
An Aladdin's Cave of iconic interior design. (p131)

○ **NH Lingotto + Lingotto Tech** Stay in the Fiat 500 factory that houses this industrial-chic hotel. (p150)

○ **Hotel Spadari Duomo**
Milan's original design hotel, with rooms like mini-galleries. (p127)

○ **10 Corso Como** Concept store, curated by Carla Sozzani, stocking designer desirables. (p132)

Romantic Interludes

○ **Bellagio, Lago di Como**
Boat cruises at sunset make dates seem as dashing as George Clooney. (p139)

○ **Cinque Terre** Cliff-edge paths lead to breathtaking views in secluded coves. (p156)

○ **Teatro Alla Scala, Milan**
Start your date on a high note: score box tickets to performances at Milan's legendary opera house. (p125)

○ **Lago Maggiore** A backdrop of belle époque splendour, grand villas and picturesque villages. (p134)

Gourmet Gifts

○ **Peck**, **Milan** A sublime selection of jams, hams and 3200 cheeses – and that's just the Parmesans. (p131)

○ **Eataly, Turin** A temple of Slow Food treats with cured meats overhead, wines underfoot and altars of truffles. (p151)

○ **Guido Golbino, Turin**
Turin's finest chocolatiers, which makes them pretty damn fine. (p152)

○ **Alba** Precious truffles and red-satin Barolo wine. (p151)

Need to Know

Aperitivo Bars

○ **Living, Milan** Crafty cocktails and an urbane crowd. (p129)

○ **10 Corso Como**, **Milan** An elegant spread under twinkling fairylights. (p129)

○ **Pandenus, Milan** Delectable bruschetta and focaccia. (p129)

ADVANCE PLANNING

○ **Three months before** Book local accommodation during Milan's Salone del Mobile or Fashion Week, or during Turin's Salone Internazionale del Gusto.

○ **Two months before** Book tickets to Teatro Alla Scala and da Vinci's *The Last Supper*, and accommodation during Aosta's winter ski season and Lake Como's summer season.

○ **One week before** Scan www.easymilano.it and www.extratorino.it to see what's on in Milan and Turin. Make restaurant reservations.

RESOURCES

○ **Milan Tourism** (www.visitamilano.it/turismo)

○ **Turin Tourism** (www.turismotorino.org)

○ **Piedmont Tourism Board** (www.piemonteitalia.eu) Itineraries, accommodation and transport links.

○ **Valle d'Aosta Tourist Board** (www.regione.vda.it/turismo)

GETTING AROUND

○ **Air** International connections to/from Milan and Turin.

○ **Walk** Perfect for cities and towns, Alpine trails and Cinque Terre.

○ **Train** Good connections between major cities and towns. Metro services in Milan and Turin.

○ **Boat** Handy for travel around the lakes.

○ **Car** Convenient for exploring Piedmont's vineyards.

○ **Bicycle** Ideal for Alpine trails and Piedmont's wine region.

BE FOREWARNED

○ **Museums** Most close Mondays.

○ **Restaurants** Many close in August; around the lakes and in Cinque Terre many close from November to March.

○ **Accommodation** Book a month ahead if travelling to Milan or Turin, and three months in advance of international design and food fairs; reserve ahead for summer accommodation in Cinque Terre and the lakes.

○ **Pickpockets** Operate in tourist areas and at fairs.

Left: Black truffle appetiser
Above: Living bar (p129)

Milan, the Lakes & Piedmont Itineraries

Find out where Italy gets its hottest design ideas, from platform stilettos made for power-stomping Milan runways to the rocket-ship espresso machines fuelling Turin's creative reinvention.

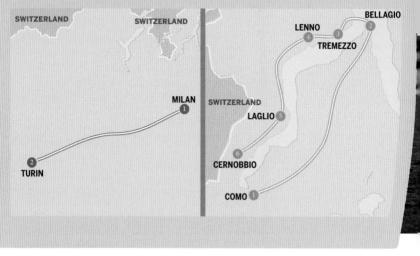

MILAN TO TURIN
TREND-SETTING CITIES

You don't have to wait for the next Salone Internazionale del Mobile, Fashion Week or Salone del Gusto to see the upcoming big trends in ❶**Milan**. You can spend days one and two here getting immersed in fashion and design. On your first morning, view the window displays of established designers such as Prada and Alessi in Galleria Vittorio Emanuele II and Quadrilatero d'Oro, then in the afternoon explore the studios of emerging designers clustered around Porta Genova station in the Navigli neighbourhood.

On day two, get inspired by the drama of the Duomo in the morning. In the afternoon

see where Italian designers find inspiration at chic bar Living's street-fashion-wise happy hours and Triennale di Milano, Milan's showcase of design objects.

On day three, hop on the fast train to ❷**Turin**, where Napoleonic ambitions and postwar industry have been channelled into contemporary art and industrial chic. A castle was invaded by Arte Povera (Poor Art) to form Museo d'Arte Contemporanea, and contemporary artists are taking over a baroque palace at Galleria Civica d'Arte Moderna e Contemporanea.

4 DAYS

LAKESIDE LOUNGING

Drive or catch a train from Milan to spiffy ① **Como**, where you can enjoy both glamorous getaways and serene retreats without ever losing sight of a dazzling shoreline. Take the vintage funicular, Funicolare Como-Brunate, to hilltop Brunate for splendid Como sunsets. The next day, retreat to villa-lined ② **Bellagio** for a day of enchanted lakeside living. Nothing need interrupt your busy Bellagio schedule of sun-tanning, except perhaps a sunset cruises in Barindelli's mahogany boats or a reservation to sample Como's lavarello fish specialties at Itturismo Da Abate.

Rejuvenated, drive around the lake or hop on a ferry to ③ **Tremezzo** to see what is arguably the world's best wedding present, the Villa Carlotta, and to enjoy a leisurely lunch on the panoramic terrace of Al Veluu. Arrange an overnight stay here, and enjoy a lakeside drive or taxi-boat ride to famous locales along the western shore: Villa Balbianello, as seen in *Casino Royale*, in ④ **Lenno;** villa-lined ⑤ **Laglio**, home to actor/director/international playboy George Clooney; and picturesque *Oceans 12* location, ⑥ **Cernobbio**.

Como (p136)
ROCCO FASANO/GETTY IMAGES ©

Discover Milan, the Lakes & Piedmont

At a Glance

○ **Milan** (p120) Runway fashion and da Vinci masterpieces by day; cocktails and opera by night.

○ **The Lakes** (p134) Living large in movie-star villas. Como silks and lakeside resorts.

○ **Piedmont** (p146) Sleek design and modern art in Turin; vineyards and Slow Food in the hills.

Vineyard, Barolo (p151)
ALAN BENSON/GETTY IMAGES ©

MILAN

POP 1.3 MILLION

Milan is Italy's city of the future, a fast-paced metropolis with New World qualities: ambition, aspiration and a highly individualistic streak. In Milan appearances really do matter and materialism requires no apology. The Milanese love beautiful things, luxurious things, and it is for that reason perhaps that Italian fashion and design maintain their esteemed global position.

But like the models that stalk the catwalks, many consider Milan to be vain, distant and dull. And it is true that the city makes little effort to seduce visitors. But this superficial lack of charm disguises a city of ancient roots and many treasures, that, unlike in the rest of Italy, you'll often get to experience without the queues. So while the Milanese may not have time to always play nice, jump in and join them in their intoxicating round of pursuits, be that precision shopping, browsing edgy contemporary galleries or loading up a plate with local delicacies while downing an expertly mixed negroni cocktail.

◉ Sights

Museo del Novecento   Art Gallery
(☏ 02 8844 4072; www.museodelnovecento.org; Piazza del Duomo 12; adult/reduced €5/3; ⊙ 9.30am-7.30pm Tue-Sun, 2.30-7.30pm Mon; Ⓜ Duomo) Overlooking the Piazza del Duomo, with fabulous views of the cathedral, is Mussolini's **Arengario** (Ⓜ Duomo), from where he would harangue huge crowds in the glory days of his regime. Now it houses Milan's museum of 20th-century art.

DENNIS K. JOHNSON/GETTY IMAGES ©

⭐ Don't Miss
Duomo

A vision in pink Candoglia marble, Milan's cathedral aptly reflects the city's creativity and ambition. Its pearly-white facade, adorned with 135 spires and 3200 statues, rises like the filigree of a fairy-tale tiara, wowing the crowds with extravagant detail. The vast interior is no less impressive, with the largest stained-glass windows in Christendom, while below is the early Christian baptistry and crypt, where the remains of the saintly Carlo Borromeo are on display in a rock crystal casket.

Begun by Giangaleazzo Visconti in 1387, the cathedral's design was originally considered unfeasible. Canals had to be dug to transport the vast quantities of marble to the centre of the city and new technologies were invented to cater for the never-before-attempted scale. There was also that small matter of style. The Gothic lines went out of fashion and were considered 'too French', so it took on several looks as the years, then centuries, dragged on. Its slow construction became the byword for an impossible task (*fabrica del Dom* in the Milanese dialect). Indeed, much of its ornament is 19th-century neo-Gothic, with the final touches only applied in the 1960s. Crowning it all is a gilded copper statue of the Madonnina (Little Madonna), the city's traditional protector.

The most spectacular view, though, is through the innumerable marble spires and pinnacles that adorn the rooftop. On a clear day you can see the Alps.

NEED TO KNOW

www.duomomilano.it; Piazza del Duomo; adult/reduced Battistero di San Giovanni €4/2, terraces stairs €7/3.50, terraces lift €12/6, treasury €2; ⊘7am-6.45pm, roof terraces 9am-6pm, baptistry 9.30am-5pm, treasury 9.30am-5pm Mon-Sat; Ⓜ Duomo

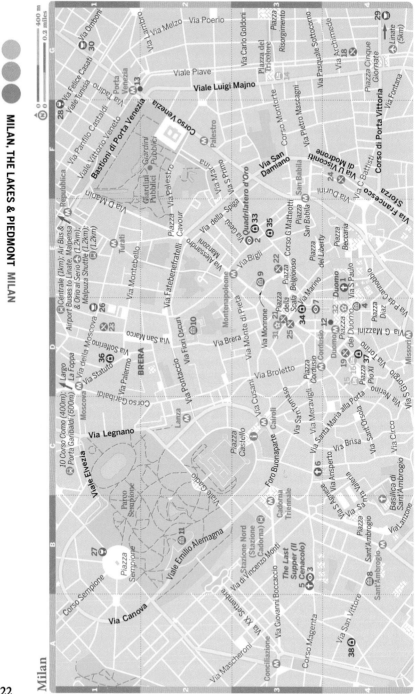

Milan

Milan

⭐ Don't Miss
The Last Supper (Il Cenacolo)

Milan's most famous mural, Leonardo da Vinci's *The Last Supper* (*Il Cenacolo*), is hidden away on a wall of the refectory adjoining the **Basilica di Santa Maria delle Grazie** (Corso Magenta; ⏱8.30am-7pm Tue-Sun; Ⓜ Conciliazione, Cadorna) FREE. Depicting Christ and his disciples at the dramatic moment when Christ reveals he is aware of the betrayal afoot, it is a masterful psychological study and one of the world's most iconic images.

Restoration of *Il Cenacolo* was completed in 1999 after more than 22 years' work. The mural was in a lamentable state after centuries of damage. Da Vinci himself is partly to blame: his experimental mix of oil and tempera was applied between 1495 and 1498, rather than within a week as is typical of fresco techniques. The Dominicans didn't help matters in 1652 by raising the refectory floor, hacking off a lower section of the scene, including Jesus' feet. The most damage was caused by restorers in the 19th century, whose alcohol and cotton-wool technique removed an entire layer. But its condition does nothing to lessen its astonishing beauty. Stare at the ethereal, lucent windows beyond the narrative action and you'll wonder if da Vinci's uncharacteristic short-sightedness wasn't divinely inspired.

When he was at work on the masterpiece a star-struck monk noted that he would sometimes arrive in the morning, stare at yesterday's effort, then promptly call it quits for the day. Your visit too will be similarly brief (15 minutes) unless you invest in **Tickitaly's** (www.tickitaly.com; guided tour €69; ⏱7.15pm & 8pm) guided, after-hours tour which allows an extended 30-minute visit.

NEED TO KNOW

☎ 02 8942 1146; www.architettonicimilano.lombardia.beniculturali.it; adult/reduced €6.50/3.25, booking fee €1.50; Ⓜ Cadorna-Triennale

Built around a futuristic spiral ramp (an ode to the Guggenheim), the lower floors are cramped, but the heady collection, which includes the likes of Boccioni, Campigli, de Chirico and Marinetti, more than distracts.

Afterwards dine in the 3rd-floor **Giacomo Arengario** (☎ 02 7209 3814; www.giacomoarengario.com; Via Guglielmo Marconi 1; meals €30-40; ⊙noon-midnight; Ⓜ Duomo) bistro overlooking the Duomo.

Teatro alla Scala   Opera House
(La Scala; www.teatroallascala.org; Via Filodram-matici 2; Ⓜ Cordusio, Duomo) Giuseppe Piermarini's grand 2800-seat theatre was inaugurated in 1778 with Antonio Salieri's *Europa Riconosciuta*. Replacing the previous theatre, which burnt down in a fire after a carnival gala. Costs were covered by the sale of *palchi* (private boxes), of which there are six gilt-and-crimson tiers. When rehearsals are not in session you can stand in boxes 13, 15 and 18 for a glimpse of the jewel-like interior.

In the **Museo Teatrale alla Scala** (La Scala Museum; ☎ 02 4335 3521; Largo Ghiringhelli 1; admission €6; ⊙9am-12.30pm & 1.30-5.30pm), harlequin costumes and a spinet inscribed with the command 'Inexpert hand, touch me not!' hint at centuries of Milanese musical drama, on and off stage.

Pinacoteca di Brera   Gallery
(☎ 02 7226 3264; www.brera.beniculturali.it; Via Brera 28; adult/reduced child €6/3; ⊙8.30am-7.15pm Tue-Sun; Ⓜ Lanza) Located upstairs from the centuries-old **Accademia di Belle Arti** (still one of Italy's most prestigious art schools) this gallery houses Milan's most impressive collection of old masters, much of the bounty 'lifted' from Venice by Napoleon. Rembrandt, Goya and van Dyck all have a place in the collection, but you're here to see the Italians: Titian, Tintoretto, glorious Veronese, ground-breaking Mantegna, the Bellini brothers and a Caravaggio.

Museo Poldi Pezzoli   House Museum
(☎ 02 79 48 89; www.museopoldipezzoli.it; Via Alessandro Manzoni 12; adult/reduced €9/6; ⊙10am-6pm Wed-Mon; Ⓜ Montenapoleone) Inheriting his vast fortune at the age of 24,

Gian Giacomo Poldi Pezzoli also inherited his mother's love of art and during extensive European travels he was inspired by the 'house museum' that was later to become London's V&A (Victoria and Albert Museum). As his collection grew, Pezzoli had the idea of transforming his apartments into a series of historically themed rooms based on the great art periods of the past (the Middle Ages, early Renaissance, baroque and rococo). Although crammed with a collection of big ticket artworks, including Botticelli, Bellini and the beautiful *Portrait of a Woman* by Pollaiuolo, these Sala d'Artista are exquisite works of art in their own right.

Museo Nazionale della Scienza e della Tecnologia   Museum
(☎ 02 48 55 51; www.museoscienza.org; Via San Vittore 21; adult/child €10/7, submarine tour €8; ⊙9.30am-5pm Tue-Fri, to 6.30pm Sat, Sun & holidays; Ⓜ Sant'Ambrogio) Kids, would-be inventors and geeks will go goggle-eyed at Milan's impressive museum of science and technology, the largest of its kind in Italy. It is a fitting tribute in a city where arch-inventor Leonardo da Vinci did much of his finest work. The 16th-century monastery, where it is housed, features a collection of more than 10,000 items, including models based on da Vinci's engineering sketches, halls devoted to physics, astronomy and horology, and outdoor hangars housing steam trains, planes, full-sized galleons and Italy's first submarine.

Chiesa di San Maurizio   Chapel, Convent
(Corso Magenta 15; ⊙9am-noon & 2-5.30pm Tue-Sun; Ⓜ Cadorna-Triennale) The 16th-century royal chapel and convent of San Maurizio is Milan's hidden crown jewel, every inch of it covered in Bernardino Luini's breath-taking frescoes. Many of them immortalise the star of Milan's literary scene at the time, Ippolita Sforza, and her family. Duck through a small doorway on the left to enter the secluded convent hall where blissful martyred women saints bear their tribulations serenely – note Santa Lucia calmly holding her lost eyes, and Santa Agata casually carrying her breasts on a platter.

Tours

When in Milan, create your own city tour by hopping on Tram No 1. This retro orange beauty, complete with wooden seats and original fittings, runs along Via Settembrini before cutting through the historic centre along Via Manzoni, through Piazza Cordusio and back up towards Piazza Cairoli and the Castello Sforzesco. A 75-minute ticket (€1.50), which is also valid for the bus and metro, should be purchased from any tobacconist before boarding and stamped in the original *obliteratrice* on the tram.

Autostradale   Guided Tour
(☏ 02 720 01 304; www.autostradale.it; ticket €60; ⏰ 9.30am Tue-Sun Sep-Jul) The tourist office sells tickets (good for the whole day) for Autostradale's three-hour city bus tours including admission to *The Last Supper*, Castello Sforzesco and La Scala's museum. Tours depart from the taxi rank on the western side of Piazza del Duomo.

Bike & the City   Cycling Tour
(☏ 346 9498623; www.bikeandthecity.it; day/ sunset tour €35/30; ⏰ morning/afternoon/ sunset tour 9.30am/3.30pm/6.30pm) Another Milan choice: make friends while you get the inside scoop on city sights on these leisurely, four-hour bike tours.

Alba Hot-Air Balloon Flights   Hot-Air Balloon
(incl transfers, wine & breakfast €220-250) Take a beautiful floating trip above the Langhe Valley on a hot-air balloon.

🛏 Sleeping

Maison Borella   Boutique Hotel €€
(☏ 02 5810 9114; www.hotelmaisonborella.com; Alzaia Naviglio Grande 8; d €140-220; ❄ @ 🛜; Ⓜ Porta Genova) With geranium-clad balconies overhanging the Naviglio Grande, striking decor and pinstriped bedlinen, Maison Borella brings a much-needed touch of class to Navigli and is, amazingly, the first canal-side hotel. The hotel is a converted house arranged around an internal courtyard and its historic rooms feature parquet floors, beamed ceilings and elegant *boiserie* (sculpted panelling).

Corso di Porta Ticinese

Foresteria Monforte
B&B €€

(☏02 7631 8516; www.foresteriamonforte.it; Piazza del Tricolore 2; d €150-250; ❄@🛜; Ⓜ San Babila) The three classy rooms in this upmarket B&B have Philippe Starck chairs, flat-screen TVs and a communal kitchen. Ceilings are high, rooms are filled with natural light and bathrooms are dizzyingly contemporary. About a 1.5km walk from the Duomo.

Hotel Gran Duca di York
Hotel €€

(☏02 87 48 63; www.ducadiyork.com; Via Moneta 1; d €160-205; ❄@🛜📶; Ⓜ Duomo) This lemon-yellow *palazzo* (mansion), literally a stone's throw from the Duomo was once a residence for scholars working in the nearby Ambrosiana library. Now it offers smiley service and 33 small, breezy rooms (some with balconies) with plump beds and neat, marble bathrooms. Our advice is to skip the rather dull breakfast and opt for five-star pastries at Princi a few blocks away.

Hotel Spadari Duomo
Design Hotel €€€

(☏02 7200 2371; www.spadarihotel.com; Via Spadari 11; d €185-345; ❄🛜; Ⓜ Duomo) Milan's original design hotel, the rooms at the Spadari are miniature galleries for the work of emerging artists. The hotel itself is the creation of respected architect-engineers Urbano Pierini and Ugo La Pietra, who designed every inch of the 'look' down to the sinuous pale-wood furniture.

Eating

Latteria di San Marco
Trattoria €

(☏02 659 76 53; Via San Marco 24; meals €18-25; ⏱7-11pm Mon-Fri; 📶; Ⓜ Moscova) If you can snare a seat in this tiny and ever-popular restaurant, you'll find old favourites like *spaghetti alla carbonara* mixed in with chef Arturo's own creations, such as *polpettine al limone* (little meatballs with lemon) or *riso al salto* (risotto fritters) on the ever-changing, mostly organic menu.

1 SALONE INTERNAZIONALE DEL MOBILE

April's furniture fair is the busiest but best time to visit Milan. You don't need to see the fair – just go see the glass Fiera Milano building (www.fieramilano.it) from outside, then head into Fiera Fuoresalone, the international selection of works by emerging designers.

2 FASHION WEEK

Unless you're in the business, skip the runway shows and go to fashion events instead. Hotel roofs, old factories and other places normally closed to the public host parties, and after the relief of getting through runway presentations, the mood is upbeat.

3 TRIENNALE DI MILANO DESIGN MUSEUM

This **museum** (www.triennaledesignmuseum.it; Viale Emilio Alemanga 6) showcases classic design objects that put Milan and Italy on the map – Memphis Group teapots, Gio Ponti chairs – as well as experimental approaches. Some shows are inspiring, some frustrating, but it's always interesting to notice your reaction to design.

4 HAPPY HOUR

The most fashionable scene in Milan is also the cheapest. From 6pm to 8.30pm you get an entire buffet for the price of a drink. Around Arco della Pace are a dozen classic happy-hour places, including Living – very stylish, sometimes snobbish.

5 STREET FASHION PHOTO-OPS

Corso Garibaldi is where you'll find people dressed to be admired, but for street fashion that's a little freaky, don't miss the scene weekdays at Corso di Porta Ticinese. For fashion photo shoots, Cimitero Monumentale (Milan's cemetery) makes an evocative setting with weathered statuary.

127

Milan's Brightest Michelin Stars

Milan's most important contemporary Italian restaurants are equally fashion- and food-oriented:

Cracco (☎02 87 67 74; www.ristorantecracco.it; Via Victor Hugo 4; meals €130-160; ☺7.30-11pm Mon & Sat, 12.30-2.30pm & 7.30-11pm Tue-Fri ; Ⓜ Duomo) Star chef Carlo Cracco conjures up exemplary deconstructive *alta cucina* (haute cuisine) in a formal contemporary environment.

Il Marchesino (☎02 7209 4338; www.ilmarchesino.it; Via Filodrammatici 2; meals €50-80, tasting menu €110; ☺8am-1am Mon-Sat; Ⓜ Duomo) Gualtiero Marchesi, Italy's most revered chef, presides over an elegant modern dining room at La Scala.

Sadler (☎02 87 67 30; www.sadler.it; Via Ascanio Sforza 77; meals €120; ☺7.30-11pm Mon-Sat; ⓂRomolo, 🚊3) On the Milanese scene since 1995, Claudio Sadler's culinary wisdom remains undisputed.

Trussardi alla Scala (☎02 8068 8201; www.trussardiallascala.com; Piazza della Scala 5; meals €120; ☺7.30am-11pm Mon-Fri, dinner Sat; Ⓜ Duomo) Gualtiero Marchesi alumni, Andrea Berton, runs the kitchen of this subdued sexy dining room overlooking La Scala.

Trattoria da Pino
Milanese €

(☎02 7600 0532; Via Cerva 14; meals €20-25; ☺noon-3pm Mon-Sat; ⓂSan Babila) In a city full of models in Michelin-starred restaurants, working-class da Pino's offers the perfect antidote. Sit elbow-to-elbow at long cafeteria-style tables and order up bowls of *bollito misto* (mixed boiled meats), handmade pasta and curried veal nuggets.

Trattoria del Nuovo Macello
Milanese €€

(☎02 5990 2122; www.trattoriadelnuovo macello.it; Via Cesare Lombroso 20; meals €28-50; ☺noon-2.15pm & 8-10.30pm Mon-Fri, 8-10.30pm Sat) A real Milanese will tell you that those thin, battered 'elephant ears' that currently masquerade in many establishments as *cotoletta alla Milanese* (Milanese schnitzel) are a poor imitation of the real deal. For authentic Milanese *cotoletta* take a taxi ride out to Nuovo Macello, in the old meat district, where you'll be presented with a thick, juicy slab of veal on the bone cooked slowly to perfection in butter.

Al Bacco
Milanese €€

(☎02 5412 1637; Via Marcona 1; meals €25-30; ☺dinner Mon-Sat) One-time pupil to the famous chef Claudio Sadler, Andrea now has his own Slow Food–recommended restaurant where he prepares Milanese classics with love. Try the homemade pasta with fava beans, pancetta and pecorino, or the rabbit with Taggiasche olives.

Dongiò
Calabrese €€

(☎02 551 13 72; Via Bernardino Corio 3; meals €30-40; ☺noon-2.30pm & 7.30-11.30pm Mon-Fri, 7.30-11.30pm Sat; 🚻; ⓂPorta Romana) One of the best value-for-money restaurants in Milan, this big-hearted Calabrese trattoria serves the spicy flavours of the south on delicious homemade pasta. Starters include bountiful platters of southern salami and piquant cheeses. Reservations recommended.

L'Antico Ristorante Boeucc
Milanese €€€

(☎02 7602 0224; www.boeucc.com; Piazza Belgioioso 2; meals €60-80; ☺lunch & dinner Mon-Fri, lunch Sun; Ⓜ Duomo) Set in the basement of the grand-looking neoclassical

Palazzo Belgioioso, Milan's oldest restaurant has been entertaining diners since 1696. Vaulted dining rooms and service reminiscent of more regal times lend your evening meal a sense of theatre. From *crespelle al prosciutto* (a kind of cross between pasta and crêpe with ham) you might move on to a *trancio di salmone al pepe verde* (slice of salmon with green pepper).

🍸 Drinking & Nightlife

Caffeteria degli Atellani
Cafe, Bar

(📞02 3653 5959; www.atellani.it; Via della Moscova 28; ⏰8.30am-9.30pm Mon-Fri, 9.30am-7.30pm Sat & Sun; 🛜; Ⓜ Moscova, Turati) Cafe Atellani's glasshouse design is modelled on a tropical greenhouse and overlooks a tranquil garden. Inside, the sleek bar is lined with an extensive selection of Italian wines, which you can enjoy after a browse in the cinema bookshop.

Torrefazione Il Caffè Ambrosiano
Cafe

(📞02 2952 5069; http://torrefazioneambrosiano.it; Corso Buenos Aires 20; ⏰7am-8pm; Ⓜ Porta Venezia) No seating, just the best coffee in Milan. There's also a **branch** (Corso XXII Marzo 18; ⏰7am-8pm; 🚌9, 23) on Corso XXII Marzo.

Pandenus
Bar

(📞02 2952 8016; www.pandenus.it; Via Alessandro Tadino 15; cocktails €8, brunch €20; ⏰7am-10pm; 🛜; Ⓜ Porta Venezia) Originally a bakery, Pandenus was named after the walnut bread that used to emerge from its still-active oven. Now the focaccia, *pizzetta* and bruschetta on its burgeoning *aperitivo* bar are some of the best in town. Given its proximity to the Marconi Foundation (which is dedicated to

contemporary art) expect a good-looking, arty crowd.

10 Corso Como
Bar

(📞02 2901 3581; www.10corsocomo.com; Corso Como 10; ⏰12.30pm-midnight Mon-Fri, 11.30am-1.30am Sat & Sun; Ⓜ Garibaldi) A picture-perfect courtyard, world-class people-watching and an elegant *aperitivo* scene lit at night by a twinkling canopy of fairy lights make Corso Como the best lifestyle concept bar in Milan.

Living
Bar

(📞02 3310 0824; www.livingmilano.com; Piazza Sempione 2; ⏰8am-2am Mon-Fri, 9am-2am Sat & Sun; Ⓜ Moscova) Living has one of the city's prettiest settings, with a corner position and floor-to-ceiling windows overlooking the Arco della Pace. The bounteous *aperitivo* spread draws a crowd of smart-casual 20- and 30-somethings. Their sister bar, **Refeel** (📞02 5832 4227; www.refeel.it; Viale Sabotino 20; ⏰7am-2am Mon-Sat, noon-4pm Sun; Ⓜ Porta Romana), in Porta Romana, is also worth a trip.

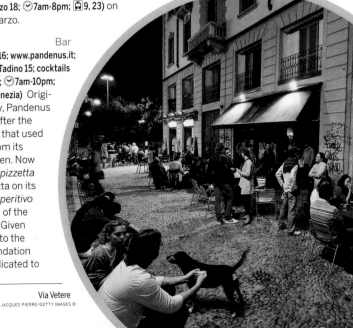

Via Vetere
JACQUES PIERRE/GETTY IMAGES ©

⭐ Entertainment

La Salumeria della Musica   Club

(📞02 5680 7350; www.lasalumeriadellamusica.com; Via Pasinetti 4; ⏰9pm-2am Mon-Sat Sep-Jun; 🚊24) This 'delicatessen of music' is a firm favourite with Milan's alternative scene. Come here to see new acts, literary salons, cultural events and jazz. Shows start around 10.30pm and if you get the munchies grab a plate of cheese and cold cuts.

Blue Note   Jazz

(📞02 6901 6888; www.bluenotemilano.com; Via Borsieri 37; tickets €20-35; ⏰Tue-Sun Sep-Jul; Ⓜ Zara, Garibaldi) Top-class jazz acts perform here from around the world; get tickets by phone, online or at the door from 7.30pm. It also does a popular easy-listening Sunday brunch (€35 or €55 for two adults and two children).

Teatro alla Scala   Opera

(📞02 8 87 91; www.teatroallascala.org; Piazza della Scala; Ⓜ Duomo) You'll need perseverance and luck to secure opera tickets at La Scala (€13 to €210, up to €2000 for opening night), which go on sale two months in advance of performances at the **box office** (Galleria del Sagrato, Piazza del Duomo; ⏰noon-6pm; Ⓜ Duomo). On performance days, 140 tickets for the gallery are sold two hours before the show (one ticket per customer). Queue early.

The opera season runs from November through July, but you can see theatre, ballet and concerts at Teatro alla Scala year-round, with the exception of in August.

San Siro Stadium   Football

(Stadio Giuseppe Meazza; 📞02 404 24 32; www.sansiro.net; Via dei Piccolomini 5, museum & tours Gate 14; museum admission €7, plus guided tour adult/reduced €13/10; ⏰nonmatch days 10am-6pm; Ⓜ Lotto) The city's two football clubs are the 1899-established AC Milan, owned by former prime minister Silvio Berlusconi and the 1908-established FC Internazionale Milano (aka 'Inter'). They play on alternate Sundays during the season at the stadium. Guided tours of the stadium, built in the 1920s, take you behind the scenes to the players' locker rooms and include a visit to the **Museo Inter e Milan** (📞02 404 24 32; www.sansiro.net; Via Piccolomini 5, Gate 21; museum & tour

Galleria Vittorio Emanuele II

adult/concession €13/10; ☉10am-6pm, tours every 20 mins; ♿; Ⓜ Lotto, 🚲16, shuttle from Piazzale Lotto to the stadium) museum, a shrine of memorabilia, papier-mâché caricatures of players, and film footage. Take tram 24, bus 95, 49 or 72, or the metro to the Lotto stop, from where a free bus shuttles to the stadium.

🔒 Shopping

Peck
Deli, Enoteca

(☎ 02 802 31 61; www.peck.it; Via Spadari 7-9; ☉3-7.30pm Mon, 8.45am-7.30pm Tue-Sat; Ⓜ Duomo) Forget *The Last Supper*: gourmands head to the food and wine emporium Peck. This Milanese institution first opened its doors as a deli in 1883. Since then, it's expanded to a restaurant-bar upstairs and an *enoteca* (wine bar). The Aladdin's-cave-like food hall is the best in Milan, stocked with some 3200 variations of *parmigiano reggiano* (Parmesan) at its cheese counter, just for starters.

Spazio Rossana Orlandi
Design Store

(☎ 02 467 44 71; www.rossanaorlandi.com; Via Matteo Bandello 14; ☉3.30-7.30pm Mon, 10am-7.30pm Tue-Fri; Ⓜ Conciliazione) Installed in a former tie factory in the Magenta district, finding this iconic interior design studio is a challenge in itself. Once inside though, you'll find it hard to leave this dream-like treasure trove stacked with vintage and contemporary limited-edition pieces from young and upcoming artists.

La Vetrina Di Beryl
Shoes

(☎ 02 65 42 78; Via Statuto 4; Ⓜ Moscova) Barbara Beryl's name was known to cultists around the world way before 'Manolo' shoes became a byword for female desire. Stumbling upon this deceptively nondescript shop is like chancing upon the shoe racks at a *Vogue Italia* photo shoot.

Borsalino Outlet
Accessories

(☎ 02 8901 5436; www.borsalino.com; Galleria Vittorio Emanuele II 92; ☉3-7pm Mon, 10am-7pm Tue-Sat; Ⓜ Duomo) The iconic Alessandrian

❤ If You Like…
Italian Design

Milan is design heaven, whether it's architecture, interiors or fashion that floats your boat.

1 FIERA MILANO
(www.fieramilano.it) Massimiliano Fuksas' brilliantly engineered Fiera Milano exhibition holds the most high profile of Milan's fairs, the **Salone Internazionale del Mobile** (www.cosmit.it) held annually in April. The space was built on the Agip oil refinery in Rho-Pero, around 40 minutes out of Milan by metro. In action since 2006, its billowing glass-and-steel sail floats over 1.4km of various halls and supporting areas, capable of holding up to half a million visitors.

2 GALLERIA VITTORIO EMANUELE II
(Piazza del Duomo; Ⓜ Duomo) So much more than a shopping arcade, the neoclassical Galleria Vittorio Emanuele is a soaring iron-and-glass structure known locally as *il salotto bueno,* the city's fine drawing room.

3 TRIENNALE DI MILANO
(☎ 02 72 43 41; www.triennaledesignmuseum. it; Viale Emilio Alemanga 6; adult/reduced €8/6.50; ☉10.30am-8.30pm Tue, Wed, Sat & Sun, to 11pm Thu & Fri; Ⓟ; Ⓜ Cadorna) Italy's first Triennale took place in 1923 in Monza. It aimed to promote interest in Italian design and applied arts, from 'the spoon to the city,' and its success led to the creation of Giovanni Muzio's **Palazzo d'Arte** in Milan in 1933. Since then it has championed design in all its forms, although the triennale formula has since been replaced by long annual events, with international exhibits as part of the program.

milliner has worked with design greats such as Achille Castiglioni, who once designed a pudding-bowl bowler hat. This outlet in Galleria Vittorio Emanuele II stocks seasonal favourites. Otherwise you can visit the **main showroom** (☎ 02 7601 7072; www.borsalino.com; Via Sant'Andrea 5; Ⓜ Montenapoleone).

RAINER MARTINI/GETTY IMAGES ©

⭐ Don't Miss
Quadrilatero d'Oro

For anyone interested in the fall of a frock or the cut of a jacket, a stroll around the Quadrilatero d'Oro, the world's most fabled shopping district, is a must. This quaintly cobbled quadrangle of streets may have always been synonymous with elegance and money (Via Monte Napoleone was where Napoleon's government managed loans), but the Quad's legendary fashion status belongs firmly to Milan's postwar reinvention. During the boom years of the 1950s the city's fashion houses established ateliers in the area bounded by Via Monte Napoleone, Via Sant'Andrea, Via della Spiga and Via Alessandro Manzoni, and by the 1960s Milan had outflanked Florence and Rome to become the country's haute couture capital. Nowadays, the world's top designers unveil their women's collections in February/March and September/October, while men's fashion hits the runways in January and June/July.

NEED TO KNOW

Golden Quad

G Lorenzi Design Store
(☑02 7602 2848; www.lorenzi.it; Via Monte Napoleone 9; ⏱3-7.30pm Mon, 9am-12.30pm & 3-7.30pm Tue-Sat; Ⓜ San Babila) One of Milan's extant early-20th-century gems, G Lorenzi specialises in the finest-quality grooming and kitchen paraphernalia. There are things here – handcrafted pocket knives set into stag antlers, say – so fine and functional that they stand as classic examples of utilitarian design.

10 Corso Como Fashion
(☑02 2900 2674; www.10corsocomo.com; Corso Como 10; ⏱10.30am-7.30pm Tue & Fri-Sun, to 9pm Wed & Thu, 3.30-7.30pm Mon; Ⓜ Garibaldi) It might be the world's most hyped 'con-

cept shop', but Carla Sozzani's selection of desirable things (Lanvin ballet flats, Alexander Girard wooden dolls, a demi-couture frock by a designer you've not read about *yet*) makes 10 Corso Como a tempting shopping experience. Next to the gallery upstairs is a bookshop with art and design titles.

ℹ️ Information

Tourist Information

Milan Tourist Office (☎ 02 7740 4343; www.turismo.milano.it; Piazza Castello 1; ☺9am-6pm Mon-Fri, 9am-1.30pm & 2-6pm Sat, to 5pm Sun; Ⓜ Duomo)

Stazione Centrale Tourist Office (☎ 02 7740 4318; opposite platform 13, Stazione Centrale; ☺9am-6pm Mon-Fri, 9am-1.30pm & 2-6pm Sat, to 5pm Sun)

Linate Airport Information Desk (☎ 02 7020 0443; Linate Airport, Arrivals, Ground Floor; ☺7.30am-11.30pm)

Malpensa Airport Information Desk (☎ 02 5858 0080; Malpensa Airport, Terminal B, Ground Floor; ☺8am-8pm)

ℹ️ Getting There & Away

Air

Orio al Serio Airport (☎ 035 32 63 23; www.sacbo.it)

Linate Airport (☎ 02 23 23 23; www.sea-aeroportimilano.it) Located 7km east of the city century; domestic and some European flights.

Malpensa Airport (☎ 02 23 23 23; www.sea-aeroportimilano.it) About 50km northwest of the city; northern Italy's main international airport.

Bus

National and international buses depart from **Lampugnano bus station** (**Via Giulia Natta**) (next to the Lampugnano metro stop), 5km west of central Milan. The main national operator is **Autostradale** (☎ 02 720 01 304; www.autostradale.it). Tickets can be purchased at the main tourist office.

Train

International, high-speed trains from France, Switzerland and Germany arrive in Milan's

Stazione Centrale (**Piazza Duca d'Aosta**). The ticketing office and left luggage are located on the ground floor and the tourist information booth is opposite platform 13. For regional trips, skip the queue and buy your tickets from the multilingual, touch-screen vending machines, which accept both cash and credit card. Daily international and long-distance destinations include:

Florence (€19 to €50, 1½ to 3½ hours, hourly)

Rome (€55 €58, three hours, half hourly)

Venice (€16 to €37; 2½ to 3½ hours, half hourly)

ℹ️ Getting Around

To/From the Airport

Bus

Air Bus (www.atm-mi.it) Coaches, run by ATM, depart from the Piazza Luigi di Savoi, next to Stazione Centrale, for **Linate Airport** (adult/child €5/2.50, 25 minutes) every 30 minutes from 6am to 11pm.

Autostradale (☎ 02 720 01 304; www.autostradale.it) Runs buses from **Orio al Serio Airport** every 30 minutes between 2.45am and 11.30pm from Piazza Luigi di Savoia to Orio al Serio airport, near Bergamo (adult/child €5/3.50, one hour).

Malpensa Shuttle (☎ 02 585 83 185; www.malpensashuttle.it; ticket €10) Departs from Piazza Luigi di Savoi, next to Stazione Centrale, every 20 minutes from 3.45am to 12.30am, taking 50 minutes to **Malpensa Airport**.

Taxi

There is a flat fee of €90 to and from Malpensa Airport to central Milan. The drive should take 50 minutes outside peak times. For travellers to Terminal 2, this might prove the quickest option. The taxi fare to Linate Airport is from €10 to €20.

Train

Malpensa Express (☎ 02 7249 4494; www.malpensaexpress.it) Coaches depart Malpensa Airport every 30 minutes from Terminal 1 for Stazione Centrale (adult/child €10/5, 50 minutes) and Cadorna Nord (**Stazione Nord**; www.ferrovienord.it; Piazza Luigi Cadorna) (adult/child €11/5, 30 minutes) between 5.25am and 11.40pm. Passengers arriving or departing from Terminal 2 will need to catch the free shuttle bus to Terminal 1 train station.

Detour:
Certosa di Pavia

One of the Italian Renaissance's most notable buildings is the splendid **Certosa di Pavia** (Pavia Charterhouse; ☎0382 92 56 13; www.certosadipavia.com; Viale Monumento; donations appreciated; ⊙9-11.30am & 2.30-5.30pm Tue-Sun) FREE . Giangaleazzo Visconti of Milan founded the monastery, 10km north of Pavia, in 1396 as a private chapel and mausoleum for the Visconti family. Originally intended as an architectural companion piece to Milan's Duomo, the same architects worked on its design although the final result, completed over a century later, was a unique hybrid between late-Gothic and new Renaissance styles.

While the airy interior is indeed predominantly Gothic, the exterior is almost entirely a creature of the Renaissance. The church is fronted by a spacious courtyard and flanked by a small cloister, which itself leads onto a much grander, second cloister, under whose arches are 24 cells, each a self-contained living area for one monk. Several cells are open to the public, but you need to join one of the guided tours (Italian only) to access these. In the former sacristy is a giant sculpture, dating from 1409 and made from hippopotamus teeth, including 66 small bas-reliefs and 94 statuettes. In the chapels you'll find frescoes by, among others, Bernardino Luini and the Umbrian master, Il Perugino.

Sila bus 175 (Pavia–Binasco–Milano) links Pavia bus station and Certosa di Pavia (15 minutes, at least seven daily).

Public Transport

ATM (☎800 80 81 81; www.atm.it) runs the metro, buses and trams. The metro is the most convenient way to get around and consists of three main lines and the blue Passante Ferroviario, which run from 6am and 12.30am, after which a night service runs to 2.30am. A ticket costs €1.50 and is valid for one metro ride or up to 90 minutes' travel on ATM buses and trams. Tickets are sold at metro stations, tobacconists and newspaper stands. Tickets must be validated on trams and buses.

Bus and tram route maps are available at ATM Info points, or download the iATM app. There are several good money-saving passes available for public transport:

One-day ticket Valid 24 hours, €4.50

Three-day ticket Valid 72 hours, €8.25

Carnet of 10 tickets Valid for 90 minutes each, €13.80

Taxi

Taxis are only available at designated taxi ranks; you cannot flag them down. Alternatively, call ☎02 40 40, ☎02 69 69 or ☎02 85 85. The average short city ride costs €10. Be aware that when you call for a cab, the meter runs from receipt of call, not pick up.

THE LAKES

Lago Maggiore

More than Como and Garda, Lake Maggiore retains the belle époque air of its 19th-century heyday when the European *haute bourgeoisie* flocked to buy and build grand lakeside villas and establish a series of extraordinarily rich gardens.

The northern end of the lake where it narrows between the mountains and enters Switzerland is the prettier, more secluded end. And it's well worth taking the delightful shoreline drive south along the SS34 and SS33.

❶ Getting There & Around

Boat

Car Ferries Connect Verbania Intra and Laveno. Ferries run every 20 minutes; one-way transport costs from €6.90 to €11.50 for a car and driver or €4.30 for a bicycle and cyclist.

Navigazione Lago Maggiore (☎800 551801; www.navigazionelaghi.it) Operates ferries and hydrofoils. There are ticket booths in each town next to the embarkation quay; the main office is in Arona. Day passes cost from €15.50/8.80 to €21.50/11.80 per adult/child, depending on the departure port, and include the Swiss town of Locarno as a stop.

Bus

SAF (☎0323 55 21 72; www.safduemila.com) offers a daily service from Stresa to Milan (€8.75, 1½ hours), and also serves Verbania Pallanza (€2.25, 20 minutes) and Arona (€2.25, 20 minutes), departing from the waterfront.

Train

Stresa is on the Domodossola–Milan train line. Domodossola, 30 minutes northwest, is on the Swiss border, from where the train line leads to Brig and on to Geneva.

Lago di Como

Set in the shadow of the snow-covered Rhaetian Alps and hemmed in on both sides by steep, wooded hills, Lago di Como (also known as Lake Lario) is the most spectacular and least visited of the three major lakes. Shaped like an upside-down letter Y, its winding shoreline is scattered with villages, including de-lightful Bellagio, which sits at the centre of the two southern branches on a small promontory. Where the southern and western shores converge is the lake's main town, Como.

❶ Getting There & Around

Boat

Navigazione Lago di Como (☎800 551801, 031 57 92 11; www.navigazionelaghi.it; Piazza Cavour) ferries and hydrofoils criss-cross the lake, departing year-round from the jetty at the northern end of Como's Piazza Cavour. One-way fares range from €2.50 (Como–Cernobbio) to €12.60 (Como–Lecco or Como–Gravedona). Hydrofoil fast services entail a supplement of €1.40 to €4.90.

Ceiling of the Certosa di Pavia

Car ferries link Cadenabbia on the west shore with Varenna on the eastern shore and Bellagio.

Bus

ASF Autolinee (☏031 24 72 47; www.sptlinea. it) operates regular buses around the lake, which depart from the bus station on Piazza Giacomo Matteotti. Key routes include Como–Colico (€5.90, 1½ hours, three to five daily), via all the villages on the western shore, and Como–Bellagio (€3.20, one hour 10 minutes, hourly).

Train

Como's main train station (Como San Giovanni) is served from Milan's Stazione Centrale and Porta Garibaldi station (€4.55 to €13, 30 minutes to one hour, hourly); some continue on to Switzerland. Trains from Milan's Stazione Nord (€4.10, one hour) use Como's lakeside Stazione FNM (aka Como Nord Lago). Trains from Milan to Lecco continue north along the eastern shore. If you're going to Bellagio, it is better to continue on the train to Varenna and make the short ferry crossing from there.

COMO
POP 85,300

With its charming historic centre, 12th-century city walls and self-confident air, Como is an elegant and prosperous town. Built on the wealth of the silk industry, it remains Europe's most important producer of silk products; you can buy scarves and ties here for a fraction of the cost elsewhere.

◎ Sights & Activities

Como's lakeside location is stunning and flower-laden; lakeside promenades make for pleasant walks to the various sights. The tourist office has walking and cycling information.

Villa Olmo   Villa, Museum
(☏031 57 61 69; www.grandimostrecomo.it; Via Cantoni 1; adult/reduced €10/8; ⏲villa during exhibitions 9am-12.30pm & 2-5pm Mon-Sat; gardens 7.30am-7pm Sep-May, 7.30am-11pm Jun-Aug) Set grandly facing the lake, the creamy facade of neoclassical Villa Olmo

is one of Como's landmarks. The extravagant structure was built in 1728 by the Odescalchi family, related to Pope Innocent XI. If there's an art exhibition inside, you'll get to admire the sumptuous Liberty-style interiors. Otherwise, you can enjoy the Italianate and English gardens, which are open all day.

During summer the **Lido di Villa Olmo** (www.lidovillaolmo.it; Via Cernobbio 2; adult/reduced day €6/4, half-day €4.50/2.50; 9am-7pm mid-May–Sep), an open-air swimming pool and lakeside bar, is open to the public.

Funicolare Como-Brunate Funicular
(031 30 36 08; www.funicolarecomo.it; Piazza de Gasperi 4, Como; adult one way/return €2.90/5.25, child €1.90/3.20; half-hourly departures 8am-midnight mid-Apr–mid-Sep, to 10.30pm mid-Sep–mid-Apr) Northeast along the waterfront, past Piazza Matteotti and the train station, is the Como–Brunate cable car, which was built in 1894. It takes seven minutes to reach hilltop **Brunate**

(720m), a quiet village offering splendid views. In **San Maurizio**, a 30-minute, steep walk from Brunate's funicular stop, scales 143 steps to the top of the lighthouse, built in 1927 to mark the centenary of Alessandro Volta's death.

Aero Club Como Scenic Flights
(031 57 44 95; www.aeroclubcomo.com; Viale Masia 44, Como; 2 people €140; Como) For a touch of Hollywood glamour, take one of the 30-minute seaplane tours from the Aero Club and buzz Bellagio. Longer excursions over Lago Maggiore and Lago Lugano are also possible. During summer you'll need to reserve at least three or four days in advance.

🛏 Sleeping & Eating

Le Stanze del Lago Apartment €
(339 5446515; www.lestanzedellago.com; Via Rodari 6; 2-/4-person apt €100/130;) Five cosy apartments, nicely decked out in

137

Como

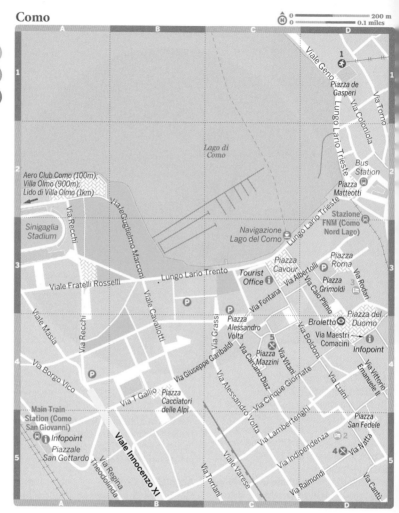

Como

modern but understated fashion, make for a good deal in the heart of Como. For stays of five days or longer you can use the kitchen too. All apartments feature a double bed, sofa bed, timber ceiling and tiled floor.

Avenue Hotel   Boutique Hotel €€
(☏ 031 27 21 86; www.avenuehotel.it; Piazzole Terragni 6; d/ste from €170/220; ✳ 🛜) Combining a quiet location deep in the old town with ultra-modern rooms in which bold colours offset a minimalist white

background, Avenue Hotel is deservedly popular. The free bicycle rental is a nice touch, as is the laptop safe box and flat-screen TVs. The service, too, is warm but discreet.

Natta Café
Cafe €

(☎ 031 26 91 23; Via Natta 16; meals €10-15; ⏰ 9.30am-3.30pm Mon, 9.30am-midnight Tue-Thu, 9.30am-2am Fri, 11.30am-2pm Sat; 🛜) This funky space in the old town but ever-so-slightly removed from the busier thoroughfares is Como's antidote to traditional trattorias and osterie. A funky cafe with free wifi, it serves up light meals that change regularly, baguettes, salads, wine by the glass and well-priced cocktails (€5 to €8). It's a lovely, laid-back little spot.

Osteria del Gallo
Italian €€

(☎ 031 27 25 91; www.osteriadelgallo-como.it; Via Vitani 16; meals €25-30; ⏰ 12.30pm-3pm Mon, to 9pm Tue-Sat) This ageless osteria is a must. Cheerful green and white gingham is draped over the little timber tables. All around are shelves of wine and other goodies. The menu is recited by staff (in French if you wish) and might include an entrée of giant ravioli, followed by lightly fried lake-fish fillets. Otherwise, pop by for a glass of wine.

ℹ️ Information

Tourist Office (☎ 031 26 97 12; www.lakecomo. org; Piazza Cavour 17; ⏰ 9am-1pm & 2-5pm Mon-Sat) There is an information kiosk (⏰ 10am-1pm & 2-5pm) next to the Duomo, and another at the train station (10am-1pm & 2-5pm).

BELLAGIO

It's impossible not to be smitten by Bellagio's waterfront of bobbing boats, its maze of steep stone staircases, red-roofed and green-shuttered buildings, dark cypress groves and rhododendron-filled gardens. Like the prow of a beautiful vessel, it sits at the crux of the inverted Y that is Lake Como; the Como and Lecco arms of the lake wash off to port and starboard.

Bellagio is hardly a secret. On summer weekends, foreign tourists are overwhelmed by hordes of day

Local Knowledge

Lago di Como

RECOMMENDATIONS FROM
RITA ANNUNZIATA, LAKE COMO
NATIVE & TOUR GUIDE

1 **WALKING TRAILS & TOURS**
Walking tours of the mountains surrounding the towns of Bellagio, Lenno and Tremezzo offer an insight into the lake's lesser-known villages and landscapes. The 6km walk from Bellano to Varenna along the ancient Viandante trail is particularly beautiful. On the western shore, head to the Chiesa di San Martino, 400m above tiny Cadenabbia, for spectacular views. You'll find information on walking trails and tours at the local tourist offices.

2 **ROMANTIC GARDENS**
Quite simply, Lake Como's gardens are marvellous. To catch the spring blooming of azaleas, rhododendrons and camellias, visit before 10 May. Among the most beautiful gardens are those of Villas Serbelloni, Balbianello and Carlotta. In summer, enchanting classical concerts are held in some of the gardens, mostly at Villa Carlotta (p140). For schedules, check the villas' websites or those of the local tourist offices.

3 **BELLAGIO**
Most visitors are surprised that Bellagio is even more stunning in real life than it is on postcards. Aside from its glorious lakeside gardens, there's a great selection of shops, cafes and restaurants. Every Monday, local history buff Lucia Sala runs a guided tour exploring some of the 22 hamlets, and she'll even show you her wonderful local ethnographic collection. PromoBellagio (www. bellagiolakecomo.com) can provide details.

trippers up from Milan. Try to come midweek if you want a modicum of peace. It makes a nice base for ferry trips to other locations on the lake. You can also take a boat trip with **Barindelli's** (☎ 338 2110337; www.barindellitaxiboats.com; Piazza

Mazzini; 1hr-long tour €140). Stay at the good-value **Hotel Silvio** (☎031 95 03 22; www.bellagiosilvio.com; Via Carcano 10-12, Bellagio; d from €180; ⏰Mar–mid-Nov & Christmas; P✻☎), which has lovely views, and eat at Slow Food–recommended **Ittiturismo Da Abate** (☎338 584 38 14; www.ittiturismodabate.it; Frazione Villa 4, Lezzeno; meals €25-35; ⏰7-10.30pm Tue-Sat, noon-2.30pm & 7-10.30pm Sun; ⛟; ☘Lezzeno), which is 8km south of Bellagio.

Small buses rattle more or less hourly from Como to Bellagio (€3.25, 70 minutes).

THE WESTERN SHORE

Scenes from *Ocean's 12* were filmed in the Lago di Como village of **Cernobbio**. If you're driving, follow the lower lakeside road (Via Regina Vecchia) north from Cernobbio, which skirts the lake shore past a fabulous row of 19th-century villas around **Moltrasio**. A few kilometres north is the villa-lined hamlet of **Laglio**, home to George Clooney.

Finally, in **Lenno**, the **Villa Balbianello** (☎0344 5 61 10; www.fondoambiente.it; Via Comoedia 5, Località Balbianello; villa & gardens adult/child €13/7, with prior reservation €10/5, gardens only adult/child €7/3; ⏰gardens 10am-6pm Tue & Thu-Sun mid-Mar–mid-Nov) takes the prize for the lake's most dramatically situated gardens, dripping down the sides of the high promontory like sauce off a melting ice-cream. Scenes from *Star Wars: Episode II* and 2006's James Bond remake *Casino Royale* were shot here. If you want to see inside, you must join a guided tour (generally in Italian) by 4.15pm. Visitors are only allowed to walk the 1km from the Lenno landing stage to the estate on Tuesday and at weekends; other days, you have to take a taxi boat from Lenno.

Tremezzo is high on everyone's list for a visit to the 17th-century **Villa Carlotta** (☎0344 4 04 05; www.villacarlotta.it; Via Regina 2; adult/reduced €9/5; ⏰9am-5pm Easter-Sep, 10am-4pm mid-Mar–Easter & Oct–mid-Nov; ☘Cadenabbia), whose botanic gardens are filled with orange trees knitted into pergolas and some of Europe's finest rhododendrons, azaleas and camellias. The villa, which is strung with paintings, alabaster-white sculptures (especially those by Antonio Canova) and tapestries, takes its name from the Prussian princess who was given the palace in 1847 as a wedding present from her mother. The other highlight of Tremezzo is excellent **Al Velulu** (☎0344 4 05 10; www.alveluu.com; Via Rogaro 11, Tremezzo; meals €50-70; ⏰Wed-Mon; ⛟; ☘Cadenabbia) restaurant, which serves wild asparagus and polenta backed by panoramic views from its hillside terrace. Upstairs there are two comfortable suites, each sleeping up to four people. Staff offer a pick-up from the dock.

Gardens at Villa Carlotta
DAMIEN SIMONIS/GETTY IMAGES ©

Lago di Garda

Poets and politicians, divas and dictators, they've all been drawn to Lake Garda. At 370 sq km it is the largest of the Italian lakes, straddling the border between Lombardy and the Veneto, with soaring mountains to the north and softer hills to the south. Vineyards, olive groves and citrus orchards range up the slopes, while villages sit around a string of natural harbours. In the southwest corner, Desenzano del Garda has good transport connections.

Garda is the most developed of the lakes and, despite a plethora of accommodation, booking ahead is advised.

❶ Getting There & Around

Air

Verona-Villafranca Airport (☎045 809 56 66; www.aeroportoverona.it) Verona's airport is most convenient for the lake. Regular trains connect Verona with Peschiera del Garda (€2.85, 15 minutes) and Desenzano del Garda (€3.80, 25 minutes).

Boat

Navigazione Lago di Garda (☎800 551801; www.navigazionelaghi.it; Piazza Matteotti 2, Desenzano del Garda) Operates ferries year-round. A one-day ticket allowing unlimited travel in the Alto Garda (Upper Garda) costs €24.30/17.60 per adult/child, while the Basso Garda (Lower Garda) ticket costs €27.40/16.40 per adult/child.

Motorists can cross the lake using the car ferry between Toscolano-Maderno and Torri del Benaco, or seasonally between Limone and Malcesine. A car costs €10.70 one way.

Bus

APTV (☎045 805 78 11; www.aptv.it) Connects Desenzano del Garda train station with Riva del Garda (€4.70, two hours, up to six daily). Peschiera del Garda train station is on the Riva del Garda–Malcesine–Garda–Verona APTV bus route, with hourly buses to both Riva (€4.10, one hour 40 minutes) and Verona (€3.20, 30 minutes).

Lago di Garda's Best Beaches

Rocca di Manerba A designated nature reserve 10km south of Salò.

Parco la Fontanella A white-pebble beach north of Gargnano, backed by olive groves.

Campione del Garda A cliff-backed beach north of Gargnano where windsurfers set sail.

Riva del Garda A family-friendly landscaped waterfront that runs for 3km.

Punta San Vigilio A cypress-lined headland that curls out into the lake 3km north of Garda.

Trasporti Brescia (☎030 440 61; www.trasportibrescia.it; Via Cassale 3/a, Brescia) Operates services from Brescia up the western side of the lake to Riva del Garda.

Trentino Trasporti (☎0461 821 000; www.ttesercizio.it) Connects Riva del Garda with Arco (20 minutes) and Trento (€4.20, 1¾ hours).

Train

Desenzano del Garda and Peschiera del Garda are on the Milan–Venice train line.

SIRMIONE

POP 7420

Sitting on an impossibly narrow peninsula on the southern shore, Sirmione is Garda's most picturesque village. Throughout the centuries it has attracted the likes of Roman poet Catullus and Maria Callas, and today thousands follow in their footsteps.

The **tourist office** (☎030 91 61 14; Viale Marconi 8; ⏱9am-12.30pm & 3-6pm Mon-Fri, 9am-12.30pm Sat) adjoins the bus station. Motorised vehicles are banned beyond this point, except for those with a hotel booking.

Below: Bellagio (p139)
Right: Windsurfers on Lago di Garda (p141)

(BELOW) ROBERTO SONCIN GEROMETTA /GETTY IMAGES © & (RIGHT) BUENA VISTA IMAGES/GETTY IMAGES ©

some three storeys high. It's the largest domestic Roman villa in northern Italy and wandering its terraced hillsides offers fantastic views.

⊙ Sights & Activities

Rocca Scaligera _Castle_
(Castello Scaligero; adult/reduced €4/2; ⊗8.30am-7pm Tue-Sun) Expanding their influence northwards, the Scala family built this enormous square-cut castle right at the entrance to the island. It guards the only footbridge into Sirmione, looming over it with impressive crenellated turrets and towers. There's not a lot inside, but the climb to the top (146 steps to the top of the tower) affords beautiful views over Sirmione's rooftops and the enclosed harbour.

Grotte di Catullo _Historic Site_
(☎030 91 61 57; adult/reduced €4/2; ⊗8.30am-8pm Tue-Sat, 9.30am-6.30pm Sun Mar-Oct, 8.30am-2pm Tue-Sun Nov-Mar) Occupying 2 hectares at Sirmione's northern tip, this ruined, 1st-century AD Roman villa is a picturesque complex of teetering stone arches and tumbledown walls,

Aquaria _Spa_
(☎030 91 60 44; www.termedisirmione.com; Piazza Don Angelo Piatti; pools day/evening €33/27, treatments from €25; ⊗pools 2-10pm Mon, 10am-10pm Tue-Sun Mar-Dec, hours vary Jan & Feb) Sirmione is blessed with a series of offshore thermal springs that pump out water at a natural 37°C. At the Aquaria spa you can wallow in two thermal pools – the outdoor one is set right beside the lake. Bring along your swimsuit and flip-flops (thongs), and towels and robes will be provided. Swim suits are also available for purchase.

🛏 Sleeping & Eating

An inordinate number of hotels are crammed into Sirmione, many of which close from the end of October to March.

Four campgrounds lie near the town and the tourist office can advise on others around the lake.

Hotel Marconi   Hotel €€

(✆030 91 60 07; www.hotelmarconi.net; Via Vittorio Emanuele II 51, Sirmione; s €45-75, d €80-135; P❄) Blue-and-white striped umbrellas line the lakeside deck at this stylish, family-run hotel. The restrained rooms are all subtle shades and crisp fabrics, and the breakfasts and homemade pastries are a treat.

La Fiasca   Trattoria €€

(✆030 990 61 11; www.trattorialafiasca.it; Via Santa Maria Maggiore; meals €30; ☉noon-2.30pm & 7-10.30pm Thu-Tue) Serving up the kind of sauces you can't help dunking your bread into, this authentic trattoria is tucked away in a back street just off the main square. The atmosphere is warm and bustling, and the dishes are packed with traditional Lake Garda produce: tagliatelle with perch and porcini, and duck with cognac and juniper.

GARDONE RIVIERA
POP 2700

Gardone's glory days were in the late 19th and early 20th centuries, and today the resort's opulent villas and ornate architecture make it one of the lake's most elegant holiday spots. About 12km north of Gardone is **Gargnano** (population 3050), a tiny harbour that fills with million-dollar yachts come September when sailing fans gather for the **Centomiglia**, the lake's most prestigious sailing regatta.

The **tourist office** (✆0365 374 87 36; Corso della Repubblica 8; ☉9am-12.30pm & 2.30-6pm Mon-Sat) stocks information on activities.

◎ Sights

Il Vittoriale degli Italiani   Museum

(✆0365 29 65 11; www.vittoriale.it; Piazza Vittoriale; gardens & museums adult/reduced €16/12; ☉grounds 8.30am-8pm Apr-Sep, to 5pm Oct-Mar, museums to 7pm Tue-Sun Apr-Sep, 9am-1pm & 2-5pm Tue-Sun Oct-Mar; P) Poet, soldier, hypochondriac and proto-Fascist, Gabriele

143

d'Annunzio (1863–1938) defies easy definition, and so does his estate. Bombastic, extravagant and unsettling, it's home to every architectural and decorative excess imaginable and the decor helps shed light on the eccentric man. In the 1920s d'Annunzio became a strong supporter of Fascism and Mussolini, while his affairs with wealthy women were legendary.

Giardino Botanico Fondazione André Heller   Garden

(☏336 41 08 77; www.hellergarden.com; Via Roma 2; adult/child €10/5; ⊙9am-7pm Mar-Oct) Gardone's heyday was due in large part to its consistently mild climate, and this mildness benefits the thousands of exotic blooms that fill artist André Heller's sculpture garden. Laid out in 1912 by Arturo Hruska, a dentist who did rather well tending to European royalty, the garden is zoned into pocket-sized climate zones and dotted with 30 pieces of contemporary sculpture, including pieces by Keith Haring and Roy Lichtenstein.

🛏 Sleeping

Locanda Agli Angeli   Rural Inn €€

(☏036 52 08 32; www.agliangeli.com; Piazza Garibaldi 2, Gardone Riviera; s €45-70, d €80-180; P ❄ ≋) A delightful renovation has produced an 18th-century *locanda* (inn) of old polished wood, gauzy curtain fabrics and bursts of lime, orange and aquamarine. The terrace has a compact pool and views across rooftops and the lake beyond. The restaurant is also good, serving classic Lake Garda cooking (meals €25 to €35).

RIVA DEL GARDA

POP 15,800

Even on a lake blessed with dramatic scenery, Riva del Garda still comes out on top. Encircled by towering rock faces and a looping strip of beach, its appealing centre is a medley of elegant architecture, maze-like streets and wide squares. Riva lies across the border from Lombardy in the Alpine region of Trentino-Alto Adige; for centuries the town's strategic position saw it fought over by the competing powers of the bishops of Trento, the republic of Venice, Milan's Viscontis and

Verona's Della Scala families. It remained part of Austria until 1919, subsequently saw fierce fighting in the Italian wars of independence, and was home to anti-Nazi resistance groups in WWII.

◉ Sights & Activities

Riva makes a natural starting point for a host of activities, including hiking and biking trails around Monte Rocchetta (1575m). More gentle pursuits are possible along the gorgeous landscaped lakefront: swimming, sunbathing and cycling the 3km lakeside path to Torbole. Windsurfing schools hire out equipment on Porfina Beach.

🛏 Sleeping & Eating

Residence Filanda   Aparthotel €€

(☏0464 55 47 34; www.residencefilanda.com; Via Sant'Alessandro, 51; d €105-135, qd €165-210; P ❄ @ ≋ ♟) Located 2km outside Riva, this bright, burnt-orange residence situated amid olive groves is a haven for families. Rooms and apartments overlook lush grounds that incorporate a heated pool, tennis and volleyball courts and 1 hectare of child-friendly gardens. Facilities are top-notch, too, with fully equipped kitchenettes, a laundrette and all the necessary paraphernalia for young children.

Lido Palace   Luxury Hotel €€€

(☏0464 02 18 99; www.lido-palace.it; Viale Carducci 10, Riva del Garda; d €270-380, ste €450-550; P ❄ @ 🛜 ≋) If you're going to splash the cash, this is the place to do it. Riva's historic Lido palace dates back to 1899 and is an absolute stunner. Sensitive renovations have installed uncompromisingly modern interiors within the grand Liberty-style palace, complete with Michelin-starred restaurant, peerless views over lawns and lake, and sumptuous spa facilities (open to non-hotel guests by reservation).

Cristallo Caffè   Gelato €

(☏0464 55 38 44; www.cristallogelateria.com; Piazza Catena 11; cones €2.50; ⊙7-1am) Over 60 flavours of artisanal ice cream served in giant sundaes. This is also a good spot for a spritz with views across the lake.

Osteria Le Servite

Osteria, Gardese €€

(☏ 0464 55 74 11; www.leservite.com; Via Passirone 68, Arco; meals €30-45; ☺ 7-10.30pm Tue-Sun Apr-Sep, 7-10.30pm Thu-Sun Oct-Mar; 🚹) Tucked away amid Arco's vineyards is this elegant little *osteria* where Alessandro and his wife serve *mimosa* gnocchi, tender *salmerino* and pork fillet with grape must. In summer you can sit out on the patio sipping small-production DOC Trentino wines.

MALCESINE

POP 3650

With the lake lapping right up to the tables of its harbourside restaurants and the vast ridge of Monte Baldo looming behind, Malcesine is another Garda hot spot. Like Riva del Garda and Torbole, it is a windsurfing centre and its streets are cobbled with thousands of lake pebbles. It is crowned by the chalky-white **Castello Scaligero**, where Goethe was temporarily imprisoned after being mistaken for a spy.

Malcesine's cable car, **Funivia Malcesine-Monte Baldo** (☏ 045 740 02 06; www.funiviedelbaldo.it; Via Navene Vecchia; adult/reduced return €19/15; ☺ 8am-7pm Apr-Aug, to 6pm Sep, to 5pm Oct) whisks you 1760m above the lake in rotating, glass cabins. The mountain is actually part of a 40km-long chain, and the ridges are the starting point for mountain-biking tours and paragliding, as well as skiing in winter. Getting off the cable car at the intermediate station of **San Michele** (one way/return €5/7) is the starting point for some excellent hikes. The hour-long walk back to Malcesine along quiet roads and rocky mountain paths reveals a rural world far from the throngs at the lake. Hire bikes at **Bikextreme** (☏ 045 740 0105; www.bikextrememalcesine.com; Via Navene Vecchia

10; per day €15-30) and check into Rifugio Monte Baldo for more extended mountain explorations.

Olives harvested around Malcesine are milled into extra-virgin olive oil by **Consorzio Olivicoltori di Malcesine** (☏ 045 740 12 86; Via Navene 21; ☺ 9am-1pm & 4.30-7pm; **P**) **FREE**. The oil is renowned for its light, fruity taste with traces of almonds. Prices of the cold-pressed extra virgin DOP olive oil range start at €11 for 0.5L.

To escape the crowds head up to Michelin-starred **Vecchia Malcesine** (☏ 045 740 04 69; www.vecchiamalcesine.com; Via Pisort 6; meals €45-100; ☺ noon-2.30pm & 7-10.30pm Thu-Tue) for artful food and 'meteorite' chocolates filled with Garda olive oil. Otherwise, **Speck Stube** (☏ 0457 40 11 77; www.speckstube.com; Via Navene Vecchia 139, Campagnola; meals €8-20; ☺ noon-midnight Mar-Oct; 🚹) is a fun barbeque place on the outskirts of town.

The **tourist office** (☏ 045 658 99 04; www.malcesinepiu.it; Via Capitanato 6; ☺ 9.30am-12.30pm & 3-6pm Mon-Sat, 9.30am-12.30pm Sun) has information on windsurfing, sailing, walking and skiing.

Rocca Scaligera (p142), Sirmione
PANORAMIC IMAGES/GETTY IMAGES ©

PIEDMONT, LIGURIA & THE ITALIAN RIVIERA

Italy's second-largest region is arguably its most elegant: a purveyor of Slow Food and fine wine, regal *palazzi* (palaces) and an atmosphere that is superficially more *français* than *italiano*. But dig deeper and you'll discover that Piedmont has 'Made in Italy' stamped all over it. Emerging from the chaos of the Austrian wars, the unification movement first exploded here in the 1850s, when the noble House of Savoy provided the nascent nation with its first prime minister and its dynastic royal family.

Turin

POP 911,800 / ELEV 240M

There's a whiff of Paris in Turin's elegant tree-lined boulevards and echoes of Vienna in its stately art nouveau cafes, but make no mistake – this city is anything but a copycat. The innovative Torinese gave the world its first saleable hard chocolate, perpetuated one of its greatest mysteries (the Holy Shroud), popularised a best-selling car (the Fiat) and inspired the black-and-white stripes of one of the planet's most iconic football teams (Juventus).

◎ Sights

Got a week? You might need it to see all the sights Turin has to offer. The time-poor can concentrate on a trio of highlights: the Museo Egizio, the Mole Antonelliana and the Museo Nazionale dell'Automobile.

Mole Antonelliana   Museum
(Via Montebello 20) The symbol of Turin, this 167m tower with its distinctive aluminium spire appears on the Italian two-cent coin. It was originally intended as a synagogue when construction began in 1862, but was never used as a place of worship. In the mid-1990s, the tower became home to the multi-floored **Museo Nazionale del Cinema** (www.museonazionaledelcinema.

org; Via Montebello 20; adult/reduced €9/7, incl panoramic lift €12/9; ◷9am-8pm Tue-Fri & Sun, to 11pm Sat)

The museum takes you on a fantastic tour through cinematic history, from the earliest magic lanterns, stereoscopes and other optical toys to the present day. Movie memorabilia on display includes Marilyn Monroe's black lace bustier, Peter O'Toole's robe from *Lawrence of Arabia* and the coffin used by Bela Lugosi's Dracula. At the heart of the museum, the vast Temple Hall is surrounded by 10 interactive 'chapels' devoted to various film genres.The Mole's glass **panoramic lift** whisks you 85m up through the centre of the museum to the Mole's roof terrace in 59 seconds.

Museo della Sindone   Museum
(www.sindone.org; Via San Domenico 28; adult/reduced €6/5; ◷9am-noon & 3-7pm) Encased in the crypt of Santo Sudario church, this fascinating museum documents one of the most studied objects in human history: the Holy Shroud. Whatever your position on the shroud's authenticity, its story unfolds like a gripping suspense mystery, with countless plots, subplots and revelations.

Museo Egizio   Museum
(Egyptian Museum; www.museoegizio.org; Via Accademia delle Scienze 6; adult/reduced €8/6; ◷8.30am-7.30pm Tue-Sun) 'The road through Memphis and Thebes passes through Turin' trumpeted French hieroglyphic decoder Jean-François Champollion in the early 19th century, and he wasn't far wrong. Opened in 1824, this legendary museum in the **Palazzo dell'Accademia delle Scienze** (Via Accademia delle Scienze 6) houses the most important collection of Egyptian treasure outside Cairo.

Duomo di San Giovanni   Cathedral
(Piazza San Giovanni) Turin's cathedral was built between 1491 and 1498 on the site of three 14th-century basilicas and, before that, a Roman theatre. Most ignore the fairly plain interior and focus

ALESSANDRO RIZZI/GETTY IMAGES ©

⭐ Don't Miss
Reggia di Venaria Reale

Humungous, ostentatious, regal yet strangely under-publicised. This Unesco-listed palace complex was built as a glorified hunting lodge by the frivolous duke of Savoy Carlo Emanuele II in 1675 and is Italy's proverbial Versailles. Sure, it may not enjoy the weighty fame of its French counterpart, but this is one of the largest royal residences in the world, rescued from ruin after decades of neglect by a €235 million 10-year-long restoration project, concluded in 2010. Among the jewels bequeathed by its erstwhile royal rulers are a vast garden complex, a glittering stag fountain (with water shows), a Louis XIV-worthy Grand Gallery, plus the attached Capella di Sant'Uberto and Juvarra stables. The last three were all designed by the great Sicilian architect Filippo Juvarra in the 1720s.

To enjoy the permanent exhibition you'll need to walk 2km through the aptly named Theatre of History and Magnificence, a museum trajectory that relates the 1000-year history of the Savoy clan that's bivouacked in their former royal residential quarters and taking in the Grand Gallery and *capella*. On top of this are numerous high-profile temporary exhibitions, regular live concerts, an on-site cafe and restaurant, and an adjacent *borgo* (old village), now engulfed by Turin's suburbs, that's full of cosy places to eat and drink. Take note, there's a lot to digest and you'll need the best part of a day to see it. You can reach the palace complex (10km northwest of Turin's city centre) on bus 11 from Porta Nuova station.

NEED TO KNOW
www.lavenaria.it; Piazza della Repubblica; admission €20, Reggia & gardens only €15, gardens only €5; 🕙 9am-5pm Tue-Fri, to 8pm Sat & Sun

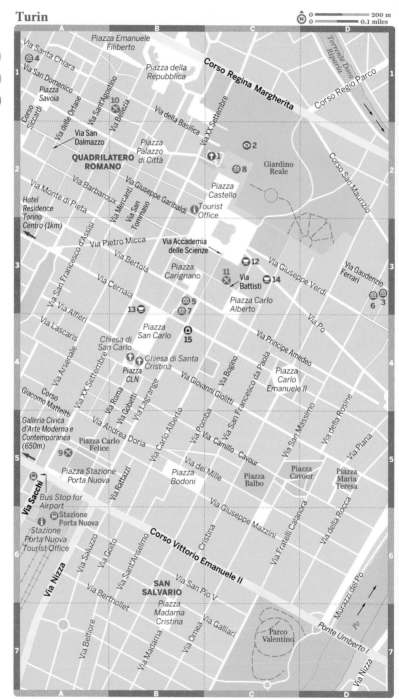

Turin

Turin

on a far bigger myth: the church is home to the famous **Shroud of Turin** (alleged to be the burial cloth in which Jesus' body was wrapped). A copy of the cloth is on permanent display to the left of the cathedral altar.

Palazzo Reale   Museum

(Piazza Castello; adult/reduced €10/5; ⏱8.30am-7.30pm Tue-Sun) Statues of the mythical twins Castor and Pollux guard the entrance to this eye-catching palace and, according to local legend, also watch over the border between the sacred ('white magic') and diabolical ('black magic') halves of the city that date back to Roman times. Built for Carlo Emanuele II around 1646, its lavishly decorated rooms house an assortment of furnishings, porcelain and other knick-knacks. The surrounding **Giardino Reale** (Royal Garden; admission free; ⏱9am-1hr before sunset) FREE, north and east of the palace, was designed in 1697 by André le Nôtre, who also created the gardens at Versailles.

Galleria Civica d'Arte Moderna e Contemporanea   Art Gallery

(GAM; www.gamtorino.it; Via Magenta 31; adult/reduced €10/8; ⏱10am-6pm Tue-Sun) Italy can sometimes feel strangely light on modern art, until you come to Turin. GAM has an astounding 45,000 works in its vaults dedicated to 19th- and 20th-century artists, including de Chirico, Otto Dix

Mole Antonelliana (p146)

RODOLFO RODRÍGUEZ CASTRO/GETTY IMAGES ©

and Klee. It cleverly hires art experts to reconfigure its permanent displays on a regular basis. You never know what you're going to get.

Museo d'Arte Contemporanea
Art Gallery

(www.castellodirivoli.org; Piazza Mafalda di Savoia; adult/reduced €6.50/4.50; ⏰10am-5pm Tue-Fri, to 7pm Sat & Sun) Works by Franz Ackermann, Gilbert and George, and Frank Gehry would have been beyond the wildest imagination of the Savoy family, who once resided in the 17th-century **Castello di Rivoli**, where the cutting edge of Turin's contemporary art scene has been housed since 1984.

Museo Nazionale dell'Automobile
Museum

(📞011 67 76 66; www.museoauto.it; Corso Unità d'Italia 40; adult/reduced €8/6; ⏰10am-7pm Wed, Thu & Sun, to 9pm Fri & Sat, to 2pm Mon, 2-7pm Tue; Ⓜ Lingotto) Reopened after extensive renovations in 2012, and now befitting of a city that is the HQ of one of the world's leading car manufacturers (the 'T' in Fiat stands for 'Torino'), this dashing museum pays homage to the motor car and is anchored by a precious collection of over 200 automobiles – everything from an 1892 Peugeot to a 1980 Ferrari 308 (in red, of course).

🛏 Sleeping

Hotel Residence Torino Centro
Hotel €

(📞011 433 82 23; www.hoteltorinocentro.it; Corso Inghilterra 33; d/tr €84/105; P ❄ 🛜) The best player in the field by a good stretch is this chic, upgraded convent right behind the Porta Susa train station. Smart modern furnishings combine with old mosaic floors in huge rooms with all the mod cons. Service is professional and efficient and there's a funky coffee bar (Coffee Lab Inghiliterra) downstairs in which to enjoy a complimentary breakfast.

NH Lingotto + Lingotto Tech
Luxury Hotel €€€

(📞011 664 20 00; www.nh-hotels.com; Via Nizza 262; NH Lingotto d €270-300, NH Lingotto Tech d €390-410; P ❄ 🛜) Stay in luxury in the old Fiat factory with a few unusual perks thrown in – the 1km running track on the roof is Fiat's former testing track and featured in the film *The Italian Job*. Newly acquired by the NH chain, this giant hotel is in Lingotto and its ex-factory status means rooms are huge and bright with large windows.

✖ Eating

Sfashion
Pizzeria €

(📞011 516 00 85; Via Cesare Battisti 13; pizzas/mains from €6/8.50; ⏰8am-midnight) Best pizza in Turin? Mention Sfashion and you'll get more than a few takers. Naples-thick and with wonderfully rustic ingredients (and not too

Turin
RAINER MARTINI/GETTY IMAGES ©

much cheese), they fly like hot bullets from the ovens of comic Torinese TV presenter Piero Chiambretti, whose funky postmodern city-centre set-up pitches retro toys amid an outlandish interior. The other in-house classic is mussels in tomato sauce.

Eataly   Cafe, Deli €
(www.eatalytorino.it; Via Nizza 230; ☯10am-8pm Tue-Sun) 🍴 Adjacent to the Lingotto congress centre is the Slow Food Movement's supermarket. Set in a vast converted factory, this gastronomic wonderland houses a staggering array of sustainable food and beverages, with a separate area for each, including a fantastic selection of cheese, bread, meat, fish, pasta, chocolate and much more.

Grom   Gelato €
(www.grom.it; Piazza Pietro Paleocapa; ☯11am-midnight Sun-Thu, to 1am Fri & Sat) 🍴 If you haven't heard of Grom, you haven't been in Turin long. The Slow Food-championed, artisan ice cream chain founded their first store right here in 2003 promising to put the same care and attention into ice cream production as oenologists put into wine. Long queues testify to a burgeoning legend.

L'Acino   Piedmontese €€
(☎011 521 70 77; Via San Domenico 2A; €30-35; ☯7.30pm-midnight Mon-Sat) Half a dozen tables and a legion of enamoured followers mean this inviting restaurant is hard to get into. Book ahead or arrive on the stroke of 7.30pm (it doesn't open for lunch) if you want to get your taste buds around snails, tripe and beef stew cooked in Roero wine. Overtures are provided by classic Piedmontese pasta staples.

🍷 Drinking & Nightlife

Caffè Mulassano   Cafe
(Piazza Castello 15; ☯7.30am-10.30pm) With dozens of customers and only five dwarf-sized tables, the art nouveau Mulassano

❤ If You Like...
Slow Food

1 BRA
Bra is the small, unassuming Piedmontese town where the Slow Food Movement first took root in 1986. There are no cars and no supermarkets here, just small, family-run shops (which shut religiously for a 'slowdown' twice a week), replete with organic sausages, handcrafted chocolates and fresh local farm produce. The Slow Food headquarters harbours a homey little eatery, **Osteria del Boccondivino** (☎0172 42 56 74; www.boccondivinoslow.it; Via Mendicità Istruita 14; set menus €26-28; ☯noon-2.30pm & 7-10pm Tue-Sat). Trains link Bra with Turin.

2 ALBA
In the gastronomic heaven that is Italy, Alba is a leading player courtesy of its truffles, dark chocolate and wine – including the incomparable Barolo. **Consorzio Turistico Langhe Monferrato Roero** (☎0173 36 25 62; www.tartufoevino.it; Piazza Risorgimento 2) organises a wide variety of gastronomic tours and courses. Truffle hunting can be arranged seasonally for white (September to December) or black (May to September) truffles for €80 per person. Alternatively, you can tour a hazelnut farm for €30, or take part in a four-hour cooking course for €130. At rustic **Osteria dei Sognatori** (Via Macrino 8b; €12-20; ☯noon-2pm & 7-11pm Thu-Tue), you get whatever's in the pot and it's always delicious. Hourly trains connect Alba with Turin, via Bra.

3 BAROLO
A wine village for centuries, Barolo dates from the 13th century, and is lorded over by **Castello Falletti** (www.baroloworld.it; Piazza Falletti; ☯Enoteca Regionale del Barolo 10am-12.30pm & 3-6.30pm Fri-Wed). Today the castle hosts the Museo del Vino a Barolo and, in its cellars, the Enoteca Regionale del Barolo, organised and run by the region's 11 wine-growing communities.

Below: Porta Palatina, Turin (p146)
Right: Vineyard, Barolo (p151)

(BELOW) JENNY ACHESON/GETTY IMAGES © & (RIGHT) HANS-PETER SIFFERT/GETTY IMAGES ©

is where regulars sink white-hot espresso *in piedi* (standing) while discussing Juventus' current form with the knowledgeable bow-tied barista.

Caffè San Carlo   Cafe
(Piazza San Carlo 156; ⏰8am-midnight Tue-Fri, to 1am Sat, to 9pm Mon) Perhaps the most gilded of the gilded, this glittery cafe dates from 1822. You'll get neckache admiring the weighty chandelier and heartache contemplating your bill (a hefty €4.50 for a cappuccino).

Fiorio   Cafe
(Via Po 8; ⏰8.30am-1am Tue-Sun) Garner literary inspiration in Mark Twain's old window seat as you contemplate the gilded interior of a cafe where 19th-century students once plotted revolutions and the Count of Cavour deftly played whist. The bittersweet hot chocolate ain't bad either.

🔒 Shopping

Guido Golbino   Chocolate
(www.guidogolbino.it; Via Lagrange 1; ⏰10am-8pm Tue-Sun, 3-8pm Mon) Chocolate heaven even by Turin standards, Guido's is currently the Torinese chocolatier of choice. This outlet has a slim little seating area tucked away behind its delectable chocolate shop where you can sit down to sample fondues, *gianduias* (hazelnut chocolates), and other such belt-looseners.

ℹ️ Information

Tourist Office (☎011 53 51 81; www.turismotorino.org; Piazza Castello; ⏰9am-6pm) Central, multilingual, open daily.

Stazione Porta Nuova Tourist Office (☎011 53 51 81; Stazione Porta Nuova; ⏰9am-6pm) The office at Stazione Porta Nuova offers a free accommodation and restaurant booking service.

ℹ Getting There & Away

Air

Turin's **Caselle** (TRN; www.turin-airport.com) airport, 16km northwest of the city centre in Caselle, has connections to European and national destinations. Budget airline Ryanair operates flights to London Stansted, Barcelona and Ibiza. Alitalia links to half a dozen Italian cities.

Bus

Most international, national and regional buses terminate at the **bus station** (Corso Castelfidardo), 1km west from Stazione Porta Nuova along Corso Vittorio Emanuele II. You can also get to Milan's Malpensa airport from this station.

Trains to/from Turin

Regular daily trains connect Turin's **Stazione Porta Nuova** (Piazza Carlo Felice) to the following destinations.

DESTINATION	FARE (€)	DURATION (HR)	FREQUENCY
Milan	11.20	1¾	28
Aosta	8.40	2	21
Venice	56	4½	17
Genoa	11.20	2	16
Rome	from 57.50	7	11

Most also stop at the space-age new **Stazione Porta Susa** (Corso Inghilterra) terminal. Some trains also stop at **Stazione Torino Lingotto** (Via Pannunzio 1), though it's generally more convenient to travel between the city centre and Lingotto by metro.

153

Detour:
Aosta

Jagged Alpine peaks rise like marble cathedrals above the town of Aosta, a once-important Roman settlement that has sprawled rather untidily across the Valle d'Aosta floor since the opening of the Mont Blanc tunnel in the 1960s.

Aosta's most intriguing church, **Chiesa di Sant'Orso** (Via Sant'Orso; ☻9am-7pm) is part of a still-operating monastery, and its 2000-year-old central district is awash with **Roman ruins**.

The Valle d'Aosta allows access to three of Europe's most prestigious ski areas – **Courmayeur** (www.courmayeur.com), **Breuil-Cervinia** (www.cervinia.it) and **Monte Rosa** (www.monterosa-ski.com) – plus numerous smaller runs.

More like a palace than a family-run converted farmhouse, **Hotel Milleluci** (☎0165 4 42 74; www.hotelmilleluci.com; Loc Porossan 15; r €170-220; P ❉ @ ☙) boasts old wooden skis, traditionally carved wooden shoes, claw-foot baths, indoor and outdoor pools, a Jacuzzi, sauna and gym, and sumptuous skiers' breakfasts.

Al dente pasta is guaranteed at **Trattoria Aldente** (☎0165 19 45 96; Via Croce de Ville 34; €26-28; ☻noon-2.30pm & 7-10.30pm), whose alluring menu confection of Valdostan and wider Italian dishes is enhanced by an equally alluring interior (the back seating section resembles a cozy cave on snowy days).

Savda (www.savda.it) buses run to Milan (1½ to 3½ hours, two daily), Turin (two hours, up to 10 daily) and Courmayeur (one hour, up to eight daily). Aosta's train station, on Piazza Manzetti, is served by trains to and from most parts of Italy. Trains to Turin (€8.40, two to 2½ hours, more than 10 daily) change at Ivrea.

❶ Getting Around

To/From the Airport

Sadem (www.sadem.it) runs buses to the airport from Stazione Porta Nuova (40 minutes), also stopping at Stazione Porta Susa (30 minutes). Buses depart every 30 minutes between 5.15am and 10.30pm (6.30am and 11.30pm from the airport). Single tickets cost €5 if you buy them from Confetteria Avvignano (Piazza Carlo Felice 50), opposite where the bus stops, or €5.50 if bought on the bus.

A taxi between the airport and the city centre will cost around €35 to €40.

Bicycle

Turin's ever-expanding bike-sharing scheme, [To] Bike (www.tobike.it), was inaugurated in 2010 and is now one of the largest in Italy, with over 18,000 subscribers and 116 stations storing bright-yellow *biciclette*. Temporary usage can be procured for €8 a week or €5 a day, after which the first 30 minutes are free. You'll then pay 80c, €1 and €2 for subsequent 30-minute sessions. To buy an access card, drop by Via Santa Chiara 26F or register online.

Public Transport

The city boasts a dense network of buses, trams and a cable car run by the Gruppo Torinese Trasporti (GTT; www.torino.city-sightseeing.it; Piazza Castello; €15 for 24 hrs; ☻10am-6pm), which has an information office (☻7am-9pm) at Stazione Porta Nuova. Buses and trams run from 6am to midnight and tickets cost €1 (€13.50 for a 15-ticket carnet and €3.50 for a one-day pass).

Turin's single-line metro (www.metrotorino. it) runs from Fermi to Lingotto. It first opened for the Winter Olympics in February 2006. It was extended to Stazione Porta Nuova in October 2007 and Lingotto in March 2011. The line is currently being extended south to Piazza Bengazi, two stations south of Lingotto. Tickets cost €1.50.

Taxi

Call Centrale Radio (☎011 57 37) or Radio Taxi (☎011 57 30).

Genoa

Contrasting sharply with the elegance of Turin, Genoa is a big crawling port that's almost Dickensian in places, thanks to its narrow, twisting lanes *(caruggi)* that are more reminiscent of the clamour of Morocco than the splendour of Venice. A once-important trading centre that bred such historic game-changers as Columbus and Mazzini, the city breathes a cosmopolitan air, with remnants of empire evident in its weighty art heritage.

Deep in the maze of the gritty old town, beauty and the beast sit side by side in streets that glimmer like a film noir movie set. Old men smoke languidly outside noisy bars and prostitutes stand like sentries in dark doorways, while on the periphery memories of the great years echo through the gold-leaf halls of the Unesco-sponsored Palazzi dei Rolli – a myriad collection of 16th- and 17th-century 'lodging palaces'.

Since hosting Expo 1992 and being championed as 2004's European City of Culture, Genoa has undergone some radical renovations, with its once-tatty port area now hosting Europe's largest aquarium and one of its best maritime museums.

◎ Sights

Aside from its Ligurian cuisine, Genoa's tour de force is its Palazzi dei Rolli. Forty-two of these plush lodging palaces – built between 1576 and 1664 to host visiting European gentry – were placed on the Unesco World Heritage list in 2006. They are mostly on or around Via Garibaldi and Via Balbi.

Musei di Strada Nuova   Museum
(www.museidigenova.it; combined ticket adult/reduced €8/6; ⊗9am-7pm Tue-Fri, 10am-7pm Sat & Sun) Skirting the northern edge of what was once the city limits, pedestrianised Via Garibaldi (formerly called the Strada Nuova) was planned by Galeazzo Alessi in the 16th century. It quickly became the city's most sought-after quarter, lined with the palaces of Genoa's wealthiest

citizens. Three of these *palazzi* – Rosso, Bianco and Doria-Tursi – comprise the Musei di Strada Nuova. Between them, they hold the city's finest collection of old masters.

Tickets must be purchased at the bookshop inside **Palazzo Doria-Tursi** (www.museidigenova.it; Via Garibaldi 9).

Cattedrale di
San Lorenzo   Cathedral
(Piazza San Lorenzo; ⊗8am-noon & 3-7pm) Impressive even by Italian standards, Genoa's black-and-white-striped Gothic-Romanesque cathedral owes its continued existence to the poor quality of a British WWII bomb that failed to ignite here in 1941; it still sits on the right side of the nave like an innocuous museum piece.

Palazzo Reale   Palace, Museum
(www.palazzorealegenova.it; Via Balbi 10; adult/reduced €4/2; ⊗9am-7pm Thu-Sun, to 1.30pm Tue & Wed) If you only get the chance to visit one of the Palazzi dei Rolli, make it this one – a veritable Versailles with terraced gardens, exquisite furnishings and a fine collection of Renaissance art. The gilded Hall of Mirrors is worth the entry fee alone.

Acquario   Aquarium
(www.acquariodigenova.it; Ponte Spinola; adult/reduced €18/12; ⊗9.30am-7.30pm; ⊞) No glorified fish tank, Genoa's bright-blue aquarium is one of the largest in Europe, with more than 5000 sea creatures, including sharks, swimming in six million litres of water. Moored at the end of a walkway is the ship Nave Blu, refurbished in July 2013 as a unique floating display.

✕ Eating

Trattoria Da Maria   Trattoria €
(☑010 58 10 80; Vico Testadoro 14R; €12; ⊗11.45am-3pm Mon-Sat, 7-10.30pm Thu & Fri) Pesto is essentially a poor man's cuisine that employs basic ingredients and you'll pay poor man's prices at this no-frills trattoria stuck up a shadowy Genovese alley that opens daily for lunch (and dinner on Thursday and Friday). Tables

are shared and the food arrives with the speed and subtlety of an invading Napoleonic army.

Trattoria della Raibetta
Trattoria €€

(www.trattoriadellaraibetta.it; Vico Caprettari 10-12; mains €14; ⊙lunch & dinner Tue-Sun) The most authentic Genoese food can be procured in the family-run joints hidden in the warren of streets near the cathedral. The Raibetta's menu is unfussy and fish-biased. Try the seafood with *riso venere* (a local black rice) or the signature homemade *trofiette al pesto*.

The octopus salad makes a good overture, while the wine is a toss-up between 200 different vintages.

❶ Getting There & Away

Air

Regular domestic and international services, including Ryanair flights to London Stansted, use **Cristoforo Colombo Airport** (☎010 6 01 51; www.airport.genova.it), 6km west of the city in Sestri Ponente.

Boat

Ferries sail to/from Spain, Sicily, Sardinia, Corsica and Tunisia from the **international passenger terminal** (Terminal Traghetti; www.porto.genova.it; Via Milano 51). Only cruise ships use the 1930s passenger ship terminal on Ponte dei Mille.

Bus

Buses to international cities depart from Piazza della Vittoria, as do buses to/from Milan's Malpensa airport (€16, two hours, 6am and 3pm) and other interregional services. Tickets are sold at **Geotravels** (Piazza della Vittoria 57) and **Pesci Viaggi e Turismo** (Piazza della Vittoria 94r).

❶ Getting Around

To/From the Airport

The **AMT** (www.amt.genova.it) line 100 runs between Stazione Principe and the airport at least every hour from 5.30am to 11pm (€4, 30 minutes). Tickets can be bought from the driver.

A taxi to or from the airport costs around €15.

Cinque Terre

If you ever get tired of life, bypass the therapist and decamp immediately to Cinque Terre. Here five crazily constructed fishing villages, set amid some of the most dramatic coastal scenery on the planet, ought to provide enough ammunition to bolster the most jaded of spirits. A Unesco World Heritage Site since 1997, Cinque Terre isn't the undiscovered Eden it was 30 years ago but, frankly, who cares? Sinuous paths tempt the antisocial to traverse seemingly impregnable cliffsides, while a 19th-century railway line cut through a series of coastal tunnels ferries the less brave from village to village. Thankfully cars – those most ubiquitous of modern interferences – were banned over a decade ago.

Rooted in antiquity, Cinque Terre's five villages date from the early medieval period. Monterosso, the oldest, was founded in AD 643, when beleaguered hill dwellers moved down to the coast to escape from invading barbarians. Riomaggiore came next, purportedly established in the 8th century by Greek settlers fleeing persecution in Byzantium. The others are Vernazza, Corniglia and Manarola.

Trains to/from Genoa

Genoa's Stazione Principe and Stazione Brignole are linked by train to the following destinations.

TO	FARE (€)	DURATION (HR)	FREQUENCY
Milan	19.50	1½	up to 8 daily
Pisa	26	2	up to 8 daily
Rome	60.50	5	6 daily
Turin	19	1¾	7-10 daily

In October 2011 flash floods along the Ligurian coast wreaked havoc in Vernazza and Monterosso, burying historic streets and houses under metres of mud and killing half-a-dozen people. As of 2013, most businesses are open again, but check the status of the Sentiero Azzurro (blue walking trail) before you set out.

ℹ Information

Online information is available at www.cinque terre.it and www.cinqueterre.com.

Parco Nazionale (www.parconazionale5terre.it; ⏱7am-8pm) Offices in the train stations of all five villages and also in La Spezia station.

ℹ Getting There & Around

Boat

In summer the **Cooperativa Battellieri del Golfo Paradiso** (www.golfoparadiso.it) runs boats to the Cinque Terre from Genoa (one way/return €18/33). Seasonal boat services to/from Santa Margherita (€17.50/25.50) are handled by the **Servizio Marittimo del Tigullio** (www.traghettiportofino.it).

From late March to October, La Spezia–based **Consorzio Marittimo Turistico Cinque Terre Golfo dei Poeti** (www.navigazionegolfodeipoeti.it)

runs daily shuttle boats between all of the Cinque Terre villages (except Corniglia), costing €8 one way, including all stops, or €15 for an all-day ticket.

Car & Motorcycle

Private vehicles are not allowed beyond village entrances. If you're arriving by car or motorcycle, you'll need to pay to park in designated car parks. In some villages, minibus shuttles depart from the car parks (one way/return €1.50/2.50) – park offices have seasonal schedules.

Train

Between 6.30am and 10pm, several trains an hour trundle along the coast between Genoa and La Spezia, stopping at each of Cinque Terre's villages. Unlimited 2nd-class rail travel between Levanto and La Spezia is covered by the Cinque Terre card.

MONTEROSSO

The most accessible village by car and the only Cinque Terre settlement to sport a tourist beach, Monterosso is the furthest west and least quintessential of the quintet (it was briefly ditched from the group in the 1940s). Noted for its lemon trees and anchovies, the village is split into two parts (old and new) linked by an underground tunnel that burrows beneath the blustery San Cristoforo

Manarola (p159)

promontory. Monterosso was badly hit by the 2011 floods, but has recovered remarkably quickly. Most businesses in town are open again, although trails are still experiencing closures. Check ahead on http://www.parconazionale5terre.it/sentieri_parco.asp.

You can buy local food and wine at ultrafriendly restaurant-enoteca **La Cantina del Pescatore** (Via V Emanuele 19, Monterosso; snacks €4-9; 🛜). Their excellent jam, spreads and limoncino liqueur make it worthwhile for a snack lunch. Try the pesto on toast, salads, hot dogs (for kids) and local wine. There's free wi-fi.

VERNAZZA

Guarding the only secure landing point on the Cinque Terre coast, Vernazza's small, quintessential Mediterranean harbour guards what is perhaps the quaintest of the five villages. Lined with little cafes, Vernazza's main cobbled street, Via Roma, links seaside Piazza Marconi with the train station. Side streets lead to the village's trademark Genoa-style *caruggi* (narrow lanes).

Traditional Cinque Terre seafood (mussels, seafood, ravioli and lemon anchovies) has been served up in harbourside trattoria **Gianni Franzi** (📞0187 82 10 03; www.giannifranzi.it; Piazza Matteotti 5, Vernazza; meals €22-30, s/d €70/100; ⏾mid-Mar–early Jan) since the 1960s. More recently, they've been renting rooms with views, all of which share a communal terrace.

CORNIGLIA

Corniglia is the 'quiet' middle village that sits atop a 100m-high rocky promontory surrounded by vineyards. It is the only Cinque Terre settlement with no direct sea access (steep steps lead down to a rocky cove). Narrow alleys and colourfully painted four-storey houses characterise the ancient core, a timeless streetscape that was namechecked in Boccaccio's *Decameron*. To reach the village proper

from the railway station you must first tackle the **Lardarina,** a 377-step brick stairway.

While the rest of Corniglia siestas, **Caffe Matteo** (Piazza Taragio, Corniglia; meals €7; ☺8am-10pm) stays open all day, its chairs spilling into the tiny main square. Don't leave without trying the pesto lasagne.

MANAROLA

Bequeathed with more grapevines than any other Cinque Terre village, Manarola is famous for its sweet Sciacchetrà wine. It's also awash with priceless medieval relics, supporting claims that it is the oldest of the five. Due to its proximity to Riomaggiore (852m away), the village is heavily trafficked, especially by Italian school parties. The spirited locals speak an esoteric local dialect known as Manarolese.

RIOMAGGIORE

Cinque Terre's easternmost village, Riomaggiore is the largest of the five and acts as its unofficial HQ (the main park office is based here). Its peeling pastel buildings tumble like faded chocolate boxes down a steep ravine to a tiny harbour – the region's favourite postcard view – and glow romantically at sunset. The famous Sentiero Azzurro coastal path starts here. The first hideously busy section to Manarola is called the Via dell'Amore.

Perched within pebble-lobbing distance of Riomaggiore's snug harbour (which is crammed with fishing nets and overturned boats), **Dau Cila** (☎0187 76 00 32; www.ristorantedaucila.com; Via San Giacomo 65, Riomaggiore; mains €18; ☺8am-2am Mar-Oct) is an obvious place to tuck into the local seafood. It also has the best wine cellar in town.

Venice, Veneto & Bologna

The hype about this region is wrong – it's an understatement. A habitual overachiever, Venice isn't only beautiful; over the past millennium, the dazzling lagoon city has become musically gifted, exceptionally handy with molten glass and a single oar, and, as you'll discover over Rialto happy-hour banter, wickedly funny. Logical types may initially resist Venetian charms, grousing about gondola rates and crooked *calli* (backstreets), but then out comes the bubbly *prosecco* and tasty *cicheti* (Venetian tapas), and suddenly newcomers are attempting toasts in Venetian dialect.

A silty lagoon may seem an inconvenient spot for a city of palaces, but it's ideally located for *la bella vita* (the beautiful life). Beaches line the Lido; vineyards just outside Verona supply exceptional wines; and Bologna awaits, a train ride away – a clever university town with the best-stocked delis on the planet.

Grand Canal (p176), Venice

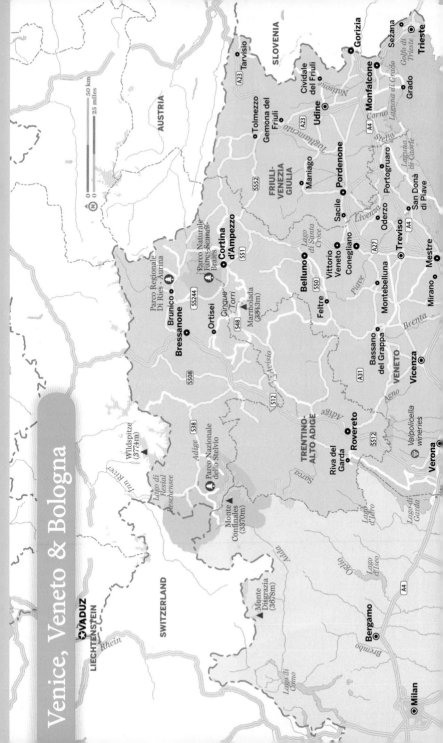

Venice, Veneto & Bologna

1 Grand Canal, Venice
2 Palazzo Ducale, Venice
3 Basilica di San Marco, Venice
4 Gallerie dell'Accademia, Venice
5 Quadrilatero, Bologna

Venice, Veneto & Bologna Highlights

Legendary Venice

This lagoon city (p170) is anchored not just by thousands of poles under the paving stones, but by a thousand years of Venetian legends. Besides the obvious – Marco Polo's travels, Casanova's escapades, star-crossed romances that inspired Shakespeare – tales unfold around every canal bend. Tour the Grand Canal past *palazzi* and film-worthy backdrops and uncover the stories for yourself.

Palazzo Ducale

Propaganda never looked as pretty as the gorgeous Gothic Palazzo Ducale (p181), covered floor to ceiling over three stories with testimonials to Venetian virtues by Titian, Veronese, Tiepolo and Tintoretto. For all its graces, this palace was a powerhouse. The *doge* (duke) lived downstairs and greeted ambassadors upstairs, while the secret service inter-rogated suspected traitors in the attic.

Basilica di San Marco

Excitement rises in multiple languages as the line of sightseers nears the Egyptian purple-marble portals of Basilica di San Marco (p175). But once you step over the threshold, the crowd hushes to a collective sigh. Millions of tiny glittering mosaics turn the basilica's domes into a billowing golden heaven, with hovering angels and skipping saints. A Unesco-certified wonder 800 years in the making, this is a uniquely uplifting experience.

ALAN BENSON/GETTY IMAGES ©

Gallerie dell'Accademia

Despite complaints from Rome for depicting angels playing stringed instruments (too worldly!), apostles dining with Germans (too Protestant!) and biblical scenes starring Venetian beauties (too alluring!), Venice kept right on painting. Hence the Gallerie dell'Accademia (p182). No ordinary museum, it is a parade of masterpieces by Titian, Bellini, Carpaccio, Tintoretto, Veronese and more. Don't miss the baroque portraits.

Bologna's Quadrilatero

Ditch your diet on the train to Bologna, Italy's most unabashedly food-loving city (and that's saying something). Lovingly nicknamed *la grassa* ('the fatty'), Bologna stocks Quadrilatero (p208) delis with celebrated local specialities, including syrupy *aceto balsamico di Modena* (aged balsamic vinegar from Modena). Walk it off with 40km of beautiful colonnaded sidewalks...or try dessert. Bottles of *aceto balsamico di Modena*

165

Venice, Veneto & Bologna's Best…

Worth-the-Trip Thrills

○ **Basilica di San Marco** Glimpsing golden mosaic heavens. (p175)

○ **Row Venice** Gliding through Venetian waterways. (p186)

○ **Murano** Watching artisans breathe life into red-hot glass. (p189)

○ **Dolomites** Zooming downhill amid snow-covered splendour. (p197)

Encore-Worthy Entertainment

○ **Roman Arena** Italy's most celebrated al fresco opera. (p203)

○ **La Fenice** A tiny, incendiary stage with world-premiere credits from Verdi, Wagner and Britten. (p196)

○ **La Biennale di Venezia** Visual art events plus top performing talents. (p187)

○ **Palazzetto Bru Zane** Exquisite musical harmonies under stucco-frosted ceilings. (p196)

Luxury Bargains

○ **Lido** Experience the original Venice beach. (p185)

○ **Al Pesador** Seafood *cicheti* along the Grand Canal. (p191)

○ **I Rusteghi** Collector's wines by the glass. (p194)

○ **Palazzo Grassi** Drink cappuccino inside an art installation. (p183)

Need to Know

Unconventional Souvenirs

○ **Marina e Susanna Sent** Murano glass soap-bubble necklaces. (p198)

○ **Càrte** Handbags made of lagoon-swirled marble paper. (p197)

○ **Quadrilatero** Syrupy balsamic vinegar aged 40 years. (p208)

○ **Gilberto Penso** Your chance to take a gondola home. (p197)

○ **Two months before** Reserve tickets to Venice's La Fenice.

○ **One month before** Book a Itinerari Segreti (Secret Itinerary) tour at the Palazzo Ducale, and a Row Venice lesson.

○ **One week before** Purchase tickets to Gallerie dell'Accademia online; reserve Laguna Eco Adventures sailing tours and make restaurant reservations.

○ **Venice Tourist Board** (www.turismovenezia.it)

○ **Venice Connected** (www.veniceconnected. com) Official sales channel for tickets to Venice events.

○ **Veneto Tourist Board** (www.veneto.to)

○ **Venezia da Vivere** (www. veneziadavivere.com) Music performances, art openings and more.

○ **Emilia Romagna Tourist Board** (www. emiliaromagnaturismo.it)

○ **Air** Connections to/ from Venice, Treviso, Verona and Bologna.

○ **Train** Excellent connections between major cities and towns.

○ **Walk** Perfect for Venice and smaller cities, towns and alpine trails.

○ **Vaporetto** Public water-buses ply Venice's Grand Canal and connect central Venice with Marco Polo airport.

○ **Gondola** Flat-bottom boats rowed with a single oar aren't just quaint: they're key to sightseeing.

○ **Traghetto** Public gondola service for crossing Venice's Grand Canal between bridges.

○ **Bus** Handy for Lido transport and inland towns not serviced by trains.

○ **Bicycle** For small towns, the Lido and alpine trails.

○ **Museums** Most close Mondays.

○ **Restaurants** Many close in August and January.

○ **Accommodation** Book months ahead for Venice in February and March during Carnevale (www. carnevale.venezia.it) or June to September during Biennale; Dolomites in winter ski season; and Bologna during spring and autumn trade fairs.

167

Venice, Veneto & Bologna Itineraries

Whether you've got island fever or a powerful rumbling in the stomach, this region will cure what ails you with an astonishing variety of island adventures, deli delicacies, and – oh yes – phenomenal wines.

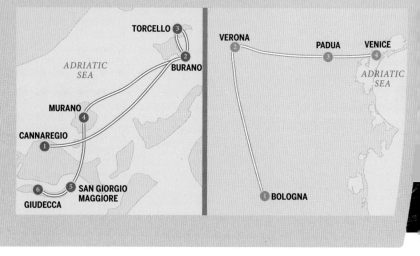

2 DAYS

CANNAREGIO TO GIUDECCA

VENETIAN ISLAND ADVENTURE

Islands in the Venetian lagoon have their own architectural styles and distinct cuisines. In the Venice neighbourhood of ❶ **Cannaregio,** at the Fondamenta Nuove stop, take the LP *vaporetto* (small passenger ferry) for a rejuvenating shock of colour on ❷ **Burano**. Unlike Venice's genteel Gothic palaces, Burano's houses look like cartoons: bubble-gum-pink cottages squat comically next to lanky cobalt-blue townhouses.

In the afternoon, take a T-line ferry to bucolic, Byzantine ❸ **Torcello**, where sheep bleat hello. Inside the 9th to 11th century Santa Maria Assunta Cathedral, sneaky

devils tip the scales in the *Final Judgment* mosaic. Don't miss the lovely Chiesa di Santa Fosca before heading back to Burano.

Catch an early LN *vaporetto* to ❹ **Murano** to witness 500 years of glass-blowing artistry at the Museo del Vetro – and beat shoppers to the bargains at Murano-glass showrooms. The 42 *vaporetto* chugs from Murano to ❺ **San Giorgio Maggiore**, where you'll find Palladio's dazzling temple-inspired church. Hop the *vaporetto* one stop to ❻ **Giudecca** and end your adventure eating at the bewitchingly romantic I Figli delle Stelle.

GOURMET TREASURE HUNT

3 DAYS

Gourmet adventures abound in ➊ **Bologna**, where the speciality in the delis of the Quadrilatero is artisan-cured prosciutto ham from nearby Parma. Climb the leaning Torre degli Asinelli to work up an appetite, and dine at Osteria dell'Orsa, which proffers heavenly food in pretension-free surroundings.

Make the most of a morning in Bologna with a cooking course, then catch the train to fair ➋ **Verona**, where the scene has been set for happy hour at Piazza delle Erbe since it was a Roman forum. At Casa di Giulietta, you can post a note requesting Juliet's help to find your own Romeo or

Juliet, but a surer bet is prized Amarone wine, which tastes like true love, with polenta and Venetian *sopressa* (soft salami) at Osteria del Bugiardo.

The next day, continue your train journey to ➌ **Padua**. If you're not moved to tears by Giotto's tender frescoes in Padua's Cappella degli Scrovegni, the homemade pasta at Godenda might do the trick. Roll back onto the train and nap to ➍ **Venice**, to reach the Rialto just as *cicheti* (Venetian tapas) appear at I Rusteghi, and corks pop on rare Ribolla Gialla white wine. *Cin-cin!*

Verona (p200)
DAVID TOMLINSON/GETTY IMAGES ©

Discover Venice, Veneto & Bologna

Gondolas, Venice
KRZYSZTOF DYDYNSKI/GETTY IMAGES ©

VENICE

POP 59,000 (VENICE CITY)

Imagine the audacity of deciding to build a city of marble palaces on a lagoon. Instead of surrendering to *acque alte* (high tide) like reasonable folk might do, Venetians flooded the world with vivid painting, baroque music, modern opera, spice-route cuisine, bohemian-chic fashions and a Grand Canal's worth of *spritz:* the signature *prosecco* and Aperol cocktail. Today cutting-edge architects and billionaire benefactors are spicing up the art scene, musicians are rocking out 18th-century instruments and backstreet *osterie* (taverns) are winning a Slow Food following. Your timing couldn't be better: the people who made walking on water look easy are well into their next act.

◉ Sights

PIAZZA SAN MARCO & AROUND

Museo Correr   Museum
(Map p178; ☏041 4273 0892; http://correr.visitmuve.it; Piazza San Marco 52; adult/reduced/child incl Palazzo Ducale €16/8/free; ⊙10am-7pm Apr-Oct, to 5pm Nov-Mar; ⊛San Marco) Napoleon filled his royal digs over Piazza San Marco with the riches of the doges, and took some of Venice's finest heirlooms to France as trophies. But the biggest treasure couldn't be lifted: Jacopo Sansovino's 16th-century **Libreria Nazionale Marciana**, covered with larger-than-life philosophers by Veronese, Titian and Tintoretto. Venice successfully reclaimed many ancient maps, statues, cameos and weapons, plus four centuries of artistic masterpieces in the **Pinacoteca**.

Torre dell'Orologio   Landmark

(Clock Tower; Map p178; ☑041 4273 0892; www.
museicivicivenezianiit; Piazza San Marco; adult/
reduced with Museum Pass €12/7; ☺tours in
English 10am & 11am Mon-Wed, 2pm & 3pm Thu-
Sun, in Italian noon & 4pm daily, in French 2pm
& 3pm Mon-Wed, 10am & 11am Thu-Sun; 🚤San
Marco) Venice's gold-leafed timepiece,
designed by Zuan Paolo Rainieri and
his son Zuan Carlo in 1493–99, had one
hitch: the clockworks required constant
upkeep by a live-in clockwatcher until
1998. After a nine-year renovation, the
clock's works are in independent working
order and tours climb the steep stairs to
the roof for giddy, close-up views of the
bare-bottomed 'Do Mori' (Two Moors),
who chime every hour.

DORSODURO

Peggy Guggenheim
Collection   Museum

(Map p178; ☑041 240 54 11; www.guggenheim-
venice.it; Palazzo Venier dei Leoni 704; adult/sen-
ior/reduced €14/11/8; ☺10am-6pm Wed-Mon;
🚤Accademia) After tragically losing her
father on the *Titanic,* heir Peggy Guggenheim befriended Dadaists, dodged Nazis
and changed art history at her palatial
home on the Grand Canal. The Palazzo
Venier dei Leoni is a showcase for surreal-
ism, futurism and abstract expressionism by some 200 breakthrough modern
artists, including Peggy's ex-husband Max
Ernst, and Jackson Pollock (among her
many rumoured lovers).

Ca' Rezzonico   Museum

(Museum of the 18th Century; Map p172; ☑041
241 01 00; www.visitmuve.it; Fondamenta Rezzonico 3136; adult/reduced €8/5.50 ; ☺10am-
6pm Wed-Mon Apr-Oct, to 5pm Nov-Mar; 🚤Ca'
Rezzonico) Baroque dreams come true
at Baldassare Longhena's Grand Canal
palace, where a marble staircase leads
to gilded ballrooms, frescoed salons and
sumptuous boudoirs. Giambattista Tiepolo's **Throne Room** ceiling is a masterpiece of elegant social climbing, showing
gorgeous Merit ascending to the Temple
of Glory clutching the Golden Book of
Venetian nobles' names – including Tiepolo's patrons, the Rezzonico family.

Making the Most of Your Euro

These passes can help you save on admission costs to Venetian sights.

Civic Museum Pass (Musei Civici Pass; ☑041 240 52 11; www.visitmuve.it; adult/reduced
€20/14) Valid for single entry to 11 civic museums for six months, or just the five
museums around Piazza San Marco (adult/child €16/8). Purchase online or at
participating museums.

Chorus Pass (☑041 275 04 62; www.chorusvenezia.org; adult/reduced/child €10/7/free)
Single entry to 11 Venice churches at any time within six months; purchase
online or at church ticket booths.

Venice Card (☑041 24 24; www.venicecard.com; adult/junior €39.90/29.90; ☺call centre
8am-7.30pm) Combines the Museum Pass and Chorus Pass as well as reduced entry
to the Guggenheim Collection and the Biennale, two public bathroom entries
and discounts on concerts, temporary exhibits and parking. Purchase at tourist
offices and at HelloVenezia booths at *vaporetto* (small passenger ferry) stops.

Rolling Venice (☑041 24 24; www.hellovenezia.com; 14-29yr €4) Entitles young visitors
to discounted access to monuments and cultural events, plus eligibility for
a 72-hour public transport pass for €18 rather than the regular price of €33.
Identification is required for purchase at tourism offices or HelloVenezia booths.

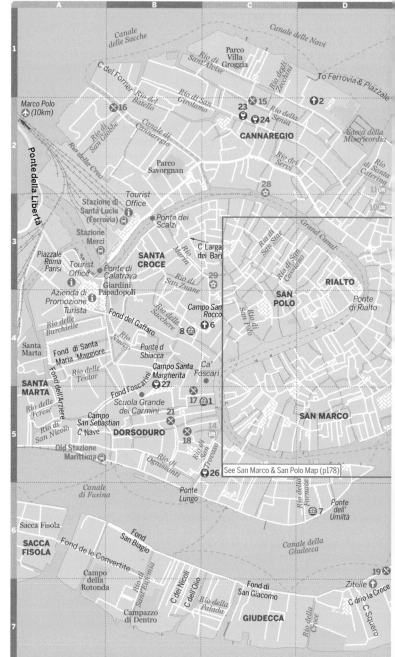

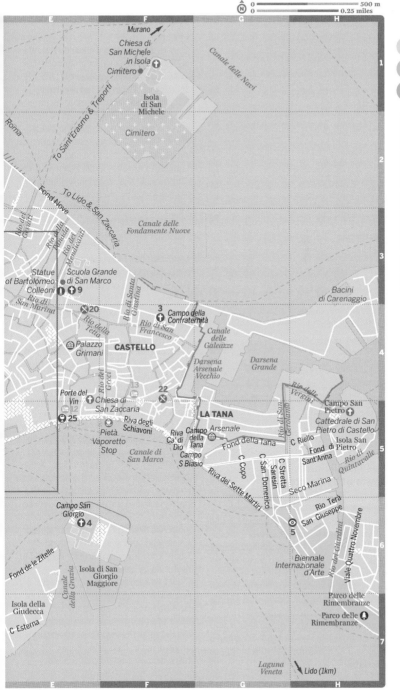

0   500 m
0   0.25 miles

Murano

Chiesa di
San Michele
in Isola
Cimitero

Canale delle Navi

Isola
di San
Michele

Cimitero

To Sant'Erasmo & Treporti

Roma

To Lido & San Zaccaria

Fond Nove

Canale delle
Fondamente Nuove

Bacini
di Carenaggio

Rio del
Gesuiti

Rio della
Panada

Rio dei
Mendicanti

Statue
of Bartolomeo
Colleoni

Scuola Grande
di San Marco 9

Rio di
San Marina

20

Rio di Santa Giustina

3
Campo della
Confraternità

Rio di San
Francesco

Canale
delle
Galeazze

Rio della
Tetta

Palazzo
Grimani

CASTELLO

Rio dei Greci

Darsena
Arsenale
Vecchio

Darsena
Grande

Rio delle
Vergini

Porte del
Vin

13

22

Chiesa di
San Zaccaria

12

25

Pietà
Vaporetto
Stop

Riva degli
Schiavoni

Canale di
San Marco

LA TANA

Riva
Ca' di
Dio

Campo
della
Tana

Campo
S Biasio

Arsenale

Fond della Tana

C Riello

Campo San
Pietro

Cattedrale di San
Pietro di Castello

Isola San
Pietro

Fond di
Sant'Anna

Rio di
Quintavalle

Rio del Gerolami

C Copo

C San Domenico

C Stretta
Saresin

Riva dei Sette Martiri

Seco Marina

Rio Terà
San Giuseppe

5

Campo San
Giorgio

4

Fond de le Zitelle

Canale della Grazia

Isola di San
Giorgio
Maggiore

Isola della
Giudecca

C Esterna

Biennale
Internazionale
d'Arte

Rio dei Giardini

Viale Quattro Novembre

Parco delle
Rimembranze

Parco delle
Rimembranze

Laguna
Veneta

Lido (1km)

173

Venice

Basilica di Santa Maria della Salute   Church

(La Salute; Map p178; 📞041 241 10 18; www.
seminariovenezia.it; Campo della Salute 1b;
admission free, sacristy adult/reduced €3/1.50;
🕑9am-noon & 3-5.30pm; 🚤Salute) A monumental sigh of relief, this splendid domed
church was commissioned by Venice's
plague survivors as thanks for salvation.
Baldassare Longhena's uplifting design
is an engineering feat that defies simple
logic, and in fact the church is said to
have mystical curative properties. Titian
eluded the plague until age 94, leaving a
legacy of 12 masterpieces now in Salute's
sacristy.

SAN POLO & SANTA CROCE

I Frari   Church

(Basilica di Santa Maria Gloriosa dei Frari; Map
p172; www.chorusvenezia.org; Campo dei Frari
3004, San Polo; adult/reduced €3/1.50; 🕑9am-
6pm Mon-Sat, 1-6pm Sun, last admittance
5.30pm; 🚤San Tomà) This soaring Italian-
brick Gothic church features marquetry
choir stalls, Canova's pyramid mausoleum, Bellini's achingly sweet *Madonna
with Child* triptych in the sacristy, and
Longhena's creepy Doge Pesaro funereal
monument hoisted by burly slaves bursting from ragged clothes like Incredible
Hulks – yet visitors are inevitably drawn
to the small altarpiece.

This is Titian's 1518 *Assumption,* in
which a radiant Madonna in a Titian-red
cloak reaches heavenward, steps onto
a cloud and escapes this mortal coil.
Both inside and outside the painting,
onlookers gasp and point out at the sight;
Titian outdid himself here, upstaging
his own 1526 Pesaro Altarpiece near the
entry. Titian was lost to the plague in
1576, but legend has it that strict rules of
quarantine were bent to allow his burial
near his masterpiece.

Scuola Grande di San Rocco   Museum

(Map p172; 📞041 523 48 64; www.scuolagrande
sanrocco.it; Campo San Rocco 3052, San Polo;
adult €8, incl Scuola Grande dei Carmini €12;
🕑9.30am-5.30pm, Tesoro to 5.15pm; 🚤San
Tomà) Everyone wanted the commission
to paint this building dedicated to the
patron saint of the plague-stricken, so
Tintoretto cheated: instead of producing
sketches like rival Veronese, he gifted
a splendid ceiling panel of patron St
Roch, knowing it couldn't be refused or
matched by other artists.

Old Testament scenes Tintoretto
painted from 1575 to 1587 for the Sala
Grande Superiore ceiling upstairs read
like a modern graphic novel: you can
almost hear the swoop! overhead as an
angel dives to feed ailing Elijah. Against
the shadowy backdrop of the Black

WIBOWO RUSLI/GETTY IMAGES ©

Basilica di San Marco

Creating Venice's architectural wonder took nearly 800 years and one barrel of lard. In AD 828, wily Venetian merchants allegedly smuggled St Mark's corpse out of Egypt in a barrel of pork fat. Venice built a golden basilica around its stolen saint, whose bones were misplaced twice during construction.

The front of the basilica ripples and crests like a wave, its five niched portals capped with shimmering mosaics. In the far-left portal, lunette mosaics dating from 1270 show St Mark's stolen body arriving at the basilica – a story reprised in 1660 lunette mosaics on the second portal from the right.

Just inside the *narthex* (vestibule) glitter the basilica's oldest mosaics: *Apostles with the Madonna,* standing sentry by the main door for over 950 years. The atrium's medieval **Dome of Genesis** depicts the separation of sky and water with surprisingly abstract motifs, anticipating modern art by 650 years. *Last Judgment* mosaics cover the atrium vault and the apocalypse looms large in vault mosaics over the gallery.

Mystical transfusions occur in the **Dome of the Holy Spirit**, where a dove's blood streams onto the heads of saints. In the central 13th-century **Cupola of the Ascension**, angels swirl overhead while dreamy-eyed St Mark rests on the pendentive. Scenes from St Mark's life unfold over the main altar, in vaults flanking the **Dome of the Prophets**.

Tucked behind the main altar containing St Mark's sarcophagus is the Pala d'Oro, studded with 2000 gemstones. But the most priceless treasures here are biblical figures in vibrant cloisonné, begun in Constantinople in AD 976 and elaborated by Venetian goldsmiths in 1209.

NEED TO KNOW

St Mark's Basilica; Map p178; ☎ 041 270 83 11; www.basilicasanmarco.it; Piazza San Marco; ⏰9.45am-5pm Mon-Sat, 2-5pm Sun & holidays, baggage storage 9.30am-5.30pm; ⛴San Marco

Grand Canal

The 3.5km route of vaporetto (passenger ferry) No 1, which passes some 50 palazzi (mansions), six churches and scene-stealing backdrops featured in four James Bond films, is public transport at its most glamorous.

The Grand Canal starts with controversy: **Ponte di Calatrava ❶** a luminous glass-and-steel bridge that cost triple the original €4 million estimate. Ahead are castle-like **Fondaco dei Turchi ❷**, the historic Turkish trading-house; Renaissance **Palazzo Vendramin ❸**, housing the city's casino; and double-arcaded **Ca' Pesaro ❹**. Don't miss **Ca' d'Oro ❺**, a 1430 filigree Gothic marvel.

Points of Venetian pride include the **Pescaria ❻**, built in 1907 on the site where fishmongers have been slinging lagoon crab for 600 years, and neighbouring **Rialto Market ❼** stalls, overflowing with island-grown produce. Cost overruns for 1592 **Ponte di Rialto ❽** rival Calatrava's, but its marble splendour stands the test of time.

The next two canal bends could cause architectural whiplash, with Sanmicheli-designed Renaissance **Palazzo Grimani ❾** and Mauro Codussi's **Palazzo Corner-Spinelli ❿** followed by Giorgio Masari-designed **Palazzo Grassi ⓫** and Baldassare Longhena's baroque jewel box, **Ca' Rezzonico ⓬**.

Wooden **Ponte dell'Accademia ⓭** was built in 1930 as a temporary bridge, but the beloved landmark was recently reinforced. Stone lions flank the **Peggy Guggenheim Collection ⓮**, where the American heiress collected ideas, lovers and art. You can't miss the dramatic dome of Longhena's **Chiesa di Santa Maria della Salute ⓯** or **Punta della Dogana ⓰**, Venice's triangular customs warehouse reinvented as a contemporary art showcase. The Grand Canal's grand finale is pink Gothic **Palazzo Ducale ⓱** and its adjoining **Ponte dei Sospiri ⓲**, currently draped in advertising.

Palazzo Grassi
French magnate François Pinault scandalised Paris when he relocated his contemporary art collection here, where there are galleries designed by Gae Aulenti and Tadao Ando.

Ca' Rezzonico
See how Venice lived in baroque splendour at this 18th-century art museum with Tiepolo ceilings, silk-swagged boudoirs and even an in-house pharmacy.

Ponte dell'Accademia

Peggy Guggenheim Collection

Chiesa di Santa Maria delle Salute

Punta della Dogana
Minimalist architect Tadao Ando creatively repurposed abandoned warehouses as galleries, which now host contemporary art installations from François Pinault's collection.

Ponte di Calatrava
With its starkly streamlined fish-fin shape, the 2008 bridge is the first to be built over the Grand Canal in 75 years.

Fondaco dei Turchi
Recognisable by its double colonnade, watchtowers, and dugout canoe parked at the Museo di Storia Naturale's ground-floor loggia.

JEAN-PIERRE LESCOURRET/GETTY IMAGES ©

Ca' d'Oro
Behind the triple Gothic arcades are priceless masterpieces: Titians looted by Napoleon, a rare Mantegna and semiprecious stone mosaic floors.

② ③ Palazzo Vendramin

④ ⑤

⑥ Pescaria

⑦ Rialto Market

⑩ Palazzo Grimani ⑨

Palazzo Corner-Spinelli

⑧ Ponte di Rialto

Ponte dei Sospiri ⑱

Palazzo Ducale ⑰

Ponte di Rialto
Antonio da Ponte beat out Palladio for the commission of this bridge, but construction costs spiralled to 250,000 Venetian ducats – about €19 million today.

KRZYSZTOF DYDYNSKI/GETTY IMAGES ©

Ca' Pesaro
Originally designed by Baldassare Longhena, this palazzo was bequeathed to the city in 1898 to house the Galleria d'Arte Moderna and Museo d'Arte Orientale.

San Marco & San Polo

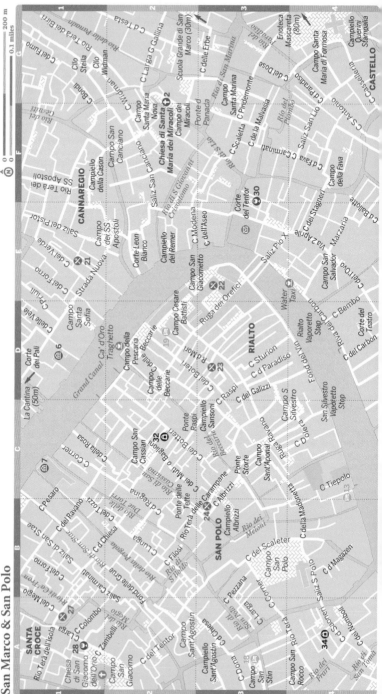

200 m
0.1 miles

SANTA CROCE

CANNAREGIO

SAN POLO

RIALTO

CASTELLO

Grand Canal

La Cantina (50m)

Scuola Grande di San Marco (30m)

Enoteca Mascareta (80m)

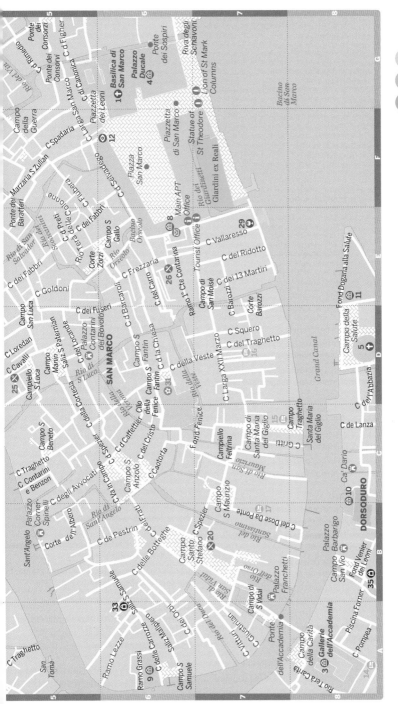

Ponte dei Consorzi
C d'Rimedio
Rio del Vin
Ponte dei Consorvi
C d'Figher

Campo della Guerra

Basilica di San Marco 1

Palazzo Ducale 4

Ponte dei Sospiri

Riva degli Schiavoni

Lion of St Mark Columns

Piazzetta San Marco
C di Canonica
C Spadaria
C Larga San Marco
Piazzetta dei Leoni

Marzaria S Zulian

Ponte dei Baratteri

12

Statue of St Theodore

Piazzetta di San Marco

Bacino di San Marco

C Fiubera

Campo S Gallo

C dei Fabbri

C de' Preti
C delle Colonne

Rio di San Salvador

Rio della Guerra

Piazza San Marco

Giardini ex Reali

Rio dei Giardinetti

Main APT Office

8

Campo S Zorzi

Rio Terà de le Colonne

Corte Zorzi

Bacino Orseolo

Rio Orseolo

Tourist Office

29

C Vallaresso

C del Fabbri

C Goldoni

C Frezzaria

26

Ramo 1ª Cte Contarina

C del Carro

C del Ridotto

C dei Fuseri

Campo di San Moisè

C del 13 Martiri

Campo San Luca

C Loredan

C Cavalli

25

C d Barcaroli

Contarini del Bovolo

C Barozzi

Corte Barozzi

Campo S Luca

Campiello S Luca

Campo Manin

Salizz Paternian

C del Locande

Palazzo Contarini del Bovolo

SAN MARCO

Campo S Fantin

Campo S Fantin
C d la Chiesa

C Squero

C del Traghetto

Fond Dogana alla Salute 11

Campo della Salute 5

Rio di S Luca

C della Cortesia

31

Rio della Veste

C della Veste

16

C Larga XXII Marzo

Grand Canal

Campo S Beneto

Rio della Fenice

Clio della Fenice

Fond Fenice

C de l'Abbazia

C de Lanza

C Traghetto
C Contarini e Benzon

Palazzo Corner-Spinelli

C degli Avvocati

C de Caffettier

C del Cristo

C S Anzolo

C Caotorta

Campiello Feltrina

Campo di Santa Maria del Giglio

Campo Traghetto

Santa Maria del Giglio

Ca' Dario 10

Rio di Sant'Angelo

C In Campo
C Spezier

Campo S Spezier

Campo S Maurizio

C del Dose Da Ponte

Corte de l'Albero

C de Pestrin

C del Frati

C de la Chiesa

Campo S Maurizio

DORSODURO

Palazzo Barbarigo

Rio del Santissimo

Sant'Angelo

San Toma

C Traghetto

Ramo Lezze

Ramo Grassi

9

Salizz Malipiero

C delle Carrozze

C del Orbo

Campo S Samuele

C delle Botteghe

Campo Santo Stefano

20

Campo di S Vidal

Palazzo Franchetti

Rio di San Vidal

Rio dell'Orso

Campo S Vidal

Ponte dell'Accademia

Palazzo Barbarigo

Campo San Vio

Fond Venier dei Leoni

35

33

C S Samuele

C Giustinian

C Vitturi

C del Pestrin

Gallerie dell'Accademia 3

Campo della Carità

Piscina Forner

C Pompea

Rio Terà della Carità

San Marco & San Polo

Death, eerie lightning-bolt illumination strikes Tintoretto's subjects in New Testament wall scenes. When Tintoretto painted these scenes, Venice's outlook was grim indeed: the plague had taken 50,000 Venetians, including the great colourist Titian.

Downstairs in the assembly hall, Tintoretto tells Mary's life story, starting on the left wall with *Annunciation* and ending with dark and cataclysmic *Ascension* opposite.

Ca' Pesaro   Museum

(Galleria Internazionale d'Arte Moderna e Museo d'Arte Orientale; Map p178; ☏ 041 72 11 27; www.visitmuve.it; Fondamenta di Ca' Pesaro 2070, Santa Croce; adult/reduced €8/5.50; ⊙10am-6pm Tue-Sun Apr-Oct, to 5pm Nov-Mar; ⛴San Stae) Like a Carnevale costume built for two, the stately exterior of this Baldassare Longhena–designed 1710 *palazzo* hides two quirky museums: **Galleria Internazionale d'Arte Moderna** and **Museo d'Arte Orientale**. The former highlights Venice's role in modern-art history, while the latter holds treasures from Prince Enrico di Borbone's epic 1887–89 souvenir-shopping spree across Asia.

CANNAREGIO

Chiesa della
Madonna dell'Orto   Church

(Map p172; Campo della Madonna dell'Orto 3520; admission €3, free with Chorus Pass; ⊙10am-5pm Mon-Sat; ⛴Madonna dell'Orto) This elegantly spare 1365 brick Gothic cathedral dedicated to the patron saint of travellers remains one of Venice's best-kept secrets. This was the parish church of Venetian Renaissance master Tintoretto, who is buried here in the corner chapel and saved two of his finest works for the apse: *Presentation of the Virgin in the Temple,* with throngs of starstruck angels and mortals vying for a glimpse of Mary, and his 1546 *Last Judgment,* where lost souls attempt to hold back a teal tidal wave while an angel rescues one last person from the ultimate *acque alte.*

Ca' d'Oro   Museum

(Map p178; ☏ 041 520 03 45; www.cadoro.org; Calle di Ca' d'Oro 3932; adult/reduced €6/3; ⊙8.15am-7.15pm Mon-Sat, 9am-12.30pm Sun; ⛴Ca' d'Oro) Along the Grand Canal, you can't miss 15th-century Ca' d'Oro's lacy **arcaded Gothic facade**, resplendent

GLENN BEANLAND/GETTY IMAGES ©

Don't Miss
Palazzo Ducale

Behind its genteel Gothic facade, the doge's palace shows a steely will to survive. After fire gutted the original palace in 1577, Antonio da Ponte won the commission to restore it with white Istrian stone and Veronese pink marble.

Climb the Scala dei Censori (Stairs of the Censors) to the Doge's Apartments, where the doge lived under 24-hour guard with a short commute to work up a secret staircase capped with Titian's painting of St Christopher. The Sala del Scudo (Shield Room) is covered with world maps that reveal the extents of Venetian power c 1483 and 1762.

Head up Sansovino's 24-carat gilt stuccowork Scala d'Oro (Golden Staircase) and emerge into rooms covered with gorgeous propaganda. In Palladio-designed Sala delle Quattro Porte (Hall of the Four Doors), ambassadors awaited ducal audiences under a lavish display of Venice's virtues by Giovanni Cambi, Titian and Tiepolo.

Few were granted an audience in the Palladio-designed Collegio (Council Room), where Veronese's 1575–78 Virtues of the Republic ceiling shows Venice as a bewitching blonde waving her sceptre over Justice and Peace. Father-son team Jacopo and Domenico Tintoretto attempt similar flattery, showing Venice keeping company with Apollo, Mars and Mercury in their *Triumph of Venice* ceiling for the Sala del Senato (Senate Hall).

Government cover-ups were never so appealing as in the Sala Consiglio dei Dieci (Trial Chambers of the Council of 10; Room 20), where Venice's star chamber plotted under Veronese's *Juno Bestowing Her Gifts on Venice,* a glowing goddess strewing gold ducats. Over the slot where anonymous treason accusations were slipped in the Sala della Bussola (Compass Room; Room 21) is his *St Mark in Glory* ceiling.

NEED TO KNOW

Ducal Palace; Map p178; 📞848 08 20 00; www.palazzoducale.visitmuve.it; Piazzetta San Marco 52; adult/reduced/child €16/8/free; ⏲8.30am-7pm Apr-Oct, to 5.30pm Nov-Mar; 🚤San Zaccaria

© JEAN-PIERRE LESCOURRET/CORBIS

Gallerie dell'Accademia

These galleries contain more murderous intrigue, forbidden romance and shameless politicking than the most outrageous Venetian parties. This former Santa Maria della Carità convent maintained its serene composure for centuries, but ever since Napoleon installed his haul of Venetian art trophies in 1807, there's been nonstop visual drama.

Rooms 1–5 To guide you through the ocular onslaught, the gallery layout is loosely organised by style and theme from the 14th to 18th centuries, though recent restorations and works on loan have shuffled around some masterpieces.

Rooms 6–10 Venice's Renaissance awaits around the corner in Room 6, featuring Titian and Tintoretto.

Rooms 11–19 As you enter Room 11, you'll notice a lighter baroque touch: gossipy Venetian socialites hang over balconies in 1743–45 lunettes by Tiepolo.

Rooms 12 & 18 Currently undergoing restoration to showcase Canaletto's sweeping views of Venice and Giorgione's highly charged *La Tempesta* (The Storm). Restored portrait galleries will feature Lorenzo Lotto's soul-searching *Portrait of a Young Scholar;* and a saucy socialite in Giambattista Piazzetta's *Fortune-Teller*.

Rooms 20–24 Finales don't come any grander than the Accademia's final suite of rooms. Room 20 is currently undergoing restorations to accommodate Gentile Bellini and Vittore Carpaccio's Venetian versions of *Miracles of the True Cross*. After careful restoration, the original convent **chapel** (Room 23) is a serene showstopper fronted by a **Bellini altarpiece**, with temporary shows in the centre.

NEED TO KNOW

Map p178; ☎ 041 520 03 45; www.gallerieaccademia.org; Campo della Carità 1050; ticket incl Palazzo Grimani adult/reduced/EU child & senior €14/11/free; ⏰ 8.15am-2pm Mon, to 7.15pm Tue-Sun, last admission 45min before closing; P; ⚓ Accademia

even without the original gold-leaf details that gave the palace its name (Golden House). Baron Franchetti donated to Venice this treasure-box palace packed with masterpieces displayed upstairs in **Galleria Franchetti**, alongside Renaissance wonders plundered from Veneto churches during Napoleon's Italy conquest.

CASTELLO

Zanipolo   Basilica
(Chiesa dei SS Giovanni e Paolo; Map p172; ☑ 041 523 59 13; www.basilicasantigiovanni epaolo.it; Campo Zanipolo; adult/student €2.50/1.25; ☉ 9am-6pm Mon-Sat, noon-6pm Sun; ☐ Ospedale) When the Dominicans began building Zanipolo in 1333 to rival the Franciscans' I Frari (p174), this barnlike church stirred passions more common to Serie A football than architecture. Both structures feature red-brick facades with high-contrast detailing, but since Zanipolo's facade remains unfinished, the Frari won a decisive early decision. Over the centuries, Zanipolo has at least tied the score with its pantheon of ducal funerary monuments and the variety of its wonderful masterpieces.

Chiesa di San Francesco della Vigna   Church
(Map p172; ☑ 041 520 61 02; www.sanfran cescodellavigna.it; Campo San Francesco del-la Vigna 2786; ☉ 9.30am-12.30pm & 3-6pm Mon-Sat, 3-6pm Sun; ☐ Celestia, Ospedale) FREE Designed and built by Jacopo Sansovino with a facade by Palladio, this enchanting Franciscan church is one of Venice's most underappreciated attractions. The Madonna positively glows in Bellini's 1507 *Madonna and Saints* in the **Cappella Santa**, just off the flower-carpeted **cloister**, while swimming angels and strutting birds steal the scene in the delightful *Virgin Enthroned*, by Antonio da Negroponte (c 1460–70). Make sure you bring €0.20 to illuminate them.

♥ If You Like...
Contemporary Art

Between billionaire benefactors and cutting-edge biennales, Venice's *palazzi* (palaces) are overflowing with new eyebrow-raising contemporary art and architecture.

1 PUNTA DELLA DOGANA
(Map p178; ☑ 041 271 90 39; www.palazzograssi.it; adult/reduced/child €15/10/free, incl Palazzo Grassi €20/15/free; ☉ 10am-7pm Wed-Mon; ☐ Salute) Fortune swung Venice's way in 2005, when bureaucratic hassles in Paris convinced billionaire art collector François Pinault to showcase his artworks in these long-abandoned customs houses. Originally built by Giuseppe Benoni in 1677 to ensure no ship entered the Grand Canal without paying duties, they now house massive, thought-provoking installations in front of cutaway views of passing ships.

2 PALAZZO GRASSI
(Map p178; ☑ box office 199 13 91 39, 041 523 16 80; www.palazzograssi.it; Campo San Samuele 3231; adult/reduced/child €15/10/free, 72hr ticket incl Punta della Dogana €20/15/free; ☉ 10am-7pm Wed-Mon; ☐ San Samuele) Grand Canal gondola riders gasp at the first glimpse of massive sculptures by contemporary artists like Thomas Houseago docked in front of Giorgio Masari's 1749 neoclassical palace. François Pinault's provocative art collection overflows Palazzo Grassi, but Tadao Ando's creatively repurposed interior architecture steals the show.

3 MAGAZZINI DEL SALE
(Map p172; ☑ 041 522 66 26; www.fondazionevedova.org; Zattere 266; donation suggested during shows; ☉ during shows 10.30am-6pm Wed-Mon; ☐ Zattere) A recent retrofit designed by Renzo Piano transformed Venice's historic salt warehouses into Fondazione Vedova art galleries, commemorating pioneering Venetian abstract painter Emilio Vedova. Shows are often literally moving and rotating: powered by renewable energy sources, 10 robotic arms designed by Vedova and Piano move major modern artworks in and out of storage slots.

DAVID C TOMLINSON/GETTY IMAGES ©

⭐ Don't Miss
Chiesa di Santa Maria dei Miracoli

A minor *miracolo* (miracle) of early-Renaissance architecture, Pietro Lombardo's little marble chapel was ahead of its time, dropping Gothic grandiosity for human-scale classical architecture. By pooling resources and scavenging multicoloured marble from San Marco slag heaps, the neighbourhood commissioned this church to house Niccolò di Pietro's Madonna icon when it miraculously started weeping in c 1480. Completing this monument to community spirit, Pier Maria Pennacchi filled 50 ceiling panels with portraits of prophets dressed as Venetians.

NEED TO KNOW

Map p178; Campo dei Miracoli 6074; admission €3 or with Chorus Pass; ⊙10am-5pm Mon-Sat; 🚤Fondamenta Nuove

---

Giardini Pubblici Garden
(Map p172; www.labiennale.org; 🚤Giardini, Biennale) Venice's public gardens were laid out between 1808 and 1812 on the orders of Napoleon, who decided the city needed a little breathing space. Never mind that an entire residential district had to be demolished. A winning combination of formal gardens and winding pathways, the park now stretches from Via Garibaldi past the Biennale pavilions to Sant'Elena, making this the largest park in Venice.

ISOLA DI SAN GIORGIO MAGGIORE

Chiesa di San Giorgio Maggiore Church
(Map p172; 📞041 522 78 27; Isola di San Giorgio Maggiore; bell tower adult/reduced €3/2; ⊙9am-12.30pm & 2.30-6.30pm Mon-Sat May-Sep, to 5pm Oct-Apr; 🚤San Giorgio Maggiore) Solar eclipses are only marginally more dazzling than Palladio's white Istrian marble facade. Begun in the 1560s, it owes more to ancient Roman temples

than the baroque of Palladio's day. Inside, ceilings billow over a generous nave, with high windows distributing filtered sunshine. Two of Tintoretto's masterworks flank the altar, and a lift whisks visitors up the 60m-high **bell tower** for stirring Ventian panoramas – a great alternative to long lines at San Marco's campanile.

THE LIDO

Only 15 minutes by *vaporetti* 1, 51, 52, 61, 62, 82 and N from San Marco, the Lido has been the beach and bastion of Venice for centuries. In the 19th century, it found a new lease of life as a glamorous bathing resort, attracting monied Europeans to its grand Liberty-style hotels. Thomas Mann's novel *Death in Venice* was set here, and you'll spot plenty of ornate villas that date from those decadent days. Walking itineraries around the most extravagant are available to download at www2.comune.venezia.it/lidoliberty.

Lido beaches, such as the Blue Moon complex, line the southern, seaward side of the island and are easily accessed from the *vaporetto* down the Gran Viale. To head further afield, hire a bike from **Lido on Bike** (**041 526 80 19; www.lidoonbike.it; Gran Viale 21b; bikes per 90min/day €5/9; 9am-7pm mid-Mar–Oct; Lido**) and cycle south across the Ponte di Borgo to tiny **Malamocco**, a miniature version of Venice right down to the lions of St Mark on medieval facades.

Activities

A gondola ride is anything but pedestrian, with glimpses into *palazzi* courtyards and hidden canals otherwise invisible on foot. Official daytime rates are €80 for 40 minutes (six passengers maximum), and it's €100 between 7pm and 8am, not including songs (negotiated separately) or tips. Additional time is charged in 20-minute increments (day/night €40/50). You may negotiate a price break in low season, overcast weather or around midday, when other travellers get hot and hungry. Agree on a price, time limit and singing in advance to

Local Knowledge

Venice

RECOMMENDATIONS FROM ALBERTO TOSO FEI, AUTHOR OF *MYSTERIES OF VENICE* AND *THE SECRETS OF THE GRAND CANAL*

1 **PALAZZO DUCALE**
Casanova escaped from the *piombi*, the attic prison of Palazzo Ducale (p181), but other prisoners had to be tough to survive hot summers under that lead roof. Still, it was better than the *poggi* (wells) in the courtyard, where prisoners shivered below water level. To house thieves, the New Prisons were built with marble probably stolen from Constantinople.

2 **BASILICA DI SAN MARCO**
Venice pulled off the heist of the millennium: smuggling the body of one of the original four evangelists, St Mark, out of Alexandria. Venice was a master thief with excellent taste – just look at the precious marble used for the basilica (p175), taken from all over the Mediterranean. Venice also appropriated St Mark's winged lion symbol as its own, which is like adopting the Coca-Cola logo as your name: instant recognition.

3 **LA FENICE**
La Fenice (p196) opera house burned down in 1996 but also in 1836, when Venice was occupied by the Austrians. When La Fenice reopened, the muses of Music and Song painted on the ceiling were dressed in red, white and green, the colours of independent Italy. Military power was temporarily Austrian, but opera belongs eternally to Italy.

4 **GRAND CANAL**
Besides Marco Polo, travellers have always played central roles in Venice, from Turkish and German traders in Grand Canal trading houses to individual visitors, whose support rescued Venice after its 1966 floods. When you cross the bridge into Venice, you are becoming a character in a marvellous story.

avoid surcharges. Gondole cluster at *stazi* (stops) along the Grand Canal, at the train station (☏041 71 85 43), the Rialto (☏041 522 49 04) and near major monuments (such as I Frari, Ponte Sospiri and Accademia), but you can also book a pick-up at a canal near you (☏041 528 50 75).

☞ Tours

From April to October, **APT (www.turismo venezia.it)** tourist offices offer guided tours ranging from the classic gondola circuit (€40 per person) to a penetrating look at Basilica di San Marco (€21 per person) and a four-hour circuit of Murano, Burano and Torcello (€20 per person).

Venice Day Trips   Cultural Tour
(☏049 60 06 72; www.venicedaytrips.com; Via Saetta 18, Padua; semi-private/private tours per person €165/275) A fantastic selec-

tion of off-the-shelf and customised tours run by the ebullient Mario, Rachel and Silvia. Keen to show you the genuine face of the Veneto, these bite-sized tours range from cooking classes in Cannaregio to cheese-making on Monte Veronese and tutored wine tastings.

Laguna Eco Adventures   Sailing Tour
(☏329 722 62 89; www.lagunaecoadventures. com; 2-8hr trips per person €40-150) Explore the far reaches of the lagoon by day or hidden Venetian canals by night in a traditional *sampierota* (a narrow twin-sailed boat).

Row Venice   Rowing
(☏345 241 52 66; www.rowvenice.com; 2hr lessons 1-2 people €80, 4 people €120) The next best thing to walking on water: rowing a *sandolo* (Venetian boat) standing up like gondoliers do, with Australian-Venetian rowing coach Jane Caporal.

Terra e Acqua — Boat Tour

(☏ 347 420 50 04; www.veneziainbarca.it; day-long trips incl lunch for 9-12 people €380-460) Spot rare lagoon wildlife, admire architectural gems of Burano and Torcello, and moor for a tasty fish-stew lunch, all via *bragosso* (Venetian barge).

✵ Festivals & Events

Carnevale — Carnival

(www.carnevale.venezia.it) Masquerade madness stretches over two weeks in February before Lent. Tickets to La Fenice's masked balls start at €200, but there's a free-flowing wine fountain to commence Carnevale, public costume parties in every *campo* (square), and a Grand Canal flotilla marking the end of festivities.

La Biennale di Venezia — Culture

(www.labiennale.org) In odd years the Art Biennale runs from June to October, while in even years the Architecture Biennale runs from September to November. The main venues are Giardini Pubblici pavilions and the **Arsenale** (Map p172; ☏ 041 521 88 28; www.labiennale.org; Campo della Tana; adult €20, reduced €12-16; ☺10am-6pm Tue-Sun; ⛴Arsenale), once the greatest medieval shipyard in Europe, founded in 1104. Every summer, the Biennale hosts avant-garde dance, theatre, cinema and music programs throughout the city.

🛏 Sleeping

The **APT tourist board** (www.turismovenezia. it) lists hundreds of B&Bs, *affittacamere* (rooms for rent) and apartments to rent in Venice proper. More can be found at **BB Planet** (www.bbplanet.it), www.guestinitaly. com and www.veniceapartment.com.

PIAZZA SAN MARCO & AROUND

Hotel Flora — Hotel €

(Map p178; ☏ 041 520 58 44; www.hotelflora.it; Calle Bergamaschi 2283a; d incl breakfast €100-358; ❄ 🛜 📶; ⛴Santa Maria del Giglio) Down a lane from glitzy Calle Larga XXII Marzo,

187

this ivy-covered retreat quietly outclasses brash designer neighbours with its delightful tearoom, breakfasts around the garden fountain, and gym offering shiatsu massage. Strollers and kids' teatime are complimentary; babysitting is available.

Novecento Boutique Hotel **€€**
(Map p178; ☎041 241 37 65; www.novecento.biz; Calle del Dose 2683/84; d €140-300; ❄ 📶; ⛴ Santa Maria del Giglio) World travellers put down roots in nine bohemian-chic rooms plush with Turkish kilim pillows, Fortuny draperies and 19th-century carved bedsteads piled with duvets. Linger over breakfasts in the garden under Indian parasols, go for a massage at sister property Hotel Flora, take a hotel-organised course in Venetian cooking or landscape drawing, or mingle with creative fellow travellers around the honesty bar.

DORSODURO

Pensione Accademia Villa Maravege Inn **€€**
(Map p172; ☎041 521 01 88; www.pensioneaccademia.it; Fondamenta Bollani 1058; d €145-340; ❄ 📶 👪; ⛴ Accademia) Step through the ivy-covered gate of this 17th-century garden villa just off the Grand Canal, and you'll forget you're a block from the Accademia. All 27 guestrooms are recently restored and effortlessly elegant, with parquet floors, antique desks, creamy walls and snug, shiny modern bathrooms – some offer four-poster beds, wood-beamed ceilings and glimpses of the canal.

Ca' Pisani Design Hotel **€€**
(Map p178; ☎041 240 14 11; www.capisanihotel.it; Rio Terà Antonio Foscarini 979a; d €140-351; ❄ 📶; ⛴ Accademia) Sprawl out in style right behind the Accademia, and luxuriate in sleigh beds, Jacuzzi tubs and walk-in closets. Mood lighting and sound-proofed padded leather walls make downstairs deco rooms right for romance, while families appreciate top-floor rooms with sleeping lofts.

SAN POLO & SANTA CROCE

Ca' Angeli Boutique Hotel **€**
(Map p178; ☎041 523 24 80; www.caangeli.it; Calle del Traghetto de la Madonnetta 1434, San Polo; d incl breakfast €70-215; ❄ 📶; ⛴ San Silvestro) 🍃 Brothers Giorgio and Matteo

Burano

EMILY RIDDELL/GETTY IMAGES ©

inherited this Grand Canal palace and restored its Murano glass chandeliers, Louis XIV love-seat and namesake 16th-century angels. Guestrooms feature beamed ceilings, antique carpets and big bathrooms; some have Grand Canal or secluded courtyard views.

Pensione Guerrato
Inn €€

(Map p178; ☑ 041 528 59 27; www.pensione guerrato.it; Calle Drio la Scimia 240a, San Polo; d/tr/q incl breakfast €145/165/185; ❄ ☎ ♿; ⚓ Rialto Mercato) In a 1227 landmark that was once a hostel for knights headed for the Third Crusade, updated guestrooms haven't lost their sense of history – some have frescoes or glimpses of the Grand Canal. A prime Rialto Market location amid gourmet *bacari* makes Pensione Guerrato the Holy Grail for visiting foodies, and newly restored apartments are equipped with kitchens. Wi-fi in lobby.

Oltre il Giardino
Boutique Hotel €€

(Map p178; ☑ 041 275 00 15; www.oltreil giardino-venezia.com; Fondamenta Contarini, San Polo 2542; d incl breakfast €180-250; ❄ @ ♿; ⚓ San Tomà) Live the design-magazine dream in this garden villa brimming with historic charm and modern comforts: marquetry composer's desks and flat-screen TVs, candelabras and minibars, 19th-century poker chairs and babysitting services. Light fills six high-ceilinged bedrooms, and though sprawling Turquoise overlooks the canal and Green hides away in the walled garden, Grey has a sexy wrought-iron bedframe under a cathedral ceiling.

CANNAREGIO

Allo Squero
B&B €

(Map p172; ☑ 041 523 69 73; www.allosquero. it; Corte dello Squero 4692; d incl breakfast €80-130; ☎ ♿; ⚓ Fondamente Nuove) Dock for the night at this historic gondola *squero* (shipyard), recently converted into a garden getaway. Gondolas passing along two canals are spotted from modern,

♥ **If You Like...**
Island Life

Serene San Giorgio Maggiore and the beachy Lido make great escapes, but don't stop there. Hop on the *vaporetto* (ferry) to discover work-of-art glass, extreme colour schemes and a near deserted island.

MURANO

Venetians have been working in crystal and glass since the 10th century, but due to fire hazards all glass-blowing was moved to the island of Murano in the 13th century. Today glass artisans ply their trade at workshops along Murano's **Fondamenta dei Vetrai** marked by Fornace (furnace) signs. Since 1861 Murano's glass-making prowess has earned pride of place in Palazzo Giustinian at **Museo del Vetro** (Glass Museum; ☑ 041 73 95 86; www.museovetro.visitmuve.it; Fondamenta Giustinian 8; adult/reduced €8/5.50; ⊙ 10am-6pm Apr-Oct, to 5pm Nov-Mar; ⚓ Museo).

BURANO

Venice's lofty Gothic architecture might leave you feeling slightly loopy, but Burano will bring you back to your senses with a reviving shock of colour. The 50-minute Laguna Nord (LN) ferry ride from the Fondamente Nuove is packed with photographers bounding into Burano's backstreets, snapping away at pea-green stockings hung to dry between hot-pink, royal-blue and caution-orange houses.

TORCELLO

On the pastoral island of Torcello, a three-minute T-line ferry-hop from Burano, sheep outnumber the 14 or so human residents. This bucolic backwater was once a Byzantine metropolis of 20,000, but of its original nine churches and two abbeys only the striking brick **Chiesa di Santa Fosca** (⊙ 10am-4.30pm; ⚓ Torcello) and splendid mosaic-filled **Santa Maria Assunta** (Piazza Torcello; adult/reduced €5/4, incl museum €8/6; ⊙ 10.30am-6pm Mar-Oct, 10am-5pm Nov-Feb; ⚓ Torcello) remain. Stay overnight at Ernest Hemingway's favoured retreat, Locanda Cipriani.

sunny upstairs guestrooms, with terrazzo marble floors and sleek mosaic-striped ensuite bathrooms, some with tubs. Hosts Andrea and Hiroko offer Venice-insider tips over cappuccino and pastry breakfasts in the fragrant, wisteria-filled garden.

Ca' Zanardi   Boutique Hotel €€
(Map p172; ☏ 041 241 33 05; www.cazanardi.eu; Calle Zanardi 4132; d €130-300; 🛜; 🚤Madonna dell'Orto) Pristine 16th-century Venetian palace, international contemporary art gallery, idyllic canalside garden: since Ca' Zanardi is all these things, calling it home for the weekend is a distinct privilege. Those throne-like chairs, tapestries and mercury-glass mirrors aren't decor but the original furnishings kept in the family over four centuries; drawing-room concerts and gala ballroom masquerades are still held here.

CASTELLO

Palazzo Soderini   B&B €€
(Map p172; ☏ 041 296 08 23; www.palazzo soderini.it; Campo di Bandiera e Mori 3611; d incl breakfast €150-200; ❄🛜; 🚤Arsenale) Whether you're coming from cutting-edge art at the Biennale or baroque master-pieces at the Palazzo Ducale, this tranquil all-white B&B with a lily pond in the garden is a welcome reprieve from the visual onslaught of Venice. Minimalist decor emphasises spare shapes and clean lines, with steel-edged modern furniture and whitewashed walls.

🍴 Eating

PIAZZA SAN MARCO & AROUND

Enoteca al Volto   Venetian, Cicheti €
(Map p178; ☏ 041 522 89 45; Calle Cavalli 4081; cicheti €2-4, meals under €25; ⏰10am-3pm & 5.30-10pm Mon-Sat; 🚤Rialto) Join the bar crowd working its way through the vast selection of wine and *cicheti,* or come early for a table outdoors (in summer). Inside the snug backroom that looks like a ship's hold, tuck into seaworthy bowls of pasta with *bottarga* (dried fish roe), steak drizzled with aged balsamic vinegar, and housemade ravioli. Cash only.

Osteria da Carla   Osteria, Cicheti €
(Map p178; ☏ 041 523 78 55; Frez-zaria 1535; meals €20-25; ⏰10am-9pm Mon-Sat; 🚤Vallaresso) For the price of hot chocolate in Piazza San Marco, din-ers in the know duck into this hidden courtyard to feast on handmade ravioli with poppyseed, pear and sheep cheese. Expect a wait at lunch and happy hour, when *gondolieri* abandon ship for DOC soave and *sopressa crostini* (soft salami on toast).

Pizza al taglio (pizza by the slice)
RICHARD I'ANSON/GETTY IMAGES ©

Tortina Rustica con Spinaci e Ricotta

Pizza Primavera

Pizza ai 5 Formaggi

Tortina Rustica con Prosciutto e Mozzarella

Tortina Rustica con Rucola e Provola

Tortina Rustica Con Verdure Fresche e Mozzarella

A Beccafico
Italian €€

(Map p178; 041 527 48 79; www.abeccafico.com; Campo Santo Stefano 2801; meals €25-45; noon-3pm & 7-11pm; Accademia) Far from clubby pubs lining Venice's alleyways, A Beccafico basks in the sunshine of Campo Santo Stefano and open Venetian admiration. Instead of cold seafood on toast, Chef Adeli serves Sicily-size bowls of mussels under a bubbling, flaky crust. He defies Venice's cardinal rule never to mix lagoon seafood with cheese, serving squid-ink pasta with lemon zest and ricotta.

DORSODURO

Ristorante La Bitta
Ristorante €€

(Map p172; 041 523 05 31; Calle Lunga San Barnaba 2753a; meals €30-40; dinner Mon-Sat; Ca' Rezzonico) The daily menu arrives on an artist's easel, and the hearty rustic fare looks like a still life and tastes like a carnivore's dream: steak comes snugly wrapped in bacon, and roast rabbit tops marinated rocket. This bistro focuses on local meats – 'bitta' means 'mooring post' – and seats only 35. Reservations essential; cash only.

Do Farai
Seafood, Venetian €€

(Map p172; 041 277 03 69; Calle del Cappeller 3278; meals €25-35; 11am-3pm & 7-10pm Mon-Sat; Ca' Rezzonico) Venetian regulars pack this hidden wood-panelled room hung with football-championship scarves and fragrant with mouthwatering seafood: pasta with shellfish and sweet prawns; herb-laced, grilled *orata* (bream); and Venetian *tris di saor sarde, scampi e sogliole* (sardines, prawns and sole in tangy Venetian *saor* marinade).

Enoteca Ai Artisti
Ristorante €€€

(Map p172; 041 523 89 44; www.enotecaaartisti.com; Fondamenta della Toletta 1169a; meals €40-50; noon-4pm & 6.30-10pm Mon-Sat; Ca' Rezzonico) Indulgent cheeses, exceptional *nero di seppia* (cuttlefish ink) pasta, and tender *tagliata* (sliced steak) drizzled with aged balsamic vinegar atop rocket are paired with exceptional wines by the glass by your oenophile hosts. Sidewalk tables for two make great people-watching.

SAN POLO & SANTA CROCE

All'Arco
Venetian €

(Map p178; 041 520 56 66; Calle dell'Ochialer 436; cicheti €1.50-4; 8am-3.30pm Mon-Sat Sep-Jun, plus 6-9pm Mon-Sat Apr-Oct; Rialto-Mercato) Father-son *maestri* Francesco and Matteo invent Venice's best *cicheti* daily with Rialto Market finds. Behind marble counters, Francesco wraps poached Bassano white asparagus with seasoned pancetta, while Matteo creates *otrega* (butterfish) *crudo* with mint–olive oil marinade and Hawaiian red-clay salt.

Antiche Carampane
Venetian €€

(Map p178; 041 524 01 65; www.antichecarampane.com; Rio Terà delle Carampane 1911, San Polo; meals €30-45; noon-2.30pm & 7-11pm Tue-Sat; San Stae) Hidden in the once-shady lanes behind Ponte delle Tette, this culinary indulgence is a trick to find. The sign proudly announcing 'no tourist menu' signals a welcome change: say goodbye to soggy lasagne and hello to silky, lagoon-fresh *crudi*, asparagus and *granseola* (lagoon crab) salad, cloudlike gnocchi, and San Pietro (whitefish) atop grilled *radicchio trevisano*.

Osteria La Zucca
Modern Italian €€

(Map p178; 041 524 15 70; www.lazucca.it; Calle del Tentor 1762, Santa Croce; meals €30-45; 12.30-2.30pm & 7-10.30pm Mon-Sat; ; San Stae) Vegetable-centric, seasonal small plates bring Venetian spice-trade influences to local produce: zucchini with ginger zing, cinnamon-tinged pumpkin flan, and raspberry spice cake. Herbed roast lamb is respectable too, but the island-grown produce is the breakout star. The snug wood-panelled interior gets toasty; reserve canalside seats in summer.

Al Pesador
Modern Italian €€€

(Map p178; 041 523 94 92; www.alpesador.it; Campo San Giacometto 125, San Polo; cicheti €1.50-5, meals €40-55; noon-3pm & 7-11pm Mon-Sat; Rialto-Mercato) Watch the world drift down the Grand Canal outside or canoodle indoors, but prepare to sit up and pay attention once the food arrives. Pesador reinvents Venetian cuisine with finesse: *cicheti* feature mackerel with balsamic-vinegar *saor* marinade and paper-thin *lardo*

VENICE, VENETO & BOLOGNA VENICE

crostini with mint oil, while *primi* (mains) include red-footed scallops kicking wild herbs across squid-ink gnocchi.

CANNAREGIO

Dalla Marisa   Venetian €

(Map p172; ☎041 72 02 11; Fondamenta di San Giobbe 652b; set menus €15-35; ☺noon-3pm & 7-11pm Tue & Thu-Sat, noon-3pm Mon & Wed; ⛴Crea) At Dalla Marisa, you'll be seated where there's room and get no menu – you'll have whatever Marisa's cooking, but you'll be informed that the menu is meat- or fish-based when you book, and house wine is included in the price. Venetian regulars confess Marisa's *fegato alla veneziana* (Venetian calf's liver) is better than their grandmothers', while fish nights bring hauls of lagoon seafood grilled, fried and perched atop pasta and rocket.

Ai Promessi
Sposi   Venetian €€

(Map p178; ☎041 241 27 47; Calle d'Oca 4367; meals €25-35; ☺11.30am-3pm & 6-11pm Tue & Thu-Sun, 6-11pm Mon & Wed; ⛴Ca' d'Oro) Bantering Venetians thronging the bar are the only permanent fixtures at this newly revived neighbourhood *osteria*, where handwritten menus created daily feature fresh Venetian seafood and Veneto meats at excellent prices.

Anice Stellato   Venetian €€€

(Map p172; ☎041 72 07 44; Fondamenta della Sensa 3272; mains €18-23; ☺noon-2pm & 7.30-11pm Wed-Sun; ⛴Madonna dell'Orto) 🍃 If finding this obscure corner of Cannaregio seems like an adventure, wait until dinner arrives: pistachio-encrusted lamb chops, succulent house-made prawn ravioli and lightly fried *moeche* (soft-shell crab) gobbled whole. Tin lamps and recycled paper placemats on communal tables keep the focus on local food and local company – all memorable. Book ahead.

CASTELLO

Osteria alla
Staffa Modern Venetian **€€**
(Map p172; ☎041 523 91 60; Calle dell'Ospedale 6397a; meals €20-35; ⏱11.30am-3pm & 6-11pm; 🚢Ospedale) With fish fresh from the Rialto every morning and a preference for organic veg and cheese, Alberto's takes on Venetian classics have flavourful foundations. But this is home cooking with a twist: the seafood selection looks like a modernist masterpiece with its creamy, coiffed *baccalà* bedded on a rich, red radicchio leaf and baby octopus set like lagoon flowers against a splash of apricot salmon.

Trattoria Corte
Sconta Modern Venetian **€€€**
(Map p172; ☎041 522 70 24; Calle del Pestrin 3886; meals €50-65; ⏱12.30-2.30pm & 7-9.30pm Tue-Sat, closed Jan & Aug; 🚢Arsenale) Well-informed visitors and celebrating locals seek out this vine-covered *corte sconta* (hidden courtyard) for its trade-mark seafood antipasti and imaginative house-made pasta, and you should too. Inventive flavour pairings transform the classics: clams zing with the hot, citrus-like taste of ginger; prawn and courgette linguine is recast with an earthy dash of saffron; and the roast eel loops like the Brenta River in a drizzle of balsamic reduction.

GIUDECCA

I Figli delle Stelle Italian **€€**
(Map p172; ☎041 523 00 04; www.ifiglidelle stelle.it; Zitelle 70; meals €30-40; ⏱12.30-2.30pm & 7-10pm Tue-Sun, closed mid-Nov–mid-Mar; 🚢Zitelle) Beware of declarations of love at one of Venice's most romantic restaurants: are you sure that's not Pugliese chef Luigi's velvety pasta and soup talking? A creamy fava-bean mash with biting chicory and fresh tomatoes coats the tongue in a naughty way, and the mixed grill for two with langoustine, sole and fresh sardines is quite a catch.

193

If You Like...
La Dolce Vita

Fans of the sweet life will find plenty of ways to lush it up in Venice.

1 GRITTI PALACE
(Map p178; ☎041 79 46 11; www.hotelgrittipalacevenice.com; Campo di Santa Maria del Giglio 2467; d €425-700, ste from €1100; ❄🅰; 🛥Santa Maria del Giglio) This landmark 1525 palace, located along the Grand Canal, reopened in 2013 after an extensive year-long restoration featuring luxe touches from Rubelli silk damask lining top-floor suites to underfloor heating beneath terrazzo marble floors in the Gritti Epicurean School. The classic Venetian rooms have also been spruced up, with restored antique fainting couches, stucco ceilings and bathrooms sheathed in rare marble.

2 HARRY'S BAR
(Map p178; ☎041 528 57 77; Calle Vallaresso 1323; cocktails €12-22; ⏰10.30am-11pm; 🛥San Marco) Aspiring auteurs hold court at bistro tables well scuffed by Ernest Hemingway, Charlie Chaplin, Truman Capote and Orson Welles, enjoying the signature €16.50 bellini (Giuseppe Cipriani's original 1948 recipe: white-peach juice and prosecco) with a side of reflected glory.

3 BAR TERAZZA DANIELI
(Map p172; ☎041 522 64 80; www.starwoodhotels.com; Riva degli Schiavoni 4196; cocktails €18-22; ⏰3-6.30pm Apr-Oct; 🛥San Zaccaria) Gondolas glide in to dock along the quay, while across the lagoon the white-marble edifice of Palladio's San Giorgio Maggiore turns from gold to pink in the waters of the canal: the late-afternoon scene from the Hotel Danieli's top-floor balcony bar definitely calls for a toast. Linger over a spritz (€10) or cocktail – preferably the sunset-tinted signature Danieli cocktail of gin, apricot and orange juices, and a splash of grenadine.

THE LIDO

Le Garzette
Farmstay €€
(☎041 712 16 53; www.legarzette.it; Lungomare Alberoni 32, Lido; meals €35-45; ⏰12.30-2.30pm & 7-10.30pm mid-Jan–mid-Dec; 👶; 🛥Lido) 🌿 Nestled amid gardens overflowing with red radicchio, astringent fennel and dark-green courgettes is the rust-red agriturismo of Renza and Salvatore. Choose between a meat or a fish menu and wait for the parade of organic dishes: crepes filled with juicy asparagus, lightly fried Malamocco artichokes and mouthwatering pear tart made with farm eggs.

La Favorita
Seafood €€
(☎041 526 16 26; Via Francesco Duodo 33; meals €35-50; ⏰12.30-2.30pm & 7.30-10.30pm Wed-Sun, 7.30-10.30pm Tue, closed Jan–mid-Feb; 🛥Lido) For long, lazy lunches, bottles of fine wine and impeccable service, look no further than La Favorita. The menu is as elegant as the surroundings; giant rhombo (turbot) simmered with capers and olives, spider-crab gnochetti (mini-gnocchi) and classic fish risotto. Book ahead for the wisteria-filled garden and well ahead during the film festival, when songbirds are practically out-sung by the ringtones of movie moguls.

🍷 Drinking & Nightlife

PIAZZA SAN MARCO & AROUND

I Rusteghi
Wine Bar
(Map p178; ☎041 523 22 05; www.osteriairusteghi.com; Corte del Tentor 5513; ⏰10.30am-3pm & 6-11.30pm Mon-Sat; 🛥Rialto) Honouring centuries of Venetian enoteca tradition, fourth-generation sommelier Giovanni d'Este will open any bottle on his shelves to pour you an ombra (half-glass of wine) – including collector's wines like Cannubi Barolo. Request 'qualcosa di particolare' (something exceptional) and Giovanni will reward you with a sensual Ribolla Gialla to pair with truffle-cheese mini-panini and platters of Spanish and Veneto ham.

DORSODURO

Cantinone Già Schiavi
Bar

(Map p172; 🕿 041 523 95 77; Fondamenta Nani 992; ⏱8.30am-8.30pm Mon-Sat; 🛳Zattere) Regulars gamely pass along orders to timid newcomers, who might otherwise miss out on tuna-leek *cicheti* with top-notch house soave, or *pallottoline* (mini-bottles of beer) with generous *sopressa* (soft salami) *panini*. Chaos cheerfully prevails at this legendary canalside spot, where Accademia art historians rub shoulders with San Trovaso gondola builders without spilling a drop.

Osteria alla Bifora
Bar

(Map p172; 🕿 041 523 61 19; Campo Santa Margherita 2930; ⏱noon-3pm & 6pm-1am Wed-Mon; 🛳Ca' Rezzonico) Other bars around this *campo* cater to *spritz*-pounding students, but this chandelier-lit medieval wine cave sets the scene for gentle flirting over big-hearted Veneto merlot. Cured-meat platters are carved to order on that Ferrari-red meat slicer behind the bar, there are placemats to doodle on and new-found friends aplenty at communal tables.

SAN POLO & SANTA CROCE

Al Prosecco
Wine Bar

(Map p178; 🕿 041 524 02 22; www.alprosecco.com; Campo San Giacomo dell'Orio, Santa Croce 1503; ⏱9am-10.30pm Mon-Sat, to 8pm winter; 🛳San Stae) 🌿 The urge to toast sunsets in Venice's loveliest *campo* is only natural – and so is the wine at Al Prosecco. This forward-thinking bar specialises in *vini naturi* (natural-process wines) – organic, biodynamic, wild yeast fermented – from the unfiltered 'cloudy' *prosecco* to the silky Veneto Venegazzú that trails across the tongue and lingers in the imagination.

CANNAREGIO

Al Timon
Wine Bar

(Map p172; 🕿 041 524 60 66; Fondamenta degli Ormesini 2754; ⏱11am-1am Thu-Tue & 6pm-1am Wed; 🛳Guglie) Find a spot on the boat moored out front along the canal and watch the motley parade of drinkers and dreamers arrive for seafood *crostini* (open-face sandwiches) and quality organic and DOC wines by the *ombra* (half-glass of wine) or carafe. Folk singers play sets canalside when the weather obliges; when it's cold, regulars scoot over to make room for newcomers at indoor tables.

Agli Ormesini
Pub

(Da Aldo; Map p172; 🕿 041 71 58 34; Fondamenta degli Ormesini 2710; ⏱8pm-1am Mon-Sat; 🛳Madonna dell'Orto) While the rest of Venice is awash in wine, Ormesini offers more than 100 brews, including reasonably priced bottles of speciality craft ales and local Birra Venezia. The cheery, beery scene often spills into the street – but keep it down, or the neighbours will get testy.

Street scene, Venice
GLENN BEANLAND/GETTY IMAGES ©

⭐ Entertainment

To find out what's on the calendar in Venice during your visit, check listings in free mags distributed citywide and online: **VeNews** (www.venezianews.it), **Venezia da Vivere** (www.veneziadavivere.com), and **2Venice** (www.2venice.it).

For blockbuster events like the Biennale or La Fenice operas, you'll need to book ahead online at the appropriate website or www.veniceconnected.com. Tickets may also be available at the venue box office, www.musicinvenice.com or from **HelloVenezia ticket outlets** (☎041 24 24; www.hellovenezia.it; tickets €15-20), located near key *vaporetto* stops.

CASINOS

Casinò Di Venezia   Casino

(Palazzo Vendramin-Calergi; Map p172; ☎041 529 71 11; www.casinovenezia.it; Palazzo Vendramin-Calergi 2040; admission €5, with €10 gaming-token purchase free; ⏱11am-2.30am Sun-Thu, to 3am Fri & Sat; 🚣San Marcuola) Fortunes have been won and lost since the 16th century inside this palatial casino. Slots open at 11am; to take on gaming

tables, arrive after 3.30pm wearing your jacket and poker face. Ask your hotel concierge for free-admission coupons, and take the casino's free water-taxi ride from Piazzale Roma – bargains, unless you count your losses. You must be at least 18 to enter the casino.

OPERA & CLASSICAL MUSIC

Teatro La Fenice   Opera

(Map p178; ☎041 78 65 11, tours ☎041 24 24; www.teatrolafenice.it; Campo San Fantin 1965; theatre visits adult/reduced €8.50/6, opera tickets from €40; ⏱tours 9.30am-6pm; 🚣Santa Maria dei Giglio) Tours are possible with advance booking, but the best way to see La Fenice is with the *loggione* – opera buffs who pass judgment from the top-tier cheap seats. When the opera is in recess, look for symphonies and chamber-music concerts.

Palazzetto Bru Zane   Classical Music

(Centre du Musique Romantique Française; Map p172; ☎041 521 10 05; www.bru-zane.com; Palazzetto Bru Zane 2368, San Polo; adult/reduced €25/15; ⏱box office 2.30-5.30pm Mon-Fri; 🚣San Tomà) Pleasure palaces don't get

The Dolomites

Detour:
Dolomites

The jagged peaks of the Dolomites, or Dolomiti, span the provinces of Trentino and Alto Adige, jutting into neighbouring Veneto. Europeans flock here in winter for highly hospitable resorts, sublime natural settings and extensive, well-coordinated ski networks. Come for downhill, cross-country and snowboarding or get ready for *sci alpinismo,* an adrenaline-spiking mix of skiing and mountaineering, freeride and a range of other winter adventure sports.

The **Sella Ronda**, a 40km circumnavigation of the Gruppo di Sella range (3151m, at Piz Boé) – linked by various cable cars and chairlifts – is one of the Alps' iconic ski routes. The tour takes in four passes and their surrounding valleys; Alto Adige's Val Gardena, Val Badia, Arabba (in the Veneto) and Trentino's Val di Fassa. Experienced skiers can complete the clockwise (orange) or anticlockwise (green) route in a day.

The region's two flexible passes are **Dolomiti Superski** (www.dolomitisuperski.com; high season 3-/6-day pass €144/254), covering the east, with access to 450 lifts and some 1200km of ski runs spread over 12 resorts, and **Superskirama** (www.skirama. it; 1/3/7-days €47/136/277), covering the western Brenta Dolomites, with 150 lifts, 380km of slopes and eight resorts.

more romantic than Palazetto Bru Zane on concert nights, when exquisite harmonies tickle Sebastiano Ricci angels tumbling across stucco-frosted ceilings. Multi-year restorations returned the 1695–97 Casino Zane's 100-seat music room to its original function, attracting world-class musicians to enjoy its acoustics.

🔒 Shopping

Cárte   Paper Products
(Map p178; ☎320 024 87 76; www.cartevenezia. it; Calle dei Cristi 1731, San Polo; ⊙11am-5pm Mon-Sat, to 3pm Nov-Mar; 🚤Rialto-Mercato)
Lagoon ripples swirl across marbled-paper statement necklaces and artist's portfolios, thanks to the steady hands and restless imagination of *carta marmorizzata* (marbled-paper) *maestra* Rosanna Corrò. After years restoring ancient Venetian books, Rosanna began creating her original beauties: aquatic marbled-paper cocktail rings, op-art jewellery boxes and hypnotically swirled handbags.

Chiarastella Cattana   Homewares
(Map p178; ☎041 522 43 69; www.chiarastella cattana.it; Salizada San Samuele 3357; ⊙10am-1pm & 3-7pm Mon-Sat; 🚤San Samuele)
Transform any home into a thoroughly modern *palazzo* with these locally woven, strikingly original Venetian linens. Whimsical cushions feature a chubby purple rhinoceros and grumpy scarlet elephants straight out of Pietro Longhi paintings, and hand-tasseled Venetian jacquard hand towels will dry your royal guests in style.

Gilberto Penzo   Artisanal, Boats
(Map p178; ☎041 71 93 72; www.veniceboats. com; Calle 2 dei Saoneri 2681, San Polo; ⊙9am-12.30pm & 3-6pm Mon-Sat; 👶; 🚤San Tomà)
Anyone fascinated by the models at Museo Storico Navale will go wild here, amid handmade wooden models of all kinds of Venetian boats, including some that are allegedly seaworthy (or at least bathtub worthy). Signor Penzo also creates kits so that the kids can have a crack at it themselves.

Marina e Susanna Sent
Glass

(Map p178; ☎041 520 81 36; www.marinaesusannasent.com; Campo San Vio 669; ⏱10am-1pm & 3-6.30pm Tue-Sat, 3-6.30pm Mon; ⛴Accademia) Wearable waterfalls and unpoppable soap-bubble necklaces are Venice style signatures, thanks to the Murano-born Sent sisters. Defying centuries-old beliefs that women can't handle molten glass, their minimalist art-glass statement jewellery is featured in museum stores worldwide.

ℹ Information

Tourist Office (Azienda di Promozione Turistica; ☎041 529 87 11; www.turismovenezia.it) There are several branches across town.

Marco Polo Airport **(Marco Polo airport, arrivals hall; ⏱9am-8pm)**

Piazzale Roma **(Map p172; Piazzale Roma, ground fl, multistorey car park; ⏱9.30am-2.30pm; ⛴Santa Chiara)**

Piazza San Marco **(Map p178; Piazza San Marco 71st fl; ⏱9am-7pm; ⛴San Marco)**

Stazione di Santa Lucia **(Map p172; Stazione di Santa Lucia; ⏱9am-7pm Nov-Mar, 1.30-7pm Apr-Oct; ⛴Ferrovia Santa Lucia).**

ℹ Getting There & Away

Air

Most flights arrive at and depart from Marco Polo airport (VCE; ☎041 260 92 60; www.

veniceairport.it), 12km outside Venice, east of Mestre. Ryanair also uses San Giuseppe airport (☎042 231 51 11; www.trevisoairport.it), about 5km southwest of Treviso and a 30km, one-hour drive from Venice.

ℹ Getting Around

To/From the Airport

Boat

Alilaguna (☎041 240 17 01; www.alilaguna.com; Marco Polo airport) operates several lines that link the airport with various parts of Venice, including the Linea Blu (Blue Line, with stops at Lido, San Marco, Stazione Marittima and various points in between), the Linea Rossa (Red Line, with stops at Murano and Lido) and Linea Arancio (Orange Line, with stops at Stazione Santa Lucia, Rialto and San Marco via the Grand Canal). Boats to Venice cost €15 and leave from the airport ferry dock (an eight-minute walk from the terminal).

Bus

ATVO (Azienda Trasporti Veneto Orientale; ☎0421 59 46 71; www.atvo.it) buses run to the airport from Piazzale Roma (€6, one hour, every 30 minutes 8am to midnight).

Vaporetto

The city's main mode of public transport is *vaporetto* – Venice's distinctive water bus. Tickets can be purchased from the HelloVenezia (☎041 24 24; www.hellovenezia.it) ticket booths at most landing stations. You can also buy tickets

Trains To/From Venice

Prompt, affordable, scenic and environmentally savvy, trains are the preferred transport option to and from Venice. Trains run frequently to Venice's Stazione Santa Lucia (signed as Ferrovia within Venice). In addition, there are direct InterCity services to major points in France, Germany, Austria and Slovenia.

TO	FARE (€)	DURATION (HR)	FREQUENCY (PER HR)
Florence	26-45	2-3	1-2
Milan	19-38	2½-3½	2-3
Naples	64-123	5½-9	1
Padua	3.50	½-1	3-4
Rome	46-80	3½-6	1-2
Verona	7.50	1¾	3-4

Vaporetto dell'Arte

New in 2012, this **vaporetto** (041 24 24; www.vaporettoarte.com; every 30 min 9am-7pm) provides a luxurious hop-on, hop-off ride down the Grand Canal. Unlike the public *vaporetti,* which can be jam-packed, the Vaporetto dell'Arte offers seating in plush red armchairs complete with seat-back monitors screening multilingual information about the attractions en route. Most people don't bother with these, as the view out the windows is far more arresting.

To get the best value from the service, buy the ticket in conjunction with your Venice Card, when the +ARTE add-on will only set you back €10. The ticket will then be valid for the same length of time as your Venice Card.

when boarding; you may be charged double with luggage, though this is not always enforced.

Instead of spending €7 for a one-way ticket, consider a Venice Card, which is a timed pass for unlimited travel (beginning when you first validate it). Passes for 12/24/36/48/72 hours cost €18/20/25/30/35. A week-long pass costs €60. Swipe your card every time you board, even if you have already validated it upon initial boarding.

Water Taxis

The standard **water taxi** (Consorzio Motoscafi Venezia; Map p178; 041 240 67 11, 24hr 041 522 23 03; www.motoscafivenezia.it) between Marco Polo airport and Venice costs €110 one way and €32 per person in a shared taxi. Official rates start at €8.90 plus €1.80 per minute, plus €6 if they're called to your hotel and more for night trips, luggage and large groups. Prices can be metered or negotiated in advance.

Glass on display, Murano (p189)

THE VENETO

Verona

Shakespeare placed star-crossed lovers Romeo Montague and Juliet Capulet in Verona for good reason: romance, drama and fatal family feuding have been the city's hallmark for centuries. From the 3rd century BC Verona was a Roman trade centre with ancient gates, a forum (now Piazza delle Erbe) and a grand Roman arena, which still serves as one of the world's great opera venues. In the Middle Ages the city flourished under the wrathful Scaligeri clan, who were as much energetic patrons of the arts as they were murderous tyrants. Their elaborate Gothic tombs, the **Arche Scaligere**, are just off Piazza dei Signori.

Under Cangrande I (1308–28) Verona conquered Padua and Vicenza, with Dante, Petrarch and Giotto benefitting from the city's patronage. But the fratricidal rage of Cangrande II (1351–59)

complicated matters, and the Scaligeri were run out of town in 1387.

The city became a Fascist control centre from 1938 to 1945, a key location for Resistance interrogation and transit point for Italian Jews sent to Nazi concentration camps. Today, as the city grapples with its changing identity as an international commercial centre, it has become a Lega Nord (Northern League) stronghold. Yet the city is a Unesco World Heritage Site and a cosmopolitan crossroads, especially in summer when the 2000-year-old arena hosts opera's biggest names.

◎ Sights

Museo di Castelvecchio Museum
(☎045 806 26 11; Corso Castelvecchio 2; adult/reduced €6/4.50, or with VeronaCard; ◷8.30am-7.30pm Tue-Sun, 1.30-7.30pm Mon) Bristling with battlements along the River Adige, Castelvecchio was built in the 1350s by Cangrande II. The fortress was so severely damaged by Napoleon and then WWII bombings that many feared it was beyond repair. But instead of erasing the past with restorations, Carlo Scarpa reinvented the building, constructing bridges over exposed foundations, filling gaping holes with glass panels, and balancing a statue of Cangrande I above the courtyard on a concrete gangplank.

Basilica di San Zeno Maggiore Basilica
(www.chieseverona.it; Piazza San Zeno; adult/child €2.50/free, combined Verona church ticket €6 or with VeronaCard; ◷8.30am-6pm Tue-Sat, 12.30-6pm Sun Mar-Oct, 10am-1pm & 1.30-5pm Tue-Sat, 12.30-5pm Sun Nov-Feb) A masterpiece of Romanesque architecture, the striped brick and stone

Casa di Giulietta (p202), Verona
JOHN FREEMAN/GETTY IMAGES ©

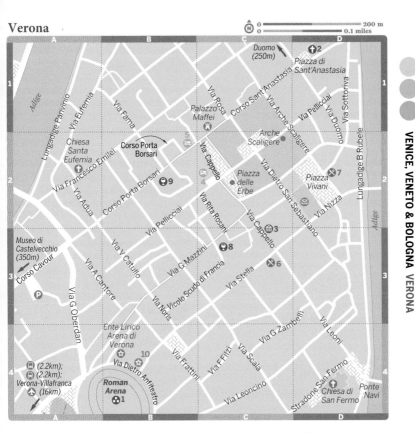

Verona

0 _____ 200 m
0 _____ 0.1 miles

basilica was built in honour of the city's patron saint. Enter through the flower-filled cloister into the nave – a vast space lined with 12th- to 15th-century frescoes. Painstaking restoration has revived Mantegna's 1457–59 *Majesty of the Virgin* altarpiece, painted with such astonishing perspective that you actually believe there are garlands of fresh fruit hanging behind the Madonna's throne.

Duomo   Cathedral
(📞045 59 28 13; www.chieseverona.it; Piazza Duomo; adult/reduced €2.50/2, or with Verona Card; ⏰10am-5.30pm Mon-Sat, 1.30-5.30pm Sun Mar-Oct, 10am-1pm & 1.30-5pm Tue-Sat, 1.30-5pm Sun Nov-Feb) Verona's 12th-century cathedral is a striking, striped Romanesque building, with bug-eyed statues

of Charlemagne's paladins Roland and Oliver, crafted by medieval master Nicolò, on the west porch. Nothing about this sober facade hints at the extravagant 16th- to 17th-century frescoed interior with angels aloft amid *trompe l'œil* architecture. At the left end of the nave is the **Cartolari-Nichesola Chapel**, designed by Renaissance master Jacopo Sansovino and featuring a vibrant Titian *Assumption*.

Basilica di Sant'Anastasia   Basilica

(www.chieseverona.it; Piazza di Sant'Anastasia; adult/reduced €6/2, or with VeronaCard; ⊙9am-6pm Tue-Sat, 1-6pm Sun Mar-Oct, 1.30-5pm Tue-Sat, 1-5pm Sun Nov-Feb) Dating from the 13th to 15th centuries, the Gothic Chiesa di Sant'Anastasia is Verona's largest church and a showcase for local art. The multitude of frescoes is overwhelming, but don't overlook Pisanello's storybook-quality fresco *St George Setting out to Free the Princess from the Dragon* in the **Pisanelli Chapel**, or the 1495 holy water font featuring a hunchback carved by Paolo Veronese's father, Gabriele Caliari.

🛏 Sleeping

Cooperativa Albergatori Veronesi (☎045 800 98 44; www.veronabooking.com) offers a no-fee booking service for two-star hotels. For homestyle stays outside the city centre, check **Verona Bed & Breakfast** (www.bedandbreakfastverona.com).

Albergo Aurora   Hotel €€

(☎045 59 47 17; www.hotelaurora.biz; Piazza XIV Novembre 2; s €90-135, d €100-160; ❄) Right off bustling Piazza delle Erbe yet cosy and blissfully quiet, this hotel has spacious, unfussy doubles, some with city views. There are cheaper single rooms with shared bathroom (€58 to €80). Head to the sunny terrace for drinks overlooking the piazza.

Hotel Gabbia d'Oro   Hotel €€€

(☎045 59 02 93; www.hotelgabbiadoro.it; Corso Porta Borsari 4a; d from €220; P❄@🤝) One of the city's top addresses and also one of its most romantic, the Gabbia d'Oro features luxe rooms inside an 18th-century *palazzo* that manage to be both elegant and cosy. The rooftop terrace and central location are icing on the wedding cake.

🍴 Eating

La Taverna di Via Stella   Veronese €€

(☎045 800 80 08; www.tavernadiviastella.com; Via Stella 5c; meals €20-30; ⊙11.30am-2.30pm & 6.30-11pm Thu-Sun & Tue, 11.30am-2.30pm Mon) Brush past the haunches of prosciutto dangling over the deli bar and make your way into a dining room, decorated Tiepolo-style with rustic murals of chivalric knights and maidens. This is the place you'll want to sample traditional Veronese

Romeo & Juliet in Verona

Shakespeare had no idea what he'd start when he set his tale of star-crossed lovers in Verona, but the city has seized the commercial possibilities with both hands – everything from *osterie* (taverns) and hotels to embroidered kitchen aprons get the R&J branding. While the play's depiction of feuding families has genuine provenance, the lead characters themselves are fictional. Undaunted, in the 1930s the authorities settled on a house in Via Cappello (think Capulet) as Juliet's and added a 14th-century-style balcony and a bronze statue of our heroine. You can squeeze through the crowds at **Casa di Giulietta** (Juliet's House; ☎045 803 43 03; Via Cappello 23; adult/reduced €6/4.50, or with VeronaCard; ⊙8.30am-7.30pm Tue-Sun, 1.30-7.30pm Mon) onto the balcony itself, or see the circus from the square below, a spot framed by a slew of scribbled love graffiti.

ALDO PAVAN/GETTY IMAGES ©

⭐ Don't Miss
Roman Arena

This Roman-era arena, built of pink-tinged marble in the 1st century AD, survived a 12th-century earthquake to become Verona's legendary open-air opera house, with seating for 30,000 people. You can visit the arena year-round, though it's at its best during the June-to-August opera season. The **ticket office** (📞045 800 51 51; Via Dietro Anfiteatro 6b) is just outside.

NEED TO KNOW

📞045 800 32 04; www.arena.it; Piazza Brà; opera tickets €21-220, adult/reduced €6/4.50, or with VeronaCard; ⏰8.30am-7.30pm Tue-Sun, 1.30-7.30pm Mon; 🚻

dishes such as *pastissada* (horse stew), bigoli with duck *ragù* and DOP Lessinia cheeses from Monte Veronese.

Pescheria I Masenini Seafood €€€
(📞045 929 80 15; www.imasenini.com; Piazzetta Pescheria 9; meals €50; ⏰12.30-2pm Wed-Sun, 7.30-10pm Tue-Sun) Located on the piazza where Verona's Roman fish market once held sway, Masenini quietly serves up Verona's most imaginative, modern fish dishes. Mullet tartare comes in a fresh tomato and basil purée, octopus is roasted with broccoli and anchovies, and scallops come gratinated with baked endives.

🍷 Drinking & Nightlife

Osteria del Bugiardo Wine Bar
(📞045 59 18 69; Corso Porta Borsari 17a; ⏰11am-11pm, to midnight Fri & Sat) On busy Corso Porta Borsari, traffic converges at Bugiardo for glasses of upstanding Valpolicella bottled specifically for the *osteria*. Polenta and *sopressa* make worthy bar snacks for the powerhouse Amarone.

Antica Bottega del Vino Wine Bar
(📞045 800 45 35; www.bottegavini.it; Vicolo Scudo di Francia 3; 3 tasting plates €27;

203

Detour:
Padua

Though under an hour from Venice, Padua seems a world away with its medieval marketplaces, Fascist-era facades and hip student population.

In **Cappella degli Scrovegni** (☎049 201 00 20; www.cappelladegliscrovegni.it; Piazza Eremitani 8; adult/reduced €13/8; ☺9am-7pm Mon, to 10pm Tue-Sun Mar-Oct, 9am-7pm Nov-Dec, by reservation only), Dante, da Vinci and Vasari all honour Giotto as the artist who ended the Dark Ages with his 1303–05 frescoes. Giotto's moving, modern approach changed how people saw themselves: not as lowly vassals but as vessels for the divine, however flawed.

Anywhere else the fresco cycle of the **Oratorio di San Giorgio** (Piazza del Santo; admission €4; ☺9am-12.30pm & 2.30-5pm Oct-Mar, to 7pm Apr-Sep) and the Titian paintings in the upstairs Scoletta del Santo would be considered highlights, but in Padua they must contend with Giotto's Scrovegni brilliance, meaning you're likely to have them to yourself.

South of the *palazzo* is the city's cathedral, built from a much altered design of Michelangelo's and completely upstaged by the adjoining 13th-century **baptistry** (☎049 65 69 14; adult/child €2.80/1; ☺10am-6pm).

Hidden under an ancient portico, airy and modern **Godenda** (☎049 877 41 92; www.godenda.it; Via Squarcione 4/6; meals €25-40; ☺10am-3pm & 6pm-2am Mon-Sat) is a local foodies' favourite.

Train is the easiest way to reach Padua from Venice (€4 to €19.50, 25 to 50 minutes, three or four per hour) or Verona (€6 to €18, 40 to 90 minutes, two or three per hour).

☺noon-11pm) Wine is the primary consideration at this historic, wood-panelled wine bar. The sommelier will gladly recommend a worthy vintage for your lobster *crudo* salad, Amarone risotto or suckling pig – some of the best wines here are bottled specifically for the bottega.

ℹ Information

Tourist Office (www.tourism.verona.it) At the airport (☎045 861 91 63; Verona-Villafranca airport; ☺10am-4pm Mon & Tue, to 5pm Wed-Sat) and on Via degli Alpini (☎045 806 86 80; Via degli Alpini 9; ☺9am-7pm Mon-Sat, 10am-4pm Sun). Extremely knowledgeable and helpful.

ℹ Getting There & Around

Air

Verona-Villafranca airport (p141) is 12km outside town and accessible by ATV Aerobus to/from the train station (€6, 15 minutes, every 20 minutes 6.30am to 11.30pm). A taxi costs €30. Flights arrive from all over Italy and some European cities, including Amsterdam, Barcelona, Berlin, Brussels, Dusseldorf, London and Paris.

Train

There are at least three trains hourly to Venice (€7.50 to €23, 1¼ to 2½ hours), Padua (€6 to €18, 40 to 90 minutes) and Vicenza (€4.70 to €16, 30 minutes to one hour). There are also regular services to Milan (€11.50 to €21.50, 1½ to two hours) and Florence (€24 to €57, 1½ to three hours) and points south, as well as direct international services to Austria and Germany.

BOLOGNA

Fusing haughty elegance with down-to-earth grit in one beautifully colonnaded medieval grid, Bologna is a city of two halves. On one side is a hard-working, hi-tech city located in the super-rich Po valley where suave opera-goers waltz out of regal theatres and reconvene in some of the nation's finest restaurants. On the other is a Bolshie, politically edgy city that hosts the world's oldest university and is famous for its graffiti-embellished piazzas filled with mildly inebriated students swapping gothic fashion tips. No small wonder Bologna has earned so many monikers. *La Grassa* (the fat one) celebrates a rich food legacy (*ragù* or bolognese sauce was first concocted here). *La Dotta* (the learned one) doffs a cap to the city university founded in 1088. *La Rossa* (the red one) alludes to the ubiquity of the terracotta medieval buildings adorned with miles of porticoes, as well as the city's longstanding penchant for left-wing politics. All three names still ring true. Bologna is the kind of city where you can be discussing Chomsky with a newspaper-seller one minute, and be eating like an erstwhile Italian king in a fine restaurant the next.

◉ Sights

PIAZZA MAGGIORE & AROUND

Fontana del Nettuno   Fountain
(Neptune's Fountain; Piazza del Nettuno) Adjacent to Piazza Maggiore, Piazza del Nettuno owes its name to this explicit bronze statue sculpted by Giambologna in 1566. Beneath the muscled sea god, four cherubs represent the winds, and four buxom sirens, water spouting from every nipple, symbolise the four known continents of the pre-Oceania world.

**Museo della
Storia di Bologna**   Museum
(✐ 051 1993 6370; Via Castiglione 8; admission €10; ◷10am-7pm Tue-Sun) Walk in a historical neophyte and walk out an A-grade honours student in Bologna's golden past. This magnificent new interactive museum skilfully encased in the regal Palazzo Pepoli is – in a word – an 'education'.

Using a 3-D film, a mock-up of an old Roman canal, and super-modern presentations of ancient relics, the innovative displays start in a futuristic open-plan lobby and progress through 34

Palazzo Comunale (p207), Bologna

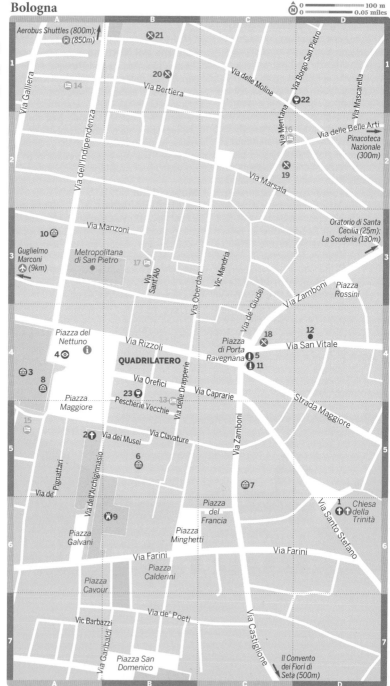

Aerobus Shuttles (800m); (850m)

21

20
Via Bertiera

Via delle Moline

Via Galliera

Via dell'Indipendenza

14

Via delle Belle Arti

22

Pinacoteca Nazionale (300m)

19
Via Marsala

Via Manzoni

10

Guglielmo Marconi (9km)

Metropolitana di San Pietro

17

Via Sant'Alò

Via Oberdan

Vic Mandria

Via de' Giudei

Via Zamboni

Piazza Rossini

Oratorio di Santa Cecilia (25m); La Scuderia (130m)

12
Via San Vitale

Piazza del Nettuno

Via Rizzoli

4

QUADRILATERO

Piazza di Porta Ravegnana

18

5
11

3

8

Via Orefici

Via delle Drapperie

Via Caprarie

Strada Maggiore

Piazza Maggiore

23
Pescherie Vecchie

13

15

2
Via dei Musei

Via Clavature

Via Zamboni

6

7

Via dell'Archiginnasio

Via de Pignattari

9

Piazza del Francia

Piazza Galvani

Piazza Minghetti

1
Chiesa della Trinità

Via Santo Stefano

Via Farini

Piazza Calderini

Via Farini

Piazza Cavour

Vic Barbazzi

Via de' Poeti

Via Garibaldi

Via Castiglione

Piazza San Domenico

Il Convento dei Fiori di Seta (500m)

Bologna

chronologically themed rooms that make Bologna's 2500-year history at once engaging and epic.

Palazzo Comunale   Art Gallery

(Piazza Maggiore; ⊙ galleries 9am-6.30pm Tue-Fri, 10am-6.30pm Sat & Sun) FREE The palace that forms the western flank of Piazza Maggiore has been home to Bologna city council since 1336. A salad of architectural styles, it owes much of its current look to makeovers in the 15th and 16th centuries.

The statue of Pope Gregory XIII, the Bolognese prelate responsible for the Gregorian calendar, was placed above the main portal in 1580, while inside, Donato Bramante's 16th-century staircase was designed to allow horse-drawn carriages to ride directly up to the 1st floor.

On the 2nd floor you'll find the *palazzo's* **Collezioni Comunali d'Arte** (☏ 051 20 36 29; adult/reduced/child €5/3/free; ⊙ 9am-6.30pm Tue-Fri, 10am-6.30pm Sat & Sun) with its interesting collection of 13th- to 19th-century paintings, sculpture and furniture.

Outside the *palazzo,* three large panels bear photos of hundreds of partisans killed in the resistance to German occupation, many on this very spot.

Palazzo Fava   Gallery

(☏ 051 1993 6305; www.genusbononiae.it; Via Manzoni 2; admission €10; ⊙ 10am-7pm Tue-Sun) This astounding museum is an exposition space encased in a Renaissance mansion given over primarily to temporary art.

The biggest draw, however, is the heavily frescoed rooms on the 1st floor painted in bright naturalistic style by the precocious young Carraccis (two brothers and a cousin) in the 1580s. There's a lovely cafe on site.

Basilica di San Petronio   Church

(Piazza Maggiore; ⊙ 8am-1pm & 3-6pm) The world's fifth-largest church, measuring 132m by 66m by 47m, hides some interesting oddities. Firstly, though construction started in 1390, the church wasn't consecrated (officially blessed) until 1954. Secondly, it has been the target of two thwarted terrorist attacks, in 2002 and 2006. Thirdly, the church exhibits an unusual scientific intrusion into a religious setting: inside, a huge sundial stretches 67.7m down the eastern aisle. Designed in 1656 by Gian Cassini and Domenico Guglielmi, the sundial was instrumental in discovering the anomalies of the Julian calendar and led to the creation of the leap year.

Lastly, take a look at the incomplete front facade and you'll quickly deduce that the church was never finished. Originally it was intended to be larger than St Peter's in Rome, but in 1561, some 169 years after building had started, Pope Pius IV blocked construction by commissioning a new university on the basilica's eastern flank. If you walk along Via dell'Archiginnasio you can see semiconstructed apses poking out oddly.

Below: Spaghetti dish
Right: Grocery shop, Bologna
(BELOW) RHKAMEN/GETTY IMAGES ©; (RIGHT) SABINE SCHECKEL/GETTY IMAGES ©

Quadrilatero — Historic Quarter

To the east of Piazza Maggiore, the grid of streets around Via Clavature (Street of Locksmiths) sits on what was once Roman Bologna. Known as the Quadrilatero, this compact district is less shabby than the adjoining university quarter, with the emphasis on old-style delis selling the region's world-famous produce, including *aceto balsamico di Modena* (aged balsamic vinegar from Modena).

SOUTH & WEST OF PIAZZA MAGGIORE

Museo Civico Archeologico — Museum

(Via dell'Archiginnasio 2; adult/reduced/child €5/3/free; ⏰9am-3pm Tue-Fri, 10am-6.30pm Sat & Sun) Impressive in its breadth of coverage of historical eras, this museum displays well-documented Egyptian and Roman artefacts along with one of Italy's best Etruscan collections.

Palazzo dell' Archiginnasio — Museum

(Piazza Galvani 1) FREE The result of Pope Pius IV's project to curtail the Basilica di San Petronio, this palace was the seat of the city university from 1563 to 1805. Today it houses Bologna's 700,000-volume **Biblioteca Comunale** (Municipal Library; ⏰9am-6.45pm Mon-Fri, 9am-1.45pm Sat) and the fascinating 17th-century **Teatro Anatomico** (⏰9am-6.45pm Mon-Fri, to 1.45pm Sat), where public body dissections were held under the sinister gaze of an Inquisition priest, ready to intervene if proceedings became too spiritually compromising.

San Colombano – Collezione Tagliavini — Museum

(☎051 1993 6366; www.genusbononiae.it; Via Parigi 5; admission €10; ⏰10am-1pm & 3-7pm Tue-Sun) A beautifully – repeat *beautifully* – restored church with original frescoes and a medieval crypt rediscovered in 2007, the San Colombano hosts a wonderful collection of over 80 musical instruments

amassed by the octogenarian organist, Luigi Tagliavini. Many of the assembled harpsichords, pianos and oboes date from the 1500s and, even more surprisingly, are still in full working order.

UNIVERSITY QUARTER

Bolshie graffiti, communist newspaper-sellers and the whiff of last night's beer characterise the scruffy but strangely contagious streets of the university quarter, the site of Bologna's former Jewish ghetto.

Le Due Torri   Tower

(Piazza di Porta Ravegnana; Torre degli Asinelli admission €3; ⏱10am-12.30pm & 3.30-6.45pm) Standing sentinel over Piazza di Porta Ravegnana, Bologna's two leaning towers are the city's main symbol. The taller of the two, the 97.6m-high **Torre degli Asinelli** (admission €3; ⏱9am-6pm, to 5pm Oct-May) is open to the public, although it's not advisable for vertigo-sufferers or owners of arthritic knees (there are 498 steps up a semi-exposed wooden staircase).

Abbazia di Santo Stefano   Church

(www.abbaziasantostefano.it; Via Santo Stefano 24; ⏱10am-12.30pm & 3.30-6.45pm) Not *just* another church, the Santo Stefano is a rather unique (and atmospheric) medieval religious complex. Originally there were seven churches – hence the basilica's nickname Sette Chiese – but only four remain.

Entry is via the 11th-century **Chiesa del Crocefisso**, which houses the bones of San Petronio and leads through to the **Chiesa del Santo Sepolcro**. This austere octagonal structure probably started life as a baptistery. Next door, the **Cortile di Pilato** is named after the central basin in which Pontius Pilate is said to have washed his hands after condemning Christ to death. In fact, it's an 8th-century Lombard artefact. Beyond the courtyard, the **Chiesa della Trinità** connects to a modest cloister and a small **museum**. The fourth church, the **Santi Vitale e Agricola**, is the city's oldest. Incorporating recycled Roman masonry and carvings, the bulk of the building dates from the 11th century. The

209

ELLEN ROONEY/GETTY IMAGES ©

⭐ Don't Miss
Basilica Santuario della Madonna di San Luca

About 3.5km southwest of Bologna city centre, this hilltop church occupies a powerful and appropriately celestial position overlooking the teeming red-hued city below. The church houses a representation of the Virgin Mary, supposedly painted by St Luke and transported from the Middle East to Bologna in the 12th century. The 18th-century sanctuary is connected to the city walls by the world's longest portico, held aloft by 666 arches, beginning at Piazza di Porta Saragozza. Take bus 20 from the city centre to Villa Spada, from where you can continue by minibus to the sanctuary. Alternatively, continue one more stop on bus 20 to the Meloncello arch and walk the remaining 2km under the arches.

NEED TO KNOW
Via di San Luca 36; ⊘7am-12.30pm & 2.30-7pm Apr-Sep, to 5pm Oct-Feb, to 6pm Mar

considerably older tombs of two saints in the side aisles once served as altars.

Oratorio di Santa Cecilia Church
(Via Zamboni 15; ⊘10am-1pm & 2-6pm) One of Bologna's unsung gems. Inside, the magnificent 16th-century frescoes by Lorenzo Costa depicting the life and Technicolor death of St Cecilia and her husband Valeriano are in remarkably good nick, their colours vibrant and their imagery bold and unabashed. The Oratorio hosts regular

free chamber music recitals. Check the board outside for upcoming events.

Pinacoteca Nazionale Art Gallery
(Via delle Belle Arti 56; admission €4; ⊘9am-1.30pm Tue-Wed, 9am-7pm Thu, 2-7pm Fri-Sun) The city's main art gallery has a powerful collection of works by Bolognese artists from the 14th century onwards, including a number of important canvases by the late-16th-century Carracci cousins Ludovico, Agostino and Annibale.

Tours

Various outfits offer guided, two-hour walking tours in English (€13). Groups assemble outside the main tourist office on Piazza Maggiore (no booking required).

La Chiocciola　　　　Walking Tour
(☎051 22 09 64; www.bolognawelcome.com/guida-turistica; Via San Vitale 22) Authorised guiding group that offers walking tours of the city.

City Red Bus　　　　Bus Tour
(www.cityredbus.com) Runs an hour-long, hop-on, hop-off bus tour of the city departing from the train station several times daily. Tickets (€12) can be bought on board.

Sleeping

Accommodation in Bologna is geared to the business market, with a glut of mid-range to top-end hotels in the convention zone to the north of the city.

Hotel University Bologna　Hotel €
(☎051 22 97 13; www.hoteluniversitybologna.com; Via Mentana 7; s/d €61/75; ❄@😊) Remember student digs? Well, heave a sigh of relief, they were nothing like this. It's good to see that the world's oldest university town can still muster up a hotel that's not a million miles beyond the price range of its large undergraduate population. The HU Bologna is billed as a three-star, but it's recently renovated and punches well above its weight.

Albergo delle Drapperie　Hotel €
(☎051 22 39 55; www.albergodrapperie.com; Via delle Drapperie 5; s/d €70/85; ❄😊) Right in the heart of the atmospheric Quadrilatero district, the Drapperie is one of those 'hidden' hotels encased in the upper floors of a larger building. Buzz in at ground level and climb the stairs to discover 21 attractive rooms with wood-beamed ceilings, the occasional brick arch and colourful ceiling frescoes. Breakfast is €5 extra.

Hotel Orologio　　Design Hotel €€
(☎051 745 74 11; www.bolognarthotels.it; Via IV Novembre 10; r from €140; P❄@😊) One of four upmarket hotels run by Bologna Art Hotels, this refined pile just off Piazza Maggiore seduces guests with its slick service, smart rooms furnished in elegant gold, blue and burgundy, swirling grey-and-white marble bathrooms, complimentary chocs and an unbeatable downtown location.

Hotel Metropolitan　Boutique Hotel €€€
(☎051 22 93 93; www.hotelmetropolitan.com; Via dell'Orso 6; r from €140; ❄@😊) Providing another lesson in Italian interior design, the Met doesn't miss a trick. It mixes functionality with handsome modern furnishings and finishes everything off with an all-pervading Thai-Buddhist theme, presumably to inject a bit of peace and tranquillity into its frenetic city-centre location. It works.

Prendiparte B&B　　　B&B €€€
(☎051 58 90 23; www.prendiparte.it; Via Sant'Alò 7; r from €350) You will never stay anywhere else like this. Forget the B&B tag: you don't just get a room here, you get an entire 900-year-old tower (Bologna's second tallest). The living area (bedroom, kitchen and lounge) is spread over three floors and there are nine more levels to explore, with a 17th-century prison halfway up and outstanding views from the terrace up top.

Il Convento dei Fiori di Seta　Boutique Hotel €€€
(☎051 27 20 39; www.silkflowersnunnery.com; Via Orfeo 34; r €140-420, ste €250-520; ❄😊) Before you get to Bologna's budget options, you have to gawp at all the pricey places, including this chic boutique hotel housed in a 14th-century convent. Religious-inspired frescoes sit alongside Mapplethorpe-style flower photos and snazzy modern light fixtures; beds come with linen sheets and bathrooms feature cool mosaic tiles.

Eating

Osteria dell'Orsa
Italian €

(☎051 23 15 76; www.osteriadellorsa.com; Via Mentana 1; meals €22-25; ⏰noon-midnight) If you were to make a list of the great wonders of Italy, hidden amid Venice's canals and Rome's Colosseum would be cheap, pretension-free *osterie* like Osteria dell'Orsa, where the food is serially sublime and the prices are giveaway cheap. So what if the waiter's wearing an AC Milan shirt and the wine is served in a water glass?

Trattoria del Rosso
Trattoria €

(☎051 23 67 30; www.trattoriadelrosso.com; Via A Righi 30; mains €7.50-10; ⏰noon-11pm) You don't have to pay big euros to eat well in Bologna. Doubters should step inside the Rosso, where unfancy decor and quick service attract plenty of hard-up single diners enjoying pop-by lunches. They say that the trattoria is the oldest in the city, proof that ancient formulas work best.

Gelateria Gianni
Gelato €

(www.gelateriagianni.com; Via San Vitale 2; ⏰noon-10pm) Edging Italy's most ubiquitous ice cream chain, Grom, into third place is this ice-cream temple where generous dollops of flavours such as white chocolate and cherry have brought a sweet ending to many an undergraduate date night.

Trattoria dal Biassanot
Trattoria €€

(☎051 23 06 44; www.dalbiassanot.it; Via Piella 16a; meals from €25; ⏰noon-2.30pm & 7-10.30pm Tue-Sat, noon-2.30pm Sun) The waiters in bow ties suggest an underlying grandiosity, but the Biassanot is about as down to earth as its earthy menu, which lists such rustic throwbacks as wild boar, goat, and veal with balsamic vinegar and mushrooms. Get in early: the check-clothed tables get busy. The pear *torta* and hot custard dessert round off proceedings very nicely.

Drinking & Nightlife

La Scuderia
Bar, Cafe

(www.lascuderia.bo.it; Piazza Verdi 2; ⏰8am-2.30am; ☎) Located on Piazza Verdi, the shabby-chic Scuderia envelops the whole square on a good night. This being Bologna, the clientele is made up of a socialist republic of pavement loungers, hairy Goths, down-but-not-quite-out students, and the odd stray opera-goer swept up in the nostalgia of their undergraduate days.

The bar occupies the Bentivoglio family's former stables and features towering columns, vaulted ceilings and arty photos.

Piazza Maggiore (p205), Bologna
RUTH EASTHAM & MAX PAOLI/GETTY IMAGES ©

Le Stanze
Wine Bar

(www.lestanzecafe.com; Via Borgo San Pietro 1; ⏲11am-3am Mon-Sat) If La Scuderia reeks of undergraduate days you'd rather forget, hit the more chic Le Stanze, a former chapel where each of the four interior rooms has its own design concept. The *aperitivo* buffet is top-notch here, with paellas, pastas and chicken drumsticks to accompany your wine or cocktail.

Osteria del Sole
Bar

(www.osteriadelsole.it; Vicolo Ranocchi 1d; ⏲10.30am-9.30pm Mon-Sat) Welcome to a rather pleasant form of chaos! The sign outside this ancient Quadrilatero dive bar tells you all you need to know – '*vino*' (wine). It's as simple as that.

ℹ Information

Tourist Office (www.bolognaturismo.info; Piazza Maggiore 1e; ⏲9am-7pm) Also offices at the airport and in the train station.

ℹ Getting There & Away

Air

Bologna's Guglielmo Marconi airport (☏051 647 96 15; www.bologna-airport.it) is 8km northwest of the city. It's served by over two dozen airlines including easyJet (daily flights to Gatwick) and Ryanair (daily flights to Stansted).

Train

Bologna is a major transport junction for northern Italy. The high-speed train to Florence (€24) takes only 37 minutes. Rome (€56, two hours 20 minutes) and Milan (regional €15.85, 2¼ hours; Eurostar €40, one hour) also offer quick links.

Frequent trains from Bologna serve cities throughout Emilia-Romagna.

ℹ Getting Around

To/From the Airport

Aerobus shuttles (www.atc.bo.it) depart from the main train station for Guglielmo Marconi airport every 15 to 30 minutes between 5.30am and 11.10pm. The 20-minute journey costs €5 (tickets can be bought on board).

Culinary Bologna & Veneto

RECOMMENDATIONS FROM ALESSANDRA SPISNI, CHEF, COOKING TEACHER AND FOOD WRITER

1 LESSER-KNOWN SPECIALITIES

Look out for highly prized Marroni di Castel Del Rio chestnuts and truffles from Savigno. In the *artisan salumerie* (delis) of Bologna and its province, don't pass up the chance to sample *salame rosa* (pink salami). It might look like *mortadella*, but it's actually prepared like regular salami then steam-cooked.

2 REGIONAL WINES

The vineyards around Modena, Reggio Emilia and Piacenza produce excellent lambrusco, and much of Romagna is celebrated for its sangiovese. The Colli Bolognesi (Bolognese Hills) produce wonderful merlot and, my personal favourite, cabernet. The latter goes perfectly with our regional dishes, whether it's *brodo da tortellini* (broth with tortellini pasta), lasagne or a fragrant *arrosto* (roast). In neighbouring Veneto, fine wines include Amarone, Valpolicella red, the lemon-zesty Soave Classico and the nutty Recioto di Soave (the latter two are whites). Emilia-Romagna's wines tend to be lighter than their Veneto counterparts.

3 GASTRONOMIC TOWNS

Top of the list is Bologna, not to mention Venice, home to the wonderfully historic Pescaria and Rialto Market, the latter operating in one form or another for 1000 years.

4 COOKING COURSES

One of the best ways to experience Italian culture is through food, and a cooking course offers both a fun window into the country and an investment in interesting future meals!

Florence, Tuscany & Umbria

When your ears hear the word 'Italy', the mind ditches work and heads to Tuscany. Leaning towers, Michelangelo's stark-naked *David*, and – oh yes – Florentine steak on the bone, washed down with some unforgettable red, all while debating Dante. Human imaginations have been captivated for centuries by Tuscany's Renaissance masterminds, who established an Italian and international ideal with sublime architectural proportions, radical notions that we now call science, and art that raises eyebrows and empties tear ducts. Amazingly, this idealistic outlook was achieved not on a sunny day in Chianti, but through generations of plague and turf warfare. Happily, the region's city-states recovered and quit fighting – now they just compete for your attention. If your perfect dreamscape involves Spoleto performance poetry instead of Florentine sculpture, Umbrian truffles instead of steak, and Orvieto white wine instead of Tuscan reds, Umbria awaits next door to Tuscany. Michelangelo won't take it personally.

Duomo (p228), Florence

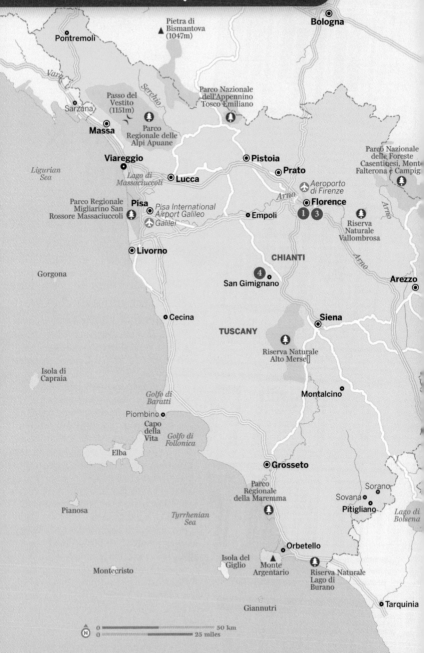

Florence, Tuscany & Umbria

Pontremoli

Pietra di
Bismantova
(1047m)

Bologna

Vara

Passo del
Vestito
(1151m)

Sarzana

Parco Nazionale
dell'Appennino
Tosco Emiliano

Serchio

Massa

Parco
Regionale delle
Alpi Apuane

Parco Nazionale
delle Foreste
Casentinesi, Monte
Falterona e Campig

Viareggio

Pistoia

Prato

Ligurian
Sea

Lago di
Massaciuccoli

Lucca

Aeroporto
di Firenze

Arno

Riserva
Naturale
Vallombrosa

Arno

Parco Regionale
Migliarino San
Rossore Massaciuccoli

Pisa

Pisa International
Airport Galileo
Galilei

Florence

1 **3**

Empoli

Livorno

Gorgona

CHIANTI

4

San Gimignano

Arezzo

Arno

Cecina

TUSCANY

Siena

Isola di
Capraia

Riserva Naturale
Alto Merse

Golfo di
Baratti

Montalcino

Piombino

Capo
della
Vita

Golfo di
Follonica

Elba

Pianosa

Tyrrhenian
Sea

Grosseto

Parco
Regionale
della Maremma

Sorano

Sovana

Pitigliano

Lago di
Bolsena

Montecristo

Isola del
Giglio

Monte
Argentario

Orbetello

Riserva Naturale
Lago di
Burano

Tarquinia

Giannutri

N

0   50 km
0   25 miles

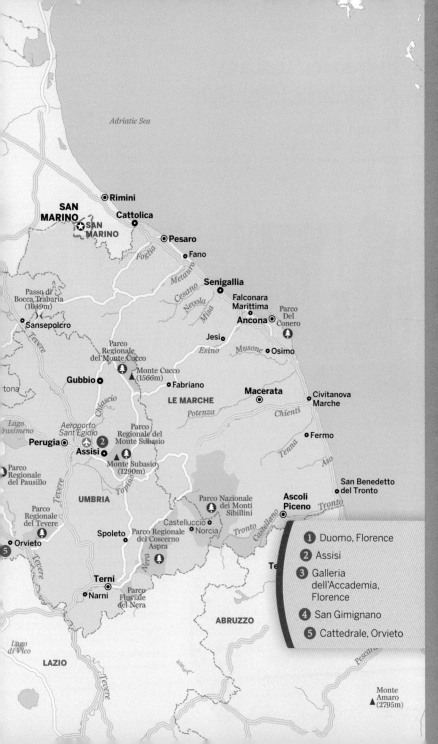

Adriatic Sea

●Rimini

**SAN
MARINO**
★SAN
MARINO

Cattolica●

●Pesaro

●Fano

Passo di
Bocca Trabaria
(1049m)

Foglia

Metauro

Cesano

●Senigallia

●Sansepolcro

Nevola

Falconara
Marittima●

Parco
Del
Conero

●Ancona

Misa

Tevere

Parco
Regionale
del Monte Cucco

●Jesi

Esino

Musone

●Osimo

Gubbio●

Chiascio

▲Monte Cucco
(1566m)

●Fabriano

tona

Lago
rasimeno

LE MARCHE

Macerata
◉

Civitanova
Marche●

Aeroporto
Sant'Egidio

Parco
Regionale del
Monte Subasio

Potenza

Chienti

Perugia◉

②

Assisi●

▲Monte Subasio
(1290m)

Topino

Tenna

●Fermo

Aso

Parco
Regionale
del Pausillo

UMBRIA

Parco Nazionale
dei Monti
Sibillini

San Benedetto
●del Tronto

Ascoli
Piceno●

Tronto

Parco
Regionale
del Tevere

Tevere

●Orvieto

⑤

Castelluccio●
●Norcia

Spoleto●

Parco Regionale
del Coscerno
Aspra

Nera

Tronto

Castellano

Te

Pescara

Terni●

●Narni

Parco
Fluviale
del Nera

ABRUZZO

Lago
di Vico

LAZIO

Tevere

① Duomo, Florence

② Assisi

③ Galleria
dell'Accademia,
Florence

④ San Gimignano

⑤ Cattedrale, Orvieto

Monte
▲Amaro
(2795m)

Florence, Tuscany & Umbria Highlights

Duomo, Florence

More than simply a monumental spiritual centrepiece, the Duomo (p228) symbolises the city's economic wealth between the years 1300 and 1500, and the incredible artistic and cultural explosion that it spurred. The building still dominates Florence, like a mountain of marble topped by a giant ruby.

1

Sacred Assisi

2

Through the life and good deeds of St Francis, patron saint of animals and the environment, Assisi (p261) has undergone a transformation from a sleepy Umbrian hill town to spiritual centre that's nothing short of miraculous. A short walk across this medieval town covers holy sites and artistic marvels that provide tangible links to the distant past, and to generations of devoted pilgrims.

FRANK WING/GETTY IMAGES ©

David, Galleria dell'Accademia

3

You may not have met him personally, but this guy is everywhere, and usually naked. Like most superstars, he goes by a single name: *David*. Before his sculpted abs appeared on fridge magnets and souvenir aprons, *David* was discovered by Michelangelo in a block of Carrara marble. Now people wait for hours to see him at Florence's Galleria dell'Accademia (p233).

San Gimignano

4

One-upmanship reached its height in medieval San Gimignano (p254), where neighbourly competition to build the biggest tower turned this small hill town into a mini-Manhattan. Of the original 72 structures, 11 have stood the test of time. Standing in the long shadow of these towering achievements will leave you with an entirely fresh perspective on the Dark Ages – and might inspire you to redesign your own backyard shed.

Orvieto's Cathedral

5

From the front, the Cattedrale di Orvieto (p268) looks like a gorgeous Gothic wedding cake. Inside, however, 'happily ever after' doesn't look likely in Signorelli's frescoes. The artist had survived plague, book burnings, earthquakes and witch hunts when he started *The End of the World* in 1500, and never has apocalypse been so vividly pictured. Five hundred years later it's a testament to our ability to survive, sometimes with flying colours.

Florence, Tuscany & Umbria's Best...

Wining & Dining

○ **Osteria il Buongustai** No-frills Florence eatery; sublime home-cooked Tuscan dishes. (p238)

○ **Trattoria Mario** Legendary family-run Florentine haunt; busy and brilliant. (p239)

○ **Il Teatro del Sale** Florentine treasure Fabio Picchi cooks up a storm; meals are followed by theatre. (p239)

○ **Ristorante la Mandragola** Wonderful restaurant built into San Gimignano's city walls. (p254)

○ **Antica Osteria de la Stella** Inventive Umbrian restaurant in Urbino. (p260)

World Heritage Treasures

○ **Florence** A-list museums, architectural wonders and killer shopping. (p224)

○ **Basilica di San Francesco** Miraculously restored, earthquake-shattered frescoes. (p262)

○ **Siena** This model medieval government ended gang warfare with public art and horse races. (p248)

○ **San Gimignano** Towering ambition put this medieval hill town on the map. (p254)

○ **Urbino** Fifteenth-century town designed by a Renaissance brain trust. (p260)

Breathtaking Views

○ **Leaning Tower** Moonlit climbs up 294 tilting steps in Pisa. (p244)

○ **Galleria dell'Accademia** Michelangelo's ageless *David* in Florence. (p233)

○ **Chianti** Drinking in the landscape – literally. (P000)

○ **Cattedrale di Orvieto** *The End of the World*, foretold in Signorelli's frescoes. (p268)

○ **Ponte Vecchio** Sunsets over the Arno in Florence. (p234)

Souvenirs That Don't Feature David

o **Officina Profumo-Farmaceutica di Santa Maria Novella** Heavenly perfume blended from monastery-grown flowers. (p241)

o **Montalcino** Rare Brunello vintages you won't find outside the cellars. (p255)

o **Giulio Giannini e Figlio** Handmade marble-paper stationery. (p241)

o **Chianti** Taste before you buy at local vineyards. (p253)

Left: Leaning Tower (p244), Pisa
Above: Vineyards, Chianti (p253)

Need to Know

ADVANCE PLANNING

o **Three months before** Book accommodation and tickets to Spoleto's summer festival.

o **One to two months before** Book high-season accommodation in Assisi and Florence.

o **Two weeks before** Book online for Pisa's Leaning Tower, and Florence's Uffizi and Galleria dell'Accademia.

o **One day before** Book your tour of Florence's Palazzo Vecchio, Cappella Brancacci, and dinner in Florence.

RESOURCES

o **APT Firenze** (www.firenzeturismo.it) Official Florence tourism website.

o **Firenze Musei** (www.firenzemusei.it) Booking for Florentine museums.

o **Tuscany Tourist Board** (www.turismo.intoscana.it) Interest-based itineraries.

o **InfoUmbria** (www.infoumbria.com) Umbria travel resource with *agriturismi* (farm-stay accommodation) listings.

GETTING AROUND

o **Air** Routes service Pisa and, to a lesser extent, Florence and Perugia.

o **Train** Good connections between major cities, with connecting buses to towns.

o **Bus** Best for reaching Siena and San Gimignano.

o **Bicycle** The scenic way to cover Chianti; handy for Florence.

o **Car** Convenient for reaching hill towns, *agriturismi* and wineries.

BE FOREWARNED

o **Museums** Many close Mondays.

o **Restaurants** Many close in August; some also close in January.

o **Accommodation** Book months ahead, especially if travelling on holiday weekends, in summer or during local festivals.

o **Wine Tasting** Vineyard visits are often free but require reservations; call direct or try the local tourist office.

Florence, Tuscany & Umbria Itineraries

So you've seen the Leaning Tower and David – two master-pieces down, untold wonders to go. Where to begin? Wander Tuscan wine country to reach spiritual enlightenment, or uncover splendours in Umbria's hill towns.

FLORENCE TO MONTALCINO
TUSCAN VINEYARDS

Sun-washed vineyards, country roads flanked by olive groves and frequent, tasty pit stops make this a mellow, indulgent trip.

Spend your first day in ❶**Florence**, visiting the Duomo and Uffizi galleries, staying in a 16th-century palazzo at Hotel Scoti and eating home-cooked food with the locals at Osteria Il Buongustai.

Next day, head south on SS222 to the historic ❷**Chianti** wine region. Visit Castello di Verrazzano in Luca to wine-taste in a castle, and browse gourmet treats like local honey and *vin santo*. Head south in the afternoon along SS2 to ❸**Siena**; explore the humbug-striped *duomo* and medieval

Campo before sampling the degustation menu at Ristorante Grotta Santa Caterina da Bagoga, and sleeping under frescoed ceilings at Pensione Palazzo Ravizza.

Day three, continue south on SS2 through Brunello wine country to ❹**Montalcino** for a Brunello tasting and dinner at Osticcio, then retreat to your rustic-chic guestroom in Hotel Vecchia Oliviera, a converted olive mill.

Before you return to Siena or Florence, stop by Montalcino's *fortezza*, a fort with a wine cellar where you can get Brunello packaged to stash in your suitcase.

5 DAYS

ORVIETO TO SPOLETO
UMBRIAN HILL TOWNS

Secretive Umbria hides its splendours on hilltops behind ancient stone walls. The adventure begins with a cliffhanger: ❶ **Orvieto**, where Signorelli's frescoed handsome devils star in the shimmering pink Gothic cathedral. Spelunk through secret passageways with Orvieto Underground, then come up for air and seasonal daily specials at Trattoria dell'Orso.

After a night in frescoed 1500s Villa Mercede, hop the train to university town ❷ **Perugia**. Explore the impressive medieval Palazzo dei Priori, which contains the Galleria Nazionale dell'Umbria's fine collection of art, from Byzantine to Renaissance, and the extravagantly adorned Nobile Collegio del Cambio.

Devote two days to ❸ **Assisi** for quiet contemplation of Giotto's moving frescoes in Basilica di San Francesco and Umbrian cooking classes at *agriturismo* Alla Madonna del Piatto. Artistic inspiration awaits in ❹ **Spoleto**, which hosts Italy's landmark summer arts festival in its Roman amphitheatre. The town is overlooked by towering Rocca Albornoziana and its Museo Nazionale del Ducato. Finish up with sophisticated local food at Tempio del Gusto.

Wine bar, Montalcino (p255)
RICHARD I'ANSON/GETTY IMAGES ©

223

Discover Florence, Tuscany & Umbria

FLORENCE

POP 357,000

Cradle of the Renaissance and home of Machiavelli, Michelangelo and the Medici, Florence (Firenze) is magnetic, romantic, unrivalled and – above all – busy.

◎ Sights

PIAZZA DEL DUOMO

Battistero di San Giovanni Baptistry

(Baptistry; Piazza di San Giovanni; combined ticket to dome, baptistry, campanile, crypt and museum adult/child under 14 €10/free; ⊙11.15am-6.30pm Mon-Sat, 8.30am-1.30pm Sun & 1st Sat of month) Lorenzo Ghiberti designed the famous gilded bronze bas-reliefs that originally adorned the eastern doors of Florence's octagonal 11th-century Romanesque baptistry (what you see now are copies, with the originals on show in the Museo dell'Opera di Santa Maria del Fiore). Dante counts among the many famous Florentines who were dunked in its baptismal font. Buy tickets from the office opposite the northern doors at Via de' Cerretani 7.

PIAZZA DELLA SIGNORIA & AROUND

Palazzo Vecchio Museum

(🕿055 276 82 24; www.musefirenze.it; Piazza della Signoria; museum adult/reduced/child €10/8/free, tower €6.50, guided tours €2; ⊙museum 9am-midnight Fri-Wed, 9am-2pm Thu summer, 9am-7pm Fri-Wed, 9am-2pm Thu winter; tower 9am-8.30pm Fri-Wed, 9am-1.30pm Thu summer, 10am-4.30pm Fri-Wed, 10am-1.30pm Thu winter) Florence's 'Old Palace' was designed by Arnolfo di Cambio between 1298 and 1314 for the *signoria* (highest level of city

Wine from Chianti (p253)
ROCCO FASANO/GETTY IMAGES ©

government). Highlights include the view from the top of the *palazzo*'s 94m-high **Torre d'Arnolfo**, and the decoration of the **Salone dei Cinquecento**, a huge room created within the original building in the 1490s for the Consiglio dei Cinquecento (Council of 500) that ruled Florence during the late 15th century. It's home to Michelangelo's sculpture *Genio della Vittoria* (Genius of Victory).

Galleria degli Uffizi   Museum
(Uffizi Gallery; www.uffizi.firenze.it; Piazzale degli Uffizi 6; adult/reduced €6.50/3.25, incl temporary exhibition €11/5.50; ☺8.15am-6.05pm Tue-Sun) Housed inside the Palazzo degli Uffizi, built between 1560 and 1580 as a government office building (*uffizi* is the Italian word for office), this world-class gallery safeguards the Medici family's private art collection, which was bequeathed to the city in 1743 on the condition that it never leaves Florence.

An ongoing and vastly overdue €65 million refurbishment and redevelopment project will see the addition of a new exit loggia designed by Japanese architect Arato Isozaki and the doubling of exhibition space. In true Italian fashion no one, including architect Antonio Godoli, will commit to a final completion date (originally 2013), and until the so-called Nuovi Uffizi (www.nuoviuffizi.it) project is finished you can expect some rooms to be temporarily closed and the contents of others changed.

The collection spans the gamut of art history from ancient Greek sculptures to 18th-century Venetian paintings, arranged in chronological order by school.

Museo del Bargello   Museum
(www.polomuseale.firenze.it; Via del Proconsolo 4; adult/reduced €4/2, temporary exhibitions €6/3; ☺8.15am-4.20pm Tue-Sun & 1st & 3rd Mon of month, to 2pm winter) It was behind the stark exterior of Palazzo del Bargello, Florence's earliest public building, that the *podestà* meted out justice from the late 13th century until 1502. Today the building safeguards Italy's most comprehensive collection of Tuscan Renaissance sculpture.

Museum Passes

The **Firenze Card** (www.firenzecard.it; €72) is valid for 72 hours and covers admission to 72 museums, villas and gardens in Florence as well as unlimited use of public transport. Buy it online (and collect upon arrival in Florence) or in Florence at tourist offices, the ticketing desks of the Uffizi (Entrance 2), Palazzo Pitti, Palazzo Vecchio, Museo del Bargello, Cappella Brancacci, Basilica e Chiostri Monumentali di Santa Maria Novella and Giardini Bardini. If you're an EU citizen your card also covers under-18s travelling with you.

Crowds clamour to see *David* in the Galleria dell'Accademia but few rush to see his creator's early works, many of which are displayed in the Bargello's downstairs **Sala di Michelangelo**.

On the 1st floor is the **Sala di Donatello** where two versions of David, a favourite subject of sculptors, are displayed. Donatello fashioned his slender, youthfully dressed image in marble in 1408 and his fabled bronze between 1440 and 1450. The latter is extraordinary – the more so when you consider it was the first freestanding naked statue to be sculpted since classical times.

SANTA MARIA NOVELLA
Basilica di Santa
Maria Novella   Church, Cloister
(www.chiesasantamarianovella.it; Piazza di Santa Maria Novella 18; adult/reduced €5/3; ☺9am-5.30pm Mon-Thu, 11am-5.30pm Fri, 9am-5pm Sat, 1-5pm Sun) This monumental complex, fronted by the green-and-white marble facade of the 13th- to 15th-century **Basilica di Santa Maria di Novella**, includes romantic church cloisters and a stunning frescoed chapel. The basilica itself is a treasure chest of artistic masterpieces, climaxing with a series of frescoes by Domenico Ghirlandaio.

The Uffizi

JOURNEY INTO THE RENAISSANCE

Navigating the Uffizi's main art collection, chronologically arranged in 45 rooms on one floor, is straightforward; knowing which of the 1500-odd masterpieces to view before gallery fatigue strikes is not. Swap coat and bag (travel light) for floor plan and audioguide on the ground floor, then meet 16th-century Tuscany head-on with a walk up the *palazzo's* magnificent bust-lined staircase (skip the lift – the Uffizi is as much about masterly architecture as art).

Allow four hours for this journey into the High Renaissance. At the top of the staircase, on the 2nd floor, show your ticket, turn left and pause to admire the full length of the first corridor sweeping south towards the Arno river. Then duck left into room 2 to witness first steps in Tuscan art – shimmering altarpieces by **Giotto** ❶ et al. Journey through medieval art to room 8 and **Piero della Francesca's** ❷ impossibly famous portrait, then break in the corridor with playful **ceiling art** ❸. After Renaissance heavyweights **Botticelli** ❹ and **da Vinci** ❺, meander past the Tribuna (potential detour) and enjoy the daylight streaming in through the vast windows and panorama of the **riverside second corridor** ❻. Lap up soul-stirring views of the Arno, crossed by Ponte Vecchio and its echo of four bridges drifting towards the Apuane Alps on the horizon. Then saunter into the third corridor, pausing between rooms 25 and 34 to ponder the entrance to the enigmatic Vasari Corridor. End on a high with High Renaissance maestro **Michelangelo** ❼.

The Ognissanti Madonna
Room 2
Draw breath at the shy blush and curvaceous breast of Giotto's humanised Virgin (*Maestà*; 1310) – so feminine compared with those of Duccio and Cimabue painted just 25 years before.

Portraits of the Duke & Duchess of Urbino
Room 8
Revel in realism's voyage with these uncompromising, warts-and-all portraits (1472–75) by Piero della Francesca. No larger than A3 size, they originally slotted into a portable, hinged frame that folded like a book.

Start of Vasari Corridor (linking the Palazzo Vecchio with the Uffizi and Palazzo Pitti)

Entrance to 2nd Floor Gallery

Palazzo Vecchio

Piazza della Signoria

Grotesque Ceiling Frescoes
First Corridor
Take time to study the make-believe monsters and most unexpected of burlesques (spot the arrow-shooting satyr outside room 15) waltzing across this eastern corridor's fabulous frescoed ceiling (1581).

JUERGEN RICHTER/GETTY IMAGES ©

The Genius of Botticelli
Room 10–14
The miniature form of *The Discovery of the Body of Holofernes* (c 1470) makes Botticelli's early Renaissance masterpiece all the more impressive. Don't miss the artist watching you in *Adoration of the Magi* (1475), left of the exit.

View of the Arno
Indulge in intoxicating city views from this short glassed-in corridor – an architectural masterpiece. Near the top of the hill, spot one of 73 outer towers built to defend Florence and its 15 city gates below.

Second Corridor

Tribuna

First Corridor

Arno River

④ ③ ② ①
⑤ ⑥ ⑦

Entrance to Vasari Corridor

VALUE LUNCHBOX

Try the Uffizi rooftop cafe or – better value – gourmet *panini* at 'Ino (www.ino-firenze.com; Via dei Georgofili 3-7r).

Third Corridor

Doni Tondo
Room 35
The creator of *David*, Michelangelo, was essentially a sculptor and no painting expresses this better than *Doni Tondo* (1506–08). Mary's muscular arms against a backdrop of curvaceous nudes are practically 3D in their shapeliness.

Tribuna
No room in the Uffizi is so tiny or so exquisite. It was created in 1851 as a 'treasure chest' for Grand Duke Francesco and in the days of the Grand Tour, the Medici Venus here was a tour highlight.

Annunciation
Room 15
Admire the exquisite portrayal of the Tuscan landscape in this painting (c 1472), one of few by Leonardo da Vinci to remain in Florence.

MATTER OF FACT

The Uffizi collection spans the 13th to 18th centuries, but its 15th- and 16th-century Renaissance works are second to none.

Don't Miss
Duomo

Florence's Duomo, the city's most iconic landmark, is among Italy's 'Big Three' (with Pisa's Leaning Tower and Rome's Colosseum). Its red-tiled dome, graceful *campanile* (bell tower) and breathtaking pink, white and green marble facade have the wow factor in spades. Begun in 1296 by Sienese architect Arnolfo di Cambio, the cathedral took almost 150 years to complete.

Cattedrale di Santa Maria del Fi or St Mary of the Flower

www.operaduomo.firenze.it

Piazza del Duomo

combined ticket to Dome, Baptistry, Campanile, Crypt and Museum adult €10

🕑 10am-5pm Mon-Wed & Fri, to 4pm Thu, to 4.45pm Sat, 1.30-4.45pm Sun; dome 8.30am-6pm Mon-Fri, to 5pm Sat; crypt 10am-5pm Mon-Wed & Fri-Sat, to 4pm Thu; campanile 8.30am-6.50pm

Exterior

Its neo-Gothic facade was designed in the 19th century by architect Emilio de Fabris to replace the uncompleted original, torn down in the 16th century. The oldest and most clearly Gothic part of the cathedral is its south flank, pierced by Porta dei Canonici (Canons' Door; you enter here to climb up inside the dome).

The dome was built between 1420 and 1436 to a design by Filippo Brunelleschi. Taking his inspiration from Rome's Pantheon, Brunelleschi arrived at an innovative engineering solution of a distinctive octagonal shape of inner and outer concentric domes resting on the drum of the cathedral rather than the roof itself, allowing artisans to build from the ground up without needing a wooden support frame. The climb up the spiral staircase (463 steps) is relatively steep, and should not be attempted if you are claustrophobic.

Interior

After the visual wham-bam of the facade and dome, the sparse decoration of the cathedral's vast interior, 155m long and 90m wide, comes as a surprise. The interior is also unexpectedly secular in places (a reflection of the sizeable chunk of the cathedral not paid for by the church): down the left aisle two immense frescoes of equestrian statues portray two *condottieri* (mercenaries) – on the left Niccolò da Tolentino by Andrea del Castagno (1456) and on the right Sir John Hawkwood by Uccello (1436).

Between the left (north) arm of the transept and the apse is the Sagrestia delle Messe (Mass Sacristy), its panelling a marvel of inlaid wood carved by Benedetto and Giuliano da Maiano. The fine bronze doors were executed by Luca della Robbia. Above the doorway is his glazed terracotta *Resurrezione* (Resurrection).

The steep 414-step climb up the 85m-high campanile, designed by Giotto, offers rewarding views that are nearly as impressive as those from the dome.

Local Knowledge

Duomo

BY PATRIZIO OSTICRESI,
OPERA DI SANTA MARIA
DEL FIORE (OPERA DEL
DUOMO) ADMINISTRATOR

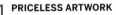

1 PRICELESS ARTWORK

The Duomo heaves with beautiful art and craftsmanship. Particularly famous is Domenico di Michelino's 1465 painting *La Divina Commedia Illumina Firenze* (Dante Explaining the Divine Comedy). Recently restored, the 15th-century stained-glass windows at the base of the dome are the work of Donatello, Lorenzo Ghiberti, Paolo Uccello and Andrea del Castagno. Above them are the wonderful *Last Judgment* dome frescoes by Giorgio Vasari and Federico Zuccari.

2 VIEWS FROM THE DOME

The panoramas are reason enough to head to the top of Brunelleschi's dome, but other incentives include a fine view of the interior's inlaid marble floors and the chance to get closer to the *Last Judgment* frescoes adorning the dome.

3 BAPTISTRY

Both the exterior and the interior of the 11th-century baptistry are feasts for the eyes, and examples of architectural and artistic genius. Especially beautiful are the 13th-century ceiling mosaics, the inlaid marble pavement, the bronze doors and the Cossa funerary monument, created by Donatello and Michelozzo in 1428.

4 MUSEO DELL'OPERA DEL DUOMO

Many precious works of art removed from the piazza's monuments are held here in order to better preserve them. Highlights include Donatello's *Maddalena* statue, the original baptistry doors by Lorenzo Ghiberti, original panels from Giotto's *campanile* and Michelangelo's *Pietà,* which he sculpted for his own tomb but was intensely unsatisfied with.

Florence

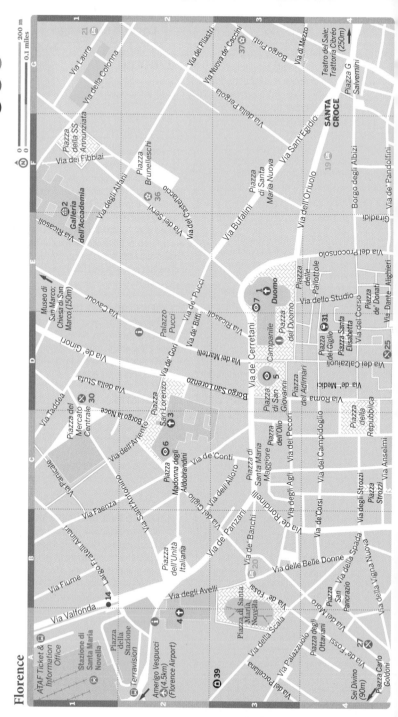

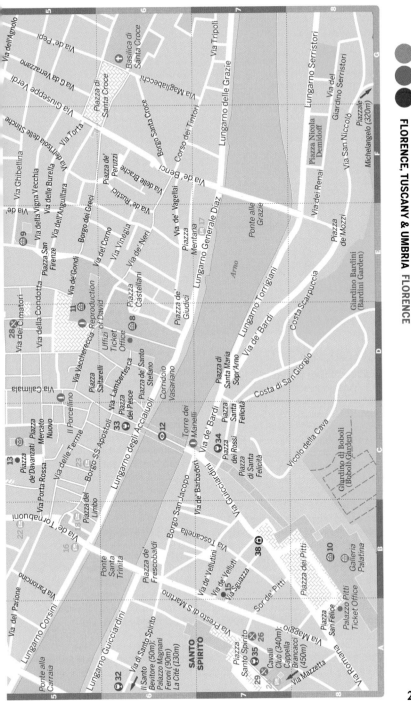

FLORENCE, TUSCANY & UMBRIA FLORENCE

231

Florence

SAN LORENZO

Basilica di San Lorenzo   Church
(Piazza San Lorenzo; admission €4.50, with Biblioteca Medicea Laurenziana €7; ⊙10am-5.30pm Mon-Sat, plus 1.30-5pm Sun Mar-Oct) In 1425 Cosimo the Elder, who lived nearby, commissioned Brunelleschi to rebuild the original 4th-century basilica on this site. The new building would become the Medici parish church and mausoleum.

Michelangelo was commissioned to design the facade in 1518 but his design in white Carrara marble was never executed, hence the building's rough unfinished appearance.

Cappelle Medicee   Mausoleum
(Medici Chapels; ☎055 294 883; www.polomuseale.firenze.it; Piazza Madonna degli Aldobrandini; adult/reduced €6/3; ⊙8.15am-1.20pm, closed 2nd & 4th Sun & 1st, 3rd & 5th Mon of month) Nowhere is the Medici conceit expressed so explicitly as in their mausoleum, the Medician Chapels. Sumptuously adorned with granite, marble, semiprecious stones

and some of Michelangelo's most beautiful sculptures, it is the burial place of 49 members of the dynasty.

SAN MARCO

Museo di San Marco   Museum
(www.polomuseale.firenze.it; Piazza San Marco 1; adult/reduced €4/2; ⊙8.15am-1.20pm Mon-Fri, to 4.20pm Sat & Sun, closed 1st, 3rd & 5th Sun & 2nd & 4th Mon of month) At the heart of Florence's university area sits the Domenican **Chiesa di San Marco** and its adjoining 15th-century monastery where both gifted painter Fra' Angelico (c 1395–1455) and the sharp-tongued Savonarola piously served God. Today the monastery, which showcases the work of Fra' Angelico, is one of Florence's most spiritually uplifting museums.

Enter via Michelozzo's **Cloister of Saint Antoninus** (1440). Turn immediately right to enter the **Sala dell'Ospizio** (Pilgrims' Hospital) where Fra' Angelico's attention to perspective and the realistic portrayal of nature

RAPHAEL VAN BUTSELE/GETTY IMAGES ©

★ Don't Miss
Galleria dell'Accademia

A lengthy queue usually marks the door to this gallery, which was built to house one of the Renaissance's greatest masterpieces, Michelangelo's *David*. Fortunately, the world's best-known statue is well worth the wait.

Carved from a single block of marble, the statue of the nude warrior assumed its pedestal in front of Palazzo Vecchio on Piazza della Signoria in 1504, providing Florentines with a powerful emblem of their city's power, liberty and civic pride.

Michelangelo was also the master behind the unfinished *San Matteo* (St Matthew; 1504–08) and four *Prigioni* ('Prisoners' or 'Slaves'; 1521–30), also displayed in the gallery. Adjacent rooms contain paintings by Andrea Orcagna, Taddeo Gaddi, Domenico Ghirlandaio, Filippino Lippi and Sandro Botticelli.

NEED TO KNOW
www.polomuseale.firenze.it; Via Ricasoli 60; adult/reduced €6.50/3.25; ⊘8.15am-6.50pm Tue-Sun

comes to life in a number of major paintings, including the *Deposition of Christ* (1432).

Giovanni Antonio Sogliani's fresco *The Miraculous Supper of St Domenic* (1536) dominates the former monks' **refectory** in the cloister; and Fra' Angelico's huge *Crucifixion and Saints* fresco (1441–42) decorates the former chapterhouse.

The museum's highlights are on the 1st floor. At the top of the stairs, Fra' Angelico's most famous work, *Annunciation* (c 1440), commands all eyes. Further on, the 44 monastic cells reveal snippets of many more religious reliefs by the Tuscan-born friar, who decorated the cells between 1440 and 1441 with deeply devotional frescoes to guide the meditation of his fellow friars.

SANTA CROCE

Basilica di Santa Croce — Church

(www.santacroceopera.it; Piazza di Santa Croce; adult/reduced €6/4, family ticket €12, combined ticket with Museo Casa Buonarroti €8.50; ⊘9.30am-5pm Mon-Sat, 2-5pm Sun) When Lucy Honeychurch, the hero of EM Forster's *A Room with a View*, is stranded in Santa Croce without a Baedeker, she looks around and wonders why the basilica is thought to be such an important building. After all, doesn't it look just like a barn? On entering, many visitors to this massive Franciscan church share the same sentiment – the austere interior is indeed a shock after the magnificent neo-Gothic facade enlivened by varying shades of coloured marble.

Although most visitors come to see the tombs of famous Florentines buried here – including Michelangelo, Galileo, Ghiberti and Machiavelli – it's the frescoes by Giotto and his school in the chapels to the right of the altar that are the real highlights.

The second of Santa Croce's two serene cloisters was designed by Brunelleschi just before his death in 1446.

THE OLTRARNO

Ponte Vecchio — Bridge

Florence's iconic bridge has twinkled with the glittering wares of jewellers ever since the 16th century, when Ferdinando I de' Medici ordered them here to replace the often malodorous presence of the town butchers, who had an unfortunate tendency to toss unwanted leftovers into the river. The bridge as it now stands dates from 1345 and was the only one saved from destruction at the hands of the retreating Germans in 1944.

Palazzo Pitti — Museum

(www.polomuseale.firenze.it; Piazza dei Pitti; adult/EU 18-25/EU child & senior Ticket 1 €8.50/4.25/free, Ticket 2 €7/3.50/free, Ticket 3 €11.50/5.75/free; ⊘8.15am-6.05pm Tue-Sun, Boboli Garden to 7.30pm Jun-Aug, shorter hrs outside summer for Museo degli Argenti, Galleria del Costume & Boboli Garden) Banker

Luca Pitti commissioned Brunelleschi to design this palace in 1457, but by the time it was completed waning family fortunes forced them to sell it to the Medici. It later became the residence of the city's rulers and, from 1865 until 1919 (when fell to the state), the residence of the Savoy royal family. Several art museums can be found inside.

Raphaels and Rubens vie for centre stage in the enviable collection of 16th- to 18th-century art amassed by the Medici and Lorraine dukes in the 1st-floor **Galleria Palatina** (☺8.15am-6.50pm Tue-Sun summer, shorter hrs winter), reached by several flights of stairs from the palace's central courtyard.

Piazzale Michelangelo   Viewpoint

(🚌13) Turn your back on the bevy of ticky-tacky souvenir stalls flogging *David* statues and boxer shorts and take in the spectacular city panorama from this vast square, pierced by one of Florence's two *David* copies (sunset here is particularly dramatic). It's a 10-minute uphill walk along the serpentine road, paths and steps that scale the hillside from the Arno and Piazza Giuseppe Poggi; from Piazza San Niccolò walk uphill and bear left up the long flight of steps signposted Viale Michelangelo.

Cappella Brancacci   Chapel

(📞055 276 82 24; www.musefirenze.it; Piazza del Carmine 14; adult/reduced €6/4.50; ☺10am-4.30pm Wed-Sat & Mon, 1-4.30pm Sun) Fire in the 18th century all but destroyed 13th-century **Basilica di Santa Maria del Carmine**, but the magnificent frescoes in its chapel, to the right of the church entrance, were miraculously spared. Visits are by guided tour (20 minutes, every 20 minutes) and advance reservations are recommended in season given only 30 people at a time are allowed in.

235

Tours

City Sightseeing Firenze
Bus Tour

(☎055 29 04 51; www.firenze.city-sightseeing. it; Piazza della Stazione 1; adult 1/2/3 days €20/25/30) Explore Florence by red open-top bus, hopping on and off at 15 bus stops around the city. Tickets, sold by the driver, are valid for 24 hours.

500 Touring Club
Vintage Car

(☎346 826 23 24; www.500touringclub.com; Via Gherardo Silvani 149a) Hook up with Florence's 500 Touring Club for a guided tour in a vintage motor – with you behind the wheel! Every car has a name in the fleet of vintage Fiat 500s from the 1960s (Giacomo is the playboy, Olivia the kind rebel). Motoring tours are guided – hop in your car and follow the leader – and themed.

ArtViva
Walking Tour

(☎055 264 50 33; www.italy.artviva.com; Via de' Sassetti 1; per person from €25) Marketed as the 'Original & Best', these excellent one- to three-hour city walks (from €25) are led by historians or art history graduates; tours include the Uffizi, the Original David tour and an Evening Walk/Murder Mystery Tour.

Ponte Vecchio (p234), Florence

Sleeping

AROUND PIAZZA DEL DUOMO & PIAZZA DELLA SIGNORIA

Hotel Scoti
Historic Hotel €

(☎055 29 21 28; www.hotelscoti.com; Via de' Tornabuoni 7; s/d/tr/q €80/125/150/175;) Wedged between Prada and McQueen, this is a splendid mix of old-fashioned charm and value for money. Run with smiling aplomb by Australian Doreen and Italian Carmello, the hotel is enthroned in a 16th-century *palazzo* on Florence's smartest shopping strip.

Hotel Cestelli
Boutique Hotel €

(☎055 21 42 13; www.hotelcestelli.com; Borgo SS Apostoli 25; d €100-115, s/d with shared bathroom €60/80, extra bed €25; ⊙closed 4 wks Jan-Feb, 3 wks Aug) A stiletto hop and skip from the Arno and fashionable Via de' Tornabuoni, this eight-room hotel in a 12th-century *palazzo* is a gem. Its large, quiet rooms ooze understated style – think washbasin with silk screen and vintage art. Before stepping out, quiz the couple, Italian photographer Alessio and gracious Japanese Asumi, on new eating, drinking and shopping openings.

Hotel Torre Guelfa
Historic Hotel €€

(☎ 055 239 63 38; www.hoteltorreguelfa.com; Borgo SS Apostoli 8; d/tr/q €200/250/300; ❄ @ ☎) Keen to kip in a Real McCoy Florentine *palazzo* without breaking the bank? If so, this 31-room hotel with fortress-style facade is the answer. Scale its 13th-century, 50m-tall tower – Florence's tallest privately owned *torre* – for a sundowner overlooking Florence and you'll be blown away. Rates are practically halved in low season.

Antica Torre di Via de' Tornabuoni 1
Boutique Hotel €€€

(☎ 055 21 92 48; www.tornabuoni1.com; Via de' Tournabuoni 1; d from €325; ⊙ reception 7am-10pm; ☎ ♿) Footsteps from the Arno, inside the beautiful 14th-century Palazzo Gianfigliazzi, languishes this raved-about hotel. Its 20 rooms are stylish, spacious and contemporary. But what completely steals the show is the stunning rooftop breakfast terrace – easily the best in the city.

SANTA MARIA NOVELLA

Hotel Azzi
Hotel €€

(Locanda degli Artisti; ☎ 055 21 38 06; www.hotelazzi.com; Via Faenza 56/88r; d €105-115, tr/q €130/150; ❄ ☎) A five-minute walk from the central market and train station only adds to the convenience of this well-maintained hotel. Its old-world style coupled with a lounge, library full of books, terrace and jacuzzi makes it particularly popular among older travellers. The hotel also has cheaper hotel rooms and self-contained apartments in nearby annexes.

Hotel L'O
Luxury Hotel €€€

(☎ 055 27 73 80; www.hotelorologioflorence.com; Piazza di Santa Maria Novella 24; d from €315; P ❄ @ ☎) The type of seductive address where James Bond would feel right at home, this super-stylish hotel oozes panache. Designed as a showcase for the (very wealthy) owner's (exceedingly expensive) luxury wristwatch collection, L'O (the hip take on its full name, Hotel L'Orologio) has four stars, rooms named after watches, and clocks pretty much everywhere. Don't be late...

SAN MARCO

Hotel Morandi alla Crocetta
Boutique Hotel €€

(☎ 055 234 47 47; www.hotelmorandi.it; Via Laura 50; s €70-120, d €100-170, tr €130-210, q €150-250; P ❄ ☎) This medieval convent-turned-hotel away from the madding crowd in San Marco is a stunner. Rooms are refined, tasteful and full of authentic period furnishings and paintings. A couple of rooms have handkerchief-sized gardens to laze in, but the pièce de résistance is frescoed room No 29, the former chapel.

SANTA CROCE

Hotel Dalí
Hotel €

(☎ 055 234 07 06; www.hoteldali.com; Via dell'Oriuolo 17; d/tr €85/110, apt from €95, with shared bathroom s/d €40/70; P @ ☎ ♿) This friendly hotel is the passion and unrelenting love of world travellers-turned-parents Marco and Samanta ('running the hotel is like travelling without moving'). The icing on the cake is a trio of gorgeous self-contained apartments – one with *duomo* view – sleeping two, four or six.

Hotel Balestri
Historic Hotel €€

(☎ 055 21 47 43; www.hotel-balestri.it; Piazza Mentana 7; d €100-160, tr €140-165; ❄ @ ☎) Dating to 1888, this hotel on the banks of the Arno remains the only riverside place to stay in downtown Florence. As part of the chic, quality-guaranteed Whythebest Florence hotel group (they're the guys behind Hotel L'O, Villa Cora and other chic pads), Balestri is comfortably contemporary while retaining a distinct old-world charm.

THE OLTRARNO

Palazzo Guadagni Hotel
Hotel €€

(☎ 055 265 83 76; www.palazzoguadagni.com; Piazza Santo Spirito 9; s €100-140, d €140-180, extra bed €35; ❄ ☎ ♿) Plump above Florence's liveliest summertime square is this legendary hotel with its impossibly romantic loggia (immortalised by Zefferelli in *Tea with Mussolini*). Florentines Laura and Ferdinando are the creative duo behind the transformation of this Renaissance palace into a brilliant-value hotel with 15 spacious rooms tastefully mixing old and new.

Palazzo Magnani Feroni
Luxury Hotel €€€

(☎055 239 95 44; www.florencepalace.com; Borgo San Frediano 5; d from €379; 🅿❄@ 🛜🛗) This extraordinary old *palazzo* is the stuff of dreams. The 12 elegant suites, which occupy four floors, with the family's private residence wedged in between, are vast, featuring authentic period furnishings, rich fabrics and Bulgari toiletries.

🍴 Eating

AROUND PIAZZA DEL DUOMO & PIAZZA DELLA SIGNORIA

Osteria Il Buongustai
Osteria €

(Via dei Cerchi 15r; meals €15; ⏱11.30am-3.30pm Mon-Sat) Run with breathtaking speed and grace by Laura and Lucia, this place heaves at lunchtime with locals who work nearby and with savvy students who flock here to fill up on tasty Tuscan homecooking at a snip of other restaurant prices. The place is brilliantly no-frills – expect to share a table and pay in cash; no credit cards.

Cantinetta dei Verrazzano
Bakery €

(Via dei Tavolini 18-20; focaccia €2.50-3; ⏱noon-9pm Mon-Sat, 10am-4.30pm Sun) A *forno* (baker's oven) and *cantinetta* (small cellar) make a heavenly match. Sit at a marble-topped table, admire prized vintages displayed behind glass wall cabinets and sip a glass of wine (€4 to €10) produced on the Verrazzano estate in Chianti.

SANTA MARIA NOVELLA

L'Osteria di Giovanni
Tuscan €€

(☎055 28 48 97; www.osteriadigiovanni.it; Via del Moro 22; meals €35; ⏱dinner Mon-Fri, lunch & dinner Sat & Sun) It's not the decor that stands out at this friendly neighbourhood eatery. It's the cuisine, which is Tuscan and creative. Think chickpea soup with octopus or pear-and-ricotta-stuffed *tortelli* (a type of ravioli) bathed in a leek and almond cream. Throw in the complimentary glass of *prosecco* and plate of *coccoli* (traditional Florentine salted fritters) as *aperitivo* and you'll return time and again.

Local produce on display, Florence

SAN LORENZO & SAN MARCO

Trattoria Mario
Tuscan €

(www.trattoriamario.com; Via Rosina 2; meals €20; ⊙noon-3.30pm Mon-Sat, closed 3 wks Aug) Arrive by noon to ensure a stool around a shared table at this noisy, busy, brilliant trattoria – a legend that retains its soul (and allure with locals) despite being in every guidebook. Charming Fabio, whose grandfather opened the place in 1953, is front of house while big brother Romeo and nephew Francesco cook with speed in the kitchen.

Antica Trattoria da Tito
Trattoria €€

(🕿055 47 24 75; www.trattoriadatito.it; Via San Gallo 112r; meals €30; ⊙lunch & dinner Mon-Sat) The 'No well-done meat here' sign strung in the window says it all: the best of Tuscan culinary tradition is the only thing this iconic trattoria serves. In business since 1913, Da Tito does everything right – tasty Tuscan dishes such as onion soup and wild boar pasta served with friendly gusto and hearty goodwill to a local crowd.

SANTA CROCE

Il Giova
Trattoria €

(🕿055 248 06 39; www.ilgiova.com; Borgo La Croce 73r; meals €25; ⊙lunch & dinner Mon-Sat) Pocket-sized and packed, this cheery trattoria is everything a traditional Florentine eating place should be. Dig into century-old dishes including *zuppa della nonna* (grandma's soup), *risotto del giorno* (risotto of the day) or *mafalde al ragù* (long-ribboned pasta with meat sauce) and pride yourself on finding a place to dine with locals.

Il Teatro del Sale
Tuscan €€

(🕿055 200 14 92; www.teatrodelsale.com; Via dei Macci 111r; breakfast/lunch/dinner €7/20/30; ⊙9-11am, 12.30-2.15pm & 7-11pm Tue-Sat, closed Aug) Florentine chef Fabio Picchi is one of Florence's living treasures, and he steals the Sant'Ambrogio show with this eccentric, good-value members-only club (everyone welcome, annual membership €7) inside an old theatre. He cooks up breakfast,

If You Like...
Gastronomy

If you not only enjoy eating but also like learning to cook, tasting wine and seeking out the finest products, then try these on for size.

1 ACCIDENTAL TOURIST
(🕿055 69 93 76; www.accidentaltourist.com) Become an Accidental Tourist (membership €10), then sign up for a wine tour (€60), cooking class (€70), gourmet picnic (€35) and so on; tours happen in and around Florence.

2 FAITH WILLINGER – LESSONS & TOURS
(www.faithwillinger.com) Food lovers' walking tour, a market stroll, gelato crawl and much more by American-born, Florence-based food writer Faith Willinger, who runs cooking courses, hands-on 'market to table' sessions, tastings, demonstrations and culinary visits, including meaty field trips to Panzano in Chianti.

3 IN TAVOLA
(🕿055 21 76 72; www.intavola.org; Via dei Velluti 18r) Take your pick from dozens of carefully crafted courses for beginners and professionals: pizza and gelato, pasta making, easy Tuscan dinners etc.

lunch and dinner culminating at 9.30pm in a live performance of drama, music or comedy arranged by his wife, artistic director and comic actor Maria Cassi.

THE OLTRARNO

Tamerò
Pasta Bar €

(🕿055 28 25 96; www.tamero.it; Piazza Santa Spirito 11r; meals €20; ⊙lunch & dinner Tue-Sun) Admire pasta cooks at work in the open kitchen while you wait for a table alongside members of the party-loving crowd that flocks here to fill up on imaginative, fresh pasta dishes (€7.50 to €10), giant salads (€7.50) and copious cheese/salami platters (€9). Weekend DJs spin sets from 10pm.

La Casalinga
Trattoria €

(☎055 21 86 24; www.trattorialacasalinga.it; Via de' Michelozzi 9r; meals €25; ☺lunch & dinner Mon-Sat) Family run and locally loved, this busy unpretentious place is one of Florence's cheapest trattorias. Don't be surprised if Paolo, the patriarch figure who conducts the mad-busy show from behind the bar, relegates you behind locals in the queue: it's a fact of life, eventually rewarded with hearty Tuscan dishes cooked to exacting perfection.

Il Santo Bevitore
Modern Tuscan €€

(☎055 21 12 64; www.ilsantobevitore.com; Via di Santo Spirito 64-66r; meals €35; ☺lunch & dinner Sep-Jul) Reserve or arrive dot-on 7.30pm to snag the last table at this raved-about address, an ode to stylish dining where gastronomes dine by candlelight in a vaulted, whitewashed, bottle-lined interior. The menu is a creative reinvention of seasonal classics, different for lunch and dinner.

🍷 Drinking & Nightlife

AROUND PIAZZA DEL DUOMO & PIAZZA DELLA SIGNORIA

La Terrazza
Bar

(www.continentale.it; Vicolo dell'Oro 6r; ☺2.30-11.30pm Apr-Sep) This rooftop bar with wooden decking terrace is accessible from the 5th floor of the chic, Ferragamo-owned Hotel Continentale. Its aperitivo buffet is a modest affair, but no one cares – the fabulous, drop-dead-gorgeous panorama of one of Europe's most beautiful cities is the major draw. Dress the part or feel out of place.

Coquinarius
Wine Bar

(www.coquinarius.com; Via delle Oche 11r; crostini & carpacci €4; ☺noon-10.30pm) With its old stone vaults, scrubbed wooden tables and refreshingly modern air, this enoteca run by the dynamic and charismatic Igor is spacious and stylish. The wine list features bags of Tuscan greats and unknowns, and a substantial crostini (toast with various toppings) and carpacci (cold sliced meats) menu ensures you won't leave hungry.

SANTA MARIA NOVELLA

Sei Divino
Wine Bar

(Borgo Ognissanti 42r; ☺10am-2am) This stylish wine bar tucked beneath a red-brick vaulted ceiling is privy to one of Florence's most happening aperitivo scenes. From the pale aqua-coloured Vespa parked inside to the music, occasional exhibition and summertime pavement action, Sei Divino is a vintage that is eternally good.

SANTA CROCE

Drogheria
Lounge Bar

(www.drogheriafirenze.it; Largo Annigoni 22; ☺10am-3am) A large vintage-chic space with dark wood furnishings and soft chairs that are perfect for lounging in for hours on end. Come spring, the action moves outside onto the terrace, plumb on the huge piazza behind Sant'Abrogio market.

THE OLTRANO

Il Santino
Wine Bar

(Via Santo Spirito 34; glass of wine & crostini €6.50-8; ☺10am-10pm) Just a few doors down from one of Florence's best gourmet addresses, Il Santo Bevitore, is this pocket-sized wine bar run by the same crew. Inside, squat modern stools contrast with old brick walls but the real action is outside, from around 9pm, when the wine-loving crowd spills onto the street.

Volume
Bar

(www.volumefirenze.com; Piazza Santo Spirito 3r; ☺9am-1.30am) Fabulous armchairs, lots of recycled and upcycled vintage furniture, books to read and a juke box give this hybrid cafe-bar-gallery in an old hat-making workshop real appeal. Watch for various music, art and DJ events and happenings.

Le Volpi e l'Uva
Wine Bar

(www.levolpieluva.com; Piazza dei Rossi 1; crostini €6.50, cheese/meat platters €8-10; ☺11am-9pm Mon-Sat) The city's best enoteca con degustazione bar none: this intimate address with marble-topped bar crowning two oak ageing wine barrels chalks up an impressive list of wines by the glass. To attain true bliss indulge in crostini (€6.50) topped with honeyed speck perhaps or lardo, or a platter of boutique Tuscan cheeses.

⭐ Entertainment

La Cité
Live Music

(www.lacitelibreria.info; Borgo San Frediano 20r; ⏰3pm-1am Mon-Thu, 5pm-2am Fri & Sat; 📶) By day this cafe-bookshop is a hip cappuccino stop with an eclectic choice of vintage seating to flop down on. From 10pm, the space morphs into a vibrant live music den. The staircase next to the bar hooks up with mezzanine seating up top.

Jazz Club
Jazz

(Via Nuovo de' Caccini 3; ⏰10pm-2am Tue-Sat, closed Jul & Aug) Catch salsa, blues, Dixieland and world music as well as jazz at Florence's top jazz venue.

Be Bop Music Club
Live Music

(Via dei Servi 76r; ⏰8pm-2am) Inspired by the swinging '60s, this beloved venue features everything from Led Zeppelin and Beatles cover bands to swing jazz and 1970s funk.

🔒 Shopping

Officina Profumo-Farmaceutica di Santa Maria Novella
Perfumery

(www.smnovella.it; Via della Scala 16; ⏰9.30am-7.30pm) In business since 1612, this perfumery began life when the Dominican friars of Santa Maria Novella began to concoct cures and sweet-smelling unguents using medicinal herbs cultivated in the monastery garden. The shop today sells a wide range of fragrances, remedies, teas and skin-care products. A real treasure, it has touchscreen catalogues and a state-of-the-art payment system, yet still oozes vintage charm.

Giulio Giannini e Figlio
Stationery

(www.giuliogiannini.it; Piazza Pitti 37r; ⏰10am-7pm Mon-Sat, 11am-6.30pm Sun) This quaint old shopfront has watched Palazzo Pitti turn pink with the evening sun since 1856. One of Florence's oldest artisan families, the Gianninis make and sell marbled paper, beautifully bound books, stationery and so on. Don't miss the workshop upstairs.

ℹ️ Information

Tourist Offices

Airport (📞055 31 58 74; Via del Termine; ⏰9am-7pm Mon-Sat, to 4pm Sun)

Piazza della Stazione (📞055 21 22 45; Piazza della Stazione 4; ⏰9am-7pm Mon-Sat, to 4pm Sun)

Via Cavour (📞055 29 08 32, www.firenzeturismo.it; Via Cavour 1r; ⏰8.30am-6.30pm Mon-Sat)

ℹ️ Getting There & Away

Air

Florence Airport (www.aeroporto.firenze.it) Also known as Amerigo Vespucci or Peretola airport, 5km northwest of the city centre; domestic and a handful of European flights.

Pisa Airport (www.pisa-airport.com) Tuscany's main international airport (named after Galileo Galilei) is near Pisa, but is well linked with Florence by public transport.

Wine bar, Florence
SIMON WATSON/GETTY IMAGES ©

Train

Florence's central train station is Stazione di Santa Maria Novella. The left-luggage counter (Deposito Bagagliamano; **first 5hr €5, then €0.70 per hr;** ☺6am-11.50pm) is located on platform 16 and the *Assistenza Disabili* (Disabled Assistance) office is on platform 5. Florence is on the Rome–Milan line. Services include the following:

Bologna €10.50 to €25, one hour to 1¾ hours

Lucca €5.10, 1½ hours to 1¾ hours, half-hourly

Milan €29.50 to €53, 2¼ hours to 3½ hours

Pisa €5.80, 45 minutes to one hour, half-hourly

Rome €17.25, 1¾ hours to 4¼ hours

Venice €24 to €43, 2¾ hours to 4½ hours

ⓘ Getting Around

To/From the Airport

Bus

A shuttle (€6, 25 minutes) travels between the airport and Florence's Stazione di Santa Maria Novella train station every 30 minutes between 6am and 11.30pm (5.30am to 11pm from city centre). Terravision (www.terravision.eu) runs daily services (one way €5, 1¼ hours, hourly) between the bus stop outside Florence's Stazione di Santa Maria Novella (under the station's digital clock) and Pisa's Galileo Galilei airport – buy tickets online, on board or from the Terravision desk inside the Deanna Bar.

Taxi

A taxi between Florence airport and town costs a flat rate of €20, plus surcharges of €2 on Sunday and holidays, €3.30 between 10pm and 6am and €1 per bag. Exit the terminal building, bear right and you'll come to the taxi rank.

Train

Regular trains link Florence's Stazione di Santa Maria Novella with Pisa's Galileo Galilei airport (€8, 1½ hours, hourly from 4.30am to 10.25pm).

Public Transport

Buses, electric *bussini* (minibuses) and trams run by ATAF (☏800 424500, 199 104245; www.ataf.net) serve the city. Most buses start/terminate at the ATAF bus stops opposite the southeastern exit of Stazione di Santa Maria Novella.

Tickets valid for 90 minutes (no return journeys) cost €1.20 (€2 on board; drivers don't give change) and are sold at kiosks, tobacconists and the ATAF ticket and information office (Piazza della Stazione; ☺7.30am-7.30pm) adjoining the train station.

A travel pass valid for 1/3/7 days is €5/12/18. Upon boarding time-stamp your ticket (punch on board) or risk a fine.

Taxi

Taxis can't be hailed in the street. Pick one up at the train station or call ☏055 42 42 or ☏055 43 90.

Battistero, Pisa

TUSCANY

....

Pisa

Once a maritime power to rival Genoa and Venice, Pisa now draws its fame from an architectural project gone terribly wrong. But the world-famous Leaning Tower is just one of many noteworthy sights in this compact and compelling city.

◎ Sights

ALONG THE ARNO

Palazzo Blu   Art Gallery

(www.palazzoblu.it; Lungarno Gambacorti 9; ◷10am-7pm Tue-Fri, to 8pm Sat & Sun) `FREE` Facing the river is this magnificently restored, 14th-century building that has a striking dusty-blue facade. Its over-the-top 19th-century interior decoration is the perfect backdrop for the Foundation CariPisa's art collection – predominantly Pisan works from the 14th to the 20th century, plus various temporary exhibitions (charges may apply for the latter).

**Museo Nazionale
di San Matteo**   Art Gallery

(Piazza San Matteo in Soarta; adult/reduced €5/2.50; ◷8.30am-7pm Tue-Sat, to 1.30pm Sun) This inspiring repository of medieval masterpieces sits in a 13th-century Benedictine convent on the Arno's northern waterfront boulevard. The collection of paintings from the Tuscan school (c 12th to 14th centuries) is notable, with works by Lippo Memmi, Taddeo Gaddi, Gentile da Fabriano and Ghirlandaio.

PIAZZA DEI MIRACOLI

Duomo   Cathedral

(www.opapisa.it; Piazza dei Miracoli; admission free with ticket for one of the other Piazza dei Miracoli sights or with coupon from ticket office; ◷10am-12.45pm & 2-4.30pm Jan-Feb & Nov-Dec, 10am-5.30pm Mar, 10am-7.30pm Apr-Sep, 10am-6.30pm Oct) Pisa's cathedral was built with funds raised from spoils brought home after Pisans attacked an Arab fleet entering Palermo in 1063. Begun a year later, the cathedral, with its striking cladding

of alternating bands of green and cream marble, became the blueprint floor for Romanesque churches throughout Tuscany. The elliptical dome, the first of its kind in Europe at the time, was added in 1380.

Inside, don't miss the extraordinary early-14th-century octagonal **pulpit** in the north aisle. Sculpted from Carrara marble by Giovanni Pisano and featuring nude and heroic figures, its depth of detail and heightening of feeling brought a new pictorial expressionism and life to Gothic sculpture.

Battistero   Baptistry

(Baptistry; www.opapisa.it; Piazza dei Miracoli; combination ticket: Battistero, Camposanto, Museo dell'Opera del Duomo & Museo delle Sinópie 1/2/3/4 sights €5/7/8/9, reduced €3/4/5/6; ◷10am-4.30pm Jan-Feb & Nov-Dec, 9am-5.30pm Mar, 8am-7.30pm Apr-Sep, 9am-6.30pm Oct) The unusual round baptistry has one dome piled on top of another, each roofed half in lead, half in tiles, and topped by a gilt bronze John the Baptist (1395). Construction began in 1152, but the building was remodelled and continued by Nicola and Giovanni Pisano more than a century later and was finally completed in the 14th century. The lower level of arcades is Pisan-Romanesque; the pinnacled upper section and dome are Gothic.

Inside, the hexagonal marble **pulpit** (1259–60) by Nicola Pisano is the highlight. Pisan scientist Galileo Galilei (who, so the story goes, came up with the laws of the pendulum by watching a lamp in Pisa's cathedral swing), was baptised in the octagonal font (1246).

Don't leave without climbing to the **Upper Gallery** to listen to the custodian demonstrate the double dome's remarkable acoustics and echo effects, which occur every half-hour.

**Museo dell'Opera
del Duomo**   Museum

(www.opapisa.it; Piazza dei Miracoli; combination ticket: Battistero, Camposanto, Museo dell'Opera del Duomo & Museo delle Sinópie 1/2/3/4 sights €5/7/8/9, reduced €3/4/5/6; ◷10am-4.30pm Jan-Feb & Nov-Dec, 9am-5.30pm Mar, 8am-7.30pm Apr-Sep, 9am-6.30pm Oct) A repository for

JOHN ELK/GETTY IMAGES ©

⭐ Don't Miss
Leaning Tower

Yes, it's true: the Leaning Tower is nowhere near straight. Construction started in 1173 but stopped a decade later when the structure's first three tiers started tilting. In 1272 work started again, with artisans and masons attempting to bolster the foundations but failing miserably. Despite this, they kept going, compensating for the lean by gradually building straight up from the lower storeys.

The tower has tilted an extra 1mm each year. By 1993 it was 4.47m out of plumb, more than five degrees from the vertical. The most recent solution saw steel braces slung around the third storey that were then joined to steel cables attached to neighbouring buildings. This held the tower in place as engineers began gingerly removing soil from below the northern foundations. After some 70 tonnes of earth had been extracted, the tower sank to its 18th-century level and, in the process, rectified the lean by 43.8cm. Experts believe that this will guarantee the tower's future for the next three centuries.

Access to the Leaning Tower is limited to 40 people at one time – children under eight are not allowed in/up and those aged eight to 12 years must hold an adult's hand. To avoid disappointment, book in advance online or go straight to a ticket office when you arrive in Pisa to book a slot for later in the day. Visits last 30 minutes and involve a steep climb up 300-odd occasionally slippery steps.

NEED TO KNOW

Torre Pendente; www.opapisa.it; Piazza dei Miracoli; incl admission to cathedral €18; ☺10am-4.30pm Dec & Jan, 9.40am-4.30pm Nov & Feb, 9am-5.30pm Mar, 8.30am-8pm Apr-Sep, 9am-6.30pm Oct

works of art once displayed in the cathedral and baptistry, this museum's highlights include Giovanni Pisano's ivory carving of the *Madonna and Child* (1299), which was made for the cathedral's high altar, as well as his mid-13th-century *Madonna del colloquio,* originally from a gate of the *duomo.* Don't miss the tranquil cloister garden with great views of the Leaning Tower.

🛏 Sleeping & Eating

Hotel Bologna   Hotel €€
(📞 05 050 21 20; www.hotelbologna.pisa.it; Via Mazzini 57; d €134-198, tr €188-278, q €194-298; ❄ @ 🛜 🚲) Well away from the Piazza dei Miracoli mayhem (but an easy 1km walk or bike ride), this four-star choice on the south side of the Arno is a 68-room oasis of peace and tranquillity. Its rooms have wooden floors and high ceilings, and some are nicely frescoed. Those for four make it a practical, if pricey, family choice. Courtyard parking/bike hire costs €10/12 per day.

Hotel Relais
dell'Orologio   Hotel €€€
(📞 05 083 03 61; www.hotelrelaisorologio.com; Via della Faggiola 12-14; s/d from €120/195; ❄ 🛜) Something of a honeymoon venue, Pisa's dreamy five-star hotel occupies a tastefully restored 14th-century fortified tower house in a quiet street. Some rooms have original frescoes and the flowery patio restaurant makes a welcome retreat from the crowds. Book through its website to bag the cheapest deal.

Osteria Bernardo   Modern Tuscan €€
(📞 05 057 52 16; www.osteriabernardo.it; Piazza San Paolo all'Orto 1; meals €30; 🕑lunch & dinner Tue-Sun) This small *osteria* on one of Pisa's loveliest squares is the perfect fusion of easy dining and gourmet excellence. Its menu is small – just four or five dishes to choose from for each course – and its cuisine is creative.

Osteria del
Porton Rosso   Osteria €€
(📞 05 058 05 66; www.portonrosso.com; Vicolo del Porton Rosso 11; meals €25; 🕑lunch & dinner

Mon-Sat) Don't be put off by the rather dank alley leading to this busy *osteria* (casual eatery) a block north of the river. Inside, you'll encounter friendly staff and excellent regional cuisine from the land and the nearby sea. Pisan specialities such as fresh ravioli with salted cod and chickpeas happily coexist with Tuscan classics such as grilled fillet steak, and the €10 lunchtime deal is unbeatable value.

ℹ Getting There & Away

Air

Galileo Galilei Airport (www.pisa-airport.com) Tuscany's main international airport, 2km south of town, has flights to most major European cities.

Train

There is a handy **left luggage office** (Deposito Bagagli; 1st 12hr €4, subsequent 12hr €2; 🕑6am-9pm) at **Pisa Centrale** (Piazza della Stazione) train station – not to be confused with north-of-town Pisa San Rossore station. Regional train services to/from Pisa Centrale:

Florence €7, 1¼ hours, frequent

Livorno €2.50, 15 minutes, frequent

Lucca €3.30, 30 minutes, every 30 minutes

ℹ Getting Around

To/From the Airport

The LAM Rossa (red) bus line (€1.10, 10 minutes, every 10 to 20 minutes) passes through the city centre and the train station en route to/from the airport. Buy tickets from the blue ticket machine, next to the bus stops to the right of the train station exit.

A taxi between the airport and city centre costs around €10. To book, call **Radio Taxi Pisa** (📞05 054 16 00; www.cotapi.it).

Trains run to/from Pisa Centrale (€2.50, five minutes, at least 30 per day); purchase and validate your ticket before boarding.

Car & Motorcycle

Parking costs up to €2 per hour, but you must be careful that the car park you choose is not in the city's ZTL. There's a free car park outside the zone on Lungarno Guadalongo near the Fortezza di San Gallo on the south side of the Arno.

Lucca

This beautiful old city elicits love at first sight with its rich history, handsome churches and excellent restaurants. Hidden behind imposing Renaissance walls, it is an essential stopover on any Tuscan tour and a perfect base for exploring the Apuane Alps and the Garfagnana.

◉ Sights

Palazzo Pfanner
Palace

(www.palazzopfanner.it; Via degli Asili 33; palace or garden adult/reduced €4.50/4, both €6/5; ⏱10am-6pm summer) Set fire to the romantic in you with a stroll around this beautiful 17th-century palace, where parts of *Portrait of a Lady* (1996) starring Nicole Kidman and John Malkovich were shot. Its baroque-style garden – the only one of substance within the city walls – is irresistible with its ornamental pond, Belle Epoque lemon house and 18th-century statues of Greek gods posing between the potted lemon trees.

City Wall
City Walls

Lucca's monumental *mura* (wall) was built around the old city in the 16th and 17th centuries and remains in almost perfect condition due to the long periods of peace the city has enjoyed. It's 12m high and 4km long; the ramparts are crowned with a tree-lined footpath that looks down on the *centro storico* and out towards the Apuane Alps.

Cattedrale di San Martino
Cathedral

(Piazza San Martino; sacristy adult/reduced €3/2, with cathedral museum & Chiesa dei SS Giovanni e Reparata €7/5; ⏱7am-6pm summer, to 5pm winter; sacristy 9.30am-4.45pm Mon-Fri, 9.30am-6.45pm Sat, 11.30am-5pm Sun) Lucca's predominantly Romanesque cathedral dates to the start of the 11th century. Its stunning facade was constructed in the prevailing Lucca-Pisan style and designed to accommodate the pre-existing *campanile*. The reliefs over the left doorway of the portico are believed to be by Nicola Pisano.

🛏 Sleeping

Tourist offices have accommodation lists and, if you visit in person, can make reservations for you (free of charge); pay 10% of the room price as on-the-spot deposit and the remainder at the hotel.

Piccolo Hotel Puccini
Hotel €

(📞05 835 54 21; www.hotelpuccini.com; Via di Poggio 9; s/d €73/98; ❄🛜) Snug around the corner from the great man himself (or at least a bronze statue) and the house where he was born is this well-run small hotel. Decor is old-fashioned, and its 14 rooms have high ceilings, modern bathrooms and vintage ceiling fans. A simple breakfast costs €3.50 and rates are around 30% lower in the depths of winter.

2italia
Apartment €€

(📞392 9960271; www.2italia.com; Via della Anfiteatro 74; apt for 2 adults & up to 4 children €190; 🛜👶) Five family-friendly self-contained apartments overlooking Piazza Anfiteatro, with a communal kids' playroom in the attic. Available on a nightly basis (minimum two nights), 2italia is the brainchild of well-travelled parents-of-three Kristin (English) and Kaare (Norwegian). Spacious apartments sleep up to six, have fully equipped kitchens, and come with sheets and towels.

Alla Corte degli Angeli
Boutique Hotel €€

(📞05 8346 9204; www.allacortedegliangeli. com; Via degli Angeli 23; s/d €120/190; ❄@🛜) Occupying three floors of a 15th-century townhouse, this four-star boutique hotel has just 10 rooms and a lovely lounge. Beautifully frescoed rooms are named after flowers: lovers in the hugely romantic Rosa room can lie beneath a pergola and swallow-filled sky, while guests in Orchidea have their own private shower-sauna.

🍴 Eating

Da Felice
Pizzeria €

(www.pizzeriadafelice.com; Via Buia 12; focaccias €1-3, pizza slices €1.30; ⏱10am-8.30pm Mon-Sat) This buzzing local, which has sat behind Piazza San Michele since 1960, is easy to spot – come noon look for the crowd packed around two tiny tables inside, spilling out the door or squatting on one of two street-side benches. *Cecina* and *castagnacci* are the raison d'être.

Trattoria da Leo
Trattoria **€**

(📞05 8349 2236; Via Tegrimi 1; meals €25; 🕐lunch & dinner Mon-Sat) A veteran everyone knows and loves, Leo is famed around town for its friendly ambience and cheap food – which ranges from plain Jane acceptable to grandma delicious. Come early in summer to snag one of 10 checked-cloth-draped tables crammed beneath parasols on the narrow street outside. No credit cards.

Cantine Bernardini
Tuscan **€€**

(📞05 8349 4336; www.cantinebernardini.com; Via del Suffragio 7; meals €40; 🕐lunch & dinner Tue-Sun) This hybrid *osteria-enoteca*, hidden in the red-brick vaulted cellars of 16th-century Palazzo Bernardini, has the balance just right. Seasonal Tuscan dishes tempt, and the wine list is exceptional. Extra kudos for the kids' menu and Friday-evening DJs.

Canuleia
Tuscan **€€**

(📞05 8346 7470; Via Canuleia 14; meals €35; 🕐lunch & dinner Tue-Sun) What makes this dining location stand out from the crowd is its secret walled garden out the back – the perfect spot to escape the tourist hordes and listen to birds tweet over partridge risotto, artichoke and prawn spaghetti or a traditional *peposa* (beef and pepper stew).

ℹ️ Information

Tourist Office (📞05 8358 3150; www.comune. lucca.it; Piazzale Verdi; 🕐9am-7pm summer, to 5.30pm winter) Free hotel reservations; bicycle hire and a left-luggage service.

ℹ️ Getting There & Away

Bus

From the bus stops around Piazzale Verdi, **Vaibus** (www.vaibus.it) runs services throughout the region, including to Pisa airport (€3.20, 45 minutes to one hour, 30 daily) and Castelnuovo di Garfagnana (€4.20, 1½ hours, eight daily)

Train

The station is south of the city walls: take the path across the moat and through the tunnel under Baluardo San Colombano.

Florence €7, 1¼ to 1¾ hours, hourly

Pisa €3.30, 30 minutes, every half hour

Viareggio €3.30, 25 minutes, hourly

Palazzo Pfanner, Lucca

PHILIP GAME/GETTY IMAGES ©

Local produce for sale

RACHEL LEWIS/GETTY IMAGES ©

Siena

The rivalry between historic adversaries Siena and Florence continues to this day, and participation isn't limited to the locals – most travellers tend to develop a strong preference for one over the other. These allegiances often boil down to aesthetic preference: while Florence saw its greatest flourishing during the Renaissance, Siena's enduring artistic glories are largely Gothic.

◎ Sights

Piazza del Campo   Piazza

This sloping piazza, popularly known as Il Campo, has been Siena's civic and social centre since being staked out by the Consiglio dei Nove in the mid-12th century. It was built on the site of a former Roman marketplace, and its pie-piece paving design is divided into nine sectors to represent the number of members of the council. At the lowest point of the square stands the spare, elegant **Palazzo Comunale (Palazzo Pubblico)**, purpose-built in the late 13th century as the piazza's centrepiece and now home

to the Museo Civico. One of the most graceful Gothic buildings in Italy, it has an ingeniously designed concave facade that mirrors the opposing convex curve formed by the piazza.

Museo Civico   Museum

(www.comune.siena.it; Palazzo Comunale, Il Campo; adult/EU reduced €8/4.50; ◎10am-6.15pm mid-Mar–Oct, to 5.15pm Nov–mid-Mar) The city's most famous museum occupies rooms richly frescoed by artists of the Sienese school. These are unusual in that they were commissioned by the governing body of the city, rather than by the Church, and many depict secular subjects instead of the favoured religious themes of the time.

Duomo   Church

(www.operaduomo.siena.it; Piazza del Duomo; admission Mar-Oct €4, Nov-Feb free; ◎10.30am-6.30pm Mon-Sat, 1.30-5.30pm Sun Mar-Oct, to 5pm Nov-Feb) Construction of the *duomo* started in 1215 and work continued well into the 14th century. The magnificent facade of white, green and red polychrome marble was designed by Giovanni Pisano (the statues of philosophers and prophets

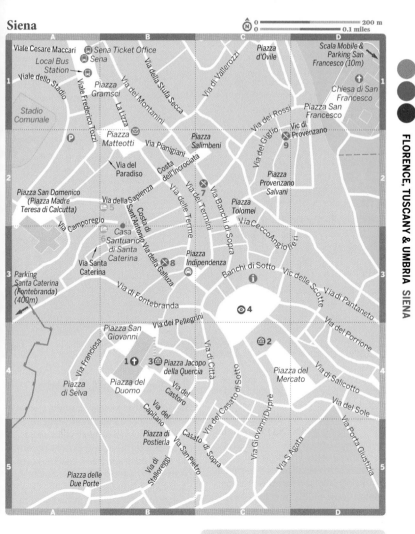

Siena

are copies; you'll find the originals in the Museo dell'Opera).

The interior is truly stunning. Walls and pillars continue the black-and-white-stripe theme of the exterior, while the vaults are painted blue with gold stars. The inlaid-marble floor, decorated with 56 panels by about 40 artists and executed over the course of 200 years (14th to 16th centuries), depicts historical and biblical subjects. Unfortunately, about half of the panels are obscured by unsightly, protective covering, and are revealed only

Siena

from 21 August through to 27 October each year (admission is €6 during this period).

Through a door from the north aisle is the enchanting **Libreria Piccolomini**, built to house the books of Enea Silvio Piccolomini, better known as Pius II. The walls of the small hall are decorated with vividly coloured narrative frescoes painted between 1502 and 1507 by Bernardino Pinturicchio and depicting events in Piccolomini's life.

Museo dell'Opera del Duomo

Museum

(Piazza del Duomo; admission €7; ⏱10.30am-6.30pm Mon-Sat, 1.30-5.30pm Sun Mar-Oct, to 5pm Nov-Feb) The collection here showcases artworks that formerly adorned the cathedral, including the 12 statues of prophets and philosophers by Giovanni Pisano that decorated the facade. Their creator designed them to be viewed from ground level, which is why they look so distorted as they crane uncomfortably forward.

🎇 Festivals & Events

Dating from the Middle Ages, the spectacular annual **Il Palio** event stages a series of colourful pageants and a wild horse race on 2 July and 16 August. Ten of Siena's 17 *contrade* (town districts) compete for the coveted *palio* (silk banner). Each *contrada* has its own traditions, symbol and colours plus its own church and *palio* museum.

🛏 Sleeping

Hotel Alma Domus

Hotel €

(📞0577 4 41 77; www.hotelalmadomus.it; Via Camporegio 37; s €40-48, d without view €60-75, d with view €65-85, q €95-125; ❄@🛜) Owned by the Catholic diocese and still home to six Dominican nuns, this convent now operates as a budget hotel. And though its prices are low, the standard of its recently renovated 4th-floor rooms is anything but. Most have new bathrooms and beds, air-con and views over the narrow green Fontebranda valley across to the *duomo*.

Pensione Palazzo Ravizza   Boutique Hotel €€

(☏0577 28 04 62; www.palazzoravizza.it; Pian dei Mantellini 34; loft r €80-150, d €100-220, ste €180-320; P❄@🛜) Occupying a Renaissance-era *palazzo* located in a quiet but convenient corner of the city, this extremely friendly hotel offers standard rooms with frescoed ceilings, huge beds and small but well-equipped bathrooms. Suites are even more impressive, with views over the delightful rear garden. The free on-site parking is a major draw and low-season rates are a huge bargain.

Campo Regio Relais   Boutique Hotel €€€

(☏0577 22 20 73; www.camporegio.com; Via della Sapienza 25; s €150-300, d €190-300, ste €250-600; ❄@🛜) Siena's most charming hotel has only six rooms, all of which are individually decorated and luxuriously equipped. Breakfast is served in the sumptuously decorated lounge or on the terrace, which has a sensational view of the *duomo* and Torre del Mangia.

🍴 Eating

Morbidi   Deli €

(www.morbidi.com; Via Banchi di Sopra 75; ⏱9am-8pm Mon-Sat, lunch buffet 12.30-2.30pm) Local gastronomes shop here as the range of cheese, cured meats and imported delicacies is the best in Siena. Also notable is the downstairs lunch buffet, which offers fantastic value. For a mere €12, you can graze on platters of *antipasti*, salads, pastas and a dessert of the day. Bottled water is supplied, wine and coffee cost extra.

Ristorante Grotta Santa Caterina da Bagoga   Tuscan €€

(☏0577 28 22 08; www.bagoga.it; Via della Galluzza 26; meals €28; ⏱12.30-2.30pm & 7.30-10.30pm Tue-Sat, 12.30-2.30pm Sun) Pierino Fagnani ('Bagogoga'), one of Siena's most famous Palio jockeys, swapped his saddle for an apron in 1973 and has been

If You Like...
Wine

Stripe upon stripe of vines over undulating, sun-drenched Tuscan hills: the source of Chianti wines is around Greve, along the SR222, 26km south of Florence. Try these local wineries to sample some of Italy's finest tipples.

1 ANTINORI NEL CHIANTI CLASSICO
(www.antinorichianticlassico.it; Via Cassia per Siena 133, Località Bargino; tour & tasting €20, bookings essential; ⏰11am-6pm Mon-Sat, to 2pm Sun) Visiting this cellar complex is a James Bond–esque experience. Show a print-out of your reservation at the gated, guarded entrance and then approach the sculptural main building, which is built into the hillside. Inside, your one-hour guided tour (English and Italian) finishes with a tasting of three Antinori wines in an all-glass tasting room suspended above barrels in the cellar (wow!).

2 BADIA A PASSIGNANO
(www.osteriadipassignano.com) This 11th-century abbey located 6km west of Montefioralle is owned by the Vallumbrosans, a Benedictine religious order. It is surrounded by a picturesque wine estate owned by the Antinoris, one of Tuscany's best known winemaking families. The main building is closed for a restoration that doesn't look as if it will be completed for many years, but the vineyards and historic cellars can be visited on a guided tour.

3 CASTELLO DI VERRAZZANO
(☎055 85 42 43; www.verrazzano.com; Via Citille, Greti) This castle 3km north of Greve was once home to Giovanni da Verrazzano (1485–1528), who explored the North American coast and is commemorated in New York by the Verrazano Narrows bridge (the good captain lost a 'z' from his name somewhere in the mid-Atlantic). Today it presides over a 220-hectare historic wine estate. There are a number of guided tours on offer, each of which incorporate a short visit to the historic wine cellar and gardens and tastings of the estate's wines (including its flagship Chianti Classico) and other products (perhaps honey, olive oil or balsamic vinegar).

operating this much-loved restaurant near the Casa Santuario di Santa Caterina ever since. Traditional Tuscan palate pleasers feature on the menu, and are perhaps best appreciated in the four-course 'tipico' (€35) or 'degustazione' (€50 with wine) menus.

Tre Cristi Seafood €€€
(☎0577 28 06 08; www.trecristi.com; Vicolo di Provenzano 1; 3-course tasting menus €35-45, 5-course menus €65; ⏰12.30-3pm & 7.30-10.30pm Mon-Sat) Seafood restaurants are thin on the ground in this meat-obsessed region, so the long existence of Tre Cristi (it's been around since 1830) should be heartily celebrated. The menu is as elegant as the decor, and added touches such as a complimentary glass of *prosecco* (dry sparkling wine) at the start of the meal only add to the quality of the experience.

ℹ Information

Tourist Office (☎0577 28 05 51; www.terresiena.it; Piazza del Campo 56; ⏰9.30am-6.30pm Easter-Sep, 9.30am-5.30pm Mon-Fri, to 12.30pm Sun Oct-Easter) Reserves accommodation, sells a map of Siena (€1), organises car and scooter hire, and sells train tickets (commission applies).

ℹ Getting There & Away

Siena isn't on a major train line so buses are generally a better alternative. Siena Mobilità (☎800 570530; www.sienamobilita.it), part of the Tiemme network, runs services between Siena and other parts of Tuscany. It has a ticket office (⏰6.30am-7.30pm Mon-Fri, 7am-7.30pm Sat & Sun) underneath the main bus station in Piazza Gramsci, where there is also a left-luggage office (per 24 hours €5.50).

Frequent *Corse Rapide* (Express) buses race up to Florence (€7.80, 1¼ hours); they are a better option than the standard *Corse Ordinarie* services, which stop in Poggibonsi and Colle di Val d'Elsa en route. Other regional destinations include the following:

/GETTY IMAGES ©

⭐ Don't Miss
Chianti

The ancient vineyards in this postcard-perfect part of Tuscany produce the grapes used in Chianti Classico, a sangiovese-dominated drop sold under the Gallo Nero (Black Cockerel/Rooster) trademark.

Split between the provinces of Florence (Chianti Fiorentino) and Siena (Chianti Sienese), Chianti is usually accessed via the SR222 (Via Chiantigiana) and is criss-crossed by a picturesque network of *strade provinciale* (provincial roads) and *strade secondaria* (secondary roads), some of which are unsealed. You'll pass immaculately maintained vineyards and olive groves, honey-coloured stone farmhouses, graceful Romanesque *pieve* (rural churches), handsome Renaissance villas and imposing castles built by Florentine and Sienese warlords during the Middle Ages.

For information about the Consorzio Vino Chianti Classico (the high-profile consortium of local producers), go to www.chianticlassico.com/en.

San Gimignano €6, one to 1½ hours, 10 daily either direct or changing in Poggibonsi

Montalcino €3.65, 1½ hours, six daily

Montepulciano €5.15, 1¾ hours

Sena (☏861 199 19 00; www.sena.it) buses run to/from Rome Tibertina (€23, 3½ hours, six daily), Fiumicino Airport (€23, 3¾ hours, two daily), Turin (€36, 8¼ hours, one daily), Milan (€36, 4¼ hours, two daily), Venice (€29, 5½ hours, one daily) and Perugia (€12, 1½ hours, one daily). Its ticket office (⊙8.30am-7.45pm Mon-Sat) is also underneath the bus station in Piazza Gramsci.

ℹ Getting Around

A Siena Mobilità bus travels between Pisa airport and Siena (one way/return €14/26, two hours), leaving Siena at 7.10am and Pisa at 1pm. Tickets should be purchased at least one day in advance from the bus station or online.

RACHEL LEWIS/GETTY IMAGES ©

★ Don't Miss
San Gimignano

As you crest the hill coming from the east, the 15 towers of this walled hill town look like a medieval Manhattan. Originally an Etruscan village, the town was named after the bishop of Modena, San Gimignano, who is said to have saved the city from Attila the Hun. It became a comune in 1199 and was very prosperous due in part to its location on the Via Francigena – building a tower taller than those built by one's neighbour (there were originally 72) became a popular way for the town's prominent families to flaunt their power and wealth.

San Gimignano's Romanesque **Collegiata** (Duomo Collegiata o Basilica di Santa Maria Assunta; Piazza del Duomo; adult/child €3.50/1.50; ⊙10am-7.10pm Mon-Fri, to 5.10pm Sat, 12.30-7.10pm Sun Apr-Oct, shorter hrs rest of year, closed 2nd half Nov & Jan) is named after the college of priests who originally managed it. Parts of the building date to the second half of the 11th century, but its remarkably vivid frescoes, which resemble a vast medieval comic strip, date from the 14th century.

The 12th-century Palazzo Comunale, housing the **Museo Civico** (Piazza del Duomo 2; adult/reduced €5/4; ⊙9.30am-7pm Apr-Sep, 11am-5.30pm Oct-Mar), has always been the centre of local government; its Sala di Dante is where the great poet addressed the town's council in 1299, urging it to support the Guelph cause, and its pinacoteca has a charming collection of paintings from the Sienese and Florentine schools of the 12th to 15th centuries.

Locals love **Ristorante la Mandragola** (☎0577 94 03 77; www.locandalamandragola. it; Via Berignano 58; meals €37, set menus €14-25, kids menu €10; ⊙noon-2.30pm & 7.30-9.30pm, closed Thu Nov-early Mar). Built into the city walls, it's big enough to seat regulars, day-tripping Italians and foreign tour groups and still have space for the rest of us.

Buses connect frequently with Florence and Siena.

Montalcino

This medieval hill town is renowned for its coveted wine, Brunello. In February each year, the new vintage is celebrated at **Benvenuto Brunello**, a weekend of tastings and award presentations organised by the Consorzio del Vino Brunello di Montalcino (www.consorziobrunellodimontalcino.it), the association of local producers.

◉ Sights

The main activity in town is visiting *enoteche*. For non-alcoholic diversion, consider popping into the modest **Museo Civico e Diocesano d'Arte Sacra** (📞0577 84 60 14; Via Ricasoli 31; adult/child €4.50/3; ⏰10am-1pm & 2-5.50pm Tue-Sun), just off Piazza Sant'Agostino. It has a fine collection of painted sculptures by the Sienese school.

Within the 14th-century **fortezza** (Piazzale Fortezza; courtyard free, ramparts adult/child €4/2, combined ticket with museum €6; ⏰9am-8pm Apr-Oct, 10am-6pm Nov-Mar) is an *enoteca* where you can sample and buy local wines (tasting of 2/3/5 Brunellos €9/13/19) and also climb up to the fort's ramparts.

🛏 Sleeping

Hotel Vecchia Oliviera   Boutique Hotel €€
(📞0577 84 60 28; www.vecchiao liviera.com; Via Landi 1; s €70-85, d €120-190, ste €200-240; ⏰closed Dec–mid-Feb; P ❄ 🛜 ≋) Just beside the Porta Cerbaia, this former olive mill has been tastefully restored and converted into a stylish small hotel. Each of the 11 rooms is individually decorated; the superior ones come with view and jacuzzi. The garden terrace has stunning views, and the pool is in an attractive garden setting.

Hotel Il Giglio   Hotel €€
(📞0577 84 81 67; www.gigliohotel.com; Via Soccorso Saloni 5; s €95, d €135-145, annex s/d €60/95, apt €100-150; P 🛜) The comfortable wrought-iron beds here are each gilded with a painted *giglio* (lily), and all doubles in the main building have a panoramic view. Room 1 has a private terrace, and the small single is very attractive.

🍴 Eating & Drinking

Osticcio   Wine Bar €€
(www.osticcio.it; Via Matteotti 23; antipasto €13-24, meals €37; ⏰noon-4pm & 7-11pm Fri-Wed, noon-7pm Thu) A huge selection of Brunello and its more modest – but still very palatable – sibling Rosso di Montalcino joins dozens of wines from around the world at this excellent *enoteca*. After browsing the wines, claim a table in the upstairs dining room for a glass with an antipasto plate.

Fiaschetteria Italiana 1888   Cafe
(Piazza del Popolo 6; ⏰7.30am-midnight, closed Thu Oct-Easter) We doff our hats to this atmosphere-laden *enoteca/*cafe on the main piazza, which has been serving

Palazzo Comunale (p248), Siena
DAVID C TOMLINSON/GETTY IMAGES ©

coffee and glasses of Brunello to locals since 1888 and has managed to retain both its decor and charm for the duration.

ℹ️ Information

Tourist Office (📞0577 84 93 31; www.prolocomontalcino.com; Costa del Municipio 1; ⏰10am-1pm & 2-5.50pm)

ℹ️ Getting There & Away

Regular Siena Mobilità buses (€4.90, 1½ hours, six daily Monday to Saturday) run to/from Siena.

Montepulciano

Exploring this reclaimed narrow ridge of volcanic rock will push your quadriceps to their failure point. When this happens, self-medicate with a generous pour of the highly reputed Vino Nobile while drinking in the spectacular views over the Val di Chiana and Val d'Orcia.

🔘 Sights

Montepulciano's streets harbour a wealth of *palazzi*, churches and fine buildings. The main street, called in stages Via di Gracciano nel Corso, Via di Voltaia nel Corso and Via dell'Opio nel Corso ('the Corso'), climbs uphill from Porta dal Prato, near the car park on Piazza Don Minzoni. Halfway along its length are Michelozzo's **Chiesa di Sant'Agostino** (Piazza Michelozzo; ⏰9am-noon & 3-6pm) and the **Torre di Pulcinella**, a medieval tower house topped by the hunched figure of Pulcinella (Punch of Punch and Judy fame), who strikes the hours on the town clock.

After passing historic **Caffè Poliziano**, which has been operating since 1868, the Corso eventually does a dog-leg at Via del Teatro, continuing uphill past **Cantine Contucci** (www.contucci.it; Via del Teatro 1; fee for tastings; ⏰9.30am-12.30pm & 2.30-6pm Mon-Fri, from 9.30am Sat & Sun), housed underneath the handsome *palazzo* of the same name. You can visit the historic cellars and taste local tipples here. Palazzo Contucci fronts onto **Piazza Grande**, the town's highest point. Also here are the 14th-century **Palazzo Comunale** (panoramic terrace €2) and the late-16th-century

duomo, with its unfinished facade. Behind the high altar is Taddeo di Bartolo's lovely *Assumption* triptych (1401).

From Piazza Grande, Via Ricci runs downhill past **Palazzo Ricci** (www.palazzoricci.com; Via Ricci 9-11); its lovely main salon hosts concerts during the year (see website for details). From the *palazzo*'s courtyard, stairs lead down to a historic wine cellar, **Cantina del Redi** (fee for tastings; ⏰10.30am-7pm mid-Mar-Jan, Sat & Sun only Jan–mid-Mar). Via Ricci continues past the **Museo Civico** (www.museocivicomontepulciano.it; Via Ricci 10; adult/reduced €5/3; ⏰10am-1pm & 3-6pm Tue-Sun Mar-July & Sep-Oct, 10am-7pm Aug, Sat & Sun only Nov-Feb), home to an eclectic collection of art works, and terminates in Piazza San Francesco, where you can admire a panoramic view of the Val di Chiana.

🍴 Eating

Osteria Acquacheta   Osteria €
(📞0578 71 70 86; www.acquacheta.eu; Via del Teatro 22; meals €20; ⏰noon-4pm & 7.30-10.30pm Wed-Mon) Hugely popular with locals and tourists alike, this bustling place specialises in *bistecca alla fiorentina* (chargrilled steak), which comes to the table in huge, exceptionally flavoursome slabs. Lunch sittings are at 12.15pm and 2.15pm; dinner at 7.30pm and 9.15pm – book ahead.

La Grotta   Traditional Italian €€€
(📞0578 75 74 79; www.lagrottamontepulciano.it; Via San Biagio 15; meals €44, 6-course tasting menu €48; ⏰12.30-2.30pm & 7.30-10pm Thu-Tue, closed mid-Jan–mid-Mar) Facing the Tempio di San Biagio on the road to Chiusi, La Grotta has elegant dining rooms and a gorgeous courtyard garden that's perfect for summer dining. The food is traditional with a modern twist or two, and service is exemplary. A hint: don't skip dessert.

ℹ️ Getting There & Around

The bus station is next to Car Park No 5. Siena Mobilità runs four buses daily between Siena and Montepulciano (€6.60, one hour via Pienza). There are three services per day to/from Florence (€11.20, 90 minutes). Regular buses connect with Chiusi-Chianciano Terme (€3.40, 40 minutes), from where you can catch a train to Florence (€12.50, two hours via Arezzo).

UMBRIA

Perugia

POP 162,100

Lifted by a hill above a valley patterned with fields, where the Tiber River runs swift and clear, Perugia is Umbria's petite and immediately likeable capital. Its *centro storico* (historic centre) rises in a helter-skelter of cobbled alleys, arched stairways and piazzas framed by magnificent *palazzi* (mansions). History seeps through every shadowy corner of these streets and an aimless wander through them can feel like time travel.

Back in the 21st century, Perugia is a party-loving, pleasure-seeking university city, with students pepping up the nightlife and filling cafe terraces.

◎ Sights

Palazzo dei Priori   Museum

Rising proudly above the main piazza, this palace, constructed between the 13th and 14th centuries, is architecturally striking with its tripartite windows, Gothic portal and fortress-like crenelations. It was formerly the headquarters of the city's magistrature.

Today it harbours some of the city's finest museums, including Umbria's foremost art gallery, the stunning **Galleria Nazionale dell'Umbria** (www.gallerianazionaleumbria.it; Corso Vannucci 19; adult/reduced €8/4; ◷8.30am-7.30pm Tue-Sun). Entered via Corso Vannucci, it's an art historian's dream, with 30 rooms of works featuring everything from Byzantine art to the Renaissance creations of homegrown heroes Pinturicchio and Perugino.

Perugia's piggy bank in medieval times, the extravagantly adorned **Nobile Collegio del Cambio** (Exchange Hall; Corso Vannucci 25; admission €4.50, combined ticket with Nobile Collegio della Mercanzia €5.50; ◷9am-12.30pm & 2.30-5.30pm Mon-Sat, 9am-1pm Sun) has three rooms: the Sala dei Legisti (Legist Chamber), with 17th-century wooden stalls carved by Giampiero Zuccari; the Sala dell'Udienza (Audience Chamber), with outstanding Renaissance frescoes by Perugino; and the Chapel of San Giovanni Battista, painted by a student of Perugino's, Giannicola di Paolo.

Perugia

JAMES BRAUND/GETTY IMAGES ©

Casa Museo di Palazzo Sorbello
Museum

(www.casamuseosorbello.org; Piazza Piccinino 9; adult/reduced €5/3; ⏰guided tours 11am-2pm) A few steps from the Piazza IV Novembre, this exquisite 17th-century mansion, once owned by the noble Sorbello family, has recently been restored to its frescoed, gilt-clad, chandelier-lit 18th-century prime. Guided tours (in Italian) let you admire the family's opulent collection of art, porcelain, embroidery and manuscripts.

🛏️ Sleeping & Eating

B&B San Fiorenzo
B&B €€

(☎393 3869987; www.sanfiorenzo.com; Via Alessi 45; r €70-120; 📶) Buried in Perugia's medieval centre is this charming 15th-century *palazzo*, where Luigi and Monica make you welcome in one of three unique rooms. A Florentine architect has carefully incorporated mod cons and marble bathrooms into spacious quarters with brick vaulting, lime-washed walls and antique furnishings.

Hotel Brufani Palace
Luxury Hotel €€€

(☎075 573 25 41; www.brufanipalace.com; Piazza Italia 12; s €115-175, d €125-220, ste €263-530; 🅿️❄️@📶♨️) From its hilltop perch, this five-star hotel has captivating views of the valley and hills beyond. The hotel builds on this splendor with frescoed public rooms, impeccably decorated bedrooms, marble bathrooms, a garden terrace for summer dining and helpful trilingual staff. Swim over Etruscan ruins in the subterranean fitness centre. There's access for disabled guests.

Pizzeria Mediterranea
Pizzeria €

(☎075 572 13 22; Piazza Piccinino 11/12; pizzas €5-12; ⏰daily) Perugians know to come here for the best pizza in town. A spaceship-sized wood-fired brick oven heats up pizzas, from the simplest *margherita* to the 12-topping 'his and hers'. It gets busy enough to queue on Saturday nights.

La Taverna
Italian €€

(☎075 572 41 28; www.ristorantelataverna.com; Via delle Streghe 8; meals €30-40; ⏰lunch &

Left: Pastries, Perugia;
Below: Fresco in Assisi (p261)
(LEFT) FRANK WING/GETTY IMAGES ©; (BELOW) DIANA MAYFIELD/GETTY IMAGES ©

SCENDI LE SCALE E TROVERAI L'OSTELLO DOVE NASQUE FRANCESCO IL POVERELLO

dinner daily) Way up there on the Perugia dining wish list, La Taverna consistently wins the praise of local foodies. Chef Claudio cooks market-fresh produce with flair and precision, while waiters treat you like one of the *famiglia*.

ℹ️ Information

Banks line Corso Vannucci. All have ATMs.

InfoUmbria (📞 075 3 26 39; www.umbriabest. com; Via della Pallotta 5; ⊙9am-1pm & 2.30-6.30pm Mon-Fri, 9am-1pm Sat) Also known as InfoTourist, it offers information on all of Umbria and is a fantastic resource for *agriturismi* (farm stay accommodation).

Tourist Office (📞 075 573 64 58; http://turismo. comune.perugia.it; Piazza Matteotti 18; ⊙9am-7pm) Housed in the 14th-century Loggia dei Lanari, Perugia's main tourist office has stacks of info on the city, maps and up-to-date bus and train timetables.

Trains To/From Perugia

In the southwest of town, Perugia's main **train station** (📞 075 963 78 91; Piazza Vittorio Veneto) has trains running to the following destinations.

TO	FARE (€)	DURATION	FREQUENCY
Assisi	2.50	20min	hourly
Florence	13.50-19	2hr	every 2 hours
Orvieto	7-14.50	1¾-3hr	10 daily
Rome	11-23	2¼-3½hr	17 daily

Detour:
Urbino

Raphael's Renaissance 'hood is the vibrant university town of Urbino. The patriarch of the Montefeltro family, Duca Federico da Montefeltro, created the hippest art scene of the 15th century, gathering the great artists, architects and scholars of his day to create a sort of think-tank. The town's splendour was made official by Unesco, which deemed the entire city centre a World Heritage Site.

A microcosm of Renaissance architecture, art and history, the **Palazzo Ducale** (www.palazzoducaleurbino.it; adult/reduced €5/2.50; ☾8.30am-7.15pm Tue-Sun, to 2pm Mon) contains the **Galleria Nazionale delle Marche**, **Museo Archeologico** and **Museo della Ceramica**. The museum triptych is housed within Federico da Montefeltro's palace, a whimsically turreted Renaissance masterpiece.

North of the Piazza della Repubblica you'll find **Casa Natale di Raffaello** (Via Raffaello 57; adult/reduced €3.50/2.50; ☾9am-1pm & 3-7pm Mon-Fri, 10am-1pm Sat & Sun summer, 9am-2pm Mon-Fri winter), the 15th-century house where Raphael was born in 1483 and spent his first 16 years. On the 1st floor is possibly one of Raphael's first frescoes, a Madonna with child.

Duck down a quiet side street to rustically elegant **Antica Osteria de la Stella** (☎0722 32 02 28; www.anticaosteriadalastella.com; Via Santa Margherita 1; meals €25-40; ☾lunch & dinner Tue-Sun), a beamed 15th-century inn once patronised by the likes of Piero della Francesca. Legendary in these parts, it puts its own inventive twist on seasonal food. Every dish strikes perfect balance, be it cocoa ravioli or venison with wild berries and polenta.

Adriabus (☎0722 37 67 38, 0800 66 43 32; www.adriabus.eu) runs hourly between Urbino and Pesaro (€3.20, 48 minutes), from where you can train to Bologna.

❶ Getting There & Away

Air

Aeroporto Sant'Egidio (PEG; ☎075 59 21 41; www.airport.umbria.it; Via dell'Aeroporto, Sant'Egidio), 13km east of the city, is small and easy to navigate, with five weekly Ryanair (www.ryanair.co.uk) flights to London Stansted.

❶ Getting Around

To/From the Airport

Umbria Mobilità (☎075 963 70 01; www.umbriamobilita.it) runs a frequent bus service from the airport to Perugia (€3, 30 minutes) and Assisi (€3, 20 minutes); you'll need the exact change. Tickets are cheaper if you buy them from the airport bar. Alternatively, a shuttle bus (€8) leaves from Piazza Italia for the airport about two hours before each flight, stopping at the train station. From the airport, buses leave once everyone is on board. A taxi costs approximately €30.

Bus

It's a steep 1.5km climb from Perugia's train station, so a bus is highly recommended (and essential for those with luggage). The bus takes you to Piazza Italia. Tickets cost €1.50 from the train-station kiosk or €2 on board. Validate your ticket on board to avoid a fine. A 10-ticket pass costs €12.90.

Minimetrò

These single-car people-movers traverse between the train station and Pincetto (just off Piazza Matteotti) every minute. A €1.50 ticket works for the bus and Minimetrò. From the train station facing the tracks, head right up a long platform.

Taxi

Available from 6am to 2am (24 hours from July to September); call ☎075 500 48 88 to arrange pick-up. A ride from the city centre to the main train station will cost about €10 to €15. Tack on €1 for each suitcase.

Assisi

POP 27,400

As if cupped in celestial hands, with the plains spreading picturesquely below and Monte Subasio rearing steep and wooded above, the mere sight of Assisi in the rosy glow of dusk is enough to send pilgrims' souls spiralling to heaven. It is at this hour, when the pitter-patter of daytripper footsteps have faded and the town is shrouded in saintly silence, that the true spirit of St Francis of Assisi, born here in 1181, can be felt most keenly.

◎ Sights

Rocca Maggiore   Fort

(Via della Rocca; adult/reduced €5/3.50; ⏱10am-sunset) Dominating the city is the massive 14th-century Rocca Maggiore, an oft-expanded, pillaged and rebuilt hill-fortress offering 360-degree views of Perugia to the north and the surrounding valleys below. Walk up winding staircases and claustrophobic passageways to reach the archer slots that served Assisians as they went medieval on Perugia.

Basilica di Santa Chiara   Church

(Piazza Santa Chiara; ⏱6.30am-noon & 2-7pm summer, to 6pm winter) Built in the 13th century in a Romanesque style, with steep ramparts and a striking white and pink facade, the basilica was raised in honour of St Clare, a spiritual contemporary of St Francis and founder of the Sorelle Povere di Santa Chiara (Order of the Poor Ladies), now known as the Poor Clares. She is buried in the church's crypt. The Byzantine cross that is said to have spoken to St Francis is also housed here.

Basilica di Santa
Maria degli Angeli   Church

(Santa Maria degli Angeli; ⏱6.15am-12.30pm & 2.30-7.30pm) That enormous domed church you can see as you approach Assisi along the Tiber Valley is the 16th-century Basilica di Santa Maria degli Angeli, the seventh largest church in the world, some 4km west and several hundred metres further down the hill from old Assisi. Built between 1565 and

1 BASILICA DI SAN FRANCESCO
Built soon after St Francis' death to house and venerate his body, the basilica (p262) is of major artistic importance. The upper church is most famous for its Giotto frescoes, while the lower church has works by Cimabue, Lorenzetti and Simone Martini. Personally, I think the lower church is the more atmospheric of the two. The crypt of St Francis is especially spiritual.

2 CHIESA DI SAN DAMIANO
This convent (p263), just outside the old city walls, has beautiful views over the Valley of Spoleto. The site itself is wonderfully silent and visually arresting. Keep an eye out for the verdant, flower-filled Giardino del Cantico, where St Francis wrote his *Cantico di Frate Sole* in approximately 1225.

3 EREMO DELLE CARCERI
These caves (p262) 4km east of Assisi are a fine example of a Franciscan hermitage. It's where St Francis would head for silent contemplation, and its location high above the town adds to the sense of isolation. It's particularly striking because it has changed very little over time.

**4 BASILICA DI SANTA
MARIA DEGLI ANGELI**
This great 16th-century basilica encases the tiny 10th-century Porziuncola chapel. On this site St Francis lived with the original members of his order, and at the site of the Cappella del Transito he passed into eternal life on 3 October 1226.

1685, its vast ornate confines house the tiny, humble **Porziuncola Chapel**, where St Francis first took refuge having found his vocation and given up his worldly goods, and which is generally regarded as the place where the Franciscan movement started. St Francis died at the site of the **Cappella del Transito** on 3 October 1226.

FRANK VAN DEN BERGH/GETTY IMAGES ©

⭐ Don't Miss
Basilica di San Francesco

Visible for miles around, the Basilica di San Francesco is the jewel in the spiritual and architectural crown of Assisi's Unesco World Heritage ensemble. For almost six centuries, its twinset of churches has been a beacon to knee-crawling, blister-footed pilgrims, brown-robed friars, Italian art lovers and saintly sightseers.

The half-light and architectural restraint of the Romanesque lower church best embodies the ascetic, introspective spirit of Franciscan life, while the brighter upper church is a Gothic wonder, containing an elaborate tableau of frescoes. Divine works by Sienese and Florentine masters like Giotto, Cimabue, Pietro Lorenzetti and Simone Martini represent an artistic weather-vane for stylistic developments across the ages.

The basilica has its own **information office** (☏ 075 819 00 84; Piazza di San Francesco; ⊙ 9.15am–noon & 2.15 –5.30pm Mon-Sat), opposite the entrance to the lower church. Here you can schedule an hour-long tour in English or Italian, led by a resident Franciscan friar. Guided tours are from 9am to 5pm Monday to Saturday; a donation of €5 to €10 per person is suggested.

NEED TO KNOW

Piazza di San Francesco; ⊙ upper church 8.30am-6.45pm summer, to 6pm winter, lower church 6am-6.45pm summer, to 6pm winter

Eremo delle Carceri   Religious

(www.eremocarceri.it; ⊙ 6.30am-7pm summer, to 6pm winter) FREE In around 1205 St Francis chose these caves above Assisi as his hermitage where he could retire to contemplate spiritual matters and be at one with nature. The *carceri* (isolated places, or 'prisons') along Monte Subasio's forested slopes are as peaceful today as in St Francis' time, albeit now surrounded by various religious buildings.

Take a contemplative walk or picnic under the oaks. It's a 4km drive (or walk) east of Assisi, and a dozen nearby hiking trails are well signposted.

Chiesa di San Damiano — Church

(Via San Damiano; ⊙10am-noon & 2-6pm, to 4.30pm winter) It's a 1.5km olive tree–lined stroll to the church where St Francis first heard the voice of God and where he wrote his *Canticle of the Creatures*. The serene surroundings are popular with pilgrims.

Foro Romano — Historic Site

(Roman Forum; Via Portica; adult/reduced €4/2.50, with Rocca Maggiore €8/5; ⊙10am-1pm & 2.30-6pm summer, to 5pm winter) On Piazza del Comune, just round the corner from the tourist office, is the entrance to the town's partially excavated Roman Forum, while on the piazza's northern side is the well-preserved facade of a 1st-century Roman temple, the **Tempio di Minerva** (admission free; ⊙7.30am-noon & 2-7pm Mon-Sat, 8.30am-noon & 2-7pm Sun), hiding a rather uninspiring 17th-century church.

Duomo di San Rufino — Church

(Piazza San Rufino; ⊙8am-1pm & 2-7pm, to 6pm winter) The 13th-century Romanesque church, remodelled by Galeazzo Alessi in the 16th century, contains the fountain where St Francis and St Clare were baptised. The facade is festooned with grotesque figures and fantastic animals.

🛏 Sleeping

Hotel Ideale — B&B €

(☎075 81 35 70; www.hotelideale.it; Piazza Matteotti 1; s/d €50/85; P ❄ 🛜) Ideal indeed, this welcoming family-run B&B sits plumb on Piazza Matteotti. Romeo the cat has the run of the shop. Many of the bright, simple rooms open onto balconies with uplifting views of the Rocca Maggiore. Breakfast is done properly, with fresh pastries, fruit and frothy cappuccino, and is served in the garden when the weather's fine.

Alla Madonna del Piatto — Agriturismo €€

(☎075 819 90 50; www.incampagna.com; Via Petrata 37; d €85-105; ⊙Mar-Nov; P 🛖) Waking up to views of meadows and olive groves sweeping up to Assisi is bound to put a spring in your step at this quiet *agriturismo*, less than 15 minutes' drive from the basilica. Each of the six rooms has been designed with care, love and character, with wrought-iron beds, antique furnishings and intricate handmade fabrics.

Nun Assisi — Luxury Hotel €€€

(☎075 815 51 50; www.nunassisi.com; Via Eremo delle Carceri 1a; s €230-280, d €280-330, ste €320-550; P @ 🛖 🛖) This former convent has been reborn as a super-stylish boutique hotel, with a clean, modern aesthetic. Stone arches and beams provide original flair in pared-down rooms with virginal white walls and flat-screen TVS. The restaurant (meals €30 to €40) puts a contemporary spin on seasonal Umbrian fare, and the gorgeous subterranean spa is set within 1st-century Roman ruins.

🍴 Eating

Trattoria Pallotta — Umbrian €€

(☎075 81 26 49; www.pallottaassisi.it; Vicolo della Volta Pinta; set menus €18-27; ⊙lunch & dinner Wed-Mon; 🍴) Head through the Volta Pinta off Piazza del Comune – being careful not to bump into someone as you gaze at the 16th-century frescoes above you – into this gorgeous setting of vaulted brick walls and wood-beamed ceilings. They cook all the Umbrian classics here: rabbit, homemade *strangozzi* (wheat noodles) and pigeon.

Osteria dei Priori — Umbrian €€

(☎075 81 21 49; Via Giotto 4; meals €25-35; ⊙Tue-Sun) Sabrina believes wholeheartedly in sourcing the best local ingredients at this wonderfully cosy osteria, where tables draped in white linen are gathered under brick vaults. Presuming you've booked ahead, you're in for quite a treat: Umbrian specialities like Norcina (pasta in a creamy mushroom-sausage sauce) and rich wild boar stew are brilliantly fresh, full of flavour and beautifully presented.

La Locanda del Podestà

Umbrian €€

(📞075 81 65 53; www.locandadelpodesta.it; Via San Giacomo 6; meals €20-30; ⏰daily) This inviting cubbyhole of a restaurant is big on old-world charm, with low arches and stone walls. Distinctly Umbrian dishes such as *torta al testo* with prosciutto and truffle-laced *strangozzi* are expertly matched by regional wines. Friendly service adds to the familiar vibe.

ℹ️ Getting There & Around

Bus

Umbria Mobilità (📞075 963 70 01; www.umbriamobilita.it) run buses run to Perugia (€4, 45 minutes, nine daily) and Gubbio (€7, 70 minutes, 11 daily) from Piazza Matteotti. Sulga (📞075 500 96 41; www.sulga.it) buses leave from Porta San Pietro for Florence (€12, 2½ hours, one daily at 7am) and Rome (€18.50, 3¼ hours, three daily).

Train

Assisi is on the Foligno–Terontola train line with regular services to Perugia (€2.50, 20 minutes, hourly). You can change at Terontola for Florence (€14.50 to €21, two to three hours, 11 daily) and at Foligno for Rome (€10 to €22, two to three hours, 14 daily). Assisi's train station is 4km west in Santa Maria degli Angeli; shuttle bus C (€1, 13 minutes) runs between the train station and Piazza Matteotti every 30 minutes. Buy tickets from the station *tabaccaio* or in town.

....

Spoleto

Presided over by a formidable medieval fortress and backed by the broad-shouldered Apennines, their summits iced with snow in winter, Spoleto is visually stunning.

Today, the town has winged its way into the limelight with its mammoth **Festival dei Due Mondi** (www.festivaldispoleto.it; ⏰late Jun–mid-Jul), a 17-day summer feast of opera, dance, music and art.

◎ Sights

Rocca Albornoziana

Fort, Museum

(Piazza Campello; adult/reduced €7.50/6.50; ⏰9.30am-7.30pm summer, to 6.30pm winter) Rising high and mighty on a hilltop above Spoleto, the Rocca, a glowering 14th-century former papal fortress, is now a fast, scenic escalator ride from Via della Ponzianina. The fortress contains the **Museo Nazionale del Ducato**, which traces the history of the Spoleto Duchy through a series of Roman, Byzantine, Carolingian and Lombard artefacts, from 5th-century sarcophagi to Byzantine jewellery.

Duomo di Spoleto

Cathedral

(Piazza Duomo; ⏰8.30am-12.30pm & 3.30-7pm summer, to 6pm winter) A flight of steps sweeps down to Spoleto's pretty pale-stone cathedral, originally built in 11th century, using huge blocks of salvaged stones from Roman buildings for its slender bell tower.

🛏️ Sleeping & Eating

Hotel San Luca

Boutique Hotel €€

(📞0743 22 33 99; www.hotelsanluca.com; Via Interna delle Mura 21; ⏰s €110-240, d €210-300; ❄️@🛜) Once a convent and now a heavenly boutique hotel, the San Luca has polished service and refined interiors to rival any of the five-stars in Umbria, yet the atmosphere is relaxed enough to cater to cyclists and walkers. Pastel tones and antique furnishings inside complement the 17th-century manicured garden. The homemade cakes are the stars of the breakfast buffet.

Tempio del Gusto

Modern Italian €€

(📞0743 4 71 12; www.iltempiodelgusto.com; Via Arco di Druso 11; meals €25-40; ⏰Fri-Wed) Intimate, inventive and unmissable, Tempio del Gusto is fine dining without the Michelin-starred price tag. The food here speaks volumes about a chef who believes in sourcing, cooking and presenting with real pride and purpose. Eros Patrizi is the whiz behind the stove. Freshly made pasta, a trio of smoked fish, herb-crusted pork – every dish strikes perfect balance.

ℹ️ Getting There & Around

Trains from the main station connect with Rome (€8 to €12.30, 1½ hours, hourly), Perugia (€4.80, one hour, nine daily) and Assisi (€3.25, 40 minutes, hourly).

Orvieto

POP 21,100

Sitting astride a volcanic plug of rock above fields streaked with vines, olive and cypress trees, Orvieto is visually stunning from the first. Like the love child of Rome and Florence and nestled midway between the two cities, history hangs over the cobbled lanes, medieval piazzas and churches of this cinematically beautiful city. And few cathedrals in Italy can hold a candle to its wedding cake of a Gothic cathedral, which frequently elicits gasps of wonder with its layers of exquisite detail.

The **Carta Unica Orvieto** (www. cartaunica.it; adult/reduced €18/15) permits entry to the town's nine main attractions (including the Cappella di San Brizio in the cathedral, Museo Claudio Faina e Civico, Orvieto Underground, Torre del Moro and Museo dell'Opera del Duomo) and a round trip on the funicular and city buses. It can be purchased at many of the attractions, the tourist office, the Piazza Cahen tourist office and the train station.

◎ Sights

Orvieto Underground   Historic Site
(www.orvietounderground.it; Piazza Duomo 24; adult/reduced €6/5; ⊙ tours 11am, 12.15pm, 4pm & 5.15pm daily) This series of 440 caves has been used for millennia by locals for various purposes, including as WWII bomb shelters, refrigerators, wells and, during many a pesky Roman or barbarian siege, as dovecotes to trap the usual one-course dinner: pigeon (still seen on local restaurant menus as *palombo*). The 45-minute English-language tours leave from in front of the tourist office.

Museo Claudio Faina e Civico   Museum
(www.museofaina.it; Piazza Duomo 29; adult/reduced €4.50/3; ⊙ 9.30am-6pm summer, 10am-5pm Tue-Sun winter) Stage your own archaeological dig at this fantastic museum opposite the cathedral. It houses one of Italy's foremost collection of Etruscan artefacts, including plenty of stone sarcophagi and terracotta pieces, as well as some significant Greek ceramic works.

Orvieto

DAVID C TOMLINSON/GETTY IMAGES ©

Orvieto

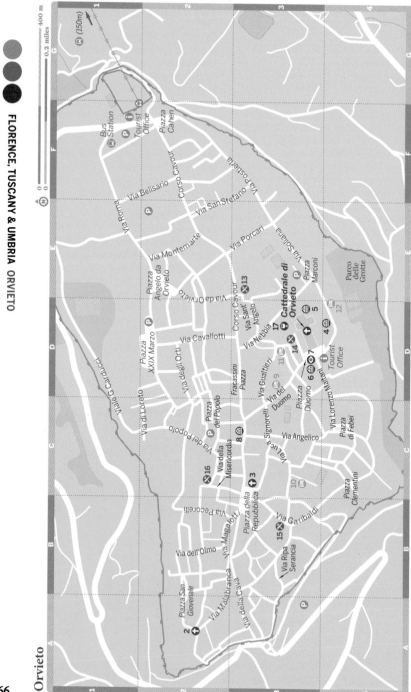

Orvieto

Torre del Moro   Historic Building

(Moor's Tower; Corso Cavour 87; adult/reduced €2.80/2; ☺10am-8pm summer, 10.30am-1pm & 2.30-5pm winter) From the Piazza Duomo, head northwest along Via del Duomo to Corso Cavour and the 13th-century Torre del Moro. Climb all 250 steps for sweeping views of the city.

Chiesa di San Giovenale   Church

(Piazza San Giovenale; ☺8am-12.30pm & 3.30-6pm) At the western end of town is this stout little church, constructed in the year 1000. Its Romanesque-Gothic art and frescoes from the later medieval Orvieto school are an astounding contrast. Just to the north, you can enjoy towering views of the countryside from the town walls.

Museo Archeologico Nazionale   Museum

(Piazza Duomo, Palazzo Papale; adult/reduced €3/1.50; ☺8.30am-7.30pm) Ensconced in the medieval Palazzo Papale, this archaeological museum holds plenty of interesting artefacts, some over 2500 years old. Etruscan ceramics, necropolis relics, bronzes and frescoed chamber tombs are all among the items on display.

Chiesa di Sant'Andrea   Church

(Piazza della Repubblica; ☺8.30am-12.30pm & 3.30-7.30pm) This 12th-century church, with its curious decagonal bell tower, presides over the Piazza della Repubblica, once Orvieto's Roman Forum and now lined with cafes. It lies at the heart of what remains of the medieval city.

A Taste of Orvieto

If you're keen to get cooking, try **Ristorante Zeppelin** (☏0763 34 14 47; www.ristorantezeppelin.it; Via Garibaldi 28; meals €30-35; ☺Mon-Sat, lunch Sun; 🖉🏠), where English-speaking chef Lorenzo Polegri whips up Umbrian feasts at one-day cookery classes. Learn to prepare specialities such as wild boar *ragout* and hand-rolled *umbricelli* pasta. He also prepares a five-course menu as the culinary climax of truffle hunts, market mornings and tours of local *pecorino*, olive oil and wine producers. Prices range from €50 to €120 per person.

Decugnano dei Barbi (☏0763 30 82 55; www.decugnanodeibarbi.com; Località Fossatello 50) estate, perched above vineyards 18km east of Orvieto, offers unique tastings and four-hour cookery classes. The winery can trace its viticultural lineage back 800 years, and the master sommelier will guide you through its cellars and talk you through a tasting of its minerally whites and full-bodied Orvieto Classico reds. Sign up in advance to assemble a four-course meal paired with homegrown wines and served in the atmospheric surrounds of a converted chapel.

DAVID C TOMLINSON/GETTY IMAGES ©

⭐ Don't Miss
Cattedrale di Orvieto

Nothing can prepare you for the visual feast that is Orvieto's Gothic cathedral, begun in 1290. The black-and-white marble banding of the main body of the church is overshadowed by the rainbow frescoes, jewel-like mosaics, bas-reliefs and delicate braids of flowers and vine – as intricate as embroidery – adorning the facade. Bathed gold at dusk, it is a soul-stirring sight to behold.

The building took 30 years to plan and three centuries to complete. It was started by Fra Bevignate and later additions were made by Sienese master Lorenzo Maitani, Andrea Pisano (of Florence Cathedral fame) and his son Nino Pisano, Andrea Orcagna and Michele Sanicheli.

Inside, Luca Signorelli's fresco cycle *The Last Judgement* shimmers with life. Look for it to the right of the altar in the **Cappella di San Brizio**. Signorelli began work on the series in 1499, and Michelangelo is said to have taken inspiration from it. Indeed, to some, Michelangelo's masterpiece runs a close second to Signorelli's work. The **Cappella del Corporale** houses a 13th-century altar cloth stained with blood that miraculously poured from the communion bread of a priest who doubted the transubstantiation.

Next to the cathedral is **MODO** (Museale dell'Opera del Duomo di Orvieto; ☎0763 34 24 77; www.museomodo.it; Piazza Duomo 26; admission €4, includes Palazzi Papali & Chiesa S Agostino; ⏱9.30am-7pm summer, 10am-5pm Wed-Mon winter), a musuem which houses a clutter of religious relics from the cathedral, as well as Etruscan antiquities and works by artists such as Simone Martini and the three Pisanos: Andrea, Nino and Giovanni.

NEED TO KNOW

☎0763 34 11 67; www.opsm.it; Piazza Duomo; admission €3; ⏱9.30am-7pm Mon-Sat, 1-6.30pm Sun summer, 9.30am-1pm & 2.30-5pm Mon-Sat, 2.30-5.30pm Sun winter

![icon] Festivals & Events

Palombella
Religious

(⏱ Pentecost Sun) For traditionalists, this rite has celebrated the Holy Spirit and good luck since 1404. For animal rights activists, the main event celebrates nothing more than scaring the living crap out of a bewildered dove. Take one dove, cage it, surround the cage with a wheel of exploding fireworks, and hurtle the cage 300m down a wire towards the cathedral steps. If the dove lives (it usually does), the couple most recently married in the cathedral becomes its caretakers.

Umbria Jazz Winter
Music

(www.umbriajazz.com; ⏱ late Dec-early Jan) This celebration of cool musical styles jazzes up the dull patches of winter, with a great feast and party on New Year's Eve.

![icon] Sleeping

It's always a good idea to book ahead in summer, on weekends, or if you're planning to come over New Year, when the Umbria Jazz Winter festival is in full swing.

B&B Michelangeli
B&B €

(☎ 0763 39 38 62; www.bbmichelangeli.com; Via Saracinelli 22; s €60-100, d €70-160; P) Francesca is your kindly host at this sweet B&B in Orvieto's historical heart, just a two-minute toddle from the Duomo. What to expect? A bright, spacious apartment, scattered with homely trinkets and with a well-stocked kitchen where you can knock up a speedy pasta dish should you so wish. We love the beautiful wood carvings and wrought-iron beds.

B&B La Magnolia
B&B €

(☎ 349 4620733, 0763 34 28 08; www.bblamagnolia.it; Via del Duomo 29; d €60-90; ❄) Tucked down a sidestreet north of the Duomo (the sign is easily missed), this light-filled Renaissance residence has delightful rooms and apartments, an English-speaking owner, a large shared kitchen and a balcony overlooking the rooftops. Serena can tell you all about Orvieto – whatever you want to know, just ask.

Villa Mercede
B&B €

(☎ 0763 34 17 66; www.villamercede.it; Via Soliana 2; s/d/tr €50/70/90; P) Heavenly close to the Duomo, with 23 rooms there's space for a gaggle of pilgrims. The building dates back to the 1500s, so the requisite frescoes adorn several rooms. High ceilings, a quiet garden and free parking seal the deal. Vacate rooms each morning by 9.30am or you'll earn the housekeepers' wrath.

Misia Resort
Boutique Hotel €€

(☎ 0763 34 23 36; Località Rocca Ripesena 51/52; s €80, d €130-160; ❄ 🛜 👪) You won't regret going the extra mile (6km

Piazza del Duomo, Urbino (p260)
FRANK WING/GETTY IMAGES ©

actually, west of Orvieto) to this boutique hotel on the rocks, with fabulous views of Orvieto from its hilltop hamlet perch. This stunning country house conversion has been designed with the utmost taste. The light, spacious rooms in soft, earthy tones come with retro-cool touches – a chesterfield sofa here, a distressed wood beam there.

Hotel Duomo
Hotel **€€**

(☎0763 34 18 87; www.orvietohotelduomo.com; Vicolo di Maurizio 7; s €70-90, d €100-130, ste €120-160; P 🛜 ♿) Orvieto's captivating Duomo is almost close enough to touch at Hotel Duomo, where the church bells will most likely be your wake-up call. This Liberty-style *palazzo*, where Orvieto-born artist Livio Orazio Valentini has left his bold, abstract imprint on the refined, neutral-hued rooms (all have marble bathrooms), has service both discreet and polite.

Eating

Pasqualetti
Gelato **€**

(Piazza Duomo 14; 3-scoop cone €3) This gelateria serves mouth-watering gelato, plus there are plenty of tables on the piazza for you to gaze at the magnificence of the cathedral while you gobble.

Trattoria dell'Orso
Trattoria **€€**

(☎0763 34 16 42; Via della Misericordia 18; meals €25-35; ☾Wed-Sun) As the owner of Orvieto's oldest restaurant, Gabriele sees no need for such modern fancies as written menus, instead reeling off the day's dishes at you as you walk in the door. Go with his recommendations – perhaps the *zuppa di farro* (spelt soup) followed by fettuccine with porcini – as he knows what he's talking about. Be prepared to take your time.

I Sette Consoli
Modern Italian **€€€**

(☎0763 34 39 11; www.isetteconsoli.it; Piazza Sant'Angelo 1a; meals €40, 6-course degustazion menu €42; ☾12.30-3pm & 7.30-10pm Thu-Tue)

Left: Assisi (p261)

(LEFT) JOHN ELK III/GETTYS IMAGES ©; (BELOW) DAVID TOMLINSON/GETTY IMAGES ©

This restaurant walks the culinary high wire in Orvieto, with inventive, artfully presented dishes, from pasta so light it floats off the fork to beautifully cooked guinea fowl stuffed with chestnuts. In good weather, try to get a seat in the garden, with the Duomo in view. Dress for dinner and reserve ahead.

Vinosus Wine Bar

(Piazza Duomo 15; ☺ **Tue-Sun)** In photo-op range of the cathedral's northwest wall is this wine bar and eatery. Try the cheese platter with local honey and pears for an elegant addition to wine. Open until the wee hours.

ⓘ Information

Tourist Office (☎**0763 34 17 72; info@iat. orvieto.tr.it; Piazza Duomo 24;** ☺**8.15am-1.50pm & 4-7pm Mon-Fri, 10am-1pm & 3-6pm Sat & Sun)** In summer, you can buy funicular, bus and Carta Unica Orvieto tickets here.

ⓘ Getting There & Away

Buses depart from the station on Piazza Cahen, stopping at the train station, and include services to Todi (€5, two hours, one daily) and Terni (€7, two hours, twice daily).

Train connections include Rome (€7.50 to €16, 1¼ hours, hourly), Florence (€15 to €21, 1½ to 2½ hours, hourly) and Perugia (€7.10 to €14.40, 1½ hours, every two hours).

ⓘ Getting Around

A century-old **funicular (each way €1;** ☺**every 10min 7.05am-8.25pm Mon-Fri, every 15min 8.15am-8pm Sat & Sun)** creaks up the wooded hill from the train station west of the centre to Piazza Cahen. The fare includes a bus ride from Piazza Cahen to Piazza Duomo.

Bus 1 runs up to the old town from the train station (€1), ATC bus A connects Piazza Cahen with Piazza Duomo and bus B runs to Piazza della Repubblica.

Naples, Pompeii & the Amalfi Coast

Inspiring, historic, swoon-worthy – and we're not only talking about the pizza. You may have already unconsciously developed a craving for Naples from its most famous dish, but nothing prepares you for the vibrant, complex flavour of this city. The street theatre over a tomato purchase in Naples' historic markets rivals performances at its groundbreaking opera house, while ancient Roman bakeries lurk underneath baroque Neapolitan church floors. Though Mt Vesuvius hasn't dusted a local pizza with ash since 1944, the volcano that buried Pompeii still looms on the local horizon. Consider this your reminder that life is short, and there's no time like the present to unwind on the beach-blessed isle of Capri, or make your romantic getaway to the Amalfi Coast. Then you'll comprehend the secret to Neapolitan pizza: it's the spice of life.

273

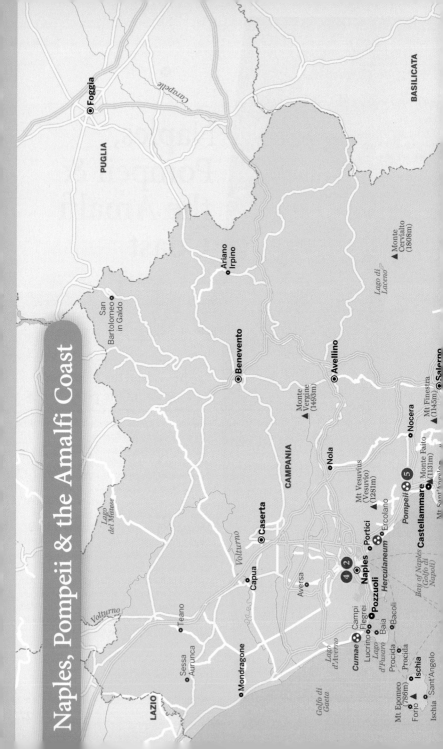

Naples, Pompeii & the Amalfi Coast

PUGLIA

Foggia

Carapelle

San
Bartolomeo
in Galdo

BASILICATA

Monte
Cervialto
(1808m)

Benevento

*Lago di
Laceno*

Ariano
Irpino

CAMPANIA

Monte
Vergine
(1493m)

Avellino

Salerno

*Lago
del Matese*

Caserta

Nola

Mt Finestra
(1145m)

Nocera

Volturno

Mt Vesuvius
(Vesuvio)
(1281m)

Monte Faito
(1131m)

Pompeii ⑤

Capua

Portici

Ercolano

Castellammare

Aversa

Naples

④ ②

Herculaneum

Teano

Pozzuoli

*Bay of Naples
Golfo di
Napoli*

Mt Sant'Angelo

LAZIO

Volturno

Campi
Flegrei

Cumae ✕

Lucrino

Baia

Bacoli

*Lago
d'Averno*

*Lago
d'Pusaro*

Sessa
Aurunca

Mondragone

Procida
Procida

*Golfo di
Gaeta*

Mt Epomeo
(786m)

Forio

Ischia

Ischia   Sant'Angelo

Battipaglia

Grotta
dell'Angelo
Pertosa

Sele

Sala Consilina

Grotta di
Castelcivita

▲ Monte
Cervati
(1900m)

4 Parco Nazionale
del Cilento e Vallo
di Diano (Cilento
National Park &
the Valley of Diana)

Paestum

Paestum ✕

Agropoli

Ascea

Pisciotta

Golfo di
Salerno

Furore

Praiano

Sant'Agata
sui due Golfi

Marina del
Cantone

Mt San
Costanza ▲
(497m)

3 **Capri
Town**

Anacapri
Capri

Tyrrhenian
Sea

N ◀

0   25 miles
0   50 km

1 Positano

2 Centro Storico, Naples

3 Grotta Azzurra, Capri

4 Museo Archeologico
Nazionale, Naples

5 Pompeii

Naples, Pompeii & the Amalfi Coast Highlights

Positano Paradise

Positano (p307) is a little like heaven, with angels in the architecture, divine seafood feasts and everlasting cliff's-edge sunsets over cobalt-blue waters. The cove may be crowded with umbrellas, but this affordable, relentlessly cheerful Amalfi Coast beach town is bound to leave the most jaded recluse in an upbeat, sociable mood.

1

Pizza in the Centro Storico

2

A fierce pizza rivalry has raged for a century between Rome and Naples, and only you can resolve this thin versus puffy crust food fight. Head to the place where even Romans concede pizza originated: Naples' *centro storico* (p291). We dare you to try to leave room for Rome...

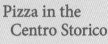

ALAN BENSON/GETTY IMAGES ©

Grotta Azzurra

With its magical blue light that glows through the cave's narrow opening and its eerie echo, the Blue Grotto (p297) is exactly the kind of place you'd expect to find mermaids singing. On recent inspection, there weren't any hanging around, though there is an ancient Roman shrine to the local water nymph. Sing a line from *The Little Mermaid* and see if you can bring any out of hiding.

Museo Archeologico Nazionale

By the 18th century, Pompeii and Herculaneum were already thoroughly looted – luckily, the most priceless booty landed in Naples' royal palace, now housing the Museo Archeologico Nazionale (p287). The Bourbon king of Naples had exceptional taste – from heroic Pompeii mosaics to Roman pornography – so the museum gives a rare, intimate glimpse of Roman life.

Ruins of Pompeii

The standard first impression heard from visitors to Pompeii (p302) is 'Amazing!'. Many are surprised by the area's vastness and assume a somewhat faraway look, as if they've been transported to another dimension. The fascination lies in the fact that each stone speaks of life and love, and of stories suspended for an eternity.

Naples, Pompeii &
the Amalfi Coast's Best...

Gourmet Landmarks

○ **Pizzeria Gino Sorbillo** Epic Neapolitan pizzas. (p291)

○ **President** For modern feasts worthy of ancient Pompeii. (p303)

○ **Ristorantino dell'Avvocato** Raffaele Cardillo's creative cuisine in Naples. (p293)

○ **Da Vincenzo** Fresh, simple seafood with an Amalfi lemon squeeze. (p307)

Places to Whisper 'Ti Amo'

○ **Villa Rufolo** On the terrace in Ravello. (p309)

○ **Teatro San Carlo** Before the end of the third act in Naples. (p293)

○ **Grotta Azzurra** In a bewitching cave in Capri. (p297)

○ **Giardini di Augusto** Capri's romantic gardens. (p297)

○ **Seggiovia del Monte Solaro** A chairlift to soul-soaring views. (p298)

Baroque Beauties

○ **Duomo** Naples' never-shy cathedral, studded with silver busts and capped with glowing frescoes. (p286)

○ **Certosa e Museo di San Martino** The least modest monastery ever, covered with frescoes. (p286)

○ **Palazzo Reale di Capodimonte** A 160-room palace is barely big enough to contain this many baroque painting masterpieces. (p289)

○ **Cattedrale di Sant'Andrea** The sweeping staircase makes every entrance to Amalfi's cathedral grand. (p306)

Affordable Luxuries

- **La Fontelina** Lovely Capri beach that enjoys day-long golden sun. (p298)

- **Hotel Lidomare** Amalfi Coast sea views and genteel elegance at affordable prices. (p306)

- **Unico Capri** Seggiovia del Monte Solaro chairlift joy-rides on Capri. (p298)

- **Villa Rufolo** Paradisical gardens in Ravello. (p309)

ADVANCE PLANNING

- **Three months before** Book accommodation, especially if hitting Capri or the Amalfi Coast between June and mid-September.

- **One to two months before** Book tickets to the Ravello Festival and tickets to opera opening nights at Naples' Teatro San Carlo.

- **One week before** Reserve a table at Palazzo Petrucci in Naples; book an urban caving tour in Naples with Naples Sotterranea (p301).

RESOURCES

- **Naples Tourist Board** (www.inaples.it)

- **Napoli Unplugged** (www.napoliunplugged.com) Sights, events, news and practicalities.

- **Capri** (www.capri.net) Listings, itineraries and ferry schedules.

GETTING AROUND

- **Air** International and domestic flights service Naples' Capodichino airport.

- **Walk** Ideal in Naples, on island beaches, in smaller towns and along coastal trails.

- **Train** Naples is a major rail hub, with frequent connections between Naples, Pompeii, Ercolano (Herculaneum) and Sorrento.

- **Bus** Regular services between Naples and the Amalfi Coast.

- **Ferries and Hydrofoils** Regular summer services between Naples and Capri, as well as to/from Sorrento and the Amalfi Coast. Reduced winter services.

BE FOREWARNED

- **Museums** Many close Mondays or Tuesdays.

- **Restaurants** In Naples, many close in August. On Capri and the Amalfi Coast, many close from November to March.

- **Accommodation** Many hotels close November to March on Capri and along the Amalfi Coast.

- **Pickpockets and bag snatchers** Active in Naples and Pompeii after sunset.

Left: Cappella di San Gennaro (p286), Naples; **Above:** Ravello (p309)

(LEFT) RICHARD I'ANSON/GETTY IMAGES ©: (ABOVE) LAURENCE DELDERFIELD/GETTY IMAGES ©

Naples, Pompeii & the Amalfi Coast Itineraries

Magic potions and time machines aren't strictly necessary in this lucky landscape, where you'll find short-cuts to romance through blue grottos and ancient Roman cities trapped in time under a still-active volcano.

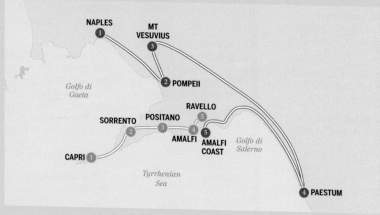

3 DAYS

NAPLES TO AMALFI
TIME-TRAVEL TRIP

Begin your time travels underground on day one in ❶ **Naples**, exploring Roman secret passages by candlelight with Napoli Sotterranea. Emerge blinking into daylight and wander into the future at MADRE, Naples' cutting-edge contemporary art showcase before stepping back into the past at Naples' baroque Duomo. Wake up and wonder what century you're in at Hotel Piazza Bellini, a new art hotel in a 16th-century palace.

Exquisite mosaics and ancient erotica take you back a couple of millennia at Museo Archeologico Nazionale on day two, but don't dawdle too long: you've got a date with destiny c AD 79 at ❷ **Pompeii**.

A volcanic eruption trapped the ancient Roman town under a layer of volcanic ash, but in the 21st century you can hop on a bus right to the source of Pompeii's troubles: the still-active cone of ❸ **Mt Vesuvius**. The next day, hurtle onwards along the coast and backwards in time by car (or more gradually by train and bus) to the breathtaking 6th century BC Greek temples of ❹ **Paestum**. Afterwards, rejoin the modern world at your leisure on the beaches of the ❺ **Amalfi Coast**.

CAPRI TO RAVELLO
AMALFI AFFAIR

5 DAYS

Romance is ready when you are, just south of Naples. Catch the ferry to **①Capri**, from whose sandy beach shores you can take a boat into the mermaid-worthy Grotta Azzurra or a chairlift to mesmerising views atop Monte Solaro.

After a night at Villa Eva or La Minerva amid balmy, lemon-scented breezes, hop on the ferry to **②Sorrento.** Spend a day strolling the cliff-straddling town, enjoying the nearby beach, and sampling the region's legendary buffalo-milk mozzarella at Inn Bufalito. Next day, take a bus to **③Positano**, spending another lazy day wandering boutique-laced lanes and

hobnobbing with Italy's glitterati in a town the colour of sugared almonds.

The next morning, take the scenic route by boat to achingly pretty **④Amalfi**. Let the Museo della Carta inspire your own medieval love-letters, or settle in at Ristorante La Caravella to work your way through the 1750-choice wine list. The following day, retreat to lofty **⑤Ravello** for sigh-worthy views from Villa Cimbrone's Infinity Terrace, and script your own Shakespearean balcony scenes at Hotel Villa Amore.

Ravello (p309)
DAVID BORLAND/GETTY IMAGES ©

Discover Naples, Pompeii & the Amalfi Coast

At a Glance

- **Naples** (p282) Street Markets, dazzling baroque and the world's best pizza.

- **Pompeii** (p302) In the long shadow of Mt Vesuvius, an ancient city incredibly preserved in lava.

- **Capri** (p296) The Mediterranean's most effortlessly chic island escape.

- **Amalfi Coast** (p306) Heart-rending, soul-stirring beauty, with cliffs towering over beach coves.

Local produce, Naples
RICHARD I'ANSON/GETTY IMAGES ©

NAPLES

POP 970,400

Italy's most misunderstood city is also one of its most intriguing – an exhilarating mess of bombastic baroque churches, cocky baristas and electrifying street life. Naples' *centro storico* (historic centre) is a Unesco World Heritage Site, its museums lay claim to some of Europe's finest archaeology and art, and its gilded royal palaces make Rome look positively provincial. But what about the pickpockets? The Camorra? Certainly, Naples has its fair share of problems, yet the city is far safer than many imagine, its streets packed with some of Italy's warmest, kindest denizens.

◉ Sights

CENTRO STORICO

Cappella Sansevero   Chapel
(☏ 081 551 84 70; www.museo sansevero.it; Via Francesco de Sanctis 19; adult/reduced €7/5; ⊙ 10am-5.40pm Mon & Wed-Sat, to 1.10pm Sun; Ⓜ Dante) It's in this Masonic-inspired chapel that you'll find Giuseppe Sanmartino's incredible sculpture, *Cristo velato* (Veiled Christ), its marble veil so realistic that it's tempting to try to lift it and view Christ underneath. It's one of several artistic wonders, which also include Francesco Queirolo's sculpture *Disinganno* (Disillusion), Antonio Corradini's *Pudicizia* (Modesty) and riotously colourful frescoes by Francesco Maria Russo, the latter untouched since their creation in 1749.

Basilica di Santa Chiara   Basilica, Cloister
(☏ 081 797 12 31; www.monasterodisantachiara. eu; Via Benedetto Croce; cloisters adult/reduced

FRANZ ABERHAM/GETTY IMAGES ©

⭐ Don't Miss
Mercato di Porta Nolana

Bellies rumble greedily at this evocative street market, one of the city's best. The market's namesake is medieval city gate **Porta Nolana**, which stands at the head of Via Sopramuro. Its two cylindrical towers, optimistically named Faith and Hope, support an arch decorated with a bas-relief of Ferdinand I of Aragon on horseback.

Below and beyond it, the *mercato* is an intoxicating place, where bellowing fishmongers and *frutti vendoli* (greengrocers) collide with fragrant delis, bakeries, and a growing number of ethnic food shops. Expect to find anything from buxom tomatoes and mozzarella to crunchy *casareccio* bread, cheap luggage and bootleg '80s compilation CDs.

NEED TO KNOW
Porta Nolana; ⊙8am-6pm Mon-Sat, to 2pm Sun; 🚎R2 to Corso Umberto I

€6/4.50; ⊙basilica 7.30am-1pm & 4.30-8pm, cloisters 9.30am-5pm Mon-Sat, 10am-2pm Sun; Ⓜ Dante) Vast, Gothic and cleverly deceptive, this mighty **basilica** is actually a 20th-century recreation of Gagliardo Primario's 14th-century Angevin original, severely damaged by Allied bombing in August 1943. The pièce de résistance, however, is the basilica's adjoining **majolica cloister**.

Pio Monte della Misericordia   Church, Museum
(☎081 44 69 44; www.piomontedellamisericordia.it; Via dei Tribunali 253; admission €6; ⊙9am-2pm Thu-Tue; 🚎C55 to Via Duomo) Caravaggio's masterpiece *Le sette opere di Misericordia* (The Seven Acts of Mercy) is considered by many to be the single most important painting in Naples. And it's in this small, octagonal 17th-century church that you'll see it.

Naples

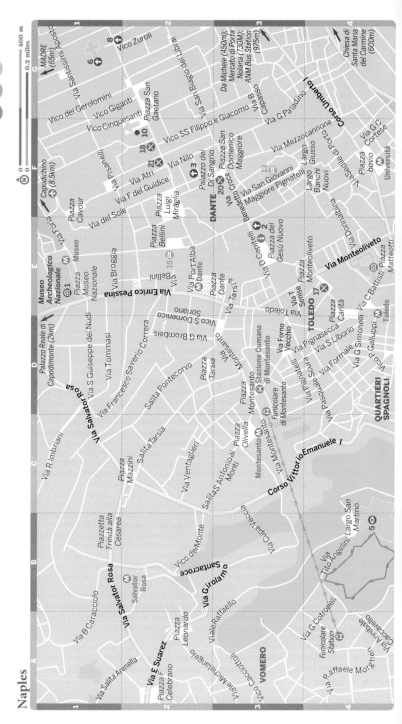

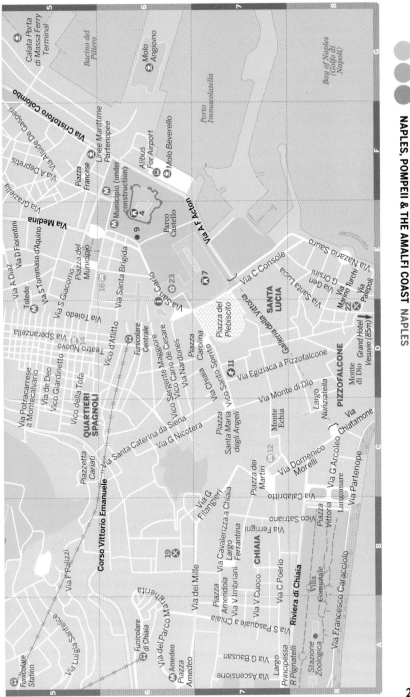

Calata Porta
di Massa Ferry
Terminal

Bacino del
Piliero

Molo
Angioino

Bay of Naples
(Golfo di
Napoli)

Via Cristoforo Colombo

Via Alcide De Gasperi

Via A Depretis

Via Graziella

Porto
Immacolatella

Molo
Beverello

Porto

Linee Marittime
Partenopee

Piazza
Francese

Alibus
For Airport

Via Medina

Via A Diaz

Via D Fiorentini

Municipio (under
construction)

4

Via A F Acton

9

Parco
Castello

Via Nazario Sauro

Via Palepoli

Via Marino Turchi

22

Via gen
G Orsini

Via Santa Lucia

SANTA
LUCIA

Via C Console

Piazza del
Municipio

Via S Tommaso d'Aquino

Via S Giacomo

Toledo

Via Toledo

Via Santa Brigida

16

Via San Carlo

23

7

Galleria della Vittoria

Piazza del
Plebiscito

Piazza
Carolina

11

Via Egiziaca a Pizzofalcone

Via Speranzella

Via Portacarrese
a Montecalvario

Via de Deo

Vico Giardinetto

Teatro Nuovo

14

Vico d'Afflitto

Funicolare
Centrale

Vico Sergente Maggiore

Vico Carlo de Cesare

Via Nardones

Piazza
Santo Spirito

Via Chiaia

Via Monte di Dio

PIZZOFALCONE

Monte
di Dio

Grand Hotel
Vesuvio (85m)

QUARTIERI
SPAGNOLI

Vico della Tofa

Piazzetta
Cariati

Via Santa Caterina da Siena

Via G Nicotera

Piazza
Santa Maria
degli Angeli

Monte
Echia

Largo
Nunziatella

Via
Chiatamone

Via Arcoleo

Via Domenico
Morelli

12

Via Partenope

Lungomare

Corso Vittorio Emanuele

Via F Palizzi

19

Via G
Filangieri

Via Cavalerizza a Chiaia

Largo
Ferrantina

Piazza dei
Martiri

Via Calabritto

CHIAIA

Via Ferrigni

Vico Satriano

Piazza
Vittoria

Via Francesco Caracciolo

Funicolare
di Chiaia

Amedeo

Via del Parco Margherita

Via dei Mille

Piazza
Amendola

Via V Imbriani

Via C Poerio

Via V Cuoco

Via S Pasquale a Chiaia

Riviera di Chiaia

Villa
Comunale

Funicolare
Station

Via Luigia Sanfelice

Piazza
Amedeo

Largo
Principessa
R Pignatelli

Stazione
Zoologica

Via Ascensione

Via G Bausan

285

Naples

Duomo — Cathedral

(☏ 081 44 90 97; www.duomodinapoli.com/it/main.htm; Via Duomo; baptistry admission €1.50; ☉ cathedral & baptistry 8am-12.30pm & 4.30-7pm Mon-Sat, 8am-1.30pm & 5-7.30pm Sun; 🚌 C55 to Via Duomo) Whether you go for Giovanni Lanfranco's fresco in the Cappella di San Gennaro (Chapel of St Janarius), the 4th-century mosaics in the baptistry, or the thrice-annual miracle of San Gennaro, don't miss Naples' spiritual centrepiece. Sitting on the site of an ancient temple to Neptune, the cathedral was initiated by Charles I of Anjou in 1272, consecrated in 1315, and largely destroyed in a 1456 earthquake. Copious alterations over the subsequent centuries have created a melange of styles and influences.

MADRE — Art Gallery

(Museo d'Arte Contemporanea Donnaregina; ☏ 081 1931 3016; www.coopculture.it; Via Set-tembrini 79; admission €7, free Mon; ☉ 10am-7.30pm Mon, Wed-Sat, to 8pm Sun; Ⓜ Piazza Cavour) Seek refuge from the ancient at Naples' impressive contemporary art museum. While the 1st floor is dedicated to specially commissioned installations – among them Rebecca Horn's eerie *Spirits* and Francesco Clemente's erotically charged Neapolitan fresco *Ave Ovo* – the 2nd floor's 'Historical Collection' of modern painting, photography, sculpture and installations includes blockbuster names like Damien Hirst, Cindy Sherman and Olafur Eliasson.

VOMERO

Certosa e Museo di San Martino — Monastery, Museum

(☏ 848 800288; www.coopculture.it; Largo San Martino 5; adult/reduced €6/3; ☉ 8.30am-7.30pm Thu-Tue, last entry 6.30pm; Ⓜ Vanvitelli, funicular Montesanto to Morghen) The high point (quite literally) of the Neapolitan baroque, this charterhouse-turned-museum was founded as a Carthusian monastery in the 14th century. Decorated, adorned and altered over the centuries by some of Italy's finest talent, most importantly Giovanni Antonio Dosio in the 16th century and baroque master Cosimo Fanzago a century later, it's now a superb repository of Neapolitan artistry.

The monastery's **church** and the rooms that flank it contain a feast of frescoes and paintings by some of Naples' greatest 17th-century artists, among them Francesco Solimena, Massimo Stanzione, Giuseppe de Ribera and Battista Caracciolo. In the nave, Cosimo Fanzago's inlaid marble work is simply extraordinary.

Adjacent to the church, the **Chiostro dei Procuratori** is the smaller of the monastery's two cloisters. A grand corridor on the left leads to the larger **Chiostro Grande** (Great Cloister), considered one of Italy's finest. Originally designed by Giovanni Antonio Dosio in the late 16th century and added to by Fanzago, it's a sublime composition of Tuscan-Doric porticoes, garden and marble statues. The sinister skulls mounted on the balustrade were a

GREG ELMS/GETTY IMAGES ©

Don't Miss
Museo Archeologico Nazionale

Head here for one of the world's finest collections of Graeco-Roman artefacts. Originally a cavalry barracks and later the seat of the city's university, the museum was established by the Bourbon king Charles VII in the late 18th century to house the rich collection of antiquities he had inherited from his mother, Elisabetta Farnese, as well as treasures looted from Pompeii and Herculaneum.

While the basement houses the Borgia collection of Egyptian relics and epigraphs, the ground-floor **Farnese collection** of colossal Greek and Roman sculptures includes the *Toro Farnese* (Farnese Bull) in Room XVI and the muscle-bound *Ercole* (Hercules) in Room XI.

If you're short on time, take in both these masterpieces before heading straight to the mezzanine floor, home to an exquisite collection of **mosaics**, mostly from Pompeii. Of the series taken from the Casa del Fauno, it is *La battaglia di Alessandro contro Dario* (The Battle of Alexander against Darius) in Room LXI that stands out. Beyond the mosaics, the **Gabinetto Segreto** (Secret Chamber) contains a small but much-studied collection of ancient erotica.

Originally the royal library, the enormous **Sala Meridiana** (Great Hall of the Sundial) on the 1st floor is home to the Farnese Atlante, a statue of Atlas carrying a globe on his shoulders, as well as various paintings from the Farnese collection. Look up and you'll find Pietro Bardellino's riotously colourful 1781 fresco depicting the Triumph of Ferdinand IV of Bourbon and Marie Caroline of Austria. The rest of the 1st floor is largely devoted to fascinating discoveries from Pompeii, Herculaneum, Boscoreale, Stabiae and Cuma.

NEED TO KNOW

📞 081 44 01 66; www.coopculture.it; Piazza Museo Nazionale 19; admission €8; ⏱ 9am-7.30pm Wed-Mon; Ⓜ Museo, Piazza Cavour

DEA / A. DAGLI ORTI/GETTY IMAGES ©

★ Don't Miss
Catacomba di San Gennaro

An evocative world of tombs, corridors and broad vestibules, the Catacomba di San Gennaro is Naples' oldest and most sacred catacomb. Not only home to 2nd-century Christian frescoes and 5th-century mosaics, it harbours the oldest known image of San Gennaro as the protector of Naples. Indeed, it was the interment of the saint's body here in the 5th century that turned this city of the dead into a Christian pilgrimage site.

NEED TO KNOW

📞 081 744 37 14; www.catacombedinapoli.it; Via Tondo di Capodimonte 13; adult/reduced €8/5; 🕙1hr tours every hour 10am-5pm Mon-Sat, to 1pm Sun

light-hearted reminder to the monks of their own mortality.

Just off the Chiostro dei Procuratori, the small **Sezione Navale** documents the history of the Bourbon navy from 1734 to 1860, and features a small collection of beautiful royal barges.

The **Sezione Presepiale** houses a whimsical collection of rare Neapolitan *presepi* (nativity scenes) from the 18th and 19th centuries, including the colossal Cuciniello creation, which covers one

wall of what used to be the monastery's kitchen.

The **Quarto del Priore** in the southern wing houses the bulk of the picture collection, as well as one of the museum's most famous pieces, Pietro Bernini's tender *La vergine col bambino e San Giovannino* (Madonna and Child with the Infant John the Baptist).

A pictorial history of Naples is told in the section **Immagini e Memorie di Napoli** (Images and Memories of Naples).

SANTA LUCIA & CHIAIA

Palazzo Reale   Palace, Museum

(Royal Palace; ☏081 40 04 54; www.coopculture.
it; Piazza del Plebiscito; adult/reduced €4/3;
☺9am-7pm Thu-Tue; ☐R2 to Via San Carlo)
Envisaged as a 16th-century monument
to Spanish glory (Naples was under
Spanish rule at the time), the magnificent
Palazzo Reale is home to the **Museo
del Palazzo Reale**, a rich and eclectic
collection of baroque and neoclassical
furnishings, porcelain, tapestries, statues
and paintings, spread across the palace's
royal apartments.

Castel Nuovo   Castle, Museum

(☏081 795 58 77; Piazza Municipio; admission
€6; ☺9am-7pm Mon-Sat, last entry 6pm; ☐R2
to Piazza Municipio) Dubbed the Maschio
Angioino (Angevin Keep), this strapping
castle was built in the late 13th century
as part of Charles I of Anjou's ambitious
urban expansion program. Christened the
Castrum Novum (New Castle) to distin-
guish it from the older Castel dell'Ovo and
Castel Capuano, the original structure's
only survivor is the Cappella Palatina. The
rest is the result of Aragonese renovations
two centuries later, as well as a meticu-
lous restoration effort prior to WWII.

CAPODIMONTE & LA SANITÀ

Palazzo Reale
di Capodimonte   Palace, Museum

(☏081 749 91 11; www.coopculture.it;
Parco di Capodimonte; museum adult/reduced
€7.50/3.75; park admission free; ☺museum
8.30am-7.30pm Thu-Tue, last entry 1hr before
closing; park 7am-8pm daily; ☐2M or 178)
On the northern edge of the city, this
colossal palace took more than a century
to build. It was originally intended as a
hunting lodge for Charles VII of Bourbon,
but as construction got under way in
1738, the plans kept on getting grander
and grander. By its completion in 1759,
Naples had a new palazzo. It's now home
to the exceptional **Museo Nazionale di
Capodimonte**.

Spread over three floors and 160
rooms, you'll never see the whole art

museum in one day. For most people,
though, a full morning or afternoon is
sufficient for an abridged best-of tour,
and forking out €5 for the insightful
audioguide is a worthy investment.

On the 1st floor you'll find works by
Bellini, Botticelli, Caravaggio, Masaccio
and Titian. While the highlights are many,
look out for Masaccio's *Crocifissione*
(Crucifixion) and Parmigianino's *Antea*.

Upstairs, the 2nd-floor galleries
display work by Neapolitan artists from
the 13th to the 19th centuries, plus
some spectacular 16th-century Belgian
tapestries. The piece that many come
to Capodimonte to see, Caravaggio's
Flagellazione (Flagellation; 1607–10),
hangs in reverential solitude in Room 78,
at the end of a long corridor.

☞ Tours

City Sightseeing Napoli   Bus Tour

(☏081 551 72 79; www.napoli.city-sightseeing.
it; adult/reduced €22/11) City Sightseeing
Napoli operates a hop-on, hop-off bus
service with four routes across the city. All
depart from Piazza Municipio–Largo Castello, and tickets are available on board.
Tour commentaries are provided in eight
languages, including English.

Tunnel Borbonico   Tour

(☏366 2484151, 081 764 58 08; www.tun-
nelborbonico.info; Vico del Grottone 4; 75min
standard tour adult/reduced €10/5; ☺ standard
tour 10am, noon, 3.30pm & 5.30pm Fri-Sun; ☐R2
to Via San Carlo) Traverse five centuries of
history along Naples' engrossing Bourbon
Tunnel. Conceived by Ferdinand II in 1853
to link the Palazzo Reale to the barracks and the sea, the never-completed
escape route is part of the 17th-century
Carmignano Aqueduct system, itself
incorporating 16th-century cisterns. Used
as an air-raid shelter and military hospital
during WWII, this underground labyrinth
rekindles the past with its evocative
wartime artifacts, from graffiti and toys,
to contraband-smuggling cars.

🛏️ Sleeping

CENTRO STORICO & PORT AREA

Hotel Piazza Bellini
Boutique Hotel €€

(📞081 45 17 32; www.hotelpiazzabellini.com; Via Santa Maria di Costantinopoli 101; s €70-140, d €80-165; ❄️@🛜; MDante) This funky art hotel inhabits a 16th-century *palazzo*, its white spaces spiked with original majolica tiles and the work of emerging artists. Rooms offer a pared-back version of cool, with designer fittings, chic bathrooms and mirror frames drawn straight on the wall.

Decumani Hotel de Charme
Boutique Hotel €€

(📞081 551 81 88; www.decumani.it; Via San Giovanni Maggiore Pignatelli 15; s €99-124, d €99-164; ❄️@🛜; 🚌R2 to Via Mezzocannone) Slumber in the former *palazzo* of Cardinal Sisto Riario Sforza, the last

bishop of the Bourbon Kingdom. The simple, stylishly decorated rooms feature high ceilings, parquet floors, 19th-century furniture and modern bathrooms with roomy showers and rustic wooden bench-tops. The deluxe rooms also boast an in-room Jacuzzi.

TOLEDO & QUARTIERI SPAGNOLI

La Ciliegina Lifestyle Hotel
Boutique Hotel €€

(📞081 1971 8800; www.cilieginahotel.it; Via PE Imbriani 30; d €170-230, junior ste €260-300; ❄️@🛜; 🚌R2 to Piazza del Municipio) All 13 spacious, minimalist rooms at this chic, fashionista favourite include top-of-the-range Hästens beds, flat-screen TVs and marble-clad bathrooms with water-jet Jacuzzi showers (one junior suite has a Jacuzzi tub). Have breakfast in bed, or on the rooftop terrace, which comes complete with sunbeds, hot tub and a view of Vesuvius.

Left: Naples;
Below: Pasta shop, Naples

(LEFT) TONY C FRENCH/GETTY IMAGES ©; (BELOW) ROCCO FASANO/GETTY IMAGES ©

Hotel Il Convento
Hotel €€

(☎081 40 39 77; www.hotelilconvento.com; Via Speranzella 137a; s €45-90, d €55-150, tr €65-140; ❄ 🔊; 🚍R2 to Via San Carlo) A soothing blend of antique furniture, erudite book shelves and candle-lit stairs, this hotel sits snugly in the atmospheric Quartieri Spagnoli. The elegant rooms combine creamy tones and dark woods with patches of 16th-century brickwork. For €80 to €180 you get a room with a private roof garden.

SANTA LUCIA & CHIAIA

B&B Cappella Vecchia
B&B €

(☎081 240 51 17; www.cappellavecchia11.it; Vico Santa Maria a Cappella Vecchia 11; s €60-65, d €80-90; ❄ @ 🔊; 🚍C24 to Piazza dei Martiri) Run by a super-helpful young couple, this B&B is a first-rate choice. Six simple, comfy rooms feature funky bathrooms and different Neapolitan themes. There's a spacious communal area for breakfast, and free internet available 24/7. Check the website for monthly packages.

Grand Hotel Vesuvio
Luxury Hotel €€€

(☎081 764 00 44; www.vesuvio.it; Via Partenope 45; s €199-500, d €215-520; ❄ @ 🔊; 🚍154 to Via Santa Lucia) Known for bedding legends – past guests include Rita Hayworth and Humphrey Bogart – this five-star heavyweight is a decadent wonderland of dripping chandeliers, period antiques and opulent rooms.

Eating

CENTRO STORICO

Pizzeria Gino Sorbillo
Pizzeria €

(☎081 44 66 43; www.accademiadellapizza. it; Via dei Tribunali 32; pizzas €3-7.30; ⏱noon-3.30pm & 7-11.30pm Mon-Sat; Ⓜ Dante) Gino Sorbillo is king of the pizza pack. Head in for gigantic, wood-fired perfection, best followed by a velvety *semifreddo;* the chocolate and *torroncino* (almond

291

nougat) combo is divine. Head in super early or expect to queue.

La Campagnola Campanian €€
(☎081 45 90 34; www.campagnolatribunali.com; Via dei Tribunali 47; meals €18; ⊗12.30-4pm & 7-11.30pm Wed-Mon; ⓂDante) Boisterous and affable, this Neapolitan stalwart serves up soul-coaxing classics. Daily specials may include a killer *genovese* (pasta with a slow-cooked lamb, tomato and onion *ragù*) or a decadent *penne alla siciliana* (pasta with fried eggplant, fior di latte cheese, tomato and basil).

Palazzo Petrucci Modern Italian €€€
(☎081 552 40 68; www.palazzopetrucci.it; Piazza San Domenico Maggiore 4; meals €50; ⊗1-2.30pm & 7.30-10.30pm Tue-Sat, dinner only Mon, lunch only Sun; ⓂDante) Progressive Petrucci thrills with new-school creations like chickpea soup with prawns and concentrated coffee, or succulent lamb with dried apricots, *pecorino* (sheep's milk cheese) and mint. Polished service and a fine-dining air make it a perfect spot to celebrate something special.

TOLEDO, QUARTIERI SPAGNOLI & VOMERO

Il Garum Italian €€
(☎081 542 32 28; Piazza Monteoliveto 2a; meals €35; ⊗noon-3.30pm & 7-11.30pm ; ⓂToledo) One of the very few restaurants open on Sunday nights, softly lit Il Garum serves up delicately flavoured, revamped classics. Stand-out dishes include an exquisite grilled calamari stuffed with seasonal vegetables and cheese.

SANTA LUCIA & CHIAIA

L'Ebbrezza di Noè Campanian €€
(☎081 40 01 04; www.lebbrezzadinoe.com; Vico Vetriera 9 ; meals €30; ⊗8.30pm-midnight Tue-Sun; ⓂPiazza Amedeo) A wine shop by day, 'Noah's Drunkenness' transforms into a culinary hotspot by night. Slip inside for vino and conversation at the bar, or settle into one of the intimate, bottle-lined dining rooms for beautiful, creative dishes dictated by the morning's market finds. Adding X-factor are over 2000 wines, artfully selected by sommelier owner Luca Di Leva.

Teatro San Carlo, Naples

Ristorantino dell'Avvocato   Campanian €€

(☏081 032 00 47; www.ilristorantinodellavvocato.it; Via Santa Lucia 115-117; meals €37, degustation menus ; ⏰noon-3pm & 7.30-11pm, lunch only Mon & Sun; 🛜; 🚍154 to Via Santa Lucia) This elegant nosh spot is home to affable chef and owner Raffaele Cardillo, whose passion for Campania's culinary heritage merges with a knack for subtle, refreshing twists – think gnocchi with fresh mussels, clams, crumbed pistachio, lemon, ginger and garlic.

⭐ Entertainment

Options run the gamut from nail-biting football games to world-class opera. For cultural listings check www.incampania.it; for the latest club news check out the free minimag *Zero* (www.zero.eu, in Italian), available from many bars.

Teatro San Carlo   Opera, Ballet

(☏081 797 23 31; www.teatrosancarlo.it; Via San Carlo 98; ⏰box office 10am-7pm Mon-Sat, to 3.30pm Sun; 🚍R2 to Via San Carlo) One of Italy's premier opera venues, the theatre stages a year-round programme of opera, ballet and concerts, though tickets can be fiendishly difficult to come by.

ℹ️ Information

Head to the following tourist bureaus for information and a map of the city:

Piazza del Gesù Nuovo 7 (Piazza del Gesù Nuovo 7; ⏰9.30am-1.30pm & 2.30-6.30pm Mon-Sat, 9am-1.30pm Sun)

Stazione Centrale (Stazione Centrale; ⏰9am-6pm)

Via San Carlo 9 (Via San Carlo 9; ⏰9.30am-1.30pm & 2.30-6.30pm Mon-Sat, 9am-1.30pm Sun; 🚍R2 to Piazza Trieste e Trento)

ℹ️ Getting There & Away

Air

Capodichino airport (NAP; ☏081 789 61 11; www.gesac.it), 7km northeast of the city centre, is southern Italy's main airport, linking Naples with most Italian and several major European cities. Budget carrier easyJet has several connections

to/from Naples, including London (Gatwick and Stansted), Paris (Orly) and Berlin (Schönefeld).

Boat

Molo Beverello, right in front of Castel Nuovo, services fast ferries and hydrofoils for Capri, Sorrento, Ischia (both Ischia Porto and Forio) and Procida. Some hydrofoils for Capri, Ischia and Procida also leave from Mergellina, 5km further west.

Molo Angioino, right beside Molo Beverello, services slow ferries for Sicily, the Aeolian Islands and Sardinia.

Calata Porta di Massa, beside Molo Angioino, services slow ferries to Ischia, Procida and Capri.

Bus

Most national and international buses leave from Corso Meridionale, on the north side of Stazione Centrale.

On Piazza Garibaldi, **Biglietteria Vecchione** (☏081 563 03 20; Piazza Garibaldi; ⏰6:30am-7.30pm Mon-Sat) displays timetables and sells tickets for most regional and inter-city buses. It also sells Unico Napoli bus and metro tickets.

Regional bus services are operated by numerous companies, the most useful of which is SITA Sud (☏089 40 51 45; www.sitasudtrasporti.it).

You can buy SITA Sud tickets and catch buses either from Porto Immacolatella, near Molo Angioino, or from outside Stazione Centrale. Tickets are also available from bars and tobacconists displaying the Unico Campania sign.

ATC (☏0823 96 90 57; www.atcbus.it) runs from Naples to Assisi (5¼ hours, twice daily) and Perugia (4½ hours, twice daily).

Train

Naples is southern Italy's main rail hub. Most national trains arrive at or depart from **Stazione Centrale** (☏081 554 31 88; Piazza Garibaldi) or underneath the main station, from Stazione Garibaldi. Some services also stop at Mergellina station.

State-owned Trenitalia (p402) runs most intercity train services, including up to 42 trains daily to Rome. Travel times and prices vary. Options to/from Rome include Frecciarossa (High Velocity; 2nd class one-way €43, 70 minutes); IC (InterCity; 2nd class one-way €24.50, two hours); and Regionale (Regional; one-way €11.20, 2¾ hours).

Privately owned **Italo** (📞060708; www. italotreno.it) runs high-velocity trains between Stazione Centrale in Naples and numerous major Italian cities, including Rome (2nd class one-way €43, 70 minutes). Note that Italo trains from Naples to Rome stop at Roma-Tiburtina station and not at the main Roma-Termini station.

Circumvesuviana (📞800 211388; www. eavcampania.it) trains connect Naples to Sorrento (€4.10, 68 minutes, around 30 daily). Stops along the way include: Ercolano (€2.20, 19 minutes) and Pompeii (€2.90, 38 minutes). Trains leave from **Stazione Circumvesuviana** (📞800 211388; www.eavcampania.it; Corso Garibaldi), adjacent to Stazione Centrale (follow the signs from the main concourse).

ⓘ Getting Around

Tickets for public transport in Naples and the surrounding Campania region are managed by **Unico Campania** (www.unicocampania.it) and sold at stations, ANM booths and tobacconists. There are various tickets, depending on where you plan to travel.

Unico Napoli (90 minutes €1.30; daily €3.70 weekdays; €3.10 weekends) Unlimited travel by bus, tram, funicular, metro, Ferrovia Cumana or Circumflegrea.

Unico 3T (3 days €20) Unlimited travel throughout Campania, including the Alibus, EAV buses to Mt Vesuvius and transport on the islands of Ischia and Procida.

Unico Capri (60 minutes €2.70; 24 hours €8.60) Unlimited bus travel on Capri. The 60-minute ticket also allows a single trip on the Seggiovia del Monte Solaro (p298) connecting Marina Grande to Capri Town; the daily ticket allows for two funicular trips.

Unico Costiera (45 minutes €2.50; 90 minutes €3.80; 1/3 days €7.60/18) A money-saver if you plan on much travelling by SITA Sud or EAV bus and/or Circumvesuvianatrain in the Bay of Naples and Amalfi Coast area.

To/From the Airport

By public transport you can catch the **Alibus** (📞800 639525; www.unicocampania.it) airport shuttle (€3, 45 minutes, every 20 to 30 minutes) to/from Molo Beverello or Piazza Garibaldi. Tickets are available on board.

Official taxi fares to the airport are as follows: €23 from a seafront hotel or from the Mergellina

hydrofoil terminal; €19 from Piazza del Municipio; and €15.50 from Stazione Centrale.

Bus

In Naples, buses are operated by the city transport company **ANM** (📞800 639525; www.anm.it). There's no central bus station, but most buses pass through Piazza Garibaldi, the city's chaotic transport hub.

Funicular

Unico Napoli tickets are valid on the funiculars. Three of Naples' four funicular railways connect the centre with Vomero (the fourth, Funicolare di Mergellina, connects the waterfront at Via Mergellina with Via Manzoni).

Funicolare Centrale Ascends from Via Toledo to Piazza Fuga.

Funicolare di Chiaia From Via del Parco Margherita to Via Domenico Cimarosa.

Funicolare di Montesanto From Piazza Montesanto to Via Raffaele Morghen.

Metro

Naples' **Metropolitana** (📞800 568866; www. metro.na.it) metro system is covered by Unico Napoli tickets.

Taxi

Official taxis are white and have meters; always ensure the meter is running. There are taxi stands at most of the city's main piazzas or you can call one of the following taxi cooperatives:

Consortaxi (📞081 22 22)

Consorzio Taxi Napoli (📞081 88 88; www. consorziotaxinapoli.it)

Radio Taxi La Partenope (📞081 01 01; www. radiotaxilapartenope.it)

The minimum taxi fare is €4.50, of which €3 is the starting fare. The minimum charge increases to €5.50 between 10pm and 7am, on Sundays and on holidays. There is also a baffling range of additional charges, including €1 for a radio taxi call and €0.50 per piece of luggage in the boot.

Official flat rates do exist on some routes, including to/from the airport, Stazione Centrale and the ferry ports. Where available, flat-rate fares must be requetsed at the beginning of your trip.

From Stazione Centrale, fixed-fare routes include Mergellina (€13.50), seafront hotels (€11.50) and Molo Beverello (€10.50).

Sorrento

POP 16,500

An unashamed resort, Sorrento is still a civilized old town. Even the souvenirs are a cut above the norm, with plenty of fine old shops selling ceramics, lacework and *intarsio* (marquetry items) – famously produced here. The main drawback is the lack of a proper beach; the town straddles the cliffs overlooking the water to Naples and Mt Vesuvius.

Activities

Bagni Regina Giovanna　　Beach

(Pollio Felix) Sorrento famously lacks a proper beach, so consider heading to Bagni Regina Giovanna, a rocky beach about 2km west of town, set among the ruins of the Roman Villa Pollio Felix. It's a picturesque spot with clear, clean water and it's possible to walk here (follow Via Capo), although you'll save your swimming (and sunbathing) strength if you get the SITA bus headed for Massa Lubrense.

City Sightseeing Sorrento　Bus Tour

(☎081 877 47 07; www.sorrento.city-sightseeing. it; adult/reduced €12/6; ☺Apr-Oct) City Sightseeing Sorrento runs a hop-on, hop-off bus tour of Sorrento and the surrounding area. Daily departures are at 9.30am, 11.30am, 1.30pm and 3.30pm from Piazza De Curtis (Circumvesuviana station). English-language commentaries are provided, and tickets, available on board, are valid for six hours.

Eating

Inn Bufalito　　Campanian €€

(☎081 365 69 75; www.innbufalito.it; Vico Fuoro 21; meals €25; ☺noon-midnight summer, reduced hrs winter; 🛜) 🍴 Owner Franco Coppola (no relation to that movie man) exudes a real passion for showcasing local produce – the restaurant is a member of the Slow Food Movement. A mozzarella bar as well as a restaurant, this effortlessly stylish place boasts a menu including delights such as Sorrento-style cheese fondue and buffalo meat *carpaccio*. Cheese tastings are a regular event, along with photography and art exhibitions, and occasional live music.

Sorrento

GREG ELMS/GETTY IMAGES ©

ⓘ Transport

Boat

Caremar (☎081 807 30 77; www.caremar.it) Runs hydrofoils to Capri (€13, 25 minutes, four daily).

Metrò del Mare (☎199 60 07 00; www.metrodelmare.net; ☉Jun-Sep) Runs ferries to Positano (€15, 35 minutes, two daily), Amalfi (€15, one hour, two daily), Naples Beverello (€11, 30 minutes, one daily) and Salerno (€15, 1 hour, 20 minutes, one daily).

Train

Circumvesuviana (☎800 211388; www.eavcampania.it) Sorrento is the last stop on the train line from Naples. Trains run every half-hour for Naples (one hour 10 minutes), via Pompeii (30 minutes) and Ercolano (50 minutes). Invest in a *Unico Costiera* card.

Bus

SITA (☎199 73 07 49; www.sitabus.it) Serves Naples, the Amalfi Coast and Sant'Agata, leaving from the bus stop across from the Circumvesuviana train station. Buy tickets at the station bar or from shops bearing the SITA sign.

Capri

POP 13,400

A stark mass of limestone rock rising sheerly through impossibly blue water, Capri (pronounced *ca*-pri) is the perfect microcosm of Mediterranean appeal – a smooth cocktail of voguish piazzas and cool cafes, Roman ruins, rugged seascapes and holidaying VIPs. While it's also a popular day-trip destination, consider staying a couple of nights to explore beyond Capri Town and its uphill rival Anacapri. It's here, in Capri's hinterland, that the island really seduces with its overgrown vegetable plots, sun-bleached stucco and indescribably beautiful walking trails.

◎ Sights

CAPRI TOWN & AROUND

Villa Jovis Ruin
(Jupiter's Villa; ☎081 837 06 86; Via Amaiuri; adult/reduced €2/1; ☉11am-3pm, closed Tue 1st-15th of month, closed Sun rest of month) A comfortable 2km walk along Via Tiberio, Villa Jovis was the largest and most sumptuous of the island's 12 Roman villas. It was also Tiberius' main Capri residence. Although reduced to ruins, wandering around will give you a good idea of the scale on which Tiberius liked to live.

Certosa di San Giacomo Monastery
(☎081 837 62 18; Viale Certosa 40; ☉9am-2pm Tue-Sun) **FREE** Generally considered the finest surviving example of Caprese architecture, this picturesque monastery now houses a school, library, temporary exhibition space and a museum with some evocative 17th-century paintings. While the

View from Monte Solaro (p298), Capri
CHRISTOPHER GROENHOUT/GETTY IMAGES ©

MAREMAGNUM/GETTY IMAGES ©

★ Don't Miss
Grotta Azzurra

Glowing in an ethereal blue light, the bewitching Grotta Azzurra is Capri's most famous single attraction.

Long known to local fishermen, the legendary sea cave was rediscovered by two Germans – writer Augustus Kopisch and painter Ernst Fries – in 1826. Subsequent research, however, revealed that Emperor Tiberius had built a quay in the cave around AD 30, complete with a *nymphaeum*. Remarkably, you can still see the carved Roman landing stage towards the rear of the grotto.

The easiest way to visit it is to take a boat tour from Marina Grande. A return trip will cost €26, comprising a return motorboat to the cave, the rowing boat into the cave itself and admission fee; allow a good hour.

NEED TO KNOW
Blue Grotto; grotto admission €12.50, return boat trip €13.50; ⊗9am-1hr before sunset

chapel has some soothing 17th-century frescoes, it's the two cloisters that have a real sense of faded glory (the smaller dates to the 14th century, the larger to the 16th century).

To reach here take Via Vittorio Emanuele, to the east of Piazza Umberto I, which meanders down to the monastery.

Giardini di Augusto Garden
(Gardens of Augustus; admission €1; ⊗9am-1hr before sunset) Get away from the Capri crowds by heading southwest from the Certosa di San Giacomo monastery where, at the end of Via G Matteotti, you'll come across the unexpected green oasis of the colourful Giardini di Augusto. Founded by the Emperor Augustus, you should spend a few minutes

contemplating the breathtaking view from here: gaze ahead to the **Isole Faraglioni**, the three dramatic limestone pinnacles that rise vertically out of the sea.

ANACAPRI & AROUND

Seggiovia del
Monte Solaro   View Point
(☎081 837 14 28; single/return €7.50/10; ⏰9.30am-4.30pm summer, to 3.30pm winter) Hop onto this *seggiovia* (chairlift) and head up to the summit of **Monte Solaro** (589m), Capri's highest point. The views from the top are utterly unforgettable – on a clear day, you can see the entire Bay of Naples, the Amalfi Coast and the islands of Ischia and Procida.

Activities

Beaches   Beach
Come summer, it's hard to resist Capri's turquoise waters. Top swimming spots include **La Fontelina** (☎081 837 08 45; www.fontelina-capri.com), reached along Via Tragara. Access to the private beach will set

you back €20 but it's right beside Capri's craggy Faraglioni stacks and is one of the few beaches with direct sunlight until late in the day.

On the west coast, **Lido del Faro** (☎081 837 17 98; www.lidofaro.com) at Punta Carena is another good option; €20 will get you access to the private beach, complete with swimming pool and a pricey but fabulous restaurant. For a free dip, opt for the neighbouring public beach, and grab a decent bite at snack bar Da Antonio. To get here from Anacapri, catch the bus to Faro (every 20 minutes, April to October) and follow the steps down to the beach.

Sercomar   Diving
(☎081 837 87 81; www.capriseaservice.com; Via Colombo 64, Marina Grande; ⏰Apr-Oct; ♿) Marina Grande is the hub of Capri's thriving water-sports business and this outfit is a solid choice for diving fans. Dives start from €100 for a single dive (maximum of three people) to €150 for an individual dive. A four-session beginner's course will set you back €350.

Left: Marina Grande, Capri
Below: Spaghetti dish

(LEFT) & (BELOW) RICHARD I'ANSON/GETTY IMAGES ©

Banana Sport Boating

(☏081 837 51 88; Marina Grande; 2hrs/day rental €120/220; ☁May-Oct) Located on the Marina Grande waterfront, Banana Sport hires out five-person motorised dinghies for exploring the island's more secluded coves and grottoes.

🛏 Sleeping

Villa Eva Hotel €€

(☏081 837 15 49; www.villaeva.com; Via La Fabbrica 8, Anacapri; d €100-140, tr €150-180, apt per person €55-65; ☁Easter-Oct; ☀) Villa Eva is a top 'budget' option, complete with small swimming pool and lush, palm-fringed gardens. Whether it's a stained glass window or a vintage fireplace, each room is distinct; some come with sea-view terraces. The four- and six-person apartments are ideal for families or groups of friends.

Casa Mariantonia Boutique Hotel €€

(☏081 837 29 23; www.casamariantonia.com; Via Guiseppe Orlandi 80, Anacapri; r €100-260; ℗❄☎☀) This fabulous boutique retreat counts Jean-Paul Sartre and Alberto Moravia among its past guests, which may well give you something to muse upon while you're lounging by the fabulous pool. Rooms deliver restrained elegance in soothing hues, and there are private terraces with gorgeous garden views.

La Minerva Boutique Hotel €€€

(☏081 837 70 67; www.laminervacapri.com; Via Occhio Marino 8, Capri Town; superior d €170-410, deluxe d €230-520; ☁mid-Mar-early Nov; ❄☎☀) This stylish, family-run hotel is highly coveted (book five to six months ahead). All 16 rooms deliver crisp, white-on-white luxury, from silk drapes, plush sofas and 100% linen sheets, to heavenly mattresses and your choice of pillows. Deluxe rooms feature Jacuzzis and larger terraces. Then there's the gorgeous pool, surrounded by lush greenery and dreamy sea views.

299

Eating

Salumeria da Aldo
Deli €

(Via Cristoforo Colombo 26, Marina Grande; panini from €3.50) Ignore the restaurant touts and head straight to this honest portside deli, where bespectacled Aldo will make you his legendary *panino alla Caprese* (crusty bread stuffed with silky mozzarella and tomatoes from his own garden). Grab a bottle of falanghina and you're set for a day at the beach.

Da Gelsomina
Campanian €€

(☏081 837 14 99; www.dagelsomina.com; Via Migliera 72, Anacapri; meals €38; ☺lunch & dinner Mon-Sun May-Sep, reduced hrs rest of year; ☎) Sublime homegrown produce and wine, sea and vineyard views; and a swimming pool for a post-prandial dip – it's no wonder you're advised to book three days ahead in the summer. Da Gelsomina ditches culinary cliches for turf classics like *coniglio alla cacciatore* (rabbit with lightly spiced tomato, sage and rosemary) and not-to-be-missed *ravioli alla caprese*, filled with Cacciotta cheese.

Pulalli
Wine Bar €€

(☏081 837 41 08; Piazza Umberto I 4, Capri Town; meals €25; ☺lunch & dinner Wed-Mon Easter-Oct) Climb the steps to the right of Capri Town's tourist office and your reward is a laid-back local hang-out, where fabulous vino meets a discerning selection of cheeses, *salumi* (charcuterie) and more substantial fare like spaghetti with zucchini flowers.

ℹ Information

Tourist Office (Marina Grande; ☺9.15am-1pm & 3-6.15pm Mon-Sat, 9am-3pm Sun Apr-Sep) The tourist office can provide a free map of the island with town plans of Capri and Anacapri, and a more detailed one for €1. For hotel listings and other useful information, ask for a free copy of *Capri è*. Branches at Capri Town (☏081 837 06 86; www.capritourism.com; Piazza Umberto I; ☺8.30am-8pm) and Anacapri (☏081 837 15 24; Via G Orlando 59; ☺9am-3pm Mon-Sat Apr-Sep).

ℹ Getting There & Away

See Naples for details of ferries and hydrofoils to the island. In summer hydrofoils connect with Positano (€17.40 to 19.30, 30 to 40 minutes) and Sorrento. Note that some companies require you to pay a small supplement for luggage, around €2.

Marina, Naples (p282)

ℹ️ Getting Around

Bus

Sippic (☏ 081 837 04 20; Via Roma, Capri Town; €1.80) runs regular buses between Capri Town, Marina Grande, Anacapri and Marina Piccola.

Staiano Autotrasporti (☏ 081 837 24 22; Via Tommaso, Anacapri; €1.80) buses serve the Grotta Azzurra and Faro of Punta Carena.

Funicular

Funicular (€1.80; ⏲ 6.30am-12.30am) connects Marina Grande to Capri Town.

Taxi

From Marina Grande, a **taxi** (☏ in Anacapri 081 837 11 75, in Capri Town 081 837 05 43) costs around €20 to Capri and €25 to Anacapri; Capri to Anacapri costs around €16.

SOUTH OF NAPLES

Mt Vesuvius

Towering darkly over Naples and its environs, Mt Vesuvius (Vesuvio, 1281m), is the only active volcano on the European mainland. Since it exploded into history in AD 79, burying Pompeii and Herculaneum and pushing the coastline out several kilometres, it has erupted more than 30 times. The most devastating of these was in 1631, the most recent in 1944.

Established in 1995, **Parco Nazionale del Vesuvio** (☏ 081 239 56 53; adult/reduced €10/8; ⏲ 9am-7pm Jul & Aug, to 5pm Apr-Jun & Sep, to 4pm Mar & Oct, to 3pm Nov-Feb, ticket office closes 1hr before the crater) attracts some 400,000 visitors annually. From a car park at the summit, an 860m path leads up to the volcano's **crater** (admission incl tour €8; ⏲ 9am-6pm Jul & Aug, to 5pm Apr-Jun & Sep, to 4pm Mar & Oct, to 3pm Nov-Feb).

Shuttle bus operator **Vesuvio Express** (☏ 081 739 36 66; www.vesuvioexpress.it) runs services from Ercolano to Mt Vesuvius, departing from Piazza Stazione Circumvesuviana, right outside Ercolano-Scavi train station. Buses depart every 40 minutes from 9.30am to 4pm daily, with a journey time of 20 minutes each way.

❤️ If You Like...
Ancient Wonders

If you're fascinated by Pompeii or the unearthed Roman artefacts at Museo Archaeologico Nazionale, check out these other ancient sites.

1 RUINS OF HERCULANEUM
(☏ 081 732 43 38; www.pompeiisites.org; Corso Resina 6, Ercolano; adult/reduced €11/5.50, combined ticket incl Pompeii €20/10; ⏲ 8.30am-7.30pm summer, to 5pm winter, last entry 90min before closing; ☒ Circumvesuviana to Ercolano-Scavi) Unfairly upstaged by Pompeii's offerings, Herculaneum has a wealth of archaeological finds. Rthis superbly conserved Roman fishing town of 4000 inhabitants is smaller and easier to navigate than Pompeii, and can be explored with a map and audioguide (€6.50). Serious archaeological work began again in 1927 and continues to this day.

2 NAPOLI SOTTERRANEA
(Underground Naples; ☏ 081 29 69 44; www.napolisotterranea.org; Piazza San Gaetano 68; tours €9; ⏲ English tours 10am, noon, 2pm, 4pm & 6pm; ☒ C55 to Via Duomo) This evocative guided tour leads you 40m below street level to explore Naples' ancient labyrinth of aqueducts, passages and cisterns.

3 MAV
(Museo Archeologico Virtuale; ☏ 081 1980 6511; www.museomav.com; Via IV Novembre 44; adult/child €7.50/6, 3D documentary €4; ⏲ 9am-4.30pm Tue-Fri, to 5.30pm Sat & Sun; ☒ Ercolano-Scavi) Using high-tech holograms and computer-generated footage, this 'virtual archaeological museum' brings ruins like Pompeii's forum and Capri's Villa Jovis back to life.

Return tickets (which include entry to the volcano summit) are €18.

From Pompeii, **Busvia del Vesuvio** (☏ 340 9352616; www.busviadelvesuvio.com) runs a shuttle service from outside Pompeii train station (hourly from 9am to 3pm) to nearby Boscoreale. From here, it's a 25-minute journey on a 4WD-style bus. Return tickets (including entry to the summit) cost €22.

Pompeii

The ruins of Pompeii are priceless. Much of the site's value lies in the fact that it wasn't simply blown away by Vesuvius in AD 79, rather it was buried under a layer of *lapilli* (burning fragments of pumice stone). The result is a remarkably well-preserved slice of ancient life, where visitors can walk down Roman streets and snoop around millennia-old abodes and businesses.

081 857 53 47

www.pompeiisites.org

entrances at Porta Marina & Piazza Anfiteatro

adult/reduced €11/5.50, combined ticket incl Herculaneum €20/10

8.30am-7.30pm summer, to 5pm winter, last entry 90min before closing

Visiting the Site

After its catastrophic demise, Pompeii receded from the public eye until 1594, when architect Domenico Fontana uncovered the ruins while digging a canal; however, exploration proper didn't begin until 1748. Of Pompeii's original 66 hectares, 44 have now been excavated. Of course that doesn't mean you'll have unhindered access to every inch of the Unesco-listed site – expect to come across areas cordoned off for no apparent reason and a noticeable lack of clear signs. Audioguides are a sensible investment and a good guidebook also helps – try *Pompeii* published by Electa Napoli (€10).

The site's main entrance is at Porta Marina, the most impressive of the seven gates that punctuated the ancient town walls. A busy passageway now as it was then, it originally connected the town with the nearby harbour, hence the gateway's name. You'll almost certainly be approached by a guide outside the *scavi* ticket office. Authorised guides wear identification tags and you can expect to pay between €100 and €120 for a two-hour tour, whether you're alone or in a group. Reputable tour operators include **Yellow Sudmarine** (334 1047036, 329 1010328; www.yellowsudmarine.com) and **Torres Travel** (081 856 78 02; www.torrestravel.it).

Need to Know

For a bite, try chandeliered **President** (081 850 72 45; www.ristorantepresident.it; Piazza Schettini 12; meals €35; 11.40am-3.30pm & 7pm-midnight Tue-Sun, closed Jan; FS to Pompei, Circumvesuviana to Pompei Scavi-Villa dei Misteri), featuring local produce in creations like eggplant *millefoglie* (flaky puff pastry) with Cetara anchovies.

Circumvesuviana trains run from Pompei-Scavi-Villa dei Misteri station to Naples (€2.90, 35 minutes) and Sorrento (€2.20, 30 minutes). **CSTP** (800 016659; www.cstp.it) bus 4 runs to/from Salerno (€2.20, 90 minutes). Shuttle buses to Vesuvius depart outside Pompei-Scavi-Villa dei Misteri train station.

Ruins of Pompeii

RECOMMENDATIONS FROM VALENTINA VELLUSI, TOUR GUIDE

1 CASA DEL FAUNO

Pompeii's greatest mosaics were uncovered at the House of the Faun, including one of Alexander the Great. The original is in Naples' Museo Archeologico Nazionale (p287), but there's a faithful copy on site. With a sophisticated use of perspective and colour, it captures the last moments of the Battle of Issos.

2 IL FORO

The Forum was the city's main piazza – a huge rectangle flanked by limestone columns. To the north stands the Tempio di Giove (Temple of Jupiter) and the Grano del Foro (Forum Granary). The Foro is particularly beautiful in the late afternoon sun, when exhausted visitors sit down and open up to the spirit of the place.

3 LA FULLONICA DI STEPHANUS

This house represents Pompeii's final period, between the earthquake of AD 63 and Vesuvius' eruption in 79. You can still see the vats used to wash, rinse and dye clothes in this wash house. Urine was commonly used to bleach clothes and assist in the dyeing process – opposite the entrance is the phallic-shaped spot where people were encouraged to relieve themselves to contribute to supplies.

4 ORTO DEI FUGGIASCHI

The plaster casts here capture the final moments of two family groups trying to flee the eruption: the screams, the hopeless attempt to shield themselves from the falling *lapilli* (burning pumice stone).

Tragedy in Pompeii

24 AUGUST AD 79

8am Buildings including the **Terme Suburbane** ❶ and the **foro** ❷ are still undergoing repair after an earthquake in AD 63 caused significant damage to the city. Despite violent earth tremors overnight, residents have little idea of the catastrophe that lies ahead.

Midday Peckish locals pour into the **Thermopolium di Vetutius Placidus** ❸. The lustful slip into the **Lupanare** ❹, and gladiators practise for the evening's planned games at the **anfiteatro** ❺. A massive boom heralds the eruption. Shocked onlookers witness a dark cloud of volcanic matter shoot some 14km above the crater.

3pm–5pm Lapilli (burning pumice stone) rains down on Pompeii. Terrified locals begin to flee; others take shelter. Within two hours, the plume is 25km high and the sky has darkened. Roofs collapse under the weight of the debris, burying those inside.

25 AUGUST AD 79

Midnight Mudflows bury the town of Herculaneum. Lapilli and ash continue to rain down on Pompeii, bursting through buildings and suffocating those taking refuge within.

4am–8am Ash and gas avalanches hit Herculaneum. Subsequent surges smother Pompeii, killing all remaining residents, including those in the **Orto dei Fuggiaschi** ❻. The volcanic 'blanket' will safeguard frescoed treasures like the **Casa del Menandro** ❼ and **Villa dei Misteri** ❽ for almost two millennia.

TOP TIPS

» Visit in the afternoon
» Allow three hours
» Wear comfortable shoes and a hat
» Bring drinking water
» Don't use flash photography

Terme Suburbane
The *laconicum* (sauna), *caldarium* (hot bath) and large, heated swimming pool weren't the only sources of heat here; scan the walls of this suburban bathhouse for some of the city's raunchiest frescoes.

Villa di Diomede

Casa del Poeta Tragico
Porta Ercolano
Casa Faur

Tempio di Apollo
Basilica
Porta Marina ❶

❷

Terme del Foro

Macellum

Teatro Grande

Quadriportico dei Teatri
Porta di Stabia
Teatro Piccolo

❹

Foro
An ancient Times Square of sorts, the forum sits at the intersection of Pompeii's main streets and was closed to traffic in the 1st century AD. The plinths on the southern edge featured statues of the imperial family.

Villa dei Misteri
Home to the world-famous *Dionysiac Frieze* fresco. Other highlights at this villa include *trompe l'oeil* wall decorations in the *cubiculum* (bedroom) and Egyptian-themed artwork in the *tablinum* (reception).

Lupanare
The prostitutes at this brothel were often slaves of Greek or Asian origin. Mattresses once covered the stone beds and the names engraved in the walls are possibly those of the workers and their clients.

Thermopolium di Vetutius Placidus
The counter at this ancient snack bar once held urns filled with hot food. The *lararium* (household shrine) on the back wall depicts Dionysus (the god of wine) and Mercury (the god of profit and commerce).

Casa dei Vettii

Porta del Vesuvio

EYEWITNESS ACCOUNT

Pliny the Younger (AD 61–c 112) gives a gripping, first-hand account of the catastrophe in his letters to Tacitus (AD 56–117).

Porta di Nola

Casa della Venere in Conchiglia

Porta di Sarno

3

7

Tempio di Iside

Grande Palestra

6

5

Orto dei Fuggiaschi
The Garden of the Fugitives showcases the plaster moulds of 13 locals seeking refuge during Vesuvius' eruption – the largest number of victims found in any one area. The huddled bodies make for a moving scene.

Anfiteatro
Magistrates, local senators and the games' sponsors and organisers enjoyed front-row seating at this veteran amphitheatre, home to gladiatorial battles and the odd riot. The parapet circling the stadium featured paintings of combat, victory celebrations and hunting scenes.

Casa del Menandro
This dwelling most likely belonged to the family of Poppaea Sabina, Nero's second wife. A room to the left of the atrium features Trojan War paintings and a polychrome mosaic of pygmies rowing down the Nile.

AMALFI COAST

Stretching about 50km along the southern side of the Sorrentine Peninsula, the Amalfi Coast (Costiera Amalfitana) is one of Europe's most breathtaking. Cliffs terraced with scented lemon groves sheer down into sparkling seas; sherbet-hued villas cling precariously to unforgiving slopes while sea and sky merge in one vast blue horizon.

Yet its stunning topography has not always been a blessing. For centuries after Amalfi's glory days as a maritime superpower, the area was poor and its isolated villages were regular victims of foreign incursions, earthquakes and landslides. It was this very isolation that first drew visitors in the early 1900s, paving the way for the advent of tourism in the latter half of the century. Today the Amalfi Coast is one of Italy's premier tourist destinations, a favourite of cashed-up jet-setters and love-struck couples.

ℹ Getting There & Away

Boat

Alicost (☎089 87 14 83; www.alicost.it; Salita Sopramuro 2, Amalfi) operates one daily ferry from Salerno to Amalfi (€7), Positano (€11) and Capri (€20.70) from April to October.

TraVelMar (☎089 87 29 50; www.travelmar.it) connects Salerno with Amalfi (€8, six daily) and Positano (€12, six daily) from April to October.

Train

From Naples, either the Circumvesuviana to Sorrento or a Trenitalia train to Salerno, then continue along the coast by SITA Sud bus.

....

Amalfi

POP 5160

Believe it or not, pretty little Amalfi, with its sun-filled piazzas and small beach, was once a maritime superpower with a population of more than 70,000. For one thing, it's not a big place – you can easily walk from one end to the other in about 20 minutes. For another, there are very few historical buildings of note. The explanation is chilling – most of the old city, and its populace, simply slid into the sea during an earthquake in 1343.

◉ Sights

Cattedrale di Sant'Andrea
Cathedral

(☎089 87 10 59; Piazza del Duomo; ⏱7.30am-7.30pm) A melange of architectural styles, Amalfi's iconic cathedral makes a striking impression from the top of its sweeping flight of stairs. Between 10am and 5pm (from 12.15pm on Sundays), entrance to the cathedral is through the adjacent Chiostro del Paradiso, where you have to pay an entrance fee of €3. It's well worth it.

Museo della Carta
Museum

(☎089 830 45 61; www.museodellacarta.it; Via delle Cartiere 23; admission €4; ⏱10am-6.30pm) Amalfi's paper museum is housed in a 13th-century paper mill (the oldest in Europe). It lovingly preserves the original paper presses, which are still in full working order, as you'll see during the 15-minute guided tour (three-day advance booking requested for English tour) which explains the original cotton-based paper production and the later wood pulp manufacturing.

🛏 Sleeping

Hotel Lidomare
Hotel €€

(☎089 87 13 32; www.lidomare.it; Largo Duchi Piccolomini 9; s/d €50/120; ❄🖧) Family run, this gracious hotel oozes character. Rooms are spacious, with appealingly haphazard decor, vintage tiles and fine antiques. Some rooms have Jacuzzi bathtubs, others have sea views and a balcony, some have both. Breakfast is laid out on top of a grand piano. Highly recommended.

Hotel Luna Convento
Hotel €€€

(☎089 87 10 02; www.lunahotel.it; Via Pantaleone Comite 33; s €230-290; d €250-300; 🅿❄@🖧🏊) This former convent founded by St Francis in 1222 has been a hotel for some 170 years. Rooms in the original building are former monks' cells, but there's nothing pokey about the bright tiles, balconies and seamless sea views. The newer wing is equally beguiling, with religious frescoes over the bed (to stop any misbehaving). The cloistered courtyard is magnificent.

GLENN BEANLAND/GETTY IMAGES ©

Don't Miss
Positano

The pearl in the pack, Positano is the coast's most photogenic and expensive town. Its steeply stacked houses are a medley of peaches, pinks and terracottas, and its near-vertical streets (many of which are, in fact, staircases) are lined with voguish shop displays, jewellery stalls, elegant hotels and smart restaurants.

Chiesa di Santa Maria Assunta (Piazza Flavio Gioia; ⊙8am-noon & 4-9pm) is the most famous sight in Positano. Inside, it's a delightfully classical affair, its pillars topped with gilded Ionic capitals and winged cherubs peeking from above every arch. Above the main altar is a 13th-century Byzantine Black Madonna and Child. To relax, **Spiaggia Grande** is the pretty, sandy town beach.

For something sleek and refreshingly contemporary, **Next2** (✆089 812 35 16; www.next2.it; Viale Pasitea 242; meals €40; ⊙6.30-11.30pm) wine bar and restaurant gives regional cooking satisfying makeovers. Whenever possible, local and organic ingredients are put to impressive use in creations such as fried ravioli with ricotta and mozzarella on fresh tomatoes, or *parmigiana di pesce bandiera,* a surf variation on the classic eggplant dish.

Da Vincenzo (✆089 87 51 28; Viale Pasitea 172-178; meals €40; ⊙noon-2.30pm & 6-11pm Wed-Mon, 6.30-11pm Tue) serves up superbly prepared dishes by the third generation of restaurateurs. The emphasis is on fish, ranging from the adventurous, like skewers of grilled octopus tentacles with deep-fried artichokes, to seasonal pasta dishes.

Positano has excellent ferry connections to the coastal towns and Capri from April to October. **Alicost** (✆089 87 14 83; www.alicost.it) operates a daily service to Amalfi (€7), Sorrento (€8.50) and Capri (€17.40). **TraVelMar** (✆089 87 29 50; www.travelmar.it) runs daily ferries to Amalfi (€8), and **Linee Marittime Partenopee** (✆081 704 19 11; www.consorziolmp.it) runs frequent hydrofoils and ferries to Capri (€19).

🍴 Eating

Le Arcate
Campanian €€

(📞089 87 13 67; www.learcate.net; Largo Orlando Buonocore, Atrani; pizzas from €6, meals €25; ⏲12.30-3pm & 7.30-11.30pm Tue-Sun, open Mon Jul & Aug) On a sunny day it's hard to beat the dreamy location at the far eastern point of the harbour, overlooking the beach with Atrani's ancient rooftops behind you. Huge white parasols shade the tables, while the dining room is a stone-walled natural cave. Tuck into bubbling pizzas or dishes like risotto with grilled swordfish; the food is good, but it's a step down from the setting.

Trattoria Il Mulino
Italian €€

(Via delle Cartiere 36; pizzas €6-11, meals €29; ⏲noon-midnight) A TV-in-the-corner, kids-running-between-the-tables sort of place, this is about as authentic a trattoria as you'll find in Amalfi. There are no culinary acrobatics, just hearty, honest pasta and simple grilled meat, fish and seafood. The *calamari alla griglia* (grilled calamari) is simple, succulent perfection.

Ristorante La Caravella
Campanian €€€

(📞089 87 10 29; www.ristorantelacaravella.it; Via Matteo Camera 12; tasting menus €50-120; ⏲noon-2.30pm & 7.30-11pm Wed-Mon) The regional food here has recently earned the restaurant a Michelin star with dishes that offer nouvelle zap, like black ravioli with cuttlefish ink, scampi and ricotta, or that are unabashedly simple, like the catch of the day served grilled on lemon leaves.

ℹ Information

Tourist Office (www.amalfitouristoffice.it; Corso delle Repubbliche Marinare 27; ⏲9am-1pm & 2-6pm Mon-Sat, 9am-1pm Sun, closed Sun Apr, May & Sep, closed Sat & Sun Oct-Mar) Good for bus and ferry timetables.

ℹ Getting There & Away

Boat

Between April and October there are daily sailings to/from Amalfi.

Left: Cattedrale di Sant'Andrea (p306), Amalfi;
Below: Gardens at Villa Cimbrone (p310), Ravello
(LEFT) MICHELE FALZONE/GETTY IMAGES ©; (BELOW) RICHARD I'ANSON/GETTY IMAGES ©

Alicost (📞089 87 14 83; www.
alicost.it) Operates one daily
service to Amalfi (€7), Sorrento (€8.50)
and Capri (€19).

TraVelMar (📞089 87 29 50; www.travelmar.it)
Runs ferries to Positano (€8, seven daily).

Linee Marittime Partenopee (📞081 704 19 11;
www.consorziolmp.it) Runs three daily hydrofoils
and four daily ferries to Capri (€21/20.50).

Coop Sant'Andrea (📞089 87 29 50; www.
coopsantandrea.com; Lungomare dei Cavalieri 1)
Connects Amalfi to Positano (€8, seven daily).

Bus

SITA Sud (📞089 40 51 45; www.sitasudtrasporti.
it) runs at least 17 daily services from Piazza
Flavio Gioia to Sorrento (€3.80, 100 minutes) via
Positano (€2.50, 50 minutes). It runs at least 24
daily services to Ravello (€2.50, 25 minutes).

There are two early-morning connections to
Naples (€4.10, two hours), with no services on
Sunday, so you're better off catching a bus to
Sorrento and then the Circumvesuviana train to
Naples.

Ravello

Sitting high in the hills above Amalfi,
refined Ravello is a polished town almost
entirely dedicated to tourism. Boasting
impeccable bohemian credentials –
Wagner, DH Lawrence and Virginia Woolf
all lounged here – it's today known for its
ravishing gardens and stupendous views.

The **tourist office** (📞089 85 70 96; www.
ravellotime.it; Via Roma 18bis; ⊙9am-8pm) has
a handy map with walking trails.

◎ Sights

Villa Rufolo   Garden
(📞089 85 76 21; Piazza Duomo; adult/
reduced €5/3; ⊙9am-sunset) To the south of
Ravello's cathedral, a 14th-century tower
marks the entrance to this villa, famed for
its beautiful cascading gardens. Created
by Scotsman Scott Neville Reid in 1853,
they are truly magnificent, commanding

309

celestial panoramic views packed with exotic colours, artistically crumbling towers and luxurious blooms.

Cathedral
Cathedral

(Piazza Duomo; museum admission €3; ⊗8.30am-noon & 5.30-8.30pm) Forming the eastern flank of Piazza Duomo, Ravello's cathedral was originally built in 1086 but has since undergone various makeovers. The facade is 16th century, even if the central bronze door, one of only about two dozen in the country, is an 1179 original; the interior is a late-20th-century interpretation of what the original must once have looked like.

Villa Cimbrone
Garden

(☎089 85 80 72; Via Santa Chiara 26; adult/reduced €6/3; ⊗9am-sunset) If Villa Rufolo's gardens leave you longing for more, the 12th-century Villa Cimbrone has you covered; we're talking vast views from delightfully ramshackle gardens.

🟣 Festivals & Events

Ravello Festival
Arts

(☎089 85 83 60; www.ravellofestival.com; ⊗Jun–mid-Sep) Come summer, the Ravello Festival turns much of the town centre into a stage. Events range from orchestral concerts and chamber music to ballet performances; film screenings and exhibitions are held in atmospheric outdoor venues, most notably the famous overhanging terrace in the Villa Rufolo gardens.

🛏 Sleeping & Eating

Hotel Villa Amore
Pension €€

(☎089 85 71 35; www.villaamore.it; Via dei Fusco 5; s/d €80/120; ⊗May-Oct; @) A welcoming family-run *pensione*, this is the best budget choice in town. All rooms have their own balcony and some have bathtubs.

Cumpà Cosimo
Campanian €€

(☎089 85 71 56; Via Roma 44-46; pizzas €7-12, meals €40; ⊗12.30-3pm & 7.30pm-midnight) Netta Bottone's rustic cooking is so good that even US celebrity Rose O'Donnell tried to get her on her show. Netta didn't make it to Hollywood but she stills rules the roost at this historic trattoria.

ℹ Getting There & Away

SITA Sud operates at least 24 buses daily from the eastern side of Piazza Flavio Gioia in Amalfi (€2.50, 25 minutes).

Villa Rufolo (p309), Ravello

GLENN BEANLAND/GETTY IMAGES ©

Detour:
Paestum

Paestum, or Poseidonia as the city was originally called (in honour of Poseidon, the Greek god of the sea), was founded in the 6th century BC by Greek settlers and fell under Roman control in 273 BC. Decline later set in following the demise of the Roman Empire. Savage raids by the Saracens and periodic outbreaks of malaria forced the steadily dwindling population to abandon the city altogether.

If you are visiting the **ruins** (📞0828 72 26 54; adult/reduced, incl museum €10/5; 🕑8.45am-2hrs before sunset) in springtime, the three temples are particularly stunning, surrounded by meadows of colourful wildflowers. Entering from the main entrance on the northern end, the first structure to take your breath away is the 6th-century-BC Tempio di Cerere (Temple of Ceres). Originally dedicated to Athena, it served as a Christian church in medieval times.

The Tempio di Nettuno (Temple of Neptune), dating from about 450 BC, is the largest and best preserved of the temples; only parts of its inside walls and roof are missing. Almost next door, the so-called basilica (in fact, a temple to the goddess Hera) is Paestum's oldest surviving monument. Dating from the middle of the 6th century BC, it's a magnificent sight, with nine columns across and 18 along the sides.

CSTP (📞089 48 70 01; www.cstp.it) bus 34 operates to Paestum from Piazza della Concordia in Salerno (€3.40, one hour 20 minutes, 12 daily).

Sicily & Southern Italy

From volcano-view beaches to cave hotels, Italy's south is set to stun. Why would anyone live under a volcano? Sicilians have their reasons: beaches, history and food, for starters. Of all those who harboured on these dramatic shores over the last 25 centuries – Greeks, Arabs, Spaniards – few seemed inclined to leave, hence the island's multicultural history. Pistachios, almonds and citrus thrive in this volcanic soil, and star in Sicily's signature pastries and gelato.

But save some travel time and appetite for the heel of Italy's boot, where Puglia and Basilicata have somehow managed to keep Unesco World Heritage sites and Italy's most satisfying rustic cuisine more or less to themselves since the 8th century BC. Here you can sleep like a caveman in a subterranean hotel or a gnome in a stone hut, without straying far from sandy beaches.

Vieste (p346)
PHILIP AND KAREN SMITH/GETTY IMAGES ©

Sicily & Southern Italy

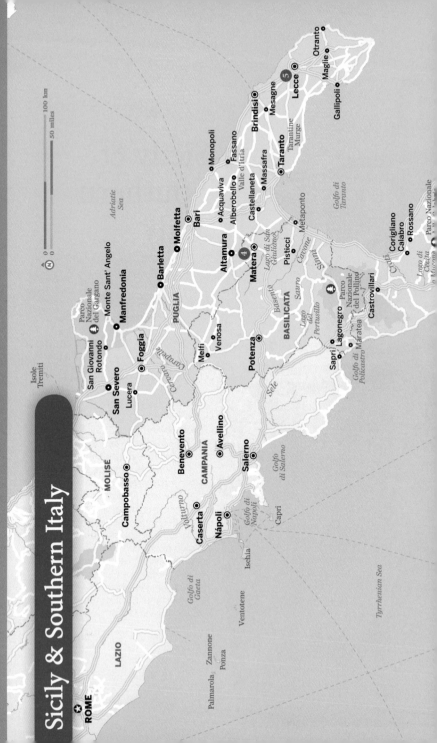

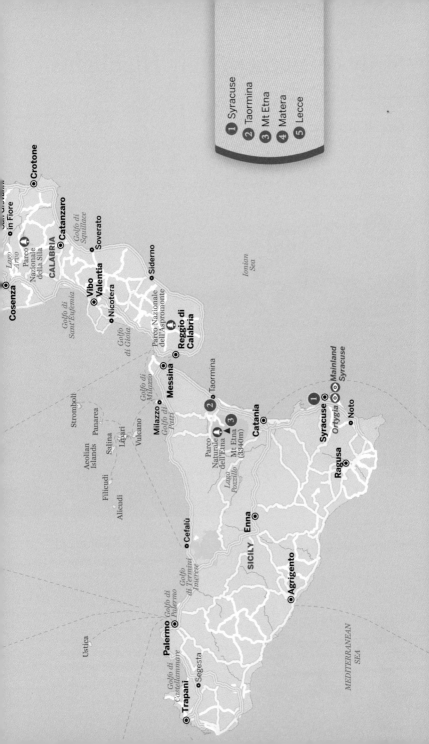

Sicily & Southern Italy Highlights

Greek Drama, Syracuse

In its Hellenic heyday, Syracuse was the Broadway of Magna Graecia, with top-billing playwrights such as Aeschylus. If productions flopped, directors could take it up with the gods a Ara di Gerone II, a sacrificial altar where up to 450 oxen were slaughtered. Today Syracuse has the only school of classical Greek drama outside Athens, with spectacular productions staged May and June at the Teatro Greco (p339).

Beachside Taormina

You're in for grand old times in the medieval beach town of Taormina. The ancier Greek theatre still hosts summer concerts, shops still sell handmade ceramics and local capers, and wooden fishir boats still bob off the cove of Isola Bell Welcome modern upgrades include cable-car access from the hillside town to Lido Mazzarò (p337) beach, and crea tive cuisine at Casa Grugno (p338).

PHILIP AND KAREN SMITH/GETTY IMAGES ©

Atop Mt Etna

3

Sicilians live dangerously in the shadow of this still-active volcano (p336), but you can top that: take the cable car and hike up to the crater zone to see Mt Etna smouldering. You probably won't see any spewing magma – and that's a good thing – but there was a lava flow as recently as 2002. To keep a safe(r) distance, hop on the Ferrovia Circumetnea train circling the volcano's base.

4

Sassi, Matera

Matera's (p347) incredible *sassi* (cave dwellings) form the most extensive troglodyte complex in the Mediterranean, one of the oldest human settlements on earth, and it's a World Heritage Site. Wander through staircases and rooms hewn from rock and you'll find ancient frescoed churches, snug pig pens and two-storied buildings – plus refurbished caves turned into hotels, complete with solar panels and subterranean swimming pools.

5

Baroque Lecce

A vibrant university town, Lecce (p346) is full of beautiful, grand buildings built out of the local sandstone. The soft building material inspired sculptors to go crazy in carving out decorations for the local baroque churches, which almost writhe with ornament. Summer nights see the streets fill with a heady mix of Italians, locals and foreigners, making this Puglia's most cosmopolitan melting pot.

Sicily & Southern Italy's Best...

Beach Spots

○ **Vieste, Puglia** Dazzling whitewashed town with white-sand beaches. (p346)

○ **Baia dei Turchi, Puglia** White sands and a wild pine forest backdrop close to Otranto. (p349)

○ **Taormina, Sicily** Hop the scenic cable car down to a sparkling cove. (p337)

○ **Cefalù, Sicily** Mountains at your back, sand at your feet, boutiques handy. (p331)

Unesco World Heritage Treasures

○ **Matera, Basilicata** Surreal cave dwellings and underground churches. (p347)

○ **Alberobello, Puglia** A truly fascinating town of *trulli:* stone cottages shaped like Santa hats. (p346)

○ **Aeolian Islands, Sicily** Green hills, black lava and turquoise waters. (p332)

○ **Syracuse, Sicily** High Greek drama atop an ancient city. (p338)

○ **Castel del Monte, Puglia** An Islamic-inspired, eight-sided castle. (p345)

Cheap Thrills

○ **Ferrovia Circumetnea** Enjoying 360-degree views of Mt Etna from the train. (p336)

○ **Mercato di Ballarò** Bargaining for beach-picnic supplies in Palermo's vibrant market. (p324)

○ **Vulcano** Restorative hot springs and pungent mud-baths. (p332)

○ **Piazza Mercantile** Dodging Bari's Colonna della Giustizia, where debtors were once whipped. (p343)

Need to Know

Foodie Experiences

○ **Ferro di Cavallo** Freshly filled Sicilian *cannoli* in Palermo. (p329)

○ **La Pescheria** Hearing the seafood vendors call at Catania's fish market. (p333)

○ **Mercato di Ballarò** Foodstuffs galore at Palermo's main market. (p324)

○ **Orecchiette** Try traditional Pugliese 'little ears' pasta in Bari (p343), Alberobello (p346) or Lecce (p346).

ADVANCE PLANNING

○ **Three months before** Book accommodation for peak beach season – late June through August – or for a stay in a Matera cave-hotel or *trullo* cottage around Alberobello or Ostuni.

○ **One to two months before** Scan the online Taormina Arte festival (www.taoarte. it) and Syracuse Greek theatre festival (www. indafondazione.org/en/) programs for promising performances.

○ **One week before** Make reservations at Trattoria Il Maestro del Brodo or Trattoria Ai Cascinari.

RESOURCES

○ **Sicilian Tourist Board** (www.regione.sicilia.it/ turismo/web_turismo)

○ **Best of Sicily** (www. bestofsicily.com)

○ **Travel in Puglia** (www. viaggiareinpuglia.it) Key info and itineraries in Puglia.

○ **Ferula Viaggi** (www. materaturismo.it) Information on Matera and surrounds.

GETTING AROUND

○ **Air** European routes service Palermo's Falcone-Borsellino airport, Catania's Fontanarossa airport and Bari's Palese airport.

○ **Train** Efficient coastal service; slower to interior towns. Frequent services between Bari and Matera and Puglian towns.

○ **Bus** Handy for crossing Sicily's interior and reaching towns not covered by trains.

○ **Car** Outside the cities, an ideal way to explore.

○ **Ferries and hydrofoils** Regular summer services between Sicily and the Aeolian Islands; reduced services the rest of the year. Services between Sicily and the mainland, especially to Calabria and overnight ferries to Naples.

BE FOREWARNED

○ **Museums** Many close Mondays or Tuesdays.

○ **Pickpockets and bag snatchers** Particularly active in Palermo; mind your belongings on crowded beaches from July to August.

Left: Sicilian pastries;
Above: Stromboli, Aeolian Islands (p332)
(LEFT) & (ABOVE) DALLAS STRIBLEY/GETTY IMAGES ©

Sicily & Southern Italy Itineraries

Between the Arabesque elegance of Sicilian seaside towns and the architectural quirks of villages in Puglia, the south may leave you breathless. To return to your senses, try local remedies: sandy beaches and gelato.

PALERMO TO CEFALÙ

ARABESQUE SICILY

With its domed roofs and sweet-and-spicy flavours, Sicily is just a mosaic tile's throw across the Mediterranean from the Middle East. Spend your first day or two exploring the heritage of ❶ **Palermo**, once the jewel of the Arab-influenced Norman Empire. Visit local landmarks, from gleaming Cappella Palatina to raucous, souk-like Mercato di Ballarò. Check out the Arabesques gracing Palermo's majolica-cupola-topped cathedral. Recover afterwards in Palermo's steamy, marble-clad *hammam*, or watch puppets re-enact ancient Arab-Norman legends of heroic battles and star-crossed romance at the Museo Internazionale delle Marionette.

Start the next morning with *pane e pannelle* (chickpea fritters) – one of several Sicilian street foods with Middle Eastern flavour. Then catch an afternoon train to ❷ **Cefalù**, one of Sicily's favourite resort towns and home to the Arab-Norman beauty Duomo di Cefalù. Another relic of Cefalù's Arabic heritage is Salita Saraceno, a staircase that winds along ancient city walls for stunning views.

 VIESTE TO MATERA
4–5 DAYS
ITALY'S WILD SOUTHWEST

The views from the heel of Italy's boot are among the country's wildest and weirdest. In this striking, sun-bleached landscape edged with sapphire sea coves, locals have made themselves at home in the most unbelievable places: two-storied cave dwellings, cone-headed stone cottages, and baroque sandstone palaces that look like elaborate sandcastles.

Ease yourself into the scenery by driving across Puglia's white bluffs to the beaches and secret sea caves of ❶ **Vieste**. Hit the road the next day to ❷ **Alberobello**, which looks like a gnome neighbourhood with tubby little *trulli* cottages capped with

comical, conical roofs. Head onwards to ❸ **Ostuni** to stroll around its all-white historic quarter and feast on dreamy views out to the azure ocean, before staying overnight in 13th-century palace La Terra. Next carry on into the sea castle sandstone beach town of ❹ **Lecce**, where you can bunk in baroque splendour at Palazzo Rollo. The tour ends with nothing like you've seen before: Basilicata's ❺ **Matera**, where the hillsides are dotted with ancient *sassi* (cave dwellings) and zig-zagged with staircases hewn from the rock.

Duomo di Cefalù (p331)
BETHUNE CARMICHAEL/GETTY IMAGES ©

Discover Sicily & Southern Italy

At a Glance

- **Palermo** (p322) Glittering palaces and Arab-Norman flavour.
- **Cefalù** (p331) Sleepy, beachy and Byzantine.
- **Taormina** (p337) Artsy, medieval beach town.
- **Catania** (p333) Carved-lava baroque under the volcano.
- **Lecce** (p346) Puglia's golden-stone university town.
- **Ostuni** (p346) Gleaming white hilltop Pugliese gem.
- **Matera** (p347) Unesco-acclaimed town built on frescoed caves.

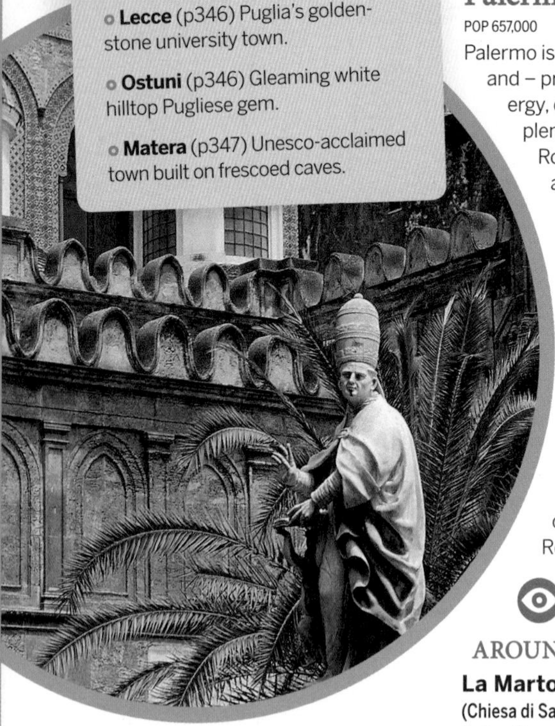

Cattedrale di Palermo (p324)

(BELOW) BETHUNE CARMICHAEL/GETTY IMAGES ©

SICILY

More of a sugar-spiked espresso than a milky cappuccino, Sicily rewards visitors with an intense, bittersweet experience. Overloaded with art treasures and natural beauty, undersupplied with infrastructure and continuously struggling against Mafia-driven corruption, Sicily's complexities sometimes seem unfathomable. To really appreciate this place, come with an open mind – and a healthy appetite.

Palermo

POP 657,000

Palermo is a city of decay and of splendour and – provided you can handle its raw energy, deranged driving and chaos – has plenty of appeal. Unlike Florence or Rome, many of the city's treasures are hidden, not scrubbed up for endless streams of tourists.

At one time an Arab emirate and seat of a Norman kingdom, Palermo became Europe's grandest city in the 12th century, then underwent another round of aesthetic transformations during 500 years of Spanish rule. The resulting treasure trove of palaces, castles and churches has a unique architectural fusion of Byzantine, Arab, Norman, Renaissance and baroque gems.

Sights & Activities

AROUND THE QUATTRO CANTI

La Martorana Church

(Chiesa di Santa Maria dell'Ammiraglio; Piazza Bellini 3; donation requested; ⏲8.30am-1pm & 3.30-5.30pm Mon-Sat, 8.30am-1pm Sun) On the southern side of Piazza Bellini, this luminously beautiful, recently restored 12th-century

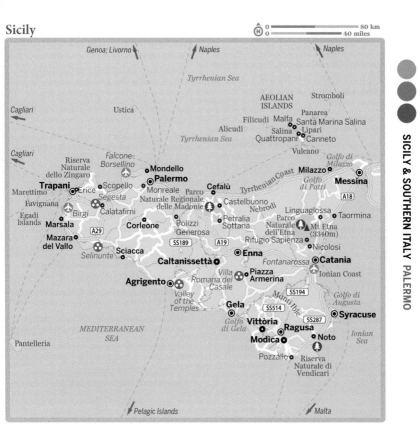

Tyrrhenian Sea

AEOLIAN ISLANDS

Stromboli

Panarea

Filicudi Malfa Santa Marina Salina

Alicudi Salina Lipari

Quattropani Canneto

Tyrrhenian Sea

Vulcano

Golfo di Milazzo

Ustica

Cagliari

Cagliari

Riserva Naturale dello Zingaro

Falcone-Borsellino

Mondello

Palermo

Milazzo

Golfo di Patti

Messina

Trapani Erice Scopello Monreale Parco Cefalù

Tyrrhenian Coast

A18

Marettimo

Segesta Naturale Regionale delle Madonie

Castelbuono

Favignana Birgi Calatafimi

Linguaglossa

Parco

Egadi Islands

Marsala

Polizzi

Petralia Sottana

Naturale dell'Etna

Taormina

Mt Etna (3340m)

Corleone

Generosa

Rifugio Sapienza

Mazara del Vallo

A29

Nicolosi

Selinunte

Sciacca

SS189 A19

Enna

Fontanarossa

Catania

Caltanissetta

Villa Romana del Casale

Piazza Armerina

Ionian Coast

Agrigento

Valley of the Temples

SS194

Monti Iblei

Golfo di Augusta

Gela

SS514

Syracuse

MEDITERRANEAN SEA

Golfo di Gela

Vittoria

SS287

Ragusa

Ionian Sea

Pantelleria

Modica

Noto

Pozzallo

Riserva Naturale di Vendicari

Genoa; Livorno

Naples

Naples

Pelagic Islands

Malta

---

church was endowed by King Roger's Syrian emir, George of Antioch, and was originally planned as a mosque.

Chiesa Capitolare di San Cataldo · Church

(Piazza Bellini 3; admission €2.50; ⏰9.30am-12.30pm & 3-6pm) This 12th-century church in Arab-Norman style is one of Palermo's most striking buildings. With its dusky-pink bijoux domes, solid square shape, blind arcading and delicate tracery, it illustrates perfectly the synthesis of Arab and Norman architectural styles.

Fontana Pretoria · Fountain

This huge and ornate fountain, with tiered basins and sculptures rippling in concentric circles, forms the centrepiece of **Piazza Pretoria**, a spacious square just south of the Quattro Canti. The city

bought the fountain in 1573; however, the flagrant nudity of the provocative nymphs proved too much for Sicilian church-goers attending Mass next door, and they prudishly dubbed it the Fountain of Shame.

ALBERGHERIA

Cappella Palatina · Chapel

(Palatine Chapel; adult €8.50; reduced for EU citizens 0-25 & 65+ years; ⏰8.15am-5pm Mon-Sat, 8.15-9.45am & 11.15am-12.15pm Sun) On the middle level of the Norman Palace's three-tiered loggia, this mosaic-clad jewel of a chapel, designed by Roger II in 1130, is Palermo's premier tourist attraction. Gleaming from a painstaking five-year restoration, its aesthetic harmony is further enhanced by the inlaid marble floors and wooden *muqarnas* ceiling, a masterpiece of Arabic-style honeycomb carving that reflects Norman Sicily's cultural complexity.

323

Palazzo dei Normanni   Palace

(Palazzo Reale; Piazza Indipendenza 1; incl Cappella Palatina adult €8.50, youth 18-25yr €6.50, senior 65+ €5, child under 18yr free; 🕑8.15am-5pm Fri, Sat & Mon, to 12.15pm Sun) On weekends, when Palermo's venerable Palazzo dei Normanni isn't being used by Sicily's parliament, visitors can take a self-guided tour of several upstairs rooms, including the gorgeous blue **Sala Pompeiana**, with its Venus & Eros frescoes, the **Sala dei Venti**, adorned with mosaics of geese, papyrus, lions, leopards and palms, and the **Sala di Ruggero II**, King Roger's mosaic-decorated bedroom.

Mercato di Ballarò   Market

Snaking for several city blocks east of Palazzo dei Normanni is Palermo's busiest street market, which throbs with activity well into the early evening. It's a fascinating mix of noises, smells and street life, and the cheapest place for everything from Chinese padded bras to fresh produce, fish, meat, olives and cheese – smile nicely and you may get a taste.

CAPO

Cattedrale di Palermo   Cathedral

(www.cattedrale.palermo.it; Corso Vittorio Emanuele; tombs & treasury adult/reduced €3/1.50; 🕑8am-7pm) A feast of geometric patterns, ziggurat crenulations, majolica cupolas and blind arches, Palermo's cathedral is a prime example of the Arab-Norman style unique to Sicily. The interior's most interesting features are the Norman tombs of Roger II and other Sicilian royalty, and the cathedral treasury, home to Constance of Aragon's fabulous gem-encrusted 13th-century crown.

VUCCIRIA

Museo Archeologico Regionale   Museum

(📞091 611 68 05; www.regione.sicilia.it/beni-culturali/salinas; Piazza Olivella 24; 🕑8.30am-1.30pm & 3-6.30pm Tue-Fri, 8.30am-1.30pm Sat & Sun) Scheduled to reopen in late 2013 after comprehensive renovations, this splendid, wheelchair-accessible museum displays some of Sicily's most valuable Graeco-Roman artefacts. The museum's crown jewel is the series of decorative friezes from the temples at Selinunte;

Cappella Palatina (p323), Palermo

RUSSELL MOUNTFORD/GETTY IMAGES ©

other treasures include the Hellenistic *Ariete di Bronzo di Siracusa* (Bronze Ram of Syracuse) and the world's largest collection of ancient anchors.

Oratories
Chapel

(Tesori della Loggia combined ticket adult/student/child under 6 €5/4/free; ⏾Tesori della Loggia 9am-1pm Mon-Sat) Vucciria's greatest architectural treasures are its two baroque oratories: **Oratorio del Rosario di Santa Zita** (Via Valverde; admission €2.50,;⏾9am-6pm Mon-Fri, 9am-3pm Sat) and **Oratorio del Rosario di San Domenico** (Via dei Bambinai 2; admission €2.50; ⏾9am-6pm Mon-Fri, 9am-3pm Sat), covered top to bottom with the ornate stuccowork of Giacomo Serpotta (1652-1732).

LA KALSA

Galleria Regionale della Sicilia
Museum

(Palazzo Abatellis; ☎091 623 00 11; www.regione.sicilia.it/beniculturali/palazzoabatellis; Via Alloro 4; adult/EU 18-25/EU under 18 & over 65 €8/4/free; ⏾9am-6pm Tue-Fri, to 1pm Sat & Sun) Housed in the stately 15th-century Palazzo Abatellis, this fine museum features works by Sicilian artists from the Middle Ages to the 18th century. Its greatest treasure is *Triunfo della Morte* (Triumph of Death), a magnificent fresco in which Death is represented as a demonic skeleton mounted on a wasted horse, brandishing a wicked-looking scythe while leaping over his hapless victims.

Galleria d'Arte Moderna
Museum

(☎091 843 16 05; www.galleriadartemoderna-palermo.it; Via Sant'Anna 21; adult €7, 19-25yr & 60+ €5, under 19 free; ⏾9.30am-6.30pm Tue-Sun) This lovely, wheelchair-accessible museum is housed in a sleekly renovated 15th-century *palazzo* (mansion), which metamorphosed into a convent in the 17th century. Divided over three floors, the wide-ranging collection of 19th- and 20th-century Sicilian art is beautifully displayed. There's a regular program of modern-art exhibitions here, as well as an excellent bookshop and gift shop. English-language audioguides cost €4.

Archaeology in Sicily

RECOMMENDATIONS FROM PROFESSOR MICHELE GALLO, TOUR GUIDE

1 VALLEY OF THE TEMPLES
Nine temples; fortifications; the Hellenistic quarter; a beautiful Greek art museum; an archaeological park covered in centuries-old almond and olive trees: these are just some of the many magical sights that you will discover in what was once the world's most beautiful city.

2 TAORMINA
Of Taormina jewels, the most precious is the antique theatre (p337) that stands in timeless scenery. You will also be astounded by the amazing setting: a view across the Ionic ocean, a magnificent coast, and Mt Etna, Europe's largest volcano.

3 MOZIA
Sicily's largest lagoon has a mirrored surface reflecting windmills and mountains of salt. There's a sense of being suspended in time as you cross it to reach the island, a place as sweet as marsala wine. Mozia presents a complex, mysterious archaeology. The *Giovinetto di Mozia*, a splendid marble sculpture of a young man (AD 450), stands proud and detached among the treasures in the Whitaker Museum.

4 SYRACUSE
If it is true that there are one hundred Sicilys, Syracuse encompasses them all: Greek, Norman, Arabic, baroque, art nouveau. Always a key Mediterranean city, its power terrified even Athens. You can walk between baroque palaces in search of beautiful Arethusa fleeing among the papyri from Alpheus. Or, you might find Plato, in search of his ideal State, seated on the steps of the West's greatest Greek theatre (p339). Syracuse will offer an art so rich and complex that you will fall in love at first sight.

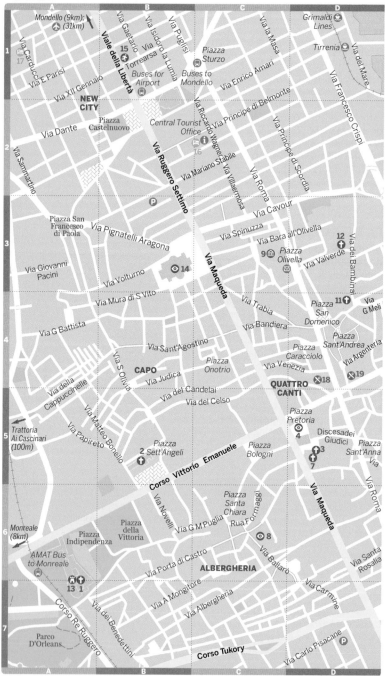

Palermo

Museo Internazionale delle Marionette
Museum

(☎091 32 80 60; www.museomarionettepalermo.
it; Piazzetta Antonio Pasqualino 5; adult/reduced
€5/3; ☺9am-1pm & 2.30-6.30pm Mon-Sat
year-round, plus 10am-1pm Sun Sep-May) This
whimsical museum houses over 3500
marionettes, puppets and shadow figures
from Palermo, Catania and Naples, as well
as from further-flung places such as Japan,
Southeast Asia, Africa, China and India.
From October through May, weekly puppet
shows (adult/child €6/4) are staged on
the museum's top floor in a beautifully
decorated traditional theatre complete
with hand-cranked music machine.

Established by the Association for the
Conservation of Folk Traditions of Palermo,
the museum takes puppeteering seriously,
researching the art, providing informative
labelling alongside museum exhibits and
hosting the annual Festa di Morgana (www.
festivaldimorgana.com), when puppeteers
from all over the world converge on the
museum for lectures and performances.

NEW CITY

Teatro Massimo   Opera House

(📞 tours 091 605 32 67; www.teatromassimo.it/
servizi/visite.php; Piazza Giuseppe Verdi; tours
adult/reduced €8/5; 🕑 9.30am-4.30pm Tue-
Sun) Palermo's grand neoclassical opera
house took over 20 years to complete
and has become one of the city's iconic
landmarks. The closing scene of *The Godfather: Part III*, with its visually stunning
juxtaposition of culture, crime, drama and
death, was filmed here. Guided 25-minute
tours are offered in English, Spanish,
French and Italian daily except Monday.

Hammam   Bathhouse

(📞 091 32 07 83; www.hammam.pa.it; Via Tor-
rearsa 17d; admission €40; 🕑 women 2-9pm
Mon & Wed, 11am-9pm Fri, couples 2-8pm Thu,
men 2-8pm Tue, 10am-8pm Sat) For a sybaritic
experience, head to this luxurious marble-
lined Moorish bathhouse, where you
can indulge in a vigorous scrub-down, a
steamy sauna and many different types of
massages and therapies. There's a one-off
charge (€10) for slippers and a hand glove.

🛏 Sleeping

B&B Amélie   B&B €

(📞 091 33 59 20; www.bb-amelie.it; Via Prinicipe
di Belmonte 94; s €40-60, d €60-80, tr €90-
100; ❄ @ 🛜) On a pedestrianised New
City street a stone's throw from Teatro
Politeama, the affable, multilingual Angela
has converted her grandmother's spacious 6th floor flat into a cheery B&B.
Rooms are colourfully decorated and the
corner triple has a sunny terrace. Angela,
a native Palermitan, generously shares
her local knowledge and serves a tasty
breakfast featuring homemade cakes and
jams.

Hotel Principe
di Villafranca   Boutique Hotel €€

(📞 091 611 85 23; www.principedivillafranca.it;
Via Turrisi Colonna 4; d €108-297; P ❄ @ 🛜)
Furnished with fine linens and antiques,
this sophisticated hotel is just west of
Viale della Libertá in one of Palermo's
most peaceful, exclusive neighbourhoods.
Public spaces include a cosy sitting area

with library, fireplace and displays of local designers' work; among the comfortable, high-ceilinged rooms, junior suite 105 stands out, decorated with artwork loaned by Palermo's modern art museum.

Eating & Drinking

Ferro di Cavallo
Trattoria €

(091 33 18 35; Via Venezia 20; meals €13-17; lunch daily, dinner Wed-Sat) Tables line the pavement and religious portraits beam down upon the bustling mix of tourists and locals at this cheerful little trattoria near the Quattro Canti. Nothing costs more than €7 on the straightforward à la carte menu of Sicilian classics. If you have a sweet tooth save room for one of Palermo's very best *cannoli* (only €1.50).

Trattoria Il Maestro del Brodo
Trattoria €€

(Via Pannieri 7; meals €19-30; 12.30-3.30pm Tue-Sun, 8-11pm Fri & Sat) This no-frills, Slow Food–recommended eatery in the Vuc-ciria offers delicious soups, an array of ultra-fresh seafood, and a sensational antipasto buffet (€8) featuring a dozen-plus homemade delicacies: *sarde a beccafico* (stuffed sardines), eggplant involtini, smoked fish, artichokes with parsley, sun-dried tomatoes, olives and more.

Trattoria Ai Cascinari
Sicilian €€

(091 651 98 04; Via d'Ossuna 43/45; meals €20-28; lunch Tue-Sun, dinner Wed-Sat) Friendly service, simple straw chairs and blue-and-white-checked tablecloths set the relaxed tone at this Slow Food–recommended neighbourhood trattoria, 1km north of the Cappella Palatina. Locals pack the labyrinth of back rooms, while waiters circulate non-stop with plates of scrumptious seasonal antipasti and divine main dishes. Save room for homemade ice cream and outstanding desserts from Palermo's beloved Pasticceria Cappello.

Kursaal Kalhesa
Bar

(✆ 091 616 21 11; www.kursaalkalhesa.it; Foro Italico Umberto I 21; ⏰ noon-3pm & 6pm-1.30am Tue-Sat, noon-1.30am Sun) This bar of choice for the city's avant-garde occupies the remnants of a handsome early-19th-century palace next to the 16th-century town gate, Porta dei Greci. Recline on silk-covered divans beneath soaring vaulted ceilings and choose from an extensive list of cocktails and snacks while listening to live music or selections from the in-house DJ.

ℹ Information

Central Tourist Office (✆ 091 58 51 72; informazionituristiche@provincia.palermo.it; Via Principe di Belmonte 42; ⏰ 8.30am-2pm & 2.30-6pm Mon-Fri) Palermo's provincial tourist office offers maps and brochures as well as the helpful booklet *Un Ospite a Palermo* (www.unospiteapalermo.it), published bi-monthly and containing listings for museums, cultural centres, tour guides and transport companies.

City Information Booth (Piazza Bellini; 8.30am-1pm & 3-7pm Mon-Sat) The most dependable of Palermo's city-run information booths, next to the churches of San Cataldo and La Martorana. Other booths around the city – at the port, the train station, Piazza Castelnuovo and Piazza Marina – are only intermittently staffed and have unpredictable hours.

Falcone-Borsellino Airport Information Office (✆ 091 59 16 98; in downstairs hall; ⏰ 8.30am-7.30pm Mon-Fri, 8.30am-2.30pm Sat)

ℹ Getting There & Away

Air
Falcone-Borsellino airport (PMO; ✆ 091 702 01 11; www.gesap.it) is at Punta Raisi, 31km west of Palermo.

Alitalia, easyJet, Ryanair and several other airlines operate between major European cities and Palermo.

Boat
The ferry terminal is located just east of the corner of Via Francesco Crispi and Via Emerico Amari.

Grandi Navi Veloci (✆ 091 58 74 04, 010 209 45 91; www.gnv.it; Calata Marinai d'Italia) Runs ferries from Palermo to Civitavecchia (from €73), Genoa (from €90), Naples (from €44) and Tunis (from €72).

Grimaldi Lines (✆ 091 611 36 91, 081 49 64 44; www.grimaldi-lines.com; Via del Mare) Ferries from Palermo to Salerno (from €65).

Tirrenia (✆ 091 976 07 73; www.tirrenia.it; Calata Marinai d'Italia) Ferries to Cagliari (from €51, Saturday only) and Naples (from €47).

Bus
The two main departure points are the brand-new **Piazzetta Cairoli bus terminal** (Piazzetta Cairoli), just south of the train station's eastern entrance, and the **intercity bus stop** on Via Paolo Balsamo, due east of the train station.

Cuffaro (✆ 091 616 15 10; www.cuffaro.info; Via Paolo Balsamo 13) Services to Agrigento (€8.70, two hours, three to eight daily).

SAIS Autolinee (✆ 091 616 60 28; www.saisautolinee.it; Piazza Cairoli) Buses to Messina (€15.80, 2¾ hours, three to five daily) and Catania (€14.90, 2½ hours, 10 to 14 daily).

Segesta (✆ 091 616 79 19; www.segesta.it; Piazza Cairoli) Services to Trapani (€9, two hours, at least 10 daily). Also sells Interbus tickets to Syracuse (€12, 3¼ hours, two to three daily).

Train
From Palermo Centrale station, just south of the centre at the foot of Via Roma, regular trains leave for Messina (from €11.80, 2¾ to 3½ hours, hourly), Agrigento (€8.30, two hours, eight to 10 daily) and Cefalù (from €5.15, one hour, hourly).

For Catania or Syracuse, you're generally better off taking the bus.

ℹ Getting Around

To/From the Airport
Prestia e Comandè (✆ 091 58 63 51; www.prestiaecomande.it) runs a half-hourly bus service from the airport to the centre of town (one way/return €6.10/11), with stops outside Teatro Politeama Garibaldi (30 minutes) and Palermo Centrale train station (45 minutes).

The Trinacria Express train (€5.80, 45 minutes to 1¼ hours) from the airport (Punta Raisi station) to Palermo takes longer and runs less frequently than the bus.

A taxi from the airport to downtown Palermo costs €45.

Cefalù

POP 14,300

This popular holiday resort wedged between a dramatic mountain peak and a sweeping stretch of sand has the lot: a great beach; a truly lovely historic centre with a grandiose cathedral; and winding medieval streets lined with restaurants and boutiques.

◎ Sights

Duomo di Cefalù · Cathedral

(☏0921 92 20 21; Piazza del Duomo; ⊗8am-7pm Apr-Sep, 8am-5pm Oct-Mar) Cefalù's cathedral is one of the jewels in Sicily's Arab-Norman crown, only equalled in magnificence by the Cattedrale di Monreale and Palermo's Cappella Palatina. Filling the central apse, a towering figure of Christ is the focal point of the elaborate Byzantine mosaics – Sicily's oldest and best preserved, predating those of Monreale by 20 or 30 years.

La Rocca · View Point

(admission €3; ⊗9am-6.45pm May-Sep, 9am-4.45pm Oct-Apr) Looming over the town, this imposing craggy mass is the site where the Arabs built their citadel, occupying it until the Norman conquest forced them down to the port below. An enormous staircase, the **Salita Saraceno**, winds up through three tiers of city walls, a 30-minute climb.

🛏 Sleeping & Eating

B&B Casanova · B&B €

(☏0921 92 30 65; www.casanovabb.it; Via Porpora 3; s €40-70, d €55-100, q €80-140; ❄ 🛜) This B&B on the water-front has rooms of varying size, from a cramped single with one minuscule window to the Ruggero room, a palatial space sleeping up to four, with a vaulted frescoed ceiling, decorative tile floors and French doors offering grand views of Cefalù's medieval centre. All guests share access to a small terrace overlooking the sea.

Hotel Kalura · Hotel €€

(☏0921 42 13 54; www.hotel-kalura.com; Via Vincenzo Cavallaro 13; d €89-179; P ❄ @ 🛥) East of town on a rocky outcrop, this German-run, family-oriented hotel has its own pebbly beach, restaurant and fabulous pool. Most rooms have sea views and the hotel arranges loads of activities, including mountain biking, hiking, canoeing, pedaloes, diving and dance nights. It's a 20-minute walk into town.

Ti Vitti · Sicilian €€

(www.ristorantetivitti.com; Via Umberto I 34; meals €30-40) At this up-and-coming eatery named after a Sicilian card game, talented young chef Vincenzo Collaro whips up divine pasta, fresh-from-the-market fish dishes and some of the best *cannoli* you'll find anywhere in Sicily.

Cefalù
KRZYSZTOF DYDYNSKI/GETTY IMAGES ©

SLOW IMAGES/GETTY IMAGES ©

⭐ Don't Miss
Aeolian Islands

The Aeolian Islands are a little piece of paradise. Stunning cobalt sea, splendid beaches, some of Italy's best hiking, and an awe-inspiring volcanic landscape are just part of the appeal. The islands also have a fascinating human and mythological history that goes back several millennia; the Aeolians figured prominently in Homer's *Odyssey*, and evidence of the distant past can be seen everywhere, most notably in Lipari's excellent archaeological museum.

The seven islands of Lipari, Vulcano, Salina, Panarea, Stromboli, Alicudi and Filicudi are part of a huge 200km volcanic ridge that runs between the smoking stack of Mt Etna and the threatening mass of Vesuvius above Naples. Collectively, the islands exhibit a unique range of volcanic characteristics, which earned them a place on Unesco's World Heritage list in 2000. In particular, volcanic Vulcano is celebrated for its therapeutic mud baths and hot springs, though the main drawcard remains the Fossa di Vulcano, or Gran Cratere (Large Crater), the steaming volcano that towers over the island's northeastern shores.

Both **Ustica Lines** (www.usticalines.it) and **Siremar** (www.siremar.it) run hydrofoils year-round from Milazzo, the mainland city closest to the islands. Regular hydrofoil and ferry services operate between the islands. Ticket offices with posted timetables can be found close to the docks on all islands.

ℹ️ Information

Tourist Office (📞 0921 42 10 50; strcefalu@ regione.sicilia.it; Corso Ruggero 77; 🕐 9am-1pm & 3-7.30pm Mon-Sat) English-speaking staff, lots of leaflets and good maps.

ℹ️ Getting There & Away

Boat

SMIV (Società Marittima Italiana Veloce; www. smiv.it) runs boats between Cefalù and the Aeolian Islands, from May to September. Rates include pick up at any Cefalù hotel. Tickets are available at **Turismez Viaggi** (☏ 0921 42 12 64; www.turismezviaggi.it) next door to the tourist office.

Train

The best way of getting to and from Cefalù. Hourly trains go to Palermo (from €5, 45 minutes to 1¼ hours) and virtually every other town on the coast.

························

Catania

POP 296,000

Catania is a true city of the volcano. Much of it is constructed from the lava that poured down the mountain and engulfed the city in the 1669 eruption in which nearly 12,000 people lost their lives. It is also lava-black in colour, as if a fine dusting of soot permanently covers its elegant buildings, most of which are the work of baroque master Giovanni Vaccarini.

◎ Sights

Piazza del Duomo   Square

A Unesco World Heritage Site, Catania's central square revolves around its grand cathedral, fringed with baroque buildings constructed in the unique local style of contrasting lava and limestone. The piazza's centrepiece is the smiling **Fontana dell'Elefante** (Piazza del Duomo), crowned by a naive black-lava elephant dating from the Roman period and surmounted by an improbable Egyptian obelisk.

Cattedrale di Sant'Agata Cathedral
(☏ 095 32 00 44; Piazza del Duomo; ◷ 8am-noon & 4-7pm) Sporting an impressive marble facade with columns from Catania's Roman amphitheatre, this cathedral honours the city's patron, St Agata. The young virgin, whose remains lie sheltered in the cool, vaulted interior, famously resisted the advances of the nefarious Quintian (AD 250) and was horribly mutilated. Her jewel-drenched effigy is ecstatically venerated on 5 February in one of Sicily's largest festivals.

La Pescheria   Market
(Via Pardo; ◷ 7am-2pm) The best show in Catania is this bustling fish market, where vendors raucously hawk their wares in

Sicilian dialect, while decapitated swordfish cast sidelong glances at you across silvery heaps of sardines on ice.

Graeco-Roman Theatre & Odeon   Ruins
(Via Vittorio Emanuele II 262; adult/reduced incl Casa Liberti €4/2; ◷ 9am-1pm & 2.30pm-1hr before sunset Tue-Sun) These twin theatres west of Piazza del Duomo constitute Catania's most impressive Graeco-Roman site. Set in a crumbling residential neighbourhood with laundry atmospherically flapping on the surrounding rooftops, the main theatre with its half-submerged stage is flanked by **Casa Liberti**, an elegantly restored 19th-century *palazzo* that now houses two millennia worth of artefacts discovered during the theatres' excavation.

🛏 Sleeping

B&B Crociferi   B&B €
(☏ 095 715 22 66; www.bbcrociferi.it; Via Crociferi 81; d €75-85, tr €100-110, 4-bed apt €120; ❀ ❄ 🤝) Affording easy access to Catania's animated nightlife, this B&B in a beautifully decorated family home makes a wonderful base. Three spacious rooms (each with bathroom across the hall) and two glorious upstairs apartments come with high ceilings, antique tiles, frescoes and artistic accoutrements from the owners' travels.

Palazzu Stidda   Apartment €
(☏ 095 34 88 26; www.palazzu-stidda.com; Vicolo della Lanterna 5; d €70-100, q €120-140; 🤝 👪) These three delightful apartments in a *palazzo* on a peaceful dead-end alley perfectly blend comfort with whimsy; all are decorated with the owners' artwork, handmade furniture, family heirlooms and finds from local antiques markets. Perfect for families, apartments 2 and 3 each come with a washing machine, kitchen, high chair and stroller. The smaller apartment 1 costs less. French and English spoken.

UNA Hotel Palace   Hotel €€
(☏ 095 250 51 11; www.unahotels.it; Via Etnea 218; s €99-125, d €125-175, ste €201-329) A top-end hotel in a city that's badly in need of some seriously upmarket options, UNA brings a bit of city slick to Catania. Part

of an Italy-wide chain, this hotel has a gleaming white interior, polished service and good rooms. The top draw are the views of Etna from the 7th floor rooftop garden bar that serves cocktails and aperitifs at sunset.

The six ivory-coloured floors lead onto equally sleek white rooms, with contrasting black-frame beds and gold lamps, and the white-black-gold combination is repeated across the four-star hotel. It has a gym and a Turkish bath, though sadly no pool. The views of the smoking cone of Etna from the rooftop terrace are mesmerising, so make sure you grab a few drinks and enjoy. It's posh all right, but prices drop significantly in winter.

Eating & Drinking

Trattoria di De Fiore   Trattoria €
(095 31 62 83; Via Coppola 24/26; meals €15-25; from 1pm Tue-Sun) This neighbourhood trattoria is presided over by septuagenarian chef Mamma Rosanna, who uses fresh, local ingredients to recreate her great-grandmother's recipes, including superb *pasta alla Norma* and *zeppoline di ricotta* (sweet ricotta fritters dusted with powdered sugar). Service can be excruciatingly slow and they don't always open promptly at 1pm, but food this good is worth the wait.

Me Cumpari Turridu   Sicilian €€
(095 715 01 42; Via Ventimiglia 15; meals €35-40; Mon-Sat) Mixing tradition with modernity both in food and decor, this quirky little spot spoils meat eaters with a variety of barbecued meat, as well as fresh pasta dishes such as ricotta and marjoram ravioli in a pork sauce. Vegetarians can opt for the Ustica lentil stew, with broad beans and fennel; there's also a wealth of Sicilian cheeses on offer.

Le Tre Bocche   Trattoria €€
(095 53 87 38; Via Mario Sangiorgi 7; meals €35-45; Tue-Sun) This fantastic Slow Food-recommended trattoria takes pride in the freshest seafood and fish – so much so, they have a stand at the Pescheria market. Short pastas come with wonderful sauces such as *bottarga* (fish roe) and artichoke, spaghetti is soaked in sea urchins or squid ink and risottos are mixed with zucchini and king prawns. It's about 800m due north of the train station.

Heaven   Bar
(Via Teatro Massimo 39; 9pm-2am) Pedestrianised Via Teatro Massimo heaves late at night as crowds swill outside the many bars. One of the best-known addresses is Heaven, a trendy lounge bar sporting kooky black and white designs and a 12m-long LED-lit bar. Outside, where most people end up, there's seating on massive black leather sofas. DJs up the ante on Wednesday, Friday and Saturday nights.

Agorá Bar   Bar
(www.agorahostel.com; Piazza Curró 6; 6pm-late) This atmospheric bar occupies a neon-lit cave 18m below ground, complete with its own subterranean river. The Romans used it as a spa; nowadays a cosmopolitan crowd lingers over late-night drinks.

Entertainment

Teatro Massimo Bellini   Opera House
(095 730 61 11; www.teatromassimobellini.it; Via Perrotta 12; Nov-Jun) Catania's premier theatre is named after the city's most famous son, composer Vincenzo Bellini. Sporting the full red-and-gilt look, it stages a year-round season of opera and an eight-month program of classical music from November to June. Tickets start around €13.

Information

Municipal Tourist Office (095 742 55 73; www.comune.catania.it; Via Vittorio Emanuele II 172; 8.15am-7.15pm Mon-Fri, to 12.15pm Sat)

Getting There & Away

Air
Catania's airport, Fontanarossa (095 723 91 11; www.aeroporto.catania.it), is 7km southwest of the city centre. To get there, take the special Alibus 457 (€1, 30 minutes, half hourly from 5am to midnight)

BETHUNE CARMICHAEL/GETTY IMAGES ©

⭐ Don't Miss
Villa Romana del Casale

The Unesco-listed Villa Romana del Casale is central Sicily's biggest attraction, and it reopened in spring 2013 after years of reconstruction. It is decorated with the finest Roman floor mosaics in existence. The mosaics cover almost the entire floor of the villa and are considered unique for their natural, narrative style, the range of their subject matter and variety of colour.

Situated in a wooded valley 5km southwest of the town of Piazza Armerina, the villa, sumptuous even by decadent Roman standards, is thought to have been the country retreat of Marcus Aurelius Maximianus, Rome's co-emperor during the reign of Diocletian (AD 286–305). Certainly, the size of the complex – four interconnected groups of buildings spread over the hillside – and the 3535 sq metres of multicoloured floor mosaics suggests a palace of imperial standing.

Following a landslide in the 12th century, the villa lay under 10m of mud for some 700 years, and was thus protected from the damaging effects of air, wind and rain. It was only when serious excavation work began in the 1950s that the mosaics were brought back to light.

The easiest way to arrive is by car. Without your own transport, the trip is more challenging: buses operated by Interbus (📞095 53 03 96; www.interbus.it) run from Catania to Piazza Armerina (€9, 1¾ hours), from where you can catch a local bus (€0.70, 30 minutes, summer only) or a taxi (€20) for the remaining 5km.

If you want to arrange a guide, contact the **Comune di Piazza Armerina** (📞093 598 22 46) or **STS Servizi Turistici** (📞093 568 70 27; www.guardalasicilia.it); otherwise you can organise one directly at the site.

NEED TO KNOW

📞093 568 00 36; www.villaromanadelcasale.it; adult/reduced €10/5; ⏰9am-6pm summer, 9am-4pm winter

PHILIP & KAREN SMITH/GETTY IMAGES ©

★ Don't Miss
Mt Etna

Dominating the landscape of eastern Sicily, Mt Etna (3323m) is Europe's largest volcano and one of the world's most active. Eruptions occur frequently, both from its four summit craters and from its slopes. The volcano's most devastating eruptions occurred in 1669 and lasted 122 days. In 2002, lava flows from Mt Etna caused an explosion in Sapienza, destroying two buildings and temporarily halting the cable-car service. More recently, in 2013 there were several dramatic instances of lava fountaining – vertical jets of lava spewing from the southeast crater.

The volcano is surrounded by Parco Naturale dell'Etna, the largest unspoilt wilderness remaining in Sicily. The southern approach to Mt Etna is the easier ascent to the craters. From Rifugio Sapienza (1923m) a cable car runs up the mountain to 2500m. From the upper cable car station it's a 3½- to four-hour return trip up the winding track to the authorised crater zone (2920m). Be sure you leave enough time to get up and down before the last cable car leaves at 4.45pm.

Gruppo Guide Alpine Etna Sud (☎ 095 791 47 55; www.etnaguide.com) is the official guide service on Etna's southern flank, with an office just below Rifugio Sapiena. **Gruppo Guide Alpine Etna** (☎ 095 777 45 02; www.guidetnanord.com) offers a similar service from Linguaglossa on the northern flank. Between May and October, **STAR** (☎ 347 495 70 91; www.funiviaetna.com/star_etna_nord.html; €40) runs 4WD excursions to the summit from Piano Provenzano.

AST (☎ 095 723 05 35; www.aziendasicilianatrasporti.it) runs daily buses from Catania to Rifugio Sapienza. You can also circle Etna on the private **Ferrovia Circumetnea** (FCE; ☎ 095 54 12 50; www.circumetnea.it; Via Caronda 352a) train line, which follows a 114km trail around the base of the volcano, giving fabulous views. Catch the metro from Catania's main train station to the FCE station at Via Caronda (metro stop Borgo) or take bus 429 or 432 going up Via Etnea and ask to be let off at the Borgo metro stop.

from outside the train station. **Etna Transporti/ Interbus** (☎095 53 03 96; www.interbus.it) also runs a regular shuttle from the airport to Taormina (€7.90, 1½ hours, six to 11 daily).

Boat
The ferry terminal is located southwest of the train station along Via VI Aprile.

TTT Lines (☎800 91 53 65, 095 34 85 86; www.tttlines.it) runs nightly ferries from Catania to Naples (seat €38 to €60, cabin per person €52 to €165, 11 hours).

Bus
All intercity buses terminate in the area just north of Catania's train station. AST buses leave from Piazza Giovanni XXIII; buy tickets at Bar Terminal on the west side of the square. Interbus/Etna and SAIS leave from a terminal one block further north, with their ticket offices diagonally across the street on Via d'Amico.

Interbus (☎095 53 03 96; www.interbus.it; Via d'Amico 187) runs buses to Syracuse (€6, 1¼ to 1½ hours, hourly Monday to Friday, fewer on weekends) and Taormina (€4.90, 1¼ to 1¾ hours, eight to 17 daily).

SAIS Trasporti (☎095 53 61 68; www. saistrasporti.it; Via d'Amico 181) goes to Agrigento (€12.40, three hours, nine to 14 daily). Its sister company **SAIS Autolinee** (www.saisautolinee.it) also runs services to Palermo (€14.90, 2¾ hours, hourly Monday to Saturday, 10 on Sunday).

Train
From Catania Centrale station on Piazza Papa Giovanni XXIII there are frequent trains.

Syracuse (€6.35 to €9.50, 1¼ hours, nine daily)

Agrigento (€10.40 to €14.50, 3¾ hours)

Palermo (€12.50 to to €15.30, three to 5¾ hours, one direct daily)

The private Ferrovia Circumetnea train circles Mt Etna, stopping at villages on the volcano's slopes.

❶ Getting Around
Several useful **AMT city buses** (☎095 751 96 11; www.amt.ct.it) terminate in front of the train station, including buses 1-4 and 4-7 (both running hourly from the station to Via Etnea) and Alibus 457 (station to airport every 30 minutes). A 90-minute ticket costs €1. From mid-June to mid-September, a special service (bus D-Est) runs from Piazza Raffaello Sanzio to the local beaches.

For a taxi, call **Radio Taxi Catania** (☎095 33 09 66).

Taormina
Spectacularly perched on the side of a mountain, Taormina is Sicily's most popular summer destination, a chic resort town beloved of holidaying high-rollers and visiting celebs. And while it is unashamedly touristy and has a main street lined with high-end designer shops, the town remains an achingly beautiful spot with gorgeous medieval churches, a stunning Greek theatre and sweeping views over the Gulf of Naxos and Mt Etna.

◉ Sights & Activities

Teatro Greco
Amphitheatre
(☎094 22 32 20; Via Teatro Greco; adult/ reduced/EU under 18 & over 65 €10/5/free; ◷9am-1hr before sunset) Taormina's premier attraction is this perfect horseshoe-shaped theatre, suspended between sea and sky, with the silhouette of Mt Etna looming on the southern horizon. Built in the 3rd century BC, it's the most dramatically situated Greek theatre in the world and the second largest in Sicily (after Syracuse).

Lido Mazzarò
Beach
Many visitors to Taormina come only for the beach scene. To reach Lido Mazzarò, directly beneath Taormina, take the **cable car** (Via Luigi Pirandello; one way €3, day pass €10; ◷8.45am-1am, every 15min). This beach is well serviced with bars and restaurants; private operators charge a fee for umbrellas and deck chairs (€10 per person per day, discountable at some hotels).

Isola Bella
Nature Reserve
Southwest of the beach is the minuscule Isola Bella, set in a stunning cove and surrounded by fishing boats . You can walk here in a few minutes but it's much more fun to rent a small boat from Mazzarò and paddle round Capo Sant'Andrea.

🍴 Eating

Casa Grugno   Gastronomic €€€
(☎094 22 12 08; www.casagrugno.it; Via Santa Maria dei Greci; meals €70-80; ⏰dinner Mon-Sat) With a walled-in terrace surrounded by plants, Taormina's most fashionable restaurant specialises in sublime modern Sicilian cuisine, under the direction of new chef David Tamburini.

Granduca   Pizzeria €
(☎0942 2 49 83; Corso Umberto 172; pizzas €7-11; ⏰dinner) Forget the staid, typically pricey Taormina restaurant upstairs; the best reason to visit Granduca is for pizza on a summer evening, served on a vast outdoor terrace overlooking Mt Etna and the sea – an unbeatable combination of view, quality and price!

ℹ️ Getting There & Away

The bus is the best way to reach Taormina. The bus station is on Via Luigi Pirandello, a 400m walk from Porta Messina, the northeastern entrance to the old town. **Etna Trasporti** (☎095 53 27 16; www.etnatrasporti.it) runs direct to/from Catania airport (€7.90, 1½ hours, six daily Monday to Saturday, four Sunday). **Interbus** (☎0942 62 53 01; Via Luigi Pirandello) services run to/from Catania (€4.80, 1½ hours, 14 daily Monday to Saturday, eight Sunday).

Syracuse

POP 124,000

A dense tapestry of overlapping cultures and civilisations, Syracuse is one of Sicily's most appealing cities. Settled by colonists from Corinth in 734 BC, this was considered to be the most beautiful city of the ancient world, rivalling Athens in power and prestige.

As the sun set on Ancient Greece, Syracuse became a Roman colony and was looted of its treasures. While modern-day Syracuse lacks the drama of Palermo and the energy of Catania, the ancient island neighbourhood of Ortygia continues to seduce visitors with its atmospheric squares, narrow alleyways and lovely waterfront, while the Parco Archaeologico della Neapolis, 2km across town, remains one of Sicily's great classical treasures.

👁️ Sights

ORTYGIA

Duomo   Cathedral
(Piazza del Duomo; ⏰8am-7pm) Built on the skeleton of a 5th-century BC Greek temple whose Doric columns are still visible underneath, Syracuse's cathedral was converted into a church when the island was evangelised by St Paul. Its most striking feature is the columned facade (1728–53), added by Andrea Palma after the church was damaged in the 1693 earthquake.

Statue of the Trinacria, Sicily
KATHRIN ZIEGLER/GETTY IMAGES ©

/GETTY IMAGES ©

★ Don't Miss
Parco Archeologico della Neapolis

For the classicist, Syracuse's real attraction is this archaeological park, with its pearly white, 5th-century-BC **Teatro Greco** (Parco Archeologico della Neapolis), hewn out of the rock above the city. This theatre saw the last tragedies of Aeschylus (including *The Persians*), which were first performed here in his presence. In summer it is brought to life again with an annual season of classical theatre.

To reach the park, take bus 1, 3 or 12 from Ortygia's Piazza Pancali and get off at the corner of Corso Gelone and Viale Teocrito. Alternatively, the walk from Ortygia will take about 30 minutes. If driving, you can park along Viale Augusto (tickets available at the nearby souvenir kiosks).

NEED TO KNOW
☑ 093 16 50 68; Viale Paradiso; adult/reduced €10/free-€5; ☯ 9am-6pm Apr-Oct, 9am-4pm Nov-Mar

---

Fontana Aretusa   Fountain

At this ancient spring, fresh water still bubbles up as it did 2500 years ago when this was Ortygia's main water supply. According to legend, the goddess Artemis transformed her beautiful handmaiden Arethusa into the spring to protect her from the river god Alpheus.

La Giudecca   Neighbourhood

Simply walking through Ortygia's tangled maze of alleys is an atmospheric experience, especially down the narrow lanes of **Via Maestranza**, the heart of the old guild quarter, and the crumbling Jewish ghetto of **Via della Giudecca**.

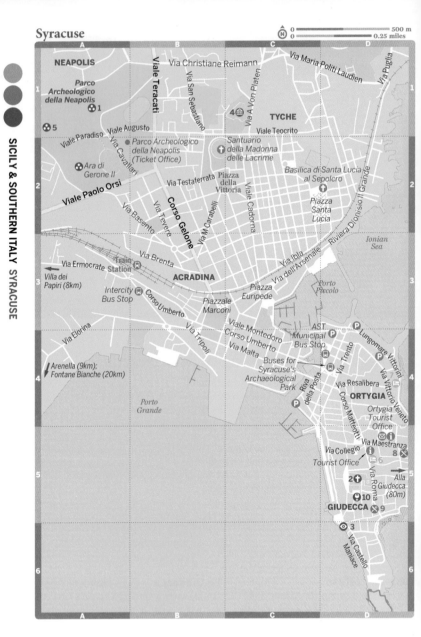

N 0 ——————— 500 m
   0 ——————— 0.25 miles

NEAPOLIS

Parco
Archeologico
della Neapolis

⊗1

⊗5

Viale Paradiso Viale Augusto

Viale Teracati

Via San Sebastiano

Via Christiane Reimann

Via A Von Platen

Via Maria Politi Laudien

Via Puglia

TYCHE

⊞4

Viale Teocrito

⊗ Ara di
Gerone II

Via Cavallari

Via Paolo Orsi

Parco Archeologico
della Neapolis
(Ticket Office)

Santuario
della Madonna
delle Lacrime

Viale Paolo Orsi

Via Testaferrata

Via Basento

Via Tevere

Via M Carabelli

Corso Gelone

Piazza
della
Vittoria

Via Cadorna

Basilica di Santa Lucia
al Sepolcro

Piazza
Santa
Lucia

Riviera Dionisio il Grande

Ionian
Sea

Via Brenta

Train
Station

Via Ermocrate

Villa dei
Papiri (8km)

ACRADINA

Via Ibla
Via dell'Arsenale

Porto
Piccolo

Piazza
Euripede

Intercity
Bus Stop

Corso Umberto

Piazzale
Marconi

Via Elorina

Via Tripoli

Viale Montedoro
Corso Umberto
Via Malta

Arenella (9km);
Fontane Bianche (20km)

Buses for
Syracuse's
Archaeological
Park

AST
Municipal
Bus Stop

Lungomare Vittorini

Via Trento

Porto
Grande

Riva
della Posta

Via Resalibera

Via Vittorio Veneto

ORTYGIA

Corso Matteotti

Ortygia
Tourist
Office

Via Collegio

Tourist Office

Via Maestranza
⊠❶
8⊗

⊗6

Via Roma

⊗2❶

Alla
Giudecca
(80m)

❷10

GIUDECCA ⊗9

⊗3

Via Castello Maniace

MAINLAND SYRACUSE

Museo Archeologico
Paolo Orsi
Museum

(📞0931 46 40 22; Viale Teocrito; adult/reduced
€8/4; ⊙9am-6pm Tue-Sat, 9am-1pm Sun) In
the grounds of Villa Landolina, about
500m east of the archaeological park, the
wheelchair-accessible museum contains
one of Sicily's largest, best organised
and most interesting archaeological
collections.

Syracuse

🛏 Sleeping & Eating

B&B dei Viaggiatori, Viandanti e Sognatori   B&B €

(☏093 12 47 81; www.bedandbreakfastsicily.it; Via Roma 156, Ortygia; s €35-50, d €55-70, tr €75-80; ❄ ☞) Decorated with verve and boasting a prime location in Ortygia, this B&B in an old *palazzo* at the end of Via Roma has a lovely bohemian feel, with books and pieces of antique furniture juxtaposed against bright walls. The sunny roof terrace with sweeping sea views makes a perfect breakfast spot. The owners also manage the nearby **B&B L'Acanto** (☏0931 46 11 29; www.bebsicily.com; Via Roma 15; s €35-50, d €55-70, tr €75-85, q €100).

Hotel Gutkowski   Hotel €€

(☏0931 46 58 61; www.guthotel.it; Lungomare Vittorini 26; s €60-80, d €75-130; ❄ @ ☞) Book ahead for one of the sea-view rooms at this calmly stylish hotel on the Ortygia waterfront, at the edge of the Giudecca neighbourhood. Rooms are divided between two buildings, both with pretty tiled floors and a minimalist mix of vintage and industrial details. There's a nice sun terrace with sea views, and a cosy lounge area with fireplace.

Le Vin De L'Assasin Bistrot   Mediterranean €€

(☏093 16 61 59; Via Roma 15; meals €30-45; ◷dinner Tue-Sun, lunch Sun) At this stylish, high-ceilinged Ortygia eatery run by the Parisian-trained Saro, chalkboard offerings include French classics such as *quiche lorraine* and *croque-monsieur*, Breton oysters, salads with impeccable vinaigrette dressing, a host of meat and fish mains and a splendid *millefoglie* of eggplant and sweet red peppers. It's a perfect late-night stop for wine by the glass or homemade, over-the-top chocolatey desserts.

Don Camillo   Modern Sicilian €€€

(☏093 16 71 33; www.ristorantedoncamillosiracusa.it; Via Maestranza 96; meals €55; ◷lunch & dinner Mon-Sat) This elegant restaurant with top-notch service is full of classy surprises: 'black' king prawns in a thick almond cream soup, red snapper with fig and lemon, *tagliata di tonno* (grilled and sliced tuna) with a red pepper 'marmalade' and blood-orange ice cream for dessert. Slow Food-recommended.

🍷 Drinking & Nightlife

Bar San Rocco   Bar

(Piazzetta San Rocco; ◷5pm-late) Head to San Rocco, the smoothest of several bars on Piazzetta San Rocco, for an early evening *aperitivi* (complete with bountiful bar snacks) or some late-night cocktails. Inside, it's a narrow, stone-vaulted affair, but the main action is outside on the vivacious piazzetta where summer crowds gather until the early hours. Occasional live music and DJ sets fuel the laid-back vibe.

✪ Entertainment

Piccolo Teatro dei Pupi   Puppet Theatre

(☏0931 46 55 40; www.pupari.com; Via della Giudecca 17) Syracuse's thriving puppet theatre hosts regular performances; see the website for a calendar. You can also buy puppets at its workshop next door.

Detour:
Valley of the Temples

Close to the modern-medieval town of Agrigento, the **Valley of the Temples** (☎092 262 16 11; www.parcovalledeitempli.it; adult/EU under 18yr & over 65yr/EU 18-25yr incl Quartiere Ellenistico-Romano €10/free/5, incl Museo Archeologico €13.50/free/7) is one of southern Europe's most compelling archaeological sites. The 1300-hectare Parco Valle dei Templi encompasses the ruins of the ancient city of Akragas. The highlight is the stunning Tempio della Concordia, one of the best-preserved Greek temples in existence and one of a series built on a ridge to act as beacons for homecoming sailors.

North of the temples, the wheelchair-accessible **Museo Archeologico** (☎092 24 01 11; Contrada San Nicola; admission incl Valley of the Temples adult/reduced €13.50/7; ⏰9am-7pm Tue-Sat, 9am-1pm Sun & Mon) is one of Sicily's finest, with a huge collection of clearly labelled artefacts from the excavated site.

Tucked up a side alley, rustic **Trattoria Concordia** (☎092 22 26 68; Via Porcello 8; meals €18-30; ⏰lunch & dinner) has exposed stone and stucco walls. It specialises in grilled fish along with traditional Sicilian *primi* such as *casarecce con pesce spada, melanzane e menta* (pasta with swordfish, eggplant and mint).

From Agrigento Centrale station (Piazza Marconi), direct trains run regularly to Palermo (€8.30, 2¼ hours, seven to 10 daily). Service to Catania (€10.40 to €14.50, four hours) is less frequent and usually requires a change of trains.

ℹ️ Information

Ortygia Tourist Office (☎093 146 42 55; Via Maestranza 33; ⏰8am-2pm & 2.30-5.30pm Mon-Fri, 8am-2pm Sat) English-speaking staff and lots of good information.

Tourist Office (☎0800 05 55 00; infoturismo@provsr.it; Via Roma 31; ⏰8am-8pm Mon-Sat, 9.15am-6.45pm Sun) English-speaking staff, city maps and other useful information.

ℹ️ Getting There & Away

Bus

Long-distance buses operate from the bus stop along Corso Umberto, just east of Syracuse's train station.

Interbus (☎093 16 67 10; www.interbus.it) runs buses to Catania (€6, 1½ hours, 15 daily Monday to Saturday, eight on Sunday) and its airport, Noto (€3.40, 55 minutes, two to four daily) and Palermo (€12, 3¼ hours, three daily).

Train

From Syracuse's **train station** (Via Francesco Crispi), several trains depart daily for Messina (InterCity/regional train €18.50/9.70, 2½ to 3¼ hours) via Catania (€9.50/6.35, 1¼ hours). For Palermo, the bus is a better option. There are also local trains from Syracuse to Noto (€3.45, 30 minutes) and Ragusa (€7.65, 2¼ hours).

ℹ️ Getting Around

For travel between the bus and train stations and Ortygia, catch the free AST shuttle bus 20 (every 20 to 60 minutes). To reach Parco Archeologico della Neapolis from Ortygia, take AST city bus 1, 3 or 12 (two-hour ticket €1.10), departing from Ortygia's Piazza Pancali.

PUGLIA

Puglia is comprised of sun-bleached seascapes, silver olive groves and picturesque hilltop and coastal towns. It is a lush, flat farming region, skirted by a long coast that alternates between glittering limestone precipices and long sandy beaches.

Bari

POP 320,200

Once regarded as the Bronx of southern Italy, Bari's reputation has gradually improved and the city, Puglia's capital and one of the south's most prosperous, deserves more than a cursory glance. Spruced up and rejuvenated, Bari Vecchia, the historic old town, is an interesting and atmospheric warren of streets.

◉ Sights

Basilica di San Nicola   Basilica
(www.basilicasannicola.it; Piazza San Nicola; ⏰7am-1pm & 4-7pm Mon-Sat, to 9pm Sun) One of the south's first Norman churches, the basilica is a splendid example of Puglian-Romanesque style, built to house the relics of St Nicholas (better known as Father Christmas), which were stolen from Turkey in 1087. His remains are said to exude a miraculous liquid with special powers.

Piazza Mercantile   Piazza
This beautiful piazza is fronted by the Sedile, the headquarters of Bari's Council of Nobles. In the northeast corner is the **Colonna della Giustizia** (Column of Justice), where debtors were once whipped.

🛌 Sleeping

B&B Casa Pimpolini   B&B €
(☎080 521 99 38; www.casapimpolini.com; Via Calefati 249; s €45-60, d €70-80; 🌬@) This lovely B&B in the new town is within easy walking distance to shops, restaurants and Bari Vecchia. The rooms are warm and welcoming, and the homemade breakfast is a treat. Great value.

Villa Romanazzi Carducci   Hotel €€€
(☎080 542 74 00; www.villaromanazzi.com; Via Capruzzi 326; d €79; 🛜) The one hotel in Bari daring to show some flare is housed in the pastel pink, 19th-century Villa Rachele. Rooms are a mixture of old and new; the decor in the villa rooms has more character.

Tempio dei Dioscuri, Valley of the Temples

JOHN ELK/GETTY IMAGES ©

Below: Purple artichokes
Right: Piazza del Duomo, Ortygia (p338)

(BELOW) MARTIN CHILD/GETTY IMAGES ©; (RIGHT) RICHARD I'ANSON/GETTY IMAGES ©

Eating & Drinking

Terranima
Pugliese €

(☎ 080 521 97 25; www.terranima.com; Via Putignani 215; meals €8-15; ☻7-11pm Mon-Sat, lunch Sun) Peep through the lace curtains into the cool interior of this rustic trattoria where worn flagstone floors and period furnishings make you feel like you're dining in someone's front room.

La Locanda di Federico
Pugliese €€

(☎ 080 522 77 05; www.lalocandadifederico.com; Piazza Mercantile 63-64; meals €30; ☻lunch & dinner) With domed ceilings, archways and medieval-style artwork on the walls, this restaurant oozes atmosphere. The menu is typical Pugliese, the food delicious and the price reasonable. *Orecchiette con le cime di rape* ('little ears' pasta with turnip tops) is highly recommended.

Information

Tourist Office (☎ 080 990 93 41; www.viaggiareinpuglia.it; 1st fl, Piazza Moro 33a; ☻8.30am-1pm & 3-6pm Mon-Fri, 10am-1pm Sat) There is also an information kiosk (☻9am-7pm May-Sep) in front of the train station in Piazza Aldo Moro.

Getting There & Away

Air

Bari's Palese **airport** (www.aeroportidipuglia.it) is served by a host of international and budget airlines, including British Airways, Alitalia and Ryanair.

Pugliairbus (http://pugliairbus. aeroportidipuglia.it) has a service from Bari airport to Matera (€5, 1¼ hours, three daily), and to Vieste (€20, 3½ hours, four daily May to September).

Bus

From Via Capruzzi, south of the main train station, SITA (☎ 080 579 01 11; www.sitabus.it) covers local destinations. **Ferrovie Appulo-Lucane** (☎ 080 572 52 29; http://ferrovieappulolucane.it) buses

serving Matera (€4.50, 1¼ hours, six daily) also depart from here.

Buses operated by **Ferrovie del Sud-Est** (FSE; ☎ 080 546 21 11; www.fseonline.it) leave from Largo Ciaia, south of Piazza Aldo Moro and service Alberobello (€3.90, 1¼ hours, hourly).

Train

From the **main train station** (☎ 080 524 43 86) trains go to Puglia and beyond, including Rome (from €50, four hours, every four hours). Ferrovie Appulo-Lucane serves Matera (€5, 1½ hours, 12 daily).

FSE trains leave from the station in Via Oberdan – cross under the train tracks south of Piazza Luigi di Savoia and head east along Via Capruzzi for about 500m, and serve Alberobello (€4.50, 1½ hours, hourly).

ⓘ Getting Around

To/From the Airport

For the airport, take the **Tempesta shuttle bus** (€4, 30 minutes, hourly) from the main train station, with pick-ups at Piazza Garibaldi and the corner of Via Andrea da Bari and Via Calefati. A taxi trip from the airport to town costs around €24.

Castel del Monte

You'll see **Castel del Monte** (☎ 0883 56 99 97; www.casteldelmonte.beniculturali.it; adult/reduced €5/2.50; ☺ 9am-6pm Oct-Feb, 10.15am-7.45pm Mar-Sep), an unearthly geometric shape on a hilltop, from miles away. Mysterious and perfectly octagonal, it's one of southern Italy's most talked-about landmarks and a Unesco World Heritage Site.

No one knows why Frederick II built it – there's no nearby town or strategic crossroads. It was not built to defend anything, as it has no moat or drawbridge, no arrow slits and no trapdoors for pouring boiling oil on invaders.

The castle has eight octagonal towers. Many of these have washing rooms with what are thought to be Europe's first flush loos – Frederick II, like the Arab world he admired, set great store by cleanliness.

It's difficult to reach here by public transport. By car, it's about 35km from Trani.

345

Vieste

POP 13,900

Vieste is an attractive whitewashed town jutting off the Gargano's easternmost promontory into the Adriatic Sea. It's the Gargano capital and sits above the area's most spectacular beach, a gleaming wide strip backed by sheer white cliffs and overshadowed by the towering rock monolith, **Scoglio di Pizzomunno**.

🛏 Sleeping & Eating

B&B Rocca sul Mare   B&B €

(📞 0884 70 27 19; www.roccasulmare.it; Via Mafrolla 32; per person €25-70; 🛜) In a former convent in the old quarter, this popular and reasonably priced place has charm, with large, comfortable high-ceilinged rooms. There's a vast rooftop terrace with panoramic views and a suite with a steam bath.

Osteria Al Duomo   Osteria €

(📞 0884 70 82 43; www.osterialduomo.it; Via Alessandro III 23; meals €25; 🕐lunch & dinner Mar-Nov) Tucked away in a picturesque narrow alley in the heart of the old town, this welcoming osteria has a cosy cave interior and outdoor seating under a shady arbour. Homemade pastas with seafood sauces feature prominently.

ℹ Getting There & Around

From May to September, **Pugliairbus** (📞 080 580 03 58; pugliairbus.aeroportidipuglia.it) runs a service to the Gargano, including Vieste, from Bari airport (€20, 3½ hours, four daily).

Alberobello

POP 11,000

Unesco World Heritage Site Alberobello resembles an urban sprawl – for gnomes. The Zona dei Trulli on the western hill of town is a dense mass of 1500 beehive-shaped houses, white-tipped as if dusted by snow.

Trattoria Amatulli (📞 080 432 29 79; Via Garibaldi 13; meals €16; 🕐Tue-Sun) is an excellent trattoria with a cheerily cluttered interior papered with photos of smiley diners. It serves superb down-to-earth dishes such as *orecchiette scure con cacioricotta pomodoro e rucola* ('little ears' pasta with cheese, tomato and rucola).

Alberobello is easily accessible from Bari (€4.50, 1½ hours, hourly) on the FSE Bari–Taranto train line.

Ostuni

POP 32,500

Ostuni shines like a pearly white tiara, extending across three hills with the magnificent gem of a cathedral as its sparkling centrepiece. It's the end of the *trulli* region and the beginning of the hot, dry Salento.

🛏 Sleeping & Eating

La Terra   Hotel €€

(📞 0831 33 66 51; www.laterrahotel.it; Via Petrarolo; d €130-170; 🅿❄🛜) This former 13th-century palace offers atmospheric and stylish accommodation with original niches, dark-wood beams and furniture, and contrasting light stonework and whitewash.

Osteria Piazzetta Cattedrale   Osteria €€

(📞 0831 33 50 26; www.piazzettacattedrale. it; Via Arcidiacono Trinchera 7; meals €25-30; 🕐Wed-Mon) Just beyond the arch opposite Ostuni's cathedral is this tiny little hostelry serving up magical food in an atmospheric setting. The menu includes plenty of vegetarian options.

ℹ Getting There & Around

Trains run frequently to Brindisi (€4, 25 minutes) and Bari (€9, 50 minutes). A half-hourly local bus covers the 2.5km between the station and town.

Lecce

POP 95,000

Historic Lecce is a beautiful baroque town; it's a glorious architectural confection of palaces and churches intricately sculpted from the soft local sandstone.

DAMIEN SIMONIS/GETTY IMAGES ©

⭐ Don't Miss
Matera

Approach Matera, in Basilicata, from virtually any direction and your first glimpse of its famous *sassi* is sure to stay in your memory forever. Haunting and beautiful, the *sassi* sprawl below the rim of a yawning ravine like a giant nativity scene.

The **Chiesa di Madonna delle Virtù & Chiesa di San Nicola del Greci** (Via Madonna delle Virtù; ⊙10am-7pm Sat & Sun) monastic complex in the Sasso Barisano is one of the most important monuments in Matera and is composed of dozens of caves spread over two floors.

In Sasso Caveoso, the **Museo della Scultura Contemporanea** (MUSMA; ✆366 9357768; www.musma.it; Via San Giacomo; adult/reduced €5/3.50; ⊙10am-2pm Tue-Sun & 4-8pm Sat & Sun Apr-Sep, 10am-2pm Tue-Sun Oct-Mar) is a fabulous contemporary sculpture museum, housed in Palazzo Pomarici.

Overnight in **Hotel in Pietra** (✆0835 34 40 40; www.hotelinpietra.it; Via San Giovanni Vecchio 22; s €70-150, d €85-160, ste €180-230; ❄@🛜), whose lobby is set in a former 13th-century chapel, complete with soaring arches. The eight rooms combine soft golden stone with the natural cave interior.

Quaint **Ristorante Il Cantuccio** (✆0835 33 20 90; Via delle Becchiere 33; meals €25; ⊙Tue-Sun) is a homey trattoria near Piazza Vittorio Veneto, and is as welcoming as its chef and owner, Michael Lella.

Pugliairbus (✆080 580 03 58; http://pugliairbus.aeroportidipuglia.it) operates a service to Bari airport (€5, 1¼ hours, four daily). **Ferrovie Appulo-Lucane** (FAL; ✆0835 33 28 61; http://ferrovieappulolucane.it) runs regular trains (€4.50, 1½ hours, 12 daily) and buses (€4.50, 1½ hours, six daily) to Bari.

⦿ Sights

Basilica di Santa Croce   Basilica

(☏ 0832 24 19 57; www.basilicasantacroce.
eu; Via Umberto I; ⏰ 9am-noon & 5-8pm) It
seems that hallucinating stonemasons
have been at work on the basilica. Sheep,
dodos, cherubs and beasties writhe
across the facade, a swirling magnificent
allegorical feast. Throughout the 16th and
17th centuries, a team of artists under
Giuseppe Zimbalo laboured to work the
building up to this pitch. Look for Zimbalo's profile on the facade.

Piazza del
Duomo   Piazza

Piazza del Duomo is a baroque feast,
the city's focal point and a sudden open
space amid the surrounding enclosed
lanes. During times of invasion the
inhabitants of Lecce would barricade
themselves in the square, which has
conveniently narrow entrances. The
12th-century **cathedral** (⏰ 8.30am-12.30pm
& 4-6.30pm) is one of Giuseppe Zimbalo's
finest works – he was also responsible for
the 68m-high bell tower.

⦿ Sleeping & Eating

Palazzo Rollo   Apartment €

(☏ 0832 30 71 52; www.palazzorollo.it; Corso
Vittorio Emanuele II 14; s €50-60, d €70-90,
ste €100-120, apt €70-90; P ❄ @) Stay in
a 17th-century palace – the Rollo family
seat for more than 200 years. The three
grand B&B suites (with kitchenettes)
have high curved ceilings and chandeliers. Downstairs, contemporary-chic
studios open onto an ivy-hung courtyard.
The rooftop garden has wonderful views.

Risorgimento Resort   Hotel €€

(☏ 0832 24 63 11; www.risorgimentoresort.it; Via
Imperatore Augusto 19; d €145-165, ste €190-290;
P ❄ @ 🛜) A warm welcome awaits at
this stylish five-star hotel in the centre of
Lecce. The rooms are spacious and refined with high ceilings, modern furniture
and contemporary details reflecting the
colours of the Salento, and the bathrooms
are enormous. There's a restaurant, wine
bar and rooftop garden.

Mamma Lupa   Osteria €

(☏ 340 7832765; Via Acaja 12; meals €20-25;
⏰ lunch Sun-Fri, dinner daily) Looking suitably
rustic, this *osteria* serves proper peasant

Trulli houses, Alberobello (p346)

Detour: Otranto

Around 45km southeast of Lecce, Otranto overlooks a pretty harbour on the turquoise Adriatic coast. In the historic centre, looming golden walls guard narrow car-free lanes, protecting countless little shops selling touristy odds and ends. In July and August it's one of Puglia's most vibrant towns.

Otranto was Italy's main port to the East for 1000 years and suffered a brutal history. There are fanciful tales that King Minos was here and St Peter is supposed to have celebrated the first Western Mass here. Otranto was sacked in 1480, when 18,000 Turks led by Ahmet Pasha besieged the town.

Otranto's **cathedral** (Piazza Basilica; ⊙8am-noon daily, 3-7pm Apr-Sep, 3-5pm Oct-Mar) was built by the Normans in the 11th century, though it's had a few facelifts since. On the floor is a vast 12th-century mosaic of a stupendous tree of life balanced on the back of two elephants. The Turks stabled their horses here when they beheaded the martyrs of Otranto on a stone preserved in the altar of the chapel.

There are some great beaches north of Otranto, especially **Baia dei Turchi**, with its translucent blue water. It's backed by fragrant pine forest and weather-worn cliffs. Much of the white-sand stretch is occupied by private beach clubs, where umbrella's go for around €20 per day.

Right by the huge Porta Terra in the historic centre, **La Bella Idrusa** (☎0836 80 14 75; Via Lungomare degli Eroi; pizzas €5; ⊙dinner Thu-Tue) has well judged pizzas and seafood standards, despite the tourist trap location.

Otranto can be reached from Lecce by FSE train (€2.60, 1½ hours) or bus (€2.60, 1½ hours).

food – such as roast tomatoes, potatoes and artichokes, or horse meatballs – in snug surroundings with just a few tables and a stone-vaulted ceiling.

Cucina Casareccia Trattoria €€
(☎0832 24 51 78; Viale Costadura 19; mains €12; ⊙lunch Tue-Sun, dinner Tue-Sat) Ring the bell to gain entry into a place that feels like a private home, with its patterned cement floor tiles, desk piled high with papers, and charming owner Carmela Perrone. In fact, it's known locally as le Zie (the aunts). Here you'll taste the true cucina povera (peasant cooking), including horsemeat done in a salsa piccante (spicy sauce). Booking is a must.

ℹ Information

InfoLecce (☎0832 52 18 77; www.infolecce.it; Piazza del Duomo 2; ⊙9.30am-1.30pm & 3.30-7.30pm Mon-Sat, from 10am Sun) Independent and helpful tourist information office. Has guided tours and bike rental (per hour/day €3/15).

ℹ Getting There & Away

Bus

STP (☎0832 35 91 42; www.stplecce.it) STP runs buses to Brindisi (€6.30, 35 minutes, nine daily) and throughout Puglia from the STP bus station (☎800 43 03 46; Viale Porta D'Europa).

FSE (☎0832 66 81 11; www.fseonline.it) FSE runs buses to Gallipoli (€2.60, one hour, four daily) and Otranto (€2.60, 1½ hours, two daily), leaving from Largo Vittime del Terrorismo.

Pugliairbus (http://pugliairbus.aeroporti dipuglia.it) Pugliairbus runs to Brindisi airport (€7, 40 minutes, nine daily). **SITA** also has buses to Brindisi airport (€6, 45 minutes, nine daily), leaving from Viale Porte d'Europa.

Train

The main **train station** runs frequent services to the following destinations:

Bari from €9, 1½ to two hours

Naples from €41, 5½ hours (transfer in Caserta)

349

Italy
In Focus

Monte Rosa (p154), Aosta
CHRISTIAN ASLUND/GETTY IMAGES ©

Italy Today

Colosseum (p70), Rome

66

Ordinary Italians are feeling the pain of austerity measures

99

if Italy were 100 people

92 would be Italian

4 would be Albanian & Eastern European

3 would be Other

1 would be North African

belief systems
(% of population)

91 Roman Catholic

4 Other Christians

3.5 Other Religions

1.5 Muslims

population per sq km

= 30 people

Rome   Italy   USA

Regardless of their politics and circumstances, locals all agree on one thing: the country is in an economic and political quagmire. Politics have long been a problem, with notoriously unstable governments – Berlusconi, with a record five-year stretch, was the longest serving prime minister since WWII. Unemployment rose from 6.2% in 2007 to 10.9% in 2012, while Italy's public debt soared above 130% of GDP in 2013.

The Economy

The country is suffering economically and ordinary Italians are feeling the pain of austerity measures coupled with seemingly perpetual recession. In addition governments continue to be fragile and divided. As taxes and prices have risen, opportunities for employment have shrunk and wages flatlined; life in Italy is bleak for many.

Berlusconi's Trials & Tribulations

In the summer of 2013, Berlusconi was successfully convicted of tax fraud, having exhausted the appeals process. The Supreme Court upheld his one-year sentence, but sent another part of the sentence – the five year bar on holding public office – back to the Court of Appeal, so at the time of writing he was still able to continue in politics. Although it's worth considering that successful conviction may not be the end of Berlusconi as a leader: Beppe Grillo, who is unable to stand for government due to a manslaughter charge following a car accident, continues to lead the Five Star Movement from the sidelines.

Berlusconi has been facing trial over several cases, including tax evasion and bribery, but the most sensational trial is 'Rubygate'. In it, Berlusconi is accused of paying for sex with Karima El Mahroug, a nightclub dancer nicknamed Ruby Rubacuori (Ruby Heartstealer), while she was 17 and therefore underage. The encounters reputedly took place at so-called 'bunga bunga' sex parties held at several of Berlusconi's villas.

Berlusconi is further accused of providing false information to a Milan police chief in order to release El Mahroug from detention on unrelated theft charges. In May 2013 a prosecutor in Milan told a court that Berlusconi paid Ruby €4.5 million in late 2010.

Despite his prosecution and the numerous other ongoing cases, the former crooner insists that the claims are part of a plot orchestrated by the political left. But could it be that Italy's tumultuous relationship with Il Cavaliere ('the Knight') is finally in its death throes?

WILL SALTER/GETTY IMAGES ©

2013 Elections

The rise of former comedian Beppe Grillo's Five Star Movement, backed by one in four voters in the February 2013 elections, is an indication of how disillusioned Italians, particularly the young, are with traditional politics. Results from the election were inconclusive, resulting in a hung parliament.

Though ex-Prime Minister Silvio Berlusconi did not take office in 2013, he retained a hold on power, as Enrico Letta's new right-left coalition depended on the support of Berlusconi's People of Freedom (PdL) movement. It may seem incredible to outsiders, observing Berlusconi's scandal-mired life, but opinion polls continue to put the PdL movement out in front.

History

RUSSELL MOUNTFORD/GETTY IMA(

Italy has seen it all – imperial domination, quarrelling city-states, international exploration, crushing poverty and postwar booms. This operatic story features a colourful cast of characters: perverted emperors, ambitious invaders, Machiavellian masterminds and, above all, ordinary Italians who have repeatedly shown themselves capable of extraordinary, history-changing feats.

Etruscans, Greeks & Ancient Rome

Long before Renaissance *palazzi* (mansions) and baroque churches, the Italian peninsula was riddled with caves and hill towns built by the Etruscans, who dominated the land by the 7th century BC. Little is known about them, since they spoke a language that today has barely

c 700,000 BC
Primitive tribes lived in caves and hunted elephants and other hefty beasts on the Italian peninsula.

been deciphered. Though impressive as seafarers, warriors and farmers, they lacked cohesion.

Greek traders set up a series of independent city-states along the coast and in Sicily in the 8th century BC, collectively known as Magna Graecia. These Greek settlements flourished until the 3rd century BC, and the remains of magnificent Doric temples still stand in Italy's south (at Paestum) and on Sicily (at Agrigento, Selinunte and Segesta).

The Etruscans tried and failed to conquer the Greek settlements, but the real threat to both civilisations came from an unexpected source – the grubby but growing Latin town of Rome.

According to legend, Italy's future capital was founded by twins Romulus and Remus on 21 April 753 BC, on the site where they had been suckled by a she-wolf as orphan infants. Romulus later killed Remus and the settlement was named Rome after him. Over the following centuries, this fearless and often ruthless town become Italy's major power, sweeping aside the Etruscans by the 2nd century AD.

The Best...
For Archaeological Booty

1 Vatican Museums (p85), Vatican City

2 Capitoline Museums (p68), Rome

3 Museo Archeologico Nazionale (p287), Naples

4 Museo Archeologico Paolo Orsi (p340), Syracuse

5 Museo e Galleria Borghese (p88), Rome

The Roman Republic

Although Roman monuments were emblazoned with the initials SPQR (Senatus Populusque Romanus, or the Senate and People of Rome), the Roman people initially had precious little say in their republic. Known as plebeians (literally 'the many'), the disenfranchised majority slowly wrested concessions from the patrician class by 280 BC, though only a small political class qualified for positions of power in government.

Slowly at first, Roman armies conquered the Italian peninsula. Defeated city-states were not taken over directly, but were obliged to become allies, providing troops on demand for the Roman army. Wars with rivals such as Carthage in the east gave Rome control of Sardinia, Sicily, Corsica, mainland Greece, Spain, most of North Africa and part of Asia Minor by 133 BC. Rome became the most important city in the Mediterranean, with a population of 300,000.

2000 BC
The Bronze Age reaches Italy. Copper and bronze are used to fashion tools and arms.

264–241 BC
War rages between Rome and the Carthage empire, across North Africa and into Spain, Sicily and Sardinia.

Beware the Ides of March

Born in 100 BC, Gaius Julius Caesar would become one of Rome's most masterful generals, lenient conquerors and capable administrators. After quelling revolts in Spain, Caesar received a Roman mandate in 59 BC to govern Gallia Narbonensis, today's southern France. Caesar raised troops to hold off an invasion of Helvetic tribes from Switzerland, and in 52 to 51 BC stamped out Gaul's last great revolt under the leader Vercingetorix. Diplomatic Caesar was generous to defeated enemies, and the Gauls became his staunchest supporters.

Jealous of the growing power of his one-time protégé, Gnaeus Pompeius Magnus (Pompey) severed his political alliance with Caesar, and convinced the Senate to outlaw Caesar in 49 BC. On 7 January, Caesar crossed the Rubicon River into Italy, sparking civil war. Caesar's three-year campaign ended in decisive victory, and upon his return to Rome in 46 BC, he assumed dictatorial powers.

Caesar launched a series of reforms, overhauled the Senate and embarked on a building program, but by 44 BC, it was clear Caesar had no plans to restore the Republic. Dissent grew in the Senate, and on the Ides (15th) of March 44 BC a band of conspirators stabbed Caesar to death in a Senate meeting.

In the years following Caesar's death, his lieutenant, Mark Antony (Marcus Antonius), and nominated heir, great-nephew Octavian, plunged into civil war against Caesar's assassins. Octavian took control of the western half of the empire and Antony headed to the east – but when Antony fell head over heels for Cleopatra VII in 31 BC, Octavian and Antony turned on one another. Octavian claimed victory over Antony and Cleopatra in Greece, and when he invaded Egypt, Antony and Cleopatra committed suicide and Egypt became a province of Rome.

Augustus & the Glories of Empire

By 27 BC Octavian was renamed Augustus (Your Eminence) and conceded virtually unlimited power by the Senate, effectively becoming Rome's emperor. Under Augustus, the arts flourished and buildings were restored and constructed, including the Pantheon.

AD 79

Mt Vesuvius showers molten rock and ash upon Pompeii and Herculaneum.

312

Constantine becomes the Roman Empire's first Christian leader.

SEAN CAFFREY /GETTY IMAGES ©

HEAD OF CONSTANTINE, CAPITOLINE MUSEUMS (P68)

Imperial Insanity

The ancient Romans suffered their fair share of eccentric leaders.

Tiberius (14–37) A steady governing hand but prone to depression, Tiberius had a difficult relationship with the Senate and withdrew in his later years to Capri, devoting himself to drinking, orgies and fits of paranoia.

Gaius (Caligula; 37–41) Sex with his sisters and violence were Caligula's idea of entertainment. He emptied the state's coffers and suggested naming a horse consul before being assassinated.

Claudius (41–54) Apparently timid as a child, he was ruthless with enemies and relished watching their executions. According to English historian Edward Gibbon, he was the only one of the first 15 emperors not to take male lovers.

Nero (54–68) Nero had his mum murdered, his first wife's veins slashed, his second wife kicked to death and his third wife's ex-husband killed. The people accused him of fiddling while Rome burned to the ground in 64; Nero blamed the disaster on the Christians. He executed the evangelists Peter and Paul, and had others thrown to wild beasts.

By AD 100, 1.5 million inhabitants thronged the capital's marble temples, public baths, theatres, circuses and libraries. Poverty was rife, and Augustus created Rome's first police force under a city prefect (*praefectus urbi*) to curb mob violence and quell dissent among the poor, politically underrepresented masses.

Under Hadrian (76–138), the empire reached its greatest extent, stretching across the continent to include Britain and most of the modern-day Middle East, from Turkey to northern Morocco. But by the time Diocletian (245–305) became emperor, the empire was faced with attacks from outside and revolts from within. Diocletian's response to the rise of Christianity was persecution, a policy reversed in 313 under Christian Constantine I (c 272–337).

The Empire was later divided in two, with the second capital in Constantinople (modern-day Istanbul) founded by Constantine in 330. The Byzantine eastern empire survived, while Italy and Rome were overrun.

962
Otto I is crowned Holy Roman Emperor in Rome, the first in a long line of Germanic rulers.

1309
Pope Clement V shifts the papacy to Avignon in France (for almost 70 years).

1321
Dante Alighieri completes epic poem *La divina commedia* (The Divine Comedy); he dies the same year.

Papal Power & Family Feuds

In a historic twist, the minority religion Emperor Diocletian tried so hard to stamp out preserved Rome's glory. While most of Italy succumbed to invasion from Germanic tribes, Byzantine reconquest and Lombards in the north, the papacy established itself in Rome as a spiritual and secular force.

In return for formal recognition of the pope's control of Rome and surrounding Papal States, the Carolingian Franks were granted a powerful position in Italy and their king, Charlemagne, was given the title of Holy Roman Emperor. The bond between the papacy and the Byzantine Empire was broken, and political power shifted north of the Alps, where it remained for more than 1000 years. Meanwhile, Rome's aristocratic families battled to control the papacy and the right to appoint politically powerful bishops.

The Wonder of the World

Marriage was the ultimate merger between Henry VI, son of Holy Roman Emperor Frederick I (Barbarossa), and Constance de Hauteville, heir to Sicily's Norman throne. The power couple's son, Frederick II (1194–1250), became one of the most colourful figures

Statue, Pompeii (p302)

1452
Leonardo da Vinci is born 15 April in Vinci, near Florence.

1506
Work starts on St Peter's Basilica in Rome, to a design by Donato Bramante.

1508–12
Pope Julius II commissions Michelangelo to paint the ceiling frescoes in the restored Sistine Chapel.

of medieval Europe. Frederick was a German who grew up in southern Italy and called Sicily home and, as Holy Roman Emperor, allowed freedom of worship to Muslims and Jews. A warrior and scholar, Frederick was nicknamed *Stupor Mundi* (the Wonder of the World) for his talents as a poet, linguist, mathematician, philosopher and military strategist.

After reluctantly carrying out a (largely diplomatic) Holy Land crusade in 1228–29 under threat of excommunication, Frederick returned to Italy to find papal troops invading Neapolitan territory. Frederick soon had them on the run, and expanded his influence to city-states in central and northern Italy. Battles ensued, which continued after Frederick's death in 1250.

Rise of the City-States

While the south of Italy tended to centralised rule, the north did not. Port cities such as Genoa, Pisa and especially Venice increasingly ignored edicts from Rome, and Florence, Milan, Parma, Bologna, Padua, Verona and Modena resisted Roman meddling in their affairs.

Between the 12th and 14th centuries, these cities developed new forms of government. Venice adopted an oligarchic 'parliamentary' system in a limited democracy. Tuscan and Umbrian city-states created a *comune* (town council), a form of republican government dominated initially by aristocrats, then by wealthy middle classes. Family dynasties shaped their hometowns, such as the Medici in Florence. War between the city-states was constant, and Florence, Milan and Venice absorbed their neighbours. Italy's dynamic, independent-minded city-states led a sea change in thinking known as the Renaissance, ushering in the modern era with scientific discoveries, publishing houses and compelling new visions for the world in art.

A Nation Is Born

Centuries of war, plague and occasional religious purges took their toll on Italy's divided city-states, whose role on the world stage was largely reduced by the 18th century to a vacation playground. Napoleon marched into Venice in 1797 without much of a fight, ending 1000 years of Venetian independence and creating the so-called Kingdom of Italy in 1805. But just 10 years later, the reactionary Congress of Vienna restored all the foreign rulers to their places in Italy.

The Best...
For Medieval Mystique

1 Siena (p248), Tuscany

2 Bologna (p205), Emilia-Romagna

3 San Gimignano (p254), Tuscany

4 Assisi (p261), Umbria

5 Verona (p200), Veneto

1582

Pope Gregory XIII replaces the Julian calendar (introduced by Caesar) with the modern-day Gregorian calendar.

1805

Napoleon is proclaimed king of the newly constituted Kingdom of Italy, comprising most of the north of the country.

1861

By the end of the 1859–61 Franco-Austrian War, Vittorio Emanuele II is proclaimed king of a newly united Italy.

Florence's Trials by Fire

In 1481, fat-lipped Dominican friar Girolamo Savonarola began prophesying apocalyptic days ahead for Florence unless the city changed its wayward habits. With the horrors of war fresh in their minds and vivid accounts of Florentine plague by Boccacio and Dante, Savonarola's blood-curdling predictions struck fear in many Florentine hearts. Savonarola developed a following, and called for the establishment of a strict theocratic government for Florence.

When Florence's Medici clan rulers fell into disgrace in 1494, the city's fathers ceded to Savonarola's demands. Books, clothes, jewellery, fancy furnishings and art were torched on 'bonfires of the vanities'. Drinking, whoring, partying, gambling, flashy fashion and other sinful behaviours were banned – and a vibrant Florentine underground scene was born. Florence's economy stagnated; no one knew what goods and services Savonarola would ban next.

Florentines soon tired of this fundamentalism, as did the rival Franciscan religious order and Pope Alexander VI (possibly the least religiously inclined pope of all time). To test Savonarola's commitment to his own methods, the Franciscans invited him to submit to trial by fire. Savonarola sent an emissary instead, but the hapless youth was saved when the trial was cancelled on account of rain. Finally the city government had the fiery friar arrested. He was hanged and burned at the stake as a heretic alongside two supporters on 22 May 1498.

Inspired by the French Revolution and outraged by their subjugation to Napoleon and Austria, Italians began to agitate for an independent, unified nationhood. Count Camillo Benso di Cavour (1810–61) of Turin, prime minister of the Savoy monarchy, became the diplomatic brains behind the Italian unification movement. He won British support for the creation of an independent Italian state and negotiated with the French in 1858 to create a northern Italian kingdom, in exchange for parts of Savoy and Nice.

The bloody 1859–61 Franco-Austrian War ensued, and is now better known as the war for Italian Independence. Pro-Independence forces took over Lombardy and forced the Austrians to relinquish the Veneto. Revolutionary Giuseppe Garibaldi claimed Sicily and southern Italy in the name of Savoy King Vittorio Emanuele II in 1860, and Cavour and the king claimed parts of central Italy (including Umbria and Le Marche). The unified Italian state was founded in 1861, with Tuscany, the Veneto and Rome incorporated into the fledgling kingdom by 1870 and parliament established in Rome in 1871.

1915

Italy enters WWI on the side of the Allies to win Italian territories still in Austrian hands.

1922

King Vittorio Emanuele III entrusts Mussolini and his Fascists with the formation of a government.

WILL SALTER/GETTY IMAGES ©

ST PETER'S BASILICA (P86), ROME

Mussolini & World Wars

When war broke out in Europe in July 1914, Italy chose to remain neutral, despite being a member of the Triple Alliance with Austria and Germany. Under the terms of the Alliance, Austria was due to hand over northern Italian territory – but Austria refused.

After Austria's deal-breaker, Italy joined the Allies, and plunged into a nightmarish 3½-year war with Austria. When the Austro-Hungarian forces collapsed in November 1918, the Italians marched into Trieste and Trento – but the postwar Treaty of Versailles failed to award Italy the remaining territories it sought.

This humiliation added insult to injury. Italy had lost 600,000 men in the war and, while a few war profiteers had benefitted, the majority of the populace was reduced to abject poverty. From this despair rose a demagogue: Benito Mussolini (1883–1945).

A former socialist newspaper editor and one-time draft dodger, Mussolini volunteered for the front and returned wounded in 1917. Frustrated at Italy's treatment in Versailles, Mussolini formed an extremist Italian right-wing militant political group. By 1921 the Fascist Party was feared and admired for its black-shirted street brawlers, Roman salute and its self-anointed Duce (Leader), Mussolini. After his march on Rome in 1922 and victory in the 1924 elections, Mussolini took full control of the country by 1926, banning other political parties, independent trade unions and free press.

As the first step to creating a 'new Roman empire', Mussolini invaded Abyssinia (Ethiopia) in 1935–36. Condemned by the League of Nations for his invasion, Mussolini allied with Nazi Germany to back Fascist rebel General Franco in Spain. Yet Italy remained aloof from WWII battles until June 1940, when Germany's blitz of Norway, Denmark and much of France made it look like a winning campaign. Instead, allying with Italy caused Germany setbacks in the Balkans and North Africa.

By the time the Allies landed in Sicily in 1943, the Italians had had enough of Mussolini and his war, and the king had the dictator arrested. Italy surrendered in September – but the Germans rescued Mussolini, occupied the northern two-thirds of the country and reinstalled the dictator.

The painfully slow Allied campaign up the peninsula was aided by the Italian Resistance sabotage of German forces, until northern Italy was finally liberated in April 1945. Resistance fighters shot Mussolini and his lover, Clara Petacci, and strung up their corpses in Milan's Piazzale Lotto.

The Best... For Renaissance Elegance

1 Duomo (p228), Florence

2 Galleria degli Uffizi (p225), Florence

3 Urbino (p260), Le Marche

4 Da Vinci's *The Last Supper* (p124), Milan

1929

Catholicism is declared Italy's sole religion and the Vatican an independent state.

1940

Italy enters WWII on Nazi Germany's side and invades Greece, which quickly proves to be a mistake.

1944

Mt Vesuvius explodes back into action on March 18.

Going the Distance for the Resistance

In 1943–44, the Assisi Underground hid hundreds of Jewish Italians in Umbrian convents and monasteries, while the Tuscan Resistance forged travel documents for them. The refugees needed the documents fast, before they were deported to concentration camps by Fascist officials. Enter the fastest man in Italy: Gino Bartali, world-famous Tuscan cyclist, Tour de France winner and three-time champion of the Giro d'Italia. After his death in 2003, documents revealed that during his 'training rides' throughout the war years, Bartali had carried Resistance intelligence and falsified documents to transport Jewish refugees to safe locations. Bartali was interrogated at the dreaded Villa Triste in Florence, where suspected anti-Fascists were routinely tortured – but he revealed nothing. Until his death, the long-distance hero downplayed his efforts to rescue Jewish refugees, saying, 'One does these things, and then that's that'.

The Grey & the Red Years

In the aftermath of war, the left-wing Resistance was disarmed and Italy's political forces scrambled to regroup. The USA, through the economic largesse of the Marshall Plan, wielded considerable political influence and used this to keep the left in check. Immediately after the war, three coalition governments succeeded one another. The third, which came to power in December 1945, was dominated by the newly formed right-wing Democrazia Cristiana (DC; Christian Democrats), led by Alcide De Gasperi, who remained prime minister until 1953. Italy became a republic in 1946 and De Gasperi's DC won the first elections under the new constitution in 1948.

Until the 1980s, the Partito Comunista Italiano (Communist Party) played a crucial role in Italy's social and political development, in spite of being systematically kept out of government. The very popularity of the party led to a grey period in the country's history, the *anni di piombo* ('years of lead') in the 1970s. Just as the Italian economy was booming, Europe-wide paranoia about the power of the Communists in Italy fuelled a secretive reaction that, it is said, was largely directed by the CIA and NATO.

The 1970s were thus dominated by the spectre of terrorism and considerable social unrest. Neo-Fascist terrorists struck with a bomb blast in Milan in 1969. In 1978 the Brigate Rosse (Red Brigades, a group of young left-wing militants responsible for several bomb blasts and assassinations), claimed their most important victim – former DC prime minister Aldo Moro. His kidnap and murder some 54 days later (the subject of the 2003 film *Buongiorno, notte*) shook the country.

1946
Italians vote in a national referendum to abolish the monarchy and create a republic.

1960
Rome hosts the Games of the XVII Olympiad.

1980
On 25 November, a 6.8-Richter-scale earthquake strikes Campania killing almost 3000 people.

Despite the disquiet, the 1970s also saw positive change. Divorce became legal, legislation allowed women to keep their own names after marriage, and abortion was legalised.

Clean Hands, Berlusconi & Five Star

A growth spurt in the aftermath of WWII saw Italy become one of the world's leading economies, but by the 1970s the economy had begun to stagnate, and by the mid-1990s a new and prolonged period of crisis had set in. Economic crisis was coupled with the Tangentopoli (Kickback City) scandal. Led by a pool of Milanese magistrates, investigations known as Mani Pulite (Clean Hands) implicated thousands of public figures in corruption scandals.

The old centre-right political parties collapsed in the wake of these trials and from the ashes rose what many Italians hoped might be a breath of fresh political air. Media magnate Silvio Berlusconi's Forza Italia (Go Italy) party swept to power in 2001 and again in April 2008. Berlusconi's blend of charisma, confidence, irreverence and promises of tax cuts appealed to many Italian voters.

Pantheon (p75), Rome
CHRISTOPHER GROENHOUT/GETTY IMAGES ©

1995
Maurizio Gucci, heir to the Gucci fashion empire, is gunned down outside his Milan offices.

2001
Silvio Berlusconi's right-wing Casa delle Libertà coalition wins an absolute majority in national polls.

2005
Pope John Paul II dies aged 84, prompting a wave of sorrow.

During Berlusconi's tenure, however, a series of laws were passed that protected his extensive business interests, and the economy continued to stagnate. In 2011 Berlusconi was forced to resign due to Italy's worsening economic situation in relation to the eurozone's sovereign debt crisis. A government of technocrats, headed by economist Mario Monti, took over until the inconclusive elections of February 2013, after which Enrico Letta, a member of the Partito Democratico (PD), was named prime minister, heading a precarious right-left coalition.

Some Italians place their hopes for a brighter political future in the Five Star Movement, started by comedian-activist Beppe Grillo. The movement won around 25% of the votes in the February 2013 election. This new, young movement subsequently refused to make any postelectoral deals with the other parties, wanting to differentiate itself from the old political class. Only time will tell if the Five Star movement will be able to generate the sea change that it desires.

San Gimignano (p254)
JEAN-PIERRE LESCOURRET/GETTY IMAGES ©

2009
Italy's Constitutional Court overturns a law giving Berlusconi immunity from prosecution while in office.

2011
After a string of scandals, Berlusconi resigns to restore confidence in the ailing Italian economy.

2013
Enrico Letta is named prime minister of a shaky left-right coalition. Berlusconi is prosecuted for fraud.

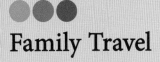

Family Travel

Pompeii (p302)

Kids love Italy: pizza and ice cream as a staple diet; white-sand beaches for bucket-and-spade magic; ancient Roman ruins for roaming around; mountains for skiing down, and lakes for splashing and boating. Gladiators, volcanoes, gondolas...it's a storybook come true. Not only that, but the feeling's mutual – Italy loves kids. You can feel relaxed eating out, there'll be no raised eyebrows if kids are out past their bedtime and the welcome is warm – babies will be particularly adored.

Inspiration

How do you get kids to go along with vacation plans, and let them think it's their idea? Italy makes it easy, with sights and activities that appeal to kids and grown-ups alike. Sprawling ancient Roman sites give kids a chance to run around, and let adults daydream about what life was like thousands of years ago. Caves and catacombs are worthy dares, though the latter are cramped and spooky enough only to be good for older kids. Grand villa estates have gardens for picnics and playtime, and art for contemplation and downtime. *Agriturismi* (farmstay accommodation) are money-savers that may include rustic meals, a pool and farm animals.

Everyone's a winner with Italian island beach vacations; there'll be plenty of other kids around and sometimes hot springs for parents. Across Italy, there is gelato and a place to run about on every major piazza.

For more information and ideas, see Lonely Planet's *Travel with Children* and the superb Italy-focused website www.italiakids.com.

Planning

Italians love children, but there are few special amenities. In this guidebook, look for the family-friendly icon ⊞ highlighting places that are especially welcoming to families. Book accommodation in advance, and ask about extra beds. Reserve train seats whenever possible to avoid finding yourselves standing.

Baby formula and sterilising solution Available at pharmacies.

Disposable nappies (diapers) Available at supermarkets and pharmacies.

High chairs Available at many restaurants.

Change facilities Rare outside airports and state-of-the-art museums.

Cots Request ahead at hotels.

Strollers Bring your own.

Infant car seats Reserve at car-rental firms.

The Best...
Destinations
for Kids

Budgeting

Stretch your family holiday budget further in Italy:

Sights Admission to many tourist attractions is free or heavily discounted for children under 18 (listed as 'reduced' in this guidebook).

Transport Discounts are often available for children under 12.

Hotels & agriturismi Many offer special rates on room and board for kids. Check the handy website www.booking.com, which details the 'kid policy' for every hotel it lists, including what extra charges apply to kids' breakfasts and extra beds.

Restaurants Kids' menus are uncommon, but you can ask for a *mezzo piatto* (half-plate), usually at half-price.

Art & Architecture

Trulli, Alberobello (p346)

OLIVER STREWE/GETTY IMAGES ©

With more Unesco World Heritage Sites than any other country, Italy is one place you can hardly throw a stone without hitting a masterpiece. Italian architecture is more than just a wall to hang the art on, with geniuses like Michelangelo creating spaces that alternately give a sense of intimacy and inclusion, steadfastness and momentum.

Classical Era

Ancient Romans initially took their cue from the Greeks – only what the Greeks did first, the Romans made bigger. The Greeks invented Doric, Ionic and Corinthian orders of columns, but Romans installed them in the Colosseum.

Harmonious proportions were key to Roman designs, including the Pantheon's carefully balanced, coffered dome showcasing a Roman innovation: concrete. Unlike the Greeks, Roman sculptors created accurate, brutally honest busts. You'll recognise Emperors Pompey, Titus and Augustus across the rooms at the Palatine Museum from their respective facial features: bulbous nose, square head, sunken eyes.

Roman emperors such as Augustus used art as a PR tool, employing it to celebrate

The Best...
Museums

great military victories – the Colonna di Traiano (Trajan's Column) and the Ara Pacis Augustae (Altar of Peace) in Rome are especially gorgeous propaganda.

Byzantine Glitz

After Constantine became Christianity's star convert, the empire's architects turned their talents to Byzantine churches: domed brick basilicas, plain on the outside, with mosaic-encrusted interiors. One early example is Cattedrale Santa Maria Assunta in Torcello. Instead of classical realism, Torcello's *Last Judgment* mosaic conveys a clear message in compelling cartoon shorthand: repent, or snickering devils will drag you off by the hair. Torcello's golden Byzantine mosaics are echoed in Venice's Basilica di San Marco and as far away as Palermo's Cappella Palatina (Palatine Chapel).

Medieval Graces

Italians didn't appreciate over-the-top French Gothic cathedrals; instead, they took Gothic further over the top. A signature Moorish Gothic style graced Venice's *palazzi* (mansions), including the Ca' d'Oro. Milan took Gothic to extremes in its flamboyant Duomo, and the Sienese came up with a novelty for Siena's cathedral: storytelling scenes inlaid in the church floor.

Florentine painter Giotto di Bondone (1266–1337) added another twist. Instead of Byzantine golden cartoon saints, Giotto featured furry donkeys in the life story of St Francis in the Basilica di San Francesco di Assisi. Pot-bellied pack animals dot Giotto's frescoed Assisi landscape, and when the donkey weeps at the death of the patron saint of animals, it's hard not to well up with him.

Meanwhile, in Siena, Ambrogio Lorenzetti (1290–1348) set a trend for secular painting with his *Allegories of Good and Bad Government* (1337–40), using convincing perspective to make good government seem perfectly achievable, with Peace, Prudence, happy merchants and a wedding party – it's like a medieval Jane Austen novel illustration.

The Renaissance

Plague cut short the talents of many artists and architects in the 14th century, and survivors regrouped. Floating, wide-eyed Byzantine saints seemed far removed from reality, where city-state wars and natural disasters loomed large. Florentine sculptors such as Lorenzo Ghiberti (1378–1455) and Donatello (1386–1466) brought Byzantine ideals down to earth, creating anatomically accurate figures with classical principles of perspective and scale.

Architect Filippo Brunelleschi (1377–1446) also looked to the classics as inspiration for Florence's Duomo – specifically Rome's Pantheon – and created a vast dome of mathematically exacting proportions to distribute its massive weight.

Critics were sure it would collapse; it still hasn't. But if Brunelleschi studied the classics, neoclassist Palladio pillaged them, borrowing architectural elements of temples, villas and forums for Venice's San Giorgio Maggiore. The idea of creative repurposing wasn't new – the art of reusing old buildings, *spolia,* had been practised in Italy for centuries – but Palladio's conceptual *spolia* was accomplished with easy grace.

Classical laws of harmonious proportions had not been mastered in Roman painting, so Sandro Botticelli (1444–1510) took on the task. Though his early works seem stiff, his *Birth of Venus* (1485) in Florence's Uffizi is a model of poise. Instead of classicism, Leonardo da Vinci (1452–1519) smudged the contours of his lines – a technique called *sfumato,* still visible in his faded *Last Supper* in Milan. Michelangelo applied the same chiselled perfection to his *David* at Florence's Galleria dell'Accademia and to his image of Adam brought to life by God on the ceiling of the Sistine Chapel.

Mannerism

By 1520, artists such as Michelangelo and Raphael had mastered naturalism, and discovered its expressive limitations – to make a point, the mannerists decided, sometimes you had to exaggerate for effect. One glorious example is *Assunta* (Ascension, 1516–18) by Titian (1490–1576) in Venice's I Frari, where the glowing Madonna rises to heaven in a swirl of red drapery.

Milanese-born Michelangelo Merisi da Caravaggio (1573–1610) had no interest in classical conventions of ideal beauty. Instead he concentrated on revealing and concealing truth through skilful contrasts of light and shadow – or *chiaroscuro* – in his *Conversion of St Paul* and the *Crucifixion of St Peter,* both in Rome's Chiesa di Santa Maria del Popolo.

The Best...
Churches

Baroque

The Renaissance's insistence on restraint and pure form led to an exuberant backlash. Baroque religious art served as a kind of spiritual cattle prod, with works by sculptor Gianlorenzo Bernini (1598–1680) simulating religious ecstasy with frantic urgency.

With sculptural flourishes, baroque architecture was well suited to the showplace piazzas of Rome and shimmering reflections in Venice's Grand Canal. But in high-density Naples, the only place to go for baroque was indoors – hence the kaleidoscope of coloured, inlaid marbles inside Naples' Certosa di San Martino.

Italian Export Art

By the 18th century, Italy was chafing under foreign domination by Napoleon and Austria. Dependent on foreign admirers, impoverished Italy turned out landscapes for European dandies as 'Grand Tour' souvenirs. The best-known *vedutisti* (landscapists) are Francesco Guardi (1712–93) and Giovanni Antonio Canaletto (1697–1768). Neoclassical sculptor Antonio Canova (1757–1822) took a more daring approach, with a nude sculpture of Napoleon's sister, Pauline Bonaparte Borghese, as a reclining *Venere Vincitrice* (Conquering Venus) in Rome's Museo e Galleria Borghese.

Modern & Contemporary

Stilted by convention and bedraggled by industrialisation, Italy found a creative outlet in European art nouveau, called 'Liberty' in Italian. But some found the style decadent and frivolous. Led by poet Filippo Tommaso Marinetti (1876–1944) and painter Umberto Boccioni (1882–1916), the 1909 *Futurist Manifesto* declared, 'Everything is in movement, everything rushes forward, everything is in constant swift change.' Though the look of futurism was co-opted by Fascism, its impulse could not have been more different: Fascism was an extreme nostalgia for a heroic Italian empire that wasn't exclusively Italian or heroic. Today, futurism is highlighted at Milan's Museo del Novecento. In the 1960s, radical Arte Povera (Poor Art) used simple and found materials to trigger associations, and the impact is still palpable at Turin's Galleria Civica d'arte Moderna e Contemporanea (GAM).

In architecture, one of the few mid-century high points is the 1956 Pirelli Tower, designed by architect Giò Ponti and engineer Pier Luigi Nervi. Today, Italian architecture is back on the world stage, ranging from Massimiliano Fuksas' whimsical glass sailboat Fiera Milano to Renzo Piano's Turin's Fiat factory creatively repurposed into Slow Food showcase, Eataly.

The Italian Table

Grocery store, Naples (p282)

FRANK ROTHE/GETTY IMAGES ©

Let's be honest, it's about the food, right? Well, sit back and enjoy: you're in for a host of treats. Just don't go expecting the stock-standards served at your local Italian back home. In reality, Italian cuisine is a handy umbrella term for the country's diverse regional cuisines. Has anything ever tasted this good? Probably not. Will it ever again? Probably tomorrow. Buon appetito!

Regional Cuisine

Italian city-state rivalries once settled with castle sieges and boiling oil poured on enemies are now settled through considerably friendlier culinary competition – though there may still be some boiling oil involved. Visitors in spring may not be allowed to leave Rome without trying *carciofi alla giudía* (Roman artichokes in the Jewish tradition, flattened into a blossom and fried) or Venice without trying *violetti di Sant'Erasmo* (tiny purple artichokes from the lagoon island of Sant'Erasmo, fried or marinated and devoured in a single mouthful). But in this stiff regional competition for gourmet affections, there is a clear winner: travellers, who get to sample regional variations on Italy's seasonal speciality produce, seafood and meats.

Rome

Italy's capital offers more than just Viagra-strength espresso at Caffè Tazza d'Oro and glorious gelato. Must-try menu items include thin-crust pizza, *saltimbocca* (literally 'leap in the mouth': veal sautéed with prosciutto and sage) and calorific pasta classics *spaghetti carbonara* (with *guanciale*, or pigs' cheeks, egg and cheese) and *bucatini all'amatriciana* (tube pasta with tomato, *pecorino romano* and *guanciale*). Rome is the spiritual home of nose-to-tail noshing, where staples such as *trippa alla Romana* (tripe with tomato and mint) and *pajata* (a pasta dish of milk-fed calf's intestines in tomato sauce) beckon brave gourmands.

Piedmont to Milan

The Piedmont town of Bra is the home of Slow Food – Italy's artisan food alternative to globalised fast-food – and Turin's Eataly fills a former Fiat factory with Italy's best artisan specialities. Piedmont's Alpine winters are perfect for rich risotto, speciality cheeses, white Alba truffles and warming Barolo red wines. No Piedmont dining extravaganza is complete without coffee roasted to nutty perfection and Turin-made chocolate at Turin's famous cafes. The Ligurian coast south of Turin is famed for pesto and focaccia, best enjoyed with staggering seaside views in the coves of Cinque Terre.

Milan specialises in *risotto alla milanese con ossobucco* (Milanese-style veal shank and marrow with saffron rice) and *bresaola* (air-dried salted beef), and the latest culinary trend is *latterie* (milk bars), comfort-food restaurants emphasising cheese, vegetables and simple homemade pasta.

Bologna to Venice

Culinary culture shock may occur between lunch and dinner in the northeast, where you can lunch on Bologna's namesake *pasta alla bolognese* (a rich beef and pork belly *ragú* usually served with tagliatelle pasta; spaghetti bolognese is a foreign adaptation) and then dine on Venetian polenta with *sarde in saor* (marinated sardines with onions, pine nuts and sultanas).

Bolognese cuisine stars two world-renowned local products: *parmigiano reggiano* (Parmesan) and *aceto balsamico di Modena* (aged Modena balsamic vinegar). While bloodlust isn't strictly required in Bologna, carnivores rejoice over meat-stuffed tortellini and cold-cut platters featuring *prosciutto di Parma* (thin-sliced cured ham from Parma), salami, mortadella, *zampone* (trotters) and *coppa,* a surprisingly tasty combo of neck meat and lard cured in brine.

Venice celebrates its lagoon location and spice-trading past in dishes such as squid-ink risotto and *granseole* (spider-crab) graced with star anise. Venetian dandies kicked off the European trend for hot chocolate at cafes ringing Piazza San Marco, and you can still enjoy a decadent, gooey cup in baroque splendour.

Tuscany & Umbria

The Tuscans have a special way with meat, herbs and olive oil – think whole boar, pheasant, rabbit on a spit, or pampered Maremma beef in *spiedino toscano* (mixed grill). Another must for carnivores is the tender, hulking *bistecca alla fiorentina,* the bone-in steak served in slabs 'three fingers thick' at Florence's Trattoria Mario. Peasant soup (*acquacotta,* literally 'cooked water') becomes a royal feast in the Tuscan town of Lucca, with the addition of farm-fresh eggs, local *pecorino* cheese, toasted bread and Lucca's prized golden olive oil.

In neighbouring Umbria, locals can be found foraging alongside the local boars for wild asparagus, mushrooms and legendary black truffles – grate some atop fresh *tagliatelle* egg pasta to discover one of the most instantly addictive flavours on the planet.

Quale Vino? Which Wine?

At a sit-down lunch or dinner, the question isn't whether you're having wine, but which one of Italy's hundreds of speciality wines will best complement the cuisine. When in doubt, keep it local: below are wines to watch for in each region.

Rome & Around Est! Est!! Est!!! (dry herbal/mineral white)

Venice & Verona *Prosecco* (Italy's most popular sparkling white), Amarone (dark, brooding red with velvety tannins), Soave (crisp, minerally white), Tocai (unctuous, fruity/floral white), Valpolicella (versatile, medium-bodied red)

Bologna Lambrusco (sparkling red)

Milan & the Lakes Franciacorta (Italy's top-quality sparkling white), Bardolino (light, satiny red)

Piedmont & Around Barolo (Italy's favourite red; elegant and structured), Asti (aka Asti Spumante; sparkling white), Cinque Terre (minerally/grassy white), Gavi (dry, aromatic white), Barbera d'Alba (pleasantly acidic, tomato-friendly red), Dolcetto (light-hearted, aromatic red), Sciacchetrá (Cinque Terre's aromatic dessert wine)

Tuscany Chianti Classico (big-hearted red, earthy character), Brunello di Montalcino (Italy's biggest, most complex vintage red), Super Tuscan IGT (bombastic, Sangiovese-based reds), Morellino di Scansano (floral, medium-weight red)

Umbria Orvieto (light, grassy/floral white), Sagrantino di Montefalco secco (dry, oak-barrel-aged Perugian red)

Naples & the Amalfi Coast Falanghina (dry, minerally white)

Sicily Marsala (sweet fortified wine), Nero d'Avola (volcanic, mineral red)

Naples & the Amalfi Coast

Sun-soaked Mediterranean flavours sparkle in Naples and its coastal turf, where hot capsicums (peppers), citrus and prized San Marzano tomatoes thrive in the volcanic soils that buried Pompeii. Local buffalo-milk mozzarella with basil and tomato sauce piled on pizza dough makes Naples' most famous export: pizza *margherita*. In Naples' *centro storico* (historic centre) you'll find sublime street food in historic *friggitorie* (fast-food kiosks), from *arancini* (mozzarella-filled rice balls) to tempura-style eggplant. Naples was the playground of French conquerors and Spanish royalty, whose influence is savoured in *sfogliatelle* (pastries filled with cinnamon-laced ricotta) and *rum baba,* French rum cake made Neapolitan with Vesuvius-like eruptions of cream.

South of Naples, you'll know you're approaching the Amalfi Coast when you get a whiff of perfumed Amalfi lemons. The local citrus stars alongside the day's seafood catch and in *limoncello,* Amalfi's sweet lemon digestive.

Sicily & Southern Italy

Born of the *cucina povera* (cooking of the poor), Pugliese fare harbours immense riches. Taste the delights of the local *burrata*, a creamier take on mozzarella, and try dishes that make the most of the fresh local seafood, such as *strascinati con la mollica* (pasta with breadcrumbs and anchovies) and *riso cozze patate* (baked rice, potatoes and mussels). Ancient Arab influences make Sicily's pasta dishes velvety and complex,

and make this one of the best places in Italy to eat dessert. Wild-caught tuna baked in a salt crust, local-anchovy-studded *fiori di zucca ripieni* (cheese-stuffed squash blossoms) and *arancini siciliani* (risotto balls) may forever spoil you for lesser versions.

Begin southern food adventures at Catania's La Pescheria, the legendary fish market, and look out for Sicilian *dolci* (sweets) that include pistachio gelato and sculpted marzipan. Save some room for Puglia, which rivals Lucca for the title of Italy's most satisfying peasant cuisine and takes the prize for Italy's crustiest bread.

Menu Decoder

Tutti a tavola! (Everyone to the table!) This is one command every Italian heeds without question. To disobey would be unthinkable – what, you're going to eat your pasta cold? And insult the cook? Even anarchists wouldn't dream of it. You're not obliged to eat three courses – or even two – but here is a rundown of your menu options.

Antipasti (Appetiser)

Tantalising offerings on the antipasti menu may include the house bruschetta (grilled bread with a variety of toppings, from chopped tomato and garlic to black-truffle spread), seasonal treats such as *prosciutto e melone* (cured ham and cantaloupe) and regional delights including *friarelle con peperoncino* (Neapolitan broccoli with chilli). At this stage, bread (and sometimes *grissini* – Turin-style breadsticks) are deposited on the table as part of your €1 to €4 *pane e coperto* (bread and 'cover', or table service).

Primo (First Course)

Starch is the star in Italian first courses, including pasta and gnocchi (especially in south and central Italy), risotto and polenta (northern Italian specialities). *Primi* menus usually include ostensibly vegetarian or vegan options, such as pasta *con pesto* – the

Vineyards, Chianti (p253)
DAMIEN SIMONIS/GETTY IMAGES ©

classic northwestern basil pasta with *parmigiano reggiano* (Parmesan) and pine nuts – or *alla Norma* (with eggplant and tomato, Sicilian style), or the extravagant *risotto al Barolo* (Piedmont risotto cooked in high-end Barolo wine). But even if a dish sounds vegetarian in theory, ask about the stock used in that risotto or polenta, or the ingredients in that suspiciously rich tomato sauce – there may be beef, ham or ground anchovies involved.

Secondo (Second Course)

Light lunchers usually call it a day after the *primo,* or skip the *primo* and just opt for a *secondo*. But if you're up for a long meal, you can follow the *primo* with meat, fish or *contorni* (side dishes) in the second course. Options may range from ambitious meats (especially in Tuscany and Rome) and elegant seafood (notably in Venice and Sicily) to lightly grilled vegetables such as *radicchio di Treviso* (feathery red rocket). A less inspiring option is *insalata mista* (mixed green salad), typically unadorned greens with vinegar and oil on the side – croutons, cheeses, nuts and other ingredients have no business in classic Italian salads.

Frutti e dolci (Fruit & Sweets)

'Siamo arrivati alla frutta' ('We've arrived at the fruit') is an idiom roughly meaning 'we've hit rock bottom' – but hey, not until you've had one last tasty morsel. Your best bets on the fruit menu are local and seasonal. *Formaggi* (cheeses) are an excellent option in Piedmont, but in the south, do the *dolci* (sweets). *Biscotti* (twice-baked biscuits) are divine dunked in wine, and consider *zabaglione* (egg and Marsala custard), tiramisu (literally 'pick me up', combining eggs, marscapone, coffee and Marsala wine), cream-stuffed profiteroles or Sicily's cream-stuffed shell pastries immortalised in *The Godfather:* 'Leave the gun. Take the *cannoli.'*

Caffè (Coffee)

Snoozing rather than sightseeing will be most attractive after a proper Italian lunch, so if you want to get things done, it's advisable to administer espresso as a final flourish. *Cappuccini* (named after the colour of Capuchin monks' habits) are usually only drunk in the morning, before around 11am, but later in the day you could indulge in an espresso with a tiny stain of milk in a *caffè macchiato*. On the hottest days of summer, a *granita di caffè* (coffee with shaved ice and whipped cream) is just the ticket.

The Best...
Wine & Cooking Courses

1 **Città del Gusto** (www.gamberorosso.it)

2 **Italian Food Artisans** (www.foodartisans.com/workshops)

3 **International Wine Academy of Roma** (www.wineacademyroma.com)

4 **Culinary Adventures** (www.peggymarkel.com)

Lifestyle

Coffee bar, Milan (p120)

MARK HORN / GETTY IMAGES

Imagine your own Freaky Friday moment: you wake up and discover you're Italian. Not that it's obvious at first – your pyjamas just have a subtly more elegant cut. But when you open your wardrobe, there's the dead giveaway: the shoes. What might it be like walking in those butter-soft, richly coloured shoes for the day, and what could you discover about Italy?

A Day in the Life of Italy

Sveglia! You're woken not by an alarm but by the burble and clatter of the *caffetiera,* the ubiquitous stovetop espresso maker. If you're between the ages of 18 and 34, there's a 60% chance that's not a roommate making your morning coffee: it's *mamma* or *papá.* This is not because Italy is a nation of pampered *mammoni* (mama's boys) and spoilt *figlie di papá* (daddy's girls) – at least, not entirely. With youth unemployment hitting 42% and many university graduates underemployed in short-term contracts, what's the hurry to leave home?

Running late, you bolt down your coffee scalding hot (an acquired Italian talent) and walk blocks out of your way for a morning paper from Bucharest-born Nicolae – your favourite news vendor and (as a Romanian) part of Italy's largest migrant community.

On your way to work you scan the headlines: the scoop on Berlusconi's latest trial, corruption allegations at another local council, today's match-fixing scandal and new EU regulations on cheese. Outrageous! The cheese regulations, that is; the rest is to be expected. At work, you're buried in paperwork until noon, when it's a relief to join friends for lunch and a glass of wine.

Afterwards you toss back another scorching espresso at your favourite bar, and find out how your barista's latest audition went – turns out you went to school with the sister of the director of the play, so you promise to put in a good word. This isn't just a nice gesture, but an essential career boost. As a Ministry of Labour study recently revealed, most people in Italy still find employment through personal connections. About 30% of Italians have landed a job through family connections, and in highly paid professions, that number rises as high as 40% to 50%. In Europe's most ancient, entrenched bureaucracy, social networks are also essential to get things done: on average, Italians spend the equivalent of two weeks annually on bureaucratic procedures required of working Italian citizens.

Back at work by 2pm, you multitask Italian-style, chatting with co-workers as you dash off work emails, text your schoolmate about the barista on your *telefonino* (mobile phone), and surreptitiously check *l'Internet* for employment listings – your work contract will expire soon. After a busy day like this, *aperitivi* are definitely in order, so at 6.30pm you head directly to the latest happy-hour hot spot. The decor is very stylish, the vibe very cool and the DJ extra hot, until suddenly it's time for your English class – everyone's learning it these days, if only for the slang.

The People

Who are the people you'd encounter every day as an Italian? On average, about half your co-workers will be women – quite a change from 10 years ago, when women represented just a quarter of the workforce. But a growing proportion of the people you'll meet are already retired: one out of five Italians is over 65. You might also notice a striking absence of children. Italy's birth rate is the lowest in Europe, at 1.2 children per woman.

Like Nicolae the news vendor, 8.2% of Italy's population today are non-EU immigrants. Though this is a relatively small number in global terms, it's a reversal of a historical trend: from 1876 to 1976, Italy was a country of net emigration. With some 30 million Italian emigrants dispersed throughout Europe, the Americas and Australia, remittances from Italians abroad helped keep Italy's economy afloat after Independence and WWII.

Political and economic upheavals in the 1980s brought new arrivals to Italy from Central Europe, Latin America and North Africa – including Italy's former colonies in Tunisia, Somalia and Ethiopia – while recent arrivals hail from the Philippines, China and Bangladesh. These new arrivals are vital for the country's economic health. Fewer Italians are entering blue-collar agricultural and industrial fields, so without immigrant workers to fill the gaps, Italy would be sorely lacking in tomato sauce and shoes. By filling low-paid service positions such as restaurant dishwashers and hotel maids, immigrants also keep Italy's vital tourism economy afloat. At the same time, Italians continue to seek their fortunes elsewhere, with 4.3 million Italians living abroad.

But not all Italians are putting out their welcome mats in return. In 2010 the shooting of an immigrant worker in Rosarno, Calabria, sparked Italy's worst race riots in years. In 2013 the entrenched racism in some parts of the establishment were also underlined when the deputy speaker of the Italian Senate, Roberto Calderoli, a leading member of the Northern League, compared Italy's first black minister (for Integration) Cecile Kyenge to an orangutan. His remarks sparked widespread condemnation.

In 2013 Pope Francis travelled to Lampedusa to weep for African refugees lost at sea. As writer Claudio Magris once observed in *The Times,* recalling Italy's recent past as a nation of emigrants, 'We, above all, should know what it is like to be strangers in a strange land'.

Religion, Loosely Speaking

Although you read about the Church in the news headlines, you didn't actually attend Mass on your day as an Italian. According to the most recent Church studies, only 15% of Italy's population regularly attends Sunday mass – yet when Pope John Paul II died in April 2005, four million mourners poured into Rome in one week, and around 150,000 descended to attend Pope Francis' inaugural mass in 2013.

The Church remains a cultural force, from the relief work of Caritas (Catholic charity) to boisterous celebrations of Christmas and Easter – no generic 'happy holidays' wishes here – plus myriad festivals organised around patron saints. Every year in Naples, thousands cram into the Duomo to witness the ancient blood of San Gennaro miraculously liquefy in the crystal vial that contains it. When the blood turns

RICHARD I'ANSON/GETTY IMAG

Football fans, Milan (p120)

'Enough!' Say Italian Women

Italian women took to the streets nationwide in 2012 to protest against priest Piero Corsi who posted a letter on a church door blaming female provocation – in both dress and behaviour – for domestic abuse. In 2011 nearly one million Italian women took to the streets, carrying signs with an unequivocal message: *Basta!* (Enough!) Sparked by allegations that Prime Minister Silvio Berlusconi had held sex parties with an underage dancer, they not only demanded his dismissal, but also an end to representation of women on Berlusconi-backed Italian media as hovering mothers or vapid *veline* (showgirls).

Unlike their popular image in Italian media, Italian women are notably accomplished. They represent 65% of college graduates, are more likely than men to pursue higher education (53% to 45%) and twice as likely to land responsible positions in public service. Yet the World Economic Forum's 2012 Global Gender Gap Report ranked Italy 80th overall for its treatment of women, well below countries such as Mozambique (23rd) and Kazakhstan (31st).

The situation isn't necessarily better at home: the latest figures from the OECD found that Italian men enjoy around an hour more leisure time daily than their female counterparts. Despite the indulgent mamma stereotype, not all Italian women relish the extra housework. According to official statistics, Italian women aged 29 to 34 are increasingly choosing careers and a home life without children. When Italian women take time out of their demanding schedules to say *basta!*, you better believe it.

from powdery to watery, the city breathes a sigh of relief – it symbolises another year safe from disaster. When it didn't in 1944, Mt Vesuvius erupted. Coincidence? Perhaps. But even the most cynical Neapolitan would rather see San Gennaro's blood wet than dry... just in case.

Italy's Other Religion: Calcio

As an Italian, your true religion is likely to be *calcio* (soccer, aka English football).

In the late 19th century, English factory barons of Turin, Genoa and Milan established teams to keep their workers fit – though during World Cups, UK supporters may wish they'd never shown the Italians how it's done. Not that it's always a fair fight: according to French forward Zinedine Zidane, Italian opponent Marco Materazzi insulted the womenfolk of his family during the 2006 World Cup finals. Zidane was red-carded for violently defending his family's honour; Italy won the Cup. The same year, match-fixing 'Calciopoli' scandals resulted in revoked championship titles and temporary demotion of Serie A (top-tier national) teams, including the mighty Juventus.

Scandals and all, Italians have an almost literal romance with their national sport. Rita Pavone's song *La partita di pallone* (The football match) topped the charts in the 1960s with a refrain that resonated nationwide: '*Perchè, perchè la domenica mi lasci sempre sola per andare a vedere la partita di pallone?*' (Why, why do you always leave me alone on Sunday so you can go and watch the football match?). That said, nine months after Italy's 2006 World Cup victory against France, hospitals in northern Italy reported a baby boom.

Outdoor Experiences

Aosta (p154)

GARETH MCCORMACK / GETTY IMAGES

Naturally blessed with rolling hills, mountain peaks, volcanic lakes and 7600km of coastline, Italy offers much more than Roman ruins and Renaissance art. Adrenaline spikes come with stirring views here: there's swimming and windsurfing in the Lakes, mountain biking and skiing in the Dolomites, and volcano summits and scuba diving in Sicily. Less daunting, Tuscany's rolling landscapes offer scenic cycling between vineyards, and Capri and the Amalfi Coast offer blissful snorkelling.

Hiking & Walking

Thousands of kilometres of *sentieri* (marked trails) criss-cross the peninsula, from mountain treks to lakeside ambles. For coastal hikes with varied challenge levels and sweeping views, don't miss Cinque Terre. Most people may think of Capri as a summer playground, but it offers fantastic walking trails away from beach crowds. The Amalfi Coast is laced with age-old paths winding through wooded mountains and ancient olive groves.

The prime volcano hike is Sicily's Mt Etna, and on the Sicilian Aeolian Island of Vulcano, you can descend to an extinct volcano's crater floor. The jagged peaks of Veneto's Dolomites provide superb walking from the end of June to September, and trails are lined with wildflowers in spring –

no wonder Unesco declared this unique mountain ecosystem a World Heritage Site in 2009.

Tourist offices and visitor centres provide some information resources and basic maps for easier tourist routes. For longer hikes and climbing information on the Dolomites, consult Club Alpino Italiano (www.cai.it).

Skiing

Most of Italy's top ski resorts are in the northern Alps. Facilities at the bigger centres in the Dolomites and around Aosta are generally world-class, with pistes ranging from nursery slopes to tough black runs.

The ski season runs from December to late March, although there is year-round skiing on Mont Blanc (Monte Bianco) and the Matterhorn in the Valle d'Aosta.

Cycling

Whether you want a gentle ride between trattorias, a 100km road race or a teeth-rattling mountain descent, you'll find a route to suit in Italy. Tourist offices can provide details on trails and guided rides, and Lonely Planet's *Cycling Italy* is handy.

Tuscany's famously rolling countryside is a favourite with cyclists, particularly the wine-producing Chianti area south of Florence. Further north, Piedmont's terraced vineyards of Barolo are also ideal for pedal-powered wine-tasting.

Puglia's rolling countryside and coastal paths make moderate challenges, while the Dolomites are a prime spot for summer mountain-biking.

Diving

Diving is one of Italy's most popular summer pursuits, and there are hundreds of schools that offer a wide range of courses, dives for all levels, and equipment for hire. Most diving schools open seasonally from June to October – but try to avoid August, when the Italian coast is swamped with visitors and prices are inflated. Information is available from local tourist offices and online at DiveItaly (www.diveitaly.com).

Prime Italian diving destinations include Sicily's Aeolian Islands, with warm waters and sea grottoes around inactive volcanoes. In the Bay of Naples, the areas around the islands of Capri, Ischia and Procida offer exceptional diving and underwater photo ops in glowing sea grottoes. To the north, Cinque Terre Marine Reserve teems with life around ancient pirate's coves.

The Best...
Cycling
Destinations

1 Chianti (p253)

2 Via Appia Antica (p81)

3 Lucca (p246)

4 Barolo (p151)

5 Bologna (p205)

Fashion & Design

Milan (p120)

JACQUES PIERRE / GETTY IMAG

Better living by design: what could be more Italian? Though the country could get by on its striking good looks, Italy is ever-mindful of design details. They are everywhere you look, and many places you don't: the acid-yellow silk lining inside a sober grey suit sleeve, the glove compartment of a newly re-issued Fiat 500, the toy duck hidden inside your chocolate uova di pasqua (Easter egg).

Italian Fashion

Italians have strong opinions about aesthetics and aren't afraid to share them. A common refrain is *Che brutta!* (How hideous!), which may strike visitors as tactless. But consider it from an Italian point of view – everyone is rooting for you to look good, and who are you to disappoint? The shop assistant who tells you with brutal honesty that yellow is not your colour is doing a public service, and will consider it a personal triumph to see you outfitted in orange instead. After all, Italy's centuries-old reputation for style is at stake.

Trend-Setters & Fashion Victims

Italians have been style trend-setters since the Middle Ages, when Venetian merchants imported dyes and silks from the East, and Florence's wool guild rose to political prominence and funded a Renaissance. Clothes became markers of social status, and not only nobles set trends: courtesans and trophy wives were so widely imitated that sumptuary laws were passed restricting low necklines and growing train lengths. Italy's local fashions went global through the dissemination of Florentine art and illustrated pamphlets from Venice's publishing houses – predecessors of billboards and Italian *Vogue*. The Venetian innovation of eyeglasses was initially mocked by monocle-sporting English dandies, who eventually saw the light – and their descendants now pay impressive sums for Italian designer sunglasses.

Italy has also had its share of fashion victims over the centuries. After political crusader Savonarola demanded Florentines surrender their extravagant statement jewellery under pain of flagellation, he was burned at the stake. So many Venetian noblewomen were hobbled emulating courtesans in their staggering platform heels that 1430 sumptuary laws set maximum shoe heights of around 2ft. Siena was more practical, requiring its prostitutes to wear flat shoes. Today, staggering platforms and chic flats still make the rounds of Milan runways.

The Best... Italian Design Icons

1 Bialetti *caffetiera*

2 Cinzano vermouth

3 Acqua di Parma cologne

4 Piaggio Vespa

5 Olivetti 'Valentine' typewriter

Italy's Fashion Powerhouses

Cobblers and tailors in Florence who once made only made-to-measure designs began to present seasonal lines in the 1950s to '60s, launching the empires of psychedelic-print maestro Emilio Pucci, logoed leather-goods magnate Guccio Gucci and shoe maven Salvatore Ferragamo. But Milan literally stole the show from Florence in 1958, hosting Italy's first Fashion Week. With its ready factories, cosmopolitan workforce and long-established media, Milan created ready-to-wear fashion for global markets from Armani, Missoni, Versace, Dolce & Gabbana and Prada. Rome remains Italy's political capitol and the home of Valentino and his signature red dress, but Milan was Italy's top (and the world's fourth-biggest) fashion exporter in 2011.

Today, Italian fashionistas are combining mass fashion with artisan-made style signatures. This trend is recession-friendly: artisan-made items are made to last and singular, hence less trend-sensitive. Fashion-forward artisan hot spots include Florence (cobblers and jewellers), Naples (tailors) and Venice (eyewear, fashion and accessories).

Bargain Fashion

Never mind the recession: Italians still rock Missoni knitwear, Fendi bags, Prada shoes and Gucci shades. Their fashion secret: annual *saldi* (sales) in January and July, offering 30% to 50% discounts. Year-round, Italians hit up discount outlets outside Milan, Florence and Rome. Some hunt down bargains at outdoor markets such as Rome's Porta Portese and Naples' Mercato Nolano where they'll find factory seconds and vintage finds.

Modern Italian Design

During centuries of domination by Napoleon and other foreign powers, Italy ceded ground as global taste-maker to French and Austrian art nouveau and English Arts and Crafts – until the industrial era. Italian futurism inspired radical, neoclassical streamlining more suited to Italian manufacturers than French decorators or English craftspeople. The dynamic deco style of futurist paintings was co-opted in Fascist propaganda posters, architecture, furniture and design, like cogs in a political machine.

The rise of Fascism required modern factories for the war industry, and after WWII, repurposed military industrial complexes in Turin and Milan became centrepieces of a new global, consumer-centric economy. Turin's strength was industrial design, from Lavazza espresso machines to the Fiat 500 car; Milan focused on fashion and home decor. As seen in Italian film and pioneering Italian lifestyle magazines such as *Domus*, Italy's mass-produced design objects seemed both aspirational and attainable.

Design Showcases

Though Italian design is distributed globally, seeing it in its home context offers fresh appreciation – and critical perspective. While the Vatican Museums showcase pre-20th-century objects of power – from saints' reliquaries to papal thrones – Milan's Triennale Museum focuses on 20th-century secular talismans, including mid-century Vespas to 1980s Memphis Group chairs. Like churches, Italian designer showcases are carefully curated to offer beauty and belonging, from the 1950s Scarpa-designed Olivetti showroom in Venice's Piazza San Marco to Alessi's new flagship store in Milan – but this fully branded lifestyle can seem impersonal. Milan's Salone del Mobile is the world's largest design fair, with 2500 companies represented – yet differences in corporate design can seem slight, and easily outshone by 700 independent designers in the satellite fair.

Fiat 500
ANGELA SORRENTINO / GETTY IMAGES ©

Survival
Guide

Cannoli
FABIO BIANCHINI/GETTY IMAGES ©

Directory

●●●

Accommodation

Accommodation in Italy can range from the sublime to the ridiculous with prices to match. The options are incredibly varied, from family-run *pensioni* and designer hotels, to characterful B&Bs, serviced apartments, *agriturismi* (farmstays), and even *rifugi* (mountain huts) for weary mountain trekkers. Capturing the imagination even more are options spanning luxurious country villas and castles, tranquil convents and monasteries.

Prices

Accommodation rates can fluctuate enormously depending on the season, with Easter, summer and the Christmas/New Year period being the typical peak tourist times. Prices also vary seasonally according to location. Expect to pay top prices in the mountains during the ski season (December to March) or along the coast in summer (July and August). Conversely, summer in the parched cities can equal low season; in August especially, many city hotels charge as little as half price.

Price also depends greatly on location. A bottom-end budget choice in Venice or Milan will set you back the price of a decent midrange option in, say, rural Campania. Where possible, we present the high-season rates for each accommodation option. Half-board equals breakfast and either lunch or dinner; full board includes breakfast, lunch and dinner.

B&Bs

B&Bs are a burgeoning sector of the Italian accommodation market and can be found throughout the country in both urban and rural settings. Options include everything from restored farmhouses, city *palazzi* (mansions) and seaside bungalows to rooms in family houses. Tariffs per person cover a wide range, from around €30 to €100. For more information see **Bed & Breakfast Italia** (www. bbitalia.it).

Convents & Monasteries

Some Italian convents and monasteries let out cells or rooms as a modest revenue-making exercise and happily take in tourists, while others only take in pilgrims or people who are on a spiritual retreat. Many impose a fairly early curfew, but prices tend to be quite reasonable.

A useful if ageing publication is Eileen Barish's *The Guide to Lodging in Italy's Monasteries*. A more recent book on the same subject is Charles M Shelton's *Beds and Blessings in Italy: A Guide to Religious Hospitality*. Other resources that can assist you in your search include:

MonasteryStays.com (www.monasterystays.com) A well-organised online booking centre for monastery and convent stays.

In Italy Online (www.initaly. com/agri/convents.htm) This website is well worth a look for monastery and convent accommodations in Abruzzo, Emilia-Romagna, Lazio, Liguria, Lombardy, Puglia, Sardinia, Sicily, Tuscany, Umbria and the Veneto. You pay US$6 to access the online newsletter, which contains all the addresses.

Chiesa di Santa Susana (www.santasusanna.org/comingtorome/convents.html) This American Catholic church in Rome has searched out convent and monastery accommodation options around the country and posted a list on its website. Note that some places are just residential

---

Book Your Stay Online

For more accommodation reviews by Lonely Planet authors, check out http://hotels. lonelyplanet.com. You'll find independent reviews, as well as recommendations on the best places to stay. Best of all, you can book online.

accommodation run by religious orders and not necessarily big on monastic atmosphere. The church doesn't handle bookings; to request a spot, you'll need to contact each individual institution directly.

Hotels & Pensioni

While the difference between an *albergo* (hotel) and a *pensione* is often minimal, a *pensione* will generally be of one- to three-star quality while an *albergo* can be awarded up to five stars. *Locande* (inns) previously fell into much the same category as *pensioni*, but the term has become a trendy one in some regions and can reveal little about the quality of an establishment. *Affittacamere* are rooms for rent in private houses. They are generally simple affairs.

Quality can vary enormously and the official star system gives limited clues. One-star hotels/*pensioni* tend to be basic and usually do not offer private bathrooms. Two-star places are similar but rooms will generally have a private bathroom. Three-star options usually offer reasonable standards. Four- and five-star hotels offer facilities such as room service, laundry and dry-cleaning.

Prices are highest in major tourist destinations. They also tend to be higher in northern Italy. A *camera singola* (single room) costs from €30. A *camera doppia* (twin beds) or *camera matrimoniale* (double room with a double bed) will cost from around €50.

Tourist offices usually have booklets with local accommodation listings. Many hotels are also signing up with (steadily proliferating) online accommodation-booking services. You could start your search here:

Alberghi in Italia (www. alberghi-in-italia.it)

All Hotels in Italy (www. hotelsitalyonline.com)

Hotels web.it (www. hotelsweb.it)

In Italia (www.initalia.it)

Travel to Italy (www.travel-to-italy.com)

Villas

Cuendet (www.cuendet. com) One of the old hands in this business; operates from Mestre, just outside Venice.

Ilios Travel (www.iliostravel. com) UK-based company with villas and apartments in Venice, Tuscany, Umbria, Lazio, Le Marche, Abruzzo and Campania.

Invitation to Tuscany (www.invitationtotuscany.com) Wide range of properties, with a strong focus on Tuscany.

Summer's Leases (www. summerleases.com) Properties in Tuscany and Umbria.

Long Travel (www.long-travel. co.uk) Specialises in Puglia, Sicily, Sardinia and other regions.

Think Sicily (www.thinksicily. com) Strictly Sicilian properties.

Cottages to Castles (www. cottagestocastles.com) UK-based operator specialising in villas.

Parker Villas (www. parkervillas.co.uk) Despite the UK web address, this is a US-based agency with an Italian office, offering exclusive listings of villas all over Italy.

Sleeping Price Ranges

The following price ranges refer to a double room with bathroom (breakfast not included) in high season.

	REST OF ITALY	ROME	VENICE
€	less than €110	€120	€120
€€	€110-200	€120-250	€120-220
€€€	more than €200	€250	€220

●●●
Customs Regulations

Anything over the following limits must be declared on arrival and the appropriate duty paid. On leaving the EU, non-EU citizens can reclaim any VAT on expensive purchases.

Duty-Free Allowances

Spirits	1L
Perfume	50g
Eau de toilette	250mL
Cigarettes	200
Other goods	up to a total value of €175

Duty-free sales within the EU no longer exist, but visitors coming into Italy from non-EU countries can import the above items duty free.

●●●
Discount Cards

Free admission to many galleries and tourist sites is available to those under 18 and over 65 years old; visitors aged between 18 and 25 often qualify for a 50% discount. In some cases, these discounts only apply to EU citizens.

In many places around Italy, you can also save money by purchasing a *biglietto cumulativo*, which allows admission to a number of associated sights for less than the combined admission fees.

●●●
Electricity

Electricity in Italy conforms to the European standard of 220V to 230V, with a frequency of 50Hz. Wall outlets typically accommodate plugs with two or three round pins (the latter grounded, the former not).

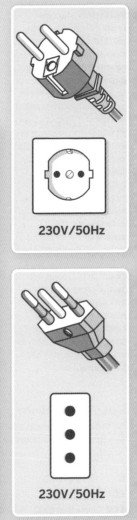

230V/50Hz

230V/50Hz

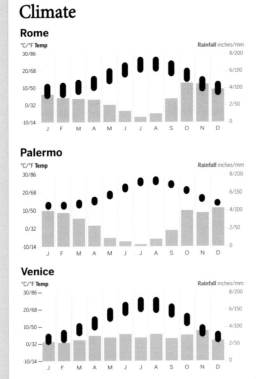

Climate

Rome

°C/°F Temp   Rainfall inches/mm

30/86 — 8/200
20/68 — 6/150
10/50 — 4/100
0/32 — 2/50
-10/14 — 0

J F M A M J J A S O N D

Palermo

°C/°F Temp   Rainfall inches/mm

30/86 — 8/200
20/68 — 6/150
10/50 — 4/100
0/32 — 2/50
-10/14 — 0

J F M A M J J A S O N D

Venice

°C/°F Temp   Rainfall inches/mm

30/86 — 8/200
20/68 — 6/150
10/50 — 4/100
0/32 — 2/50
-10/14 — 0

J F M A M J J A S O N D

Food

Note that most eating establishments add *coperto* (cover charge) of around €2 to €3. Some also include a service charge *(servizio)* of 10% to 15%.

Eating Price Ranges

The following price ranges refer to a meal of two courses, a glass of house wine, and *coperto* for one person.

€	under €25
€€	€25-45
€€€	over €45

These figures represent a halfway point between expensive cities such as Milan and Venice and the considerably cheaper towns across the south. Indeed, a restaurant rated as midrange in rural Sicily might be considered dirt cheap in Milan.

Gay & Lesbian Travellers

Homosexuality is legal in Italy and well tolerated in the major cities. Overt displays of affection by homosexual couples, however, could attract a negative response in the more conservative south and in smaller towns.

There are gay clubs in Rome, Milan and Bologna, and a handful in places such as Florence and Naples. Some coastal towns and resorts (such as the Viareggio in Tuscany or Taormina in Sicily) have more action in summer.

See the following resources for more information:

Practicalities

- **Weights and measurements** Metric

- **Smoking** Banned in all enclosed public spaces

- **Newspapers** The major national dailies are centre-left; try Rome-based *La Republicca*, and the liberal-conservative, Milan-based *Corriere della Sera*.

- **Radio** Tune into Vatican Radio (www.radiovaticana.org; 93.3 FM and 105 FM in the Rome area; in Italian, English and other languages) for a rundown of what the pope is up to; or state-owned Italian RAI-1, RAI-2 and RAI-3 (www.rai.it), which broadcast all over the country and abroad. Commercial stations such as Rome's Radio **Centro Suono** (www.centrosuono.com) and **Radio Città Futura** (www.radiocittafutura.it), Naples' Radio **Kiss Kiss** (www.kisskissnapoli.it) and Milan-based left-wing Radio **Popolare** (www.radiopopolare.it) are all good for contemporary music.

- **TV** Channels include state-run RAI-1, RAI-2 and RAI-3 (www.rai.it) and the main commercial stations **Canale 5** (www.canale5.mediaset.it), **Italia 1** (www.italia1.mediaset.it) and **Rete 4** (www.rete4.mediaset.it), run by Silvio Berlusconi's Mediaset company, as well as **La 7** (www.la7.it)

Arcigay (www.arcigay.it) Bologna-based national organisation for the LGBTI community.

Circolo Mario Mieli (www.mariomieli.org) Rome-based cultural centre that publishes *Aut,* a free monthly covering news, culture and politics.

Gay.it (www.gay.it) Website featuring LGBT news, feature articles and gossip.

Pride (www.prideonline.it) National monthly magazine of art, politics and gay culture.

Health

Required Vaccinations

No jabs are required to travel to Italy. Though the World Health Organization (WHO) recommends that all travellers should be covered for diphtheria, tetanus, the measles, mumps, rubella, polio and hepatitis B.

Health Insurance

If you're an EU citizen (or from Switzerland, Norway or Iceland), a European Health Insurance Card (EHIC) covers you for medical care in public hospitals free of charge, but not for private medical care or emergency repatriation. For more information, see http://ec.europa.eu/social/main.jsp?langId=en&catId=559. Citizens from other countries should find out if there is a reciprocal arrangement for free medical care between their country and Italy (Australia, for instance, has such an agreement; carry your Medicare card).

If you do need health insurance, make sure you get a policy that covers you for the worst possible scenario, such as an accident requiring an emergency flight home. Find out in advance if your insurance plan will make payments directly to providers or reimburse you later for overseas health expenditures.

Availability of Health Care

Health care is readily available throughout Italy, but standards can vary significantly. Public hospitals tend to be less impressive the further south you travel. Pharmacists can give you valuable advice and sell over-the-counter medication for minor illnesses.

Pharmacies generally keep the same hours as other shops, closing at night and on Sundays. However, a handful remain open on a rotation basis (*farmacie di turno*) for emergency purposes. Closed pharmacies display a list of the nearest ones open.

If you need an ambulance in Italy call ☎118. For emergency treatment, head straight to the *pronto soccorso* (casualty) section of a public hospital, where you can also get emergency dental treatment.

Insurance

A travel-insurance policy to cover theft, loss and medical problems is a very good idea. It may also cover you for cancellation or delays to your travel arrangements. Paying for your ticket with a credit card can often provide limited travel accident insurance and you may

be able to reclaim the payment if the operator doesn't deliver. Ask your credit-card company what it will cover.

Worldwide travel insurance is available at www.lonelyplanet.com/travel-insurance. You can buy, extend and claim online anytime – even if you're already on the road.

Internet Access

○ Internet access in Italy has improved markedly in the past couple of years, with Rome, Bologna, Venice and other municipalities instituting city-wide hot spots.

○ On the downside, public wi-fi and internet cafes (€2 to €6 per hour) remain thinner on the ground than elsewhere in Europe, signal strength is variable, and access is not yet as widespread in rural and southern Italy as in urban and northern areas.

○ An ever-increasing number of hotels, B&Bs, hostels and even *agriturismi* offer free wi-fi. Unfortunately, you will still have to pay at many top-end hotels (upwards of €10 per day).

○ Some internet cafes will request ID before allowing you to use their facilities.

Legal Matters

The average tourist will only have a brush with the law if robbed by a bag-snatcher or pickpocket.

Police

If you run into trouble you're likely to end up dealing with

the *polizia statale* or the *carabinieri*. The former wear powder-blue trousers with a fuchsia stripe and a navy blue jacket, the latter wear black uniforms with a red stripe and drive dark-blue cars with a red stripe.

To contact the police in an emergency, dial ☎113.

Drugs & Alcohol

○ Under Italy's tough drug laws, possession of any controlled substances, including cannabis or marijuana, can get you into hot water. Those caught in possession of 5g of cannabis can be prosecuted as traffickers. The same applies to tiny amounts of other drugs. Those caught with amounts below this threshold can be subject to minor penalties.

○ The legal limit for blood-alcohol when driving is 0.05% and random breath tests do occur.

Your Rights

○ You should be given verbal and written notice of the charges laid against you within 24 hours by arresting officers.

○ You have no right to a phone call upon arrest.

○ The prosecutor must apply to a magistrate for you to be held in preventive custody awaiting trial (depending on the seriousness of the offence) within 48 hours of arrest.

○ You have the right not to respond to questions without the presence of a lawyer.

○ If the magistrate orders preventive custody, you have the right to then contest this within the following 10 days.

●●●
Money

The euro is Italy's currency. The seven euro notes come in denominations of €500, €200, €100, €50, €20, €10 and €5. The eight euro coins are in denominations of €2 and €1, and 50, 20, 10, five, two and one cents.

ATMs & Credit Cards

○ ATMs (called 'Bancomats') are widely available throughout Italy and the best way to obtain local currency. International credit and debit cards can be used in any ATM displaying the appropriate sign.

○ Visa and MasterCard are among the most widely recognised credit cards, but others like Cirrus and Maestro are also well covered. Only some banks give cash

advances over the counter, so you're better off using ATMs.

○ Cards are also good for payment in most hotels, restaurants, shops, supermarkets and tollbooths.

○ Check any charges with your bank. Most banks now build a fee of around 2.75% into every foreign transaction. In addition, ATM withdrawals can attract a further fee, usually around 1.5%.

If your card is lost, stolen or swallowed by an ATM, you can telephone toll-free to have an immediate stop put on its use:

Amex (📞 800 928391)

Diners Club (📞 800 393939)

MasterCard (📞 800 870866)

Visa (📞 800 819014)

Moneychangers

You can change money in banks, at the post office or in a *cambio* (exchange office). Post offices and banks tend to offer the best rates; exchange offices keep longer hours, but watch for high commissions and inferior rates.

Taxes & Refunds

A value-added tax of around 22%, known as IVA (Imposta di Valore Aggiunto), is slapped onto just about everything in Italy. If you are a non-EU resident and spend more than €155 (€154.94 to be more precise!) on a purchase, you can claim a refund when you leave. The refund only applies to purchases from affiliated retail outlets that display a 'tax free for tourists' (or similar) sign. You have to complete a form at the point of sale, then have it stamped by Italian customs

Opening Hours

BUSINESS TYPE	GENERAL HOURS	NOTES
Banks	8.30am-1.30pm & 3.30-4.30pm Mon-Fri	Exchange offices usually keep longer hours.
Central post offices	8am-7pm Mon-Fri, 8.30am-noon Sat	Smaller branch post offices often close at 2pm on weekdays.
Restaurants	noon-2.30pm & 7.30-11pm or midnight	Sometimes later in summer and in the south; kitchen often shuts an hour earlier than final closing time; most places close at least one day a week.
Cafes	7.30am-8pm	
Bars, pubs & clubs	10pm-4am	May open earlier if they have eateries on the premises; things don't get seriously shaking until after midnight.
Shops	9am-1pm & 3.30-7.30pm (or 4-8pm) Mon-Sat	In larger cities, department stores and supermarkets may stay open at lunchtime or on Sundays.

as you leave. At major airports you can get an immediate cash refund; otherwise it will be refunded to your credit card. For information, visit **Tax Refund for Tourists** (www.taxrefund.it) or pick up a pamphlet on the scheme from participating stores.

Tipping

Tipping is not generally expected nor demanded in Italy as it is in some other countries. This said, a discretionary tip for good service is appreciated in some circumstances. Use the following table as a guide.

PLACE	SUGGESTED TIP
Restaurant	10-15%, if service charge not included
Bar	€0.10-0.20 if drinking at bar, 10% for table service
Top-end hotel	€2, for porter, maid, room service
Taxi	Round up to the nearest euro

Public Holidays

Most Italians take their annual holiday in August, with the busiest period occurring around 15 August, known locally as Ferragosto. As a result, many businesses and shops close for at least part of that month. Settimana Santa (Easter Holy Week) is another busy holiday period for Italians. National public holidays include:

New Year's Day (Capodanno or Anno Nuovo) 1 January

Epiphany (Epifania) 6 January

Easter Monday (Pasquetta) March/April

Liberation Day (Giorno della Liberazione) 25 April

Labour Day (Festa del Lavoro) 1 May

Republic Day (Festa della Repubblica) 2 June

Feast of the Assumption (Assunzione or Ferragosto) 15 August

All Saints' Day (Ognissanti) 1 November

Feast of the Immaculate Conception (Immaculata Concezione) 8 December

Christmas Day (Natale) 25 December

Boxing Day (Festa di Santo Stefano) 26 December

Telephone

Directory Enquiries

National and international phone numbers can be requested at 📞1254 (or online at 1254.virgilio.it).

Domestic Calls

○ Italian telephone area codes all begin with 0 and consist of up to four digits. The area code is followed by anything from four to eight digits. The area code is an integral part of the telephone number and must always be dialled, even when calling from next door.

○ Mobile-phone numbers begin with a three-digit prefix such as 📞330.

○ Toll-free (free-phone) numbers are known as *numeri verdi* and usually start with 📞800.

○ Nongeographical numbers start with 📞840, 841, 848, 892, 899, 163, 166 or 199.

○ Some six-digit national rate numbers are also in use (such as those for Alitalia, rail and postal information).

As elsewhere in Europe, Italians choose from a host of providers of phone plans and rates, making it difficult to make generalisations about costs.

International Calls

○ The cheapest options for calling internationally are free or low-cost computer programs/smartphone apps such as Skype and Viber.

○ Cut-rate call centres, found in all of the main cities, are also a cheaper option. You simply place your call from a private booth inside the centre and pay for it when you've finished.

Important Numbers

Italy's country code 📞39

International access code 📞00

Ambulance 📞118

Police 📞113

Fire 📞115

- International calling cards, sold at newsstands and tobacconists, also offer cheaper call rates. They can be used at public telephones. Dial ☎ 00 to get out of Italy, then the relevant country and area codes, followed by the telephone number.

- To call Italy from abroad, call your international access number, then Italy's country code (☎ 39) and then the area code of the location you want, including the leading 0.

Mobile Phones

- Italy uses GSM 900/1800, compatible with the rest of Europe and Australia but not with North American GSM 1900 or the totally different Japanese system.

- Most modern smart phones are multiband, meaning that they are compatible with a variety of international networks. Before bringing your own phone to Italy, check with your service provider to make sure it is compatible, and beware of calls being routed internationally (very expensive for a 'local' call).

- Unlocking your phone for use with an Italian SIM card is often the cheapest option, but always check with your home mobile-service provider to ascertain whether your handset allows use of another SIM card.

- You can get a temporary or prepaid account from most phone company stores in Italy if you already own a GSM, multiband cellular phone (take your passport). Activating a local prepaid SIM card can cost as little as €10 (sometimes with €10 worth of calls on

the card). Pay-as-you-go SIM cards are also readily available at telephone and electronics stores throughout Italy.

- You can easily top up your Italian account with recharge cards (ricariche), available from most tobacconists, some bars, supermarkets and banks.

- Another option is to buy an inexpensive Italian phone for the duration of your trip.

- Of the main mobile phone companies, TIM (Telecom Italia Mobile), Wind and Vodafone have the densest networks of outlets across the country.

Payphones & Phonecards

- Telecom Italia is the largest communications organisation in Italy. Telecom payphones are commonly found on streets, in train stations and in Telecom offices.

- Most payphones accept only carte/schede telefoniche (phonecards), although some also accept credit cards.

- Telecom offers a wide range of prepaid cards for domestic and international use; for a full list, see www.telecomitalia.it/telefono/carte-telefoniche.

- You can buy phonecards (most commonly €3 or €5) at post offices, tobacconists and newsstands. Break off the top left-hand corner of the card before use. All phonecards have an expiry date, printed on the face of the card.

●●●
Time

- Italy is one hour ahead of GMT. When it is noon in London, it is 1pm in Italy.

- Daylight-saving time (when clocks are moved forward one hour) starts on the last Sunday in March and ends on the last Sunday in October.

- Italy operates on a 24-hour clock.

●●●
Tourist Information

There are four tiers of tourist office in Italy: local, provincial, regional and national.

Local & Provincial Tourist Offices

Despite their different names, provincial and local offices offer similar services. All deal directly with the public and most will respond to written and telephone requests for information. Staff can usually provide a city map, lists of hotels and information on the major sights. In larger towns and major tourist areas, English is generally spoken, along with other languages depending on the region (for example, German in Alto Adige, French in Valle d'Aosta).

Main offices are generally open Monday to Friday; some also open on weekends, especially in urban areas or during peak summer season. Affiliated information booths (at train stations and airports, for example) may keep slightly different hours.

Regional Tourist Authorities

Regional offices are generally more concerned with planning, budgeting, marketing and promotion than with offering a public information service. However, they still maintain some useful websites. In some cases you'll need to look for the Tourism or Turismo link within the regional site.

Abruzzo
(www.abruzzoturismo.it)

Basilicata
(www.aptbasilicata.it)

Calabria (www.turiscalabria.it)

Campania
(www.incampania.com)

Emilia-Romagna
(www.emiliaromagnaturismo.it)

Friuli Venezia Giulia
(www.turismo.fvg.it)

Lazio (www.ilmiolazio.it)

Le Marche
(www.le-marche.com)

Liguria
(www.turismoinliguria.it)

Lombardy (www.turismo.
regione.lombardia.it)

Molise (www.regione.molise.
it/turismo)

Piedmont
(www.piemonteitalia.eu)

Puglia
(www.viaggiareinpuglia.it)

Sardinia
(www.sardegnaturismo.it)

Sicily
(www.regione.sicilia.it/turismo)

Trentino-Alto Adige
(www.visittrentino.it)

Tuscany
(www.turismo.intoscana.it)

Umbria
(www.regioneumbria.eu)

Valle d'Aosta
(www.regione.vda.it/turismo)

Veneto (www.veneto.to)

Tourist Offices Abroad

The **Italian National Tourist Office** (ENIT; www.enit.it) maintains offices in 23 cities on five continents. Contact information for all offices can be found on its website.

●●●

Travellers with Disabilities

Italy is not an easy country for travellers with disabilities and getting around can be a problem for wheelchair users. Even a short journey in a city or town can become a major expedition if cobblestone streets have to be negotiated. Although many buildings have lifts, they are not always wide enough for wheelchairs. Not an awful lot has been done to make life for the deaf or blind any easier either.

The Italian National Tourist Office in your country may be able to provide advice on Italian associations for travellers with disabilities and information on what help is available.

Italy's national rail company, **Trenitalia** (☎199 303 060; www.trenitalia.com), offers a national helpline for passengers with disabilities (6.45am to 9.30pm daily).

A handful of cities also publish general guides on accessibility, among them Bologna, Milan, Padua, Reggio Emilia, Turin, Venice and

Verona. In Milan, **Milano per Tutti** (www.milanopertutti.it) is a helpful resource.

Some organisations that may help include the following:

Accessible Italy (☎378 94 11 11; www.accessibleitaly.com) A San Marino–based company that specialises in holiday services for people with disabilities. This is the best first port of call.

Cooperative Integrate Onlus (COIN; ☎06 712 90 11; www.coinsociale.it) Based in Rome, CO.IN provides information on the capital (including transport and access) and is happy to share its contacts throughout Italy.

Italia (www.italia.it) Italy's official tourism website offers a number of links for travellers with disabilities, covering destinations like Rome, Campania, Piedmont and the South Tyrol.

●●●

Visas

● European citizens whose country is part of the Schengen Treaty may enter Italy with nothing more than a valid identity card or passport.

● Residents of 28 non-EU countries, including Australia, Brazil, Canada, Israel, Japan, New Zealand and the USA, do not require visas for tourist visits of up to 90 days (this list varies for those wanting to travel to the UK and Ireland).

● All non-EU and non-Schengen nationals entering Italy for more than 90 days or for any reason other than tourism (such as study or work) may need a specific visa. See www.esteri.it/visti/home_eng.asp or contact an Italian consulate for details.

○ EU citizens do not require any permits to live or work in Italy but, after three months' residence, are supposed to register at the municipal registry office where they live and offer proof of work or sufficient funds to support themselves.

○ Non-EU foreign citizens with five years' continuous legal residence may apply for permanent residence.

Permesso di Soggiorno

○ Non-EU citizens planning to stay at the same address for more than one week are supposed to report to the police station to receive a *permesso di soggiorno* (a permit to remain in the country). Tourists staying in hotels are not required to do this.

○ A *permesso di soggiorno* only really becomes a necessity if you plan to study, work (legally) or live in Italy. Obtaining one is never a pleasant experience; it involves long queues and the frustration of arriving at the counter only to find you don't have the necessary documents.

○ The exact requirements, such as specific documents, are always subject to change. Updated requirements can be found online at www.poliziadistato.it (click on 'Foreign nationals').

○ EU citizens do not require a *permesso di soggiorno*.

●●●
Women Travellers

Italy is not a dangerous country for women to travel in. As with anywhere in the world, however, women travelling alone need to take certain precautions and, in some parts of the country, be prepared for more than their fair share of unwanted attention. Eye-to-eye contact is the norm in Italy's daily flirtatious interplay. Eye contact can become outright staring the further south you travel.

Lone women may find it difficult to remain alone. In many places, local Lotharios will try it on with exasperating insistence, which can be flattering or a pain. Foreign women are particular objects of male attention in tourist towns like Florence and more generally in the south. Usually the best response to undesired advances is to ignore them. If that doesn't work, politely tell your interlocutors you're waiting for your *marito* (husband) or *fidanzato* (boyfriend) and, if necessary, walk away. Avoid becoming aggressive as this may result in an unpleasant confrontation. If all else fails, approach the nearest member of the police.

Watch out for men with wandering hands on crowded buses. Either keep your back to the wall or make a loud fuss if someone starts fondling your behind. A loud '*Che schifo!*' (How disgusting!) will usually do the trick. If a more serious incident occurs, report it to the police, who are then required to press charges.

Transport

●●●
Getting There & Away

A plethora of airlines link Italy with the rest of the world, and cut-rate carriers have significantly driven down the cost of flights from other European countries. Excellent rail and bus connections, especially with northern Italy, offer efficient overland transport, while car and passenger ferries operate to ports throughout the Mediterranean. Flights, tours and rail tickets can be booked online at lonelyplanet.com/bookings.

Entering the Country

○ EU citizens can travel to Italy with their national identity card alone. All other nationalities must have a valid passport.

○ By law you are supposed to have your passport or ID card with you at all times. You'll need one of these documents for police registration every time you check into a hotel.

○ In theory there are no passport checks at land crossings from neighbouring countries, but random customs controls do occasionally still take place between Italy and Switzerland.

Air

Airports & Airlines

Italy's main intercontinental gateways are Rome's **Leonardo da Vinci airport** (☑ 06 65 9 51; www.adr.it/fiumicino) and Milan's **Malpensa airport** (☑ 02 23 23 23; www.milanomalpensa1.eu/en). Both are served by non-stop flights from around the world. Venice's **Marco Polo airport** (☑ 041 260 92 60; www.veniceairport.it; Viale Galileo Galilei 30/1, Tessera) is also served by a handful of intercontinental flights.

Land

There are plenty of options for entering Italy by train, bus or private vehicle.

Border Crossings

Aside from the coast roads linking Italy with France and Slovenia, border crossings into Italy mostly involve tunnels through the Alps (open year-round) or mountain passes (seasonally closed or requiring snow chains). The the major points of entry include:

Austria From Innsbruck to Bolzano via A22/E45 (Brenner Pass); Villach to Tarvisio via A23/E55

France From Nice to Ventimiglia via A10/E80; Modane to Turin via A32/E70 (Fréjus Tunnel); Chamonix to Courmayeur via A5/E25 (Mont Blanc Tunnel)

Slovenia From Sežana to Trieste via SS58/E70

Switzerland From Martigny to Aosta via SS27/E27 (Grand St Bernard Tunnel); Lugano to Como via A9/E35

🚗 Car & Motorcycle

o Every vehicle travelling across an international border should display a nationality plate of its country of registration.

o Always carry proof of vehicle ownership and evidence of third-party insurance. If driving an EU-registered vehicle, your home country insurance is sufficient. Ask your insurer for a European Accident Statement (EAS) form, which can simplify matters in the event of an accident.

o A European breakdown assistance policy is a good investment and can be obtained through the Automobile Club d'Italia.

o Italy's scenic roads are tailor-made for motorcycle touring, and motorcyclists swarm into the country every summer. With a motorcycle you rarely have to book ahead for ferries and can enter restricted-traffic areas in cities. Crash helmets and a motorcycle licence are compulsory.

o The US-based **Beach's Motorcycle Adventures** (www.bmca.com) offers a number of two-week tours from April to October, with destinations including the Alps, Tuscany and Umbria, Sicily and Sardinia. For longer-term auto leasing (14 days or more) or campervan and motorhome hire, check **IdeaMerge** (www.ideamerge.com).

Direct Trains to Italy from Continental Europe

FROM	TO	FREQUENCY	DURATION (HR)	COST (€)
Geneva	Milan	four daily	4	78
Geneva	Venice	one daily	7	108
Munich	Florence	one nightly	9¼	111
Munich	Rome	one nightly	12¼	145
Munich	Venice	one nightly	9	116
Paris	Milan	three daily	7	98
Paris	Turin	three daily	5½	98
Paris	Venice	one nightly	13½	120
Vienna	Milan	one nightly	14	109
Vienna	Rome	one nightly	14	99
Zurich	Milan	six daily	3¾	69

🚆 Train

Regular trains on two western lines connect Italy with France (one along the coast and the other from Turin into the French Alps). Trains from Milan head north into Switzerland and on towards the Benelux countries. Further east, two main lines head for the main cities in Central and Eastern Europe. Those crossing the Brenner Pass go to Innsbruck, Stuttgart and Munich. Those crossing at Tarvisio proceed to Vienna, Salzburg and Prague. The main international train line to Slovenia crosses near Trieste.

Depending on distances covered, rail can be highly competitive with air travel. Those travelling from neighbouring countries to northern Italy will find it is frequently more comfortable, less expensive and only marginally more time-consuming than flying.

Those travelling longer distances (say, from London, Spain, northern Germany or Eastern Europe) will doubtless find flying cheaper and quicker. Bear in mind, however, that the train is a much greener way to go – a trip by rail can contribute up to 10 times less carbon dioxide emissions per person than the same trip by air.

○ The comprehensive *European Rail Timetable* (UK£14.99), updated monthly, is available from **Thomas Cook Publishing** (www.thomascookpublishing.com).

○ Reservations on international trains to/from Italy are always advisable, and sometimes compulsory.

○ Some international services include transport for private cars.

○ Consider taking long journeys overnight, as the supplemental fare for a sleeper costs substantially less than Italian hotels.

If travelling from the UK:
○ High-velocity passenger train **Eurostar** (www.eurostar.com) travels between London and Paris, or London and Brussels. Alternatively, you can get a train ticket that includes crossing the Channel by ferry.

○ For the latest fare information on journeys to Italy, including the Eurostar, contact the **Rail Europe Travel Centre** (www.raileurope.co.uk) or **International Rail** (www.internationalrail.com).

●●● Getting Around

Italy's network of train, bus, ferry and domestic air transport allows you to reach most destinations efficiently and relatively affordably.

With your own vehicle, you'll enjoy greater freedom, but *benzina* (petrol) and *autostrada* (motorway) tolls are expensive and Italian drivers have a style all their own. For many, the stress of driving and parking in urban areas may outweigh the delights of puttering about the countryside. One solution is to take public transport between large cities and rent a car only to reach more remote rural destinations.

Climate Change & Travel

Every form of transport that relies on carbon-based fuel generates CO_2, the main cause of human-induced climate change. Modern travel is dependent on , which might use less fuel per per person than most cars but travel much greater distances. The altitude at which aircraft emit gases (including CO_2) and particles also contributes to their climate change impact. Many websites offer 'carbon calculators' that allow people to estimate the carbon emissions generated by their journey and, for those who wish to do so, to offset the impact of the greenhouse gases emitted with contributions to portfolios of climate-friendly initiatives throughout the world. Lonely Planet offsets the carbon footprint of all staff and author travel.

✈ Air

Italy enjoys an extensive network of internal flights. The privatised national airline, Alitalia, is the main domestic carrier. A useful search engine for comparing multiple carriers' fares and purchasing low-cost domestic flights is **AZfly** (www.azfly.it).

The many cut-rate airlines within Italy include the following:

Air One (☎ 89 24 44; www.flyairone.com)

AirAlps (☎ 06 22 22; www.airalps.at)

Blu-express (📞 06 9895 6666; www.blu-express.com)

Darwin Airline (📞 06 8997 0422; www.darwinairline.com)

easyJet (📞 199 201840; www.easyjet.com)

Meridiana (📞 89 29 28; www.meridiana.it)

Ryanair (📞 899 552589; www.ryanair.com)

Volotea (📞 895 8954404; www.volotea.com)

🚲 Bicycle

Cycling is very popular in Italy. The following tips will help ensure a pedal-happy trip:

◦ If bringing your own bike, you'll need to disassemble and pack it for the journey, and you may need to pay an airline surcharge.

◦ Make sure to bring tools, spare parts, a helmet, lights and a secure bike lock.

◦ Bikes are prohibited on Italian autostradas (motorways).

◦ Bikes can be wheeled onto any domestic train displaying the bicycle logo. Simply purchase a separate bicycle ticket, valid for 24 hours (€3.50). Certain international trains, listed on Trenitalia's 'In treno con la bici' page, also allow transport of assembled bicycles for €12, paid on board. Bikes dismantled and stored in a bag can be taken for free, even on night trains.

◦ Most ferries also allow free bicycle passage.

◦ In the UK, **Cyclists' Touring Club** (CTC; www.ctc.org.uk) can help you plan

your tour or organise a guided tour. Membership costs £41 for adults, £25 for seniors and £16 for under-18s.

◦ Bikes are available for hire in most Italian towns. City bikes start at €10/50 per day/week; mountain bikes a bit more. Some municipalities, including Rimini and Ravenna, offer free bikes for visitors, as do a growing number of Italian hotels.

Boat

Craft *Navi* (large ferries) service Sicily and Sardinia, while *traghetti* (smaller ferries) and *aliscafi* (hydrofoils) service the smaller islands. Most ferries carry vehicles; hydrofoils do not.

Routes Main embarkation points for Sicily and Sardinia are Genoa, Livorno, Civitavecchia and Naples. Ferries for Sicily also leave from Villa San Giovanni and Reggio Calabria. Main arrival points in Sardinia are Cagliari, Arbatax, Olbia and Porto Torres; in Sicily they're Palermo, Catania, Trapani and Messina.

Timetables and tickets Comprehensive website **TraghettiOnline** (www.traghettionline.com) includes links to multiple Italian ferry companies, allowing you to compare prices and buy tickets.

Overnight ferries Travellers can book a two- to four-person cabin or a *poltrona*, which is an airline-type armchair. Deck class (which

allows you to sit/sleep in lounge areas or on deck) is available only on some ferries.

Bus

Routes Everything from meandering local routes to fast, reliable InterCity connections provided by numerous bus companies.

Timetables and tickets Available on bus company websites and from local tourist offices. Tickets are generally competitively priced with the train and often the only way to get to smaller towns. In larger cities most of the InterCity bus companies have ticket offices or sell tickets through agencies. In villages and even some good-sized towns, tickets are sold in bars or on the bus.

Advance booking Generally not required, but advisable for overnight or long-haul trips in high season.

🚗 Car & Motorcycle

Italy's extensive network of roads span numerous categories. The main ones include:

Autostradas An extensive, privatised network of motorways, represented on road signs by a white 'A' followed by a number on a green background. The main north–south link is the Autostrada del Sole (the 'Motorway of the Sun'), which extends from Milan to Reggio di Calabria (called the A1 from Milan to Rome, the A2 from Rome to Naples, and the A3 from Naples to Reggio di Calabria). There are tolls on most motorways, payable by cash or credit card as you exit.

Strade statali State highways are represented on maps by 'S' or 'SS'. Vary from toll-free, four-lane highways to two-lane main roads. The latter can be slow, especially in mountainous regions.

Strade regionali Regional highways connecting small villages. Coded 'SR' or 'R'.

Strade provinciali Provincial highways. Coded 'SP' or 'P'.

Strade locali Often not even paved or mapped.

For information about distances, driving times and fuel costs, see http://en.mappy.com. Information, on traffic conditions and toll costs is available at www.autostrade.it.

Automobile Associations

The **Automobile Club d'Italia** (ACI; ☏ from non-Italian phone account 800 116800, roadside assistance 803116; www.aci.it) is a driver's best resource in Italy. Foreigners do not have to join to get 24-hour roadside emergency service but instead pay a per-incident fee.

Driving Licences

All EU member states' driving licences are fully recognised throughout Europe. In practice, many non-EU licences (such as Australian, Canadian, New Zealand and US) are accepted by car-hire outfits in Italy. Travellers from other countries should obtain an International Driving Permit (IDP) through their national automobile association.

Fuel & Spare Parts

Italy's petrol prices are among the highest in Europe and vary from one service station (*benzinaio, stazione di servizio*) to another. At the time of writing, lead-free gasoline (*senza piombo; 95 octane*) was averaging €1.79 per litre, with diesel (*gasolio*) costing €1.69 per litre.

Spare parts are available at many garages or via the 24-hour ACI motorist assistance number, ☏ 803116 (or ☏ 800 116800 if calling with a non-Italian mobile phone account).

Hire

Pre-booking via the internet often costs less than hiring a car in Italy. Online booking agency **Rentalcars.com** (www.rentalcars.com) compares the rates of numerous car-rental companies.

ROAD DISTANCES (KM)

Note
Distances between Palermo and mainland towns do not take into account the ferry from Reggio di Calabria to Messina. Add an extra hour to your journey time to allow for this crossing

	Bari	Bologna	Florence	Genoa	Milan	Naples	Palermo	Perugia	Reggio di Calabria	Rome	Siena	Trento	Trieste	Turin	Venice
Bologna	681														
Florence	784	106													
Genoa	996	285	268												
Milan	899	218	324	156											
Naples	322	640	534	758	858										
Palermo	734	1415	1345	1569	1633	811									
Perugia	612	270	164	432	488	408	1219								
Reggio di Calabria	490	1171	1101	1325	1389	567	272	816							
Rome	482	408	302	526	626	232	1043	170	664						
Siena	714	176	70	296	394	464	1275	103	867	232					
Trento	892	233	339	341	218	874	1626	459	1222	641	375				
Trieste	995	308	414	336	420	948	1689	543	1445	715	484	279			
Turin	1019	338	442	174	139	932	1743	545	1307	702	460	349	551		
Venice	806	269	265	387	284	899	799	394	1296	567	335	167	165	415	
Verona	808	141	247	282	164	781	1534	377	1139	549	293	97	250	295	120

○ Renters must generally be aged 25 or over.

○ Consider hiring a small car, which will reduce your fuel expenses and help you negotiate narrow city lanes and tight parking spaces.

○ Check with your credit-card company to see if it offers a Collision Damage Waiver, which covers you for additional damage if you use that card to pay for the car.

○ Agencies throughout Italy rent motorbikes, ranging from small Vespas to larger touring bikes. Prices start at around €35/150 per day/week for a 50cc scooter, or upwards of €80/400 per day/week for a 650cc motorcycle.

Car-rental agencies include:

Auto Europe (www.autoeurope.com)

Avis (www.avis.com)

Budget (☏ 800 472 33 25; www.budget.com)

Europcar (www.europcar.com)

Hertz (www.hertz.it)

Holiday Cars (www.holidaycars.com)

Italy by Car (☏ 334 6481920; www.italybycar.it)

Maggiore (☏ 199 151120; www.maggiore.it)

Road Rules

○ Cars drive on the right side of the road and overtake on the left. Unless otherwise indicated, you must always give way to cars entering an intersection from a road on your right.

○ Seatbelt use (front and rear) is required by law; violators are subject to an on-the-spot fine.

Helmets are required on all two-wheeled transport.

○ Headlights are compulsory day and night for all vehicles on the autostradas, and advisable for motorcycles even on smaller roads.

○ In the event of a breakdown, a warning triangle is compulsory, as is use of an approved yellow or orange safety vest if you leave your vehicle. Recommended accessories include a first-aid kit, spare-bulb kit and fire extinguisher.

○ No licence is required to ride a scooter under 50cc but you must be aged 14 or over and you can't carry passengers or ride on an autostrada. To ride a motorcycle or scooter up to 125cc, you must be aged 16 or over and have a licence (a car licence will do). For motorcycles over 125cc you need a motorcycle licence. Do not venture onto the autostrada with a bike of less than 150cc.

○ Motorbikes can enter most restricted traffic areas in Italian cities, and traffic police generally turn a blind eye to motorcycles or scooters parked on footpaths.

○ Italy's blood-alcohol limit is 0.05%, and random breath tests occur. If you're in an accident while under the influence the penalties are severe.

○ Speeding fines follow EU standards and are proportionate with the number of kilometres that you are caught driving over the speed limit, reaching up to €3119 with a possible six- to 12-month suspension of your driving licence.

Speed limits are as follows:

Autostradas 130km/h to 150km/h

Other main highways 110km/h

Minor, non-urban roads 90km/h

Built-up areas 50km/h

Mopeds The speed limit is always 40km/h

Local Transport

Major cities all have good transport systems, including bus and underground-train networks. In Venice, the main public transport option is *vaporetti* (small ferries).

Bus & Metro

○ Extensive *metropolitane* (metros) exist in Rome, Milan, Naples and Turin, with smaller metros in Genoa and Catania. The space-age *Minimetrò* in Perugia connects the train station with the city centre.

○ Cities and towns of any size have an efficient *urbano* (urban) and *extraurbano* (suburban) bus system. Services are generally limited on Sundays and holidays.

○ Purchase bus and metro tickets before boarding and validate them once on board. Passengers with unvalidated tickets are subject to a fine (between €50 and €75 in most cities). Buy tickets from *tabaccaio* (tobacconist's shops), newsstands, ticket booths or dispensing machines at bus stations and in metro stations. Tickets usually cost around €1.30 to €1.80. Most cities offer good-value 24-hour or daily tourist tickets.

Taxi

∘ You can catch a taxi at the ranks outside most train and bus stations, or simply telephone for a radio taxi. Radio taxi meters start running from when you've called rather than when you're picked up.

∘ Charges vary somewhat from one region to another. Most short city journeys cost between €10 and €15. Generally, no more than four people are allowed in one taxi.

🚆 Train

Italian trains are comfortable, convenient and relatively cheap compared with other European countries. **Trenitalia** (📞199 303060; www.trenitalia.com) is the partially privatised state train system that runs most services. Its competitor **Italo** (📞06 07 08; www.italotreno.it) runs high-velocity trains on two lines between Turin and Salerno, and between Venice and Naples.

Train tickets must be validated in the yellow machines (usually found at the head of platforms) just before boarding. Failure to do so can result in fines.

Italy operates several types of trains:

Regionale/interregionale Slow and cheap, stopping at all or most stations.

InterCity (IC) Faster services operating between major cities. Their international counterparts are called Eurocity (EC).

Alta Velocità (AV) State-of-the-art, high-velocity trains, including Frecciarossa, Frecciargento, Frecciabianca and Italo trains. with speeds of up to 300km/hr and connections to the major cities. More expensive than InterCity express trains, but journey times are cut by almost half.

Classes & Costs

Prices vary according to the class of service, time of travel and how far in advance you book. Most Italian trains have 1st- and 2nd-class seating; a 1st-class ticket typically costs from a third to half more than 2nd-class.

Travel on Trenitalia's InterCity and Alta Velocità (Frecciarossa, Frecciargento, Frecciabianca) trains means paying a supplement, included in the ticket price, determined by the distance you are travelling. If you have a standard ticket for a slower train and end up hopping on an IC train, you'll have to pay the difference on board. (You can only board an Alta Velocità train if you have a

booking, so the problem does not arise in those cases.)

Reservations

∘ Reservations are obligatory on AV trains. On other services they're not and, outside of peak holiday periods, you should be fine without them.

∘ Reservations can be made on the Trenitalia and Italo websites, at train station counters and self-service ticketing machines, or through travel agents.

∘ Both Trenitalia and Italo offer a variety of advance purchase discounts. Basically, the earlier you book, the greater the saving. Discounted tickets are limited, and refunds and changes are highly restricted. For all ticket options and prices, see the Trenitalia and Italo websites.

Train Passes

Trenitalia offers various discount passes, including the Carta Verde for youth and Carta d'Argento for seniors, but these are mainly useful for residents or long-term visitors, as they only pay for themselves with regular use over an extended period.

More interesting for short-term visitors are Eurail and InterRail passes.

Trains: High-Velocity (AV) vs InterCity (IC)

FROM	TO	AV DURATION (HR)	PRICE (€)	IC DURATION (HR)	PRICE (€)
Turin	Naples	5½	105	9¾	70.50
Milan	Rome	3¼	86	6¾	55.50
Venice	Florence	2	45	3	27
Rome	Naples	1¼	43	2¼	24.50
Florence	Bologna	37min	24	1	11.50

Eurail & Interrail Passes

Generally speaking, you'll need to cover a lot of ground to make a rail pass worthwhile. Before buying, consider where you intend to travel and compare the price of a rail pass to the cost of individual tickets online at **Trenitalia** (www. trenitalia.com).

INTERRAIL

InterRail (www.interrailnet.com) passes, available online and at most major stations and student-travel outlets, are for people who have been a resident in Europe for more than six months. A Global Pass encompassing 30 countries comes in five versions, ranging from five days' travel within a 10-day period to a full month's unlimited travel. There are four age brackets: child (4 to 11), youth (12 to 25), adult (26 to 59) and senior (60 plus), with different prices for 1st and 2nd class. The InterRail one-country pass for Italy can be used for three, four, six or eight days in one month and does not offer senior discounts. See the website for full price details. Cardholders get discounts on travel in the country where they purchase the ticket.

EURAIL

Eurail (www.eurail.com) passes, available for non-European residents, are good for travel in 24 European countries (not including the UK). They can be purchased online or from travel agencies outside of Europe. The original Eurail pass, now known as the **Global Pass**, is valid for a continuous period of 10 days, 15 days, 21 days, one, two or three months. Youth under 26 are eligible for a 2nd-class pass; all others must buy the more expensive 1st-class pass (offered at half-price for children aged between four and 11). Eurail offers several alternatives to the traditional Global Pass:

Select Pass This allows five to 15 days of travel within a two-month period in three to five bordering countries of your choice.

Regional Pass This two-country (France/Italy, Spain/Italy or Greece/Italy) pass allows four to 10 days of travel within a two-month period.

One Country Pass Allows three to 10 days of travel in Italy within a two-month period.

a b c

Language

Italian pronunciation isn't difficult as most sounds are also found in English. The pronunciation of some consonants depends on which vowel follows, but if you read our pronunciation guides below as if they were English, you'll be understood just fine. Just remember to pronounce double consonants as a longer, more forceful sound than single ones. The stressed syllables in words are in italics in our pronunciation guides.

To enhance your trip with a phrasebook, visit **lonelyplanet.com**. Lonely Planet iPhone phrasebooks are available through the Apple App store.

BASICS

Hello.
Buongiorno./Ciao. (pol/inf) bwon·*jor*·no/chow
How are you?
Come sta? *ko*·me sta
I'm fine, thanks.
Bene, grazie. *be*·ne *gra*·tsye
Excuse me.
Mi scusi. mee *skoo*·zee
Yes./No.
Sì./No. see/no
Please. (when asking)
Per favore. per fa·*vo*·re
Thank you.
Grazie. *gra*·tsye
Goodbye.
Arrivederci./Ciao. (pol/inf) a·ree·ve·*der*·chee/chow
Do you speak English?
Parla inglese? *par*·la een·*gle*·ze
I don't understand.
Non capisco. non ka·*pee*·sko
How much is this?
Quanto costa? *kwan*·to *ko*·sta

ACCOMMODATION

I'd like to book a room.
Vorrei prenotare vo·*ray* pre·no·*ta*·re
una camera. *oo*·na *ka*·me·ra
How much is it per night?
Quanto costa per *kwan*·to *kos*·ta per
una notte? *oo*·na *no*·te

EATING & DRINKING

I'd like ..., please.
Vorrei ..., per favore. vo·*ray* ... per fa·*vo*·re
What would you recommend?
Cosa mi consiglia? *ko*·za mee kon·*see*·lya
That was delicious!
Era squisito! *e*·ra skwee·*zee*·to
Bring the bill/check, please.
Mi porta il conto, mee *por*·ta eel *kon*·to
per favore. per fa·*vo*·re

I'm allergic (to peanuts).
Sono allergico/a *so*·no a·*ler*·jee·ko/a
(alle arachidi). (m/f) (*a*·le a·*ra*·kee·dee)
I don't eat ...
Non mangio ... non *man*·jo ...
  fish *pesce* *pe*·she
  meat *carne* *kar*·ne
  poultry *pollame* po·*la*·me

EMERGENCIES

I'm ill.
Mi sento male. mee *sen*·to *ma*·le
Help!
Aiuto! a·*yoo*·to
Call a doctor!
Chiami un medico! *kya*·mee oon *me*·dee·ko
Call the police!
Chiami la polizia! *kya*·mee la po·lee·*tsee*·a

DIRECTIONS

I'm looking for (a/the) ...
Cerco ... *cher*·ko ...
  bank
  la banca la *ban*·ka
  ... embassy
  la ambasciata de ... la am·ba·*sha*·ta de ...
  market
  il mercato eel mer·*ka*·to
  museum
  il museo eel moo·*ze*·o
  restaurant
  un ristorante oon rees·to·*ran*·te
  toilet
  un gabinetto oon ga·bee·*ne*·to
  tourist office
  l'ufficio del turismo loo·*fee*·cho del too·*reez*·mo

Behind the Scenes

Our Readers

Many thanks to the travellers who used the last edition and wrote to us with helpful hints, useful advice and interesting anecdotes:

Andrea Mancini, Andrew Volin, Carol Buchman, Cheryl Dunne, Gustavo Michelli, Ken Ohlsen, Kim Dorin, Linda Werner, Nick Radloff, Paul Guz, Paul Seaver, Rob McDonald

Author Thanks
Abigail Blasi

A huge thank you to Joe Bindloss and Helena Smith, for giving me the chance to write about my favourite country once again. Thanks to all the Lonely Planet Italy guide authors – their work is truly fantastic – and all the Lonely Planet in-house staff, especially Angela Tinson. *Molto grazie* to Luca, Gabriel, Jack and Valentina, and to *la famiglia Blasi* for all their kindness and insight into Italian life.

Acknowledgments

Climate map data adapted from Peel MC, Finlayson BL & McMahon TA (2007) 'Updated World Map of the Köppen-Geiger Climate Classification', *Hydrology and Earth System Sciences*, 11, 163344.

Illustrations pp64-5, pp176-7, pp226-7, pp304-5 by Javier Martinez Zarracina.

Cover photographs: Front: Duomo, Florence, Medioimages/Photodisc; Back: Burano, the Veneto, © Jose Fuste Raga/Corbis.

This Book

This 3rd edition of Lonely Planet's *Discover Italy* guidebook was written and researched by Abigail Blasi, Cristian Bonetto, Kerry Christiani, Gregor Clark, Duncan Garwood, Paula Hardy, Virginia Maxwell, Brendan Sainsbury, Helena Smith and Donna Wheeler. The previous edition was coordinated by Alison Bing. This guidebook was commissioned in Lonely Planet's London office, and produced by the following:

Commissioning Editors Joseph Bindloss, Helena Smith

Coordinating Editors Samantha Forge, Susan Paterson

Book Designer Jessica Rose

Senior Cartographer Valentina Kremenchutskaya

Managing Editors Annelies Mertens, Angela Tinson

Senior Editor Catherine Naghten

Assisting Editors Alison Barber, Gabrielle Innes

Cover Research Naomi Parker

Language Content Branislava Vladisavljevic

Thanks to Lauren Egan, Ryan Evans, Larissa Frost, Genesys India, Jouve India, Kate Mathews, Virginia Moreno, Chad Parkhill, Mazzy Prinsep, Wibowo Rusli, Gerard Walker

SEND US YOUR FEEDBACK

Index

000 Map pages

000 Map pages

INDEX P-T

How to Use This Book

These symbols give you the vital information for each listing:

☎	Telephone Numbers	🛜	Wi-Fi Access	🚌	Bus	
⊙	Opening Hours	🏊	Swimming Pool	⛴	Ferry	
P	Parking	🥗	Vegetarian Selection	Ⓜ	Metro	
⊖	Nonsmoking	📖	English-Language Menu	Ⓢ	Subway	
✳	Air-Conditioning	👪	Family-Friendly	⊖	London Tube	
@	Internet Access	🐾	Pet-Friendly	🚋	Tram	

Look out for these icons:

FREE	No payment required
🍃	A green or sustainable option

Our authors have nominated these places as demonstrating a strong commitment to sustainability – for example by supporting local communities and producers, operating in an environmentally friendly way, or supporting conservation projects.

All reviews are ordered in our authors' preference, starting with their most preferred option. Additionally:

Sights are arranged in the geographic order that we suggest you visit them, and within this order, by author preference.

Eating and Sleeping reviews are ordered by price range (budget, mid-range, top end) and within these ranges, by author preference.

Map Legend

Sights
- 🏖 Beach
- 🛕 Buddhist
- 🏰 Castle
- ✝ Christian
- 🕉 Hindu
- ☪ Islamic
- ✡ Jewish
- ❗ Monument
- 🏛 Museum/Gallery
- 🏚 Ruin
- 🍷 Winery/Vineyard
- 🐘 Zoo
- ◉ Other Sight

Activities, Courses & Tours
- 🤿 Diving/Snorkelling
- 🛶 Canoeing/Kayaking
- ⛷ Skiing
- 🏄 Surfing
- 🏊 Swimming/Pool
- 🚶 Walking
- 🏄 Windsurfing
- ➕ Other Activity/Course/Tour

Sleeping
- 🛏 Sleeping
- ⛺ Camping

Eating
- 🍴 Eating

Drinking
- ☕ Drinking
- ☕ Cafe

Entertainment
- 🎭 Entertainment

Shopping
- 🛍 Shopping

Information
- ✉ Post Office
- ❶ Tourist Information

Transport
- ✈ Airport
- ⊗ Border Crossing
- 🚌 Bus
- ➕🚠➕ Cable Car/Funicular
- 🚲 Cycling
- ⛴ Ferry
- Ⓜ Monorail
- P Parking
- Ⓢ S-Bahn
- 🚕 Taxi
- ➕🚆➕ Train/Railway
- 🚋 Tram
- ⊖ Tube Station
- Ⓤ U-Bahn
- Ⓜ Underground Train Station
- • Other Transport

Routes
- Tollway
- Freeway
- Primary
- Secondary
- Tertiary
- Lane
- Unsealed Road
- Plaza/Mall
- Steps
-)= = Tunnel
- Pedestrian Overpass
- Walking Tour
- Walking Tour Detour
- Path

Boundaries
- International
- State/Province
- Disputed
- Regional/Suburb
- Marine Park
- Cliff
- Wall

Population
- ✪ Capital (National)
- ◉ Capital (State/Province)
- ● City/Large Town
- ● Town/Village

Geographic
- ❁ Hut/Shelter
- 🚩 Lighthouse
- 👁 Lookout
- ▲ Mountain/Volcano
- 🌴 Oasis
- ❶ Park
-)(Pass
- 🏞 Picnic Area
- 💧 Waterfall

Hydrography
- River/Creek
- Intermittent River
- Swamp/Mangrove
- Reef
- Canal
- Water
- Dry/Salt/Intermittent Lake
- Glacier

Areas
- Beach/Desert
- Cemetery (Christian)
- Cemetery (Other)
- Park/Forest
- Sportsground
- Sight (Building)
- Top Sight (Building)

Our Story

A beat-up old car, a few dollars in the pocket and a sense of adventure. In 1972 that's all Tony and Maureen Wheeler needed for the trip of a lifetime – across Europe and Asia overland to Australia. It took several months, and at the end – broke but inspired – they sat at their kitchen table writing and stapling together their first travel guide, *Across Asia on the Cheap*. Within a week they'd sold 1500 copies. Lonely Planet was born.

Today, Lonely Planet has offices in Melbourne, London and Oakland, with more than 600 staff and writers. We share Tony's belief that 'a great guidebook should do three things: inform, educate and amuse'.

Our Writers

ABIGAIL BLASI

Coordinating Author Abigail moved to Rome in 2003 and lived there for three years; she married an Italian and her first son was born in Rome. Nowadays the *famiglia* divide their time between Rome, Puglia and London. She has worked on four editions of Lonely Planet's *Rome* and *Italy* guides, the latest *Discover Rome* guide, the *Best of Rome* pocket guide, and cowrote the first edition of *Puglia & Basilicata*. She also regularly writes on Italy for various publications, including *Lonely Planet Magazine*, *Wanderlust* and i-escape.com.

CRISTIAN BONETTO

Naples, Pompeii & the Amalfi Coast An ex-writer of farce and TV drama, it's not surprising that Cristian clicks with Italy. Born to a Venetian father and a Piedmontese mother, the Italo-Australian scribe was proudly bred the Italian way, and has both lived and holidayed in the *bel paese* (beautiful country). His musings on the motherland have appeared in newspapers, magazines and websites across the world. When he's not in Italy hunting down perfect coffee or pastries, you'll find him scouring the rest of the globe for insight and delight. Cristian's Lonely Planet titles to date also include *New York City*, *Denmark*, *Scandinavia* and *Singapore*. You can follow his adventures on Twitter @CristianBonetto.

KERRY CHRISTIANI

Umbria Kerry's relationship with Italia began one hazy, post-graduation summer when she set off for a grand tour in a 1960s bubble caravan. Memorable moments researching this edition include spring coastal walks along Sardinia's cliff-flanked Golfo di Orosei, hill-town slow-touring in Umbria and getting stuck in a rare snow storm in Urbino. An award-winning travel writer, Kerry has authored some 20 guidebooks, including Lonely Planet's *Sardinia*, and contributes to publications including bbc.com/travel and *Lonely Planet Traveller*. She tweets @kerrychristiani and lists her latest work at www.kerrychristiani.com.

GREGOR CLARK

Sicily Gregor caught the Italy bug at age 14 while living in Florence with his professor dad, who took him to see every fresco, mosaic and museum within a 1000km radius. He's lived in Le Marche, huffed and puffed across the Dolomites, and fallen head-over-heels for Sicily while researching Lonely Planet's *Cycling Italy* and the last three editions of the *Italy* guide. A lifelong polyglot with a romance languages degree, his peak experience this trip was celebrating his birthday atop an erupting Stromboli.

More Writers

Published by Lonely Planet Publications Pty Ltd
ABN 36 005 607 983
3rd edition – Apr 14
ISBN 978 1 74220 747 6
© Lonely Planet 2014   Photographs © as indicated 2014
10 9 8 7 6 5 4 3
Printed in China

DUNCAN GARWOOD

Rome & the Vatican Born in the UK, Duncan currently lives in the Castelli Romani hills just outside Rome. He first fell for the Italian capital in 1996 after arriving at the crack of dawn on an overnight train and walking the almost-deserted streets in beautiful morning sunlight. Since then he has worked on the past five *Rome* guides and a whole host of Lonely Planet Italy titles. He has also written on Italy for newspapers and magazines.

PAULA HARDY

Milan & the Lakes, Venice & the Veneto From the slopes of Valpolicella to the shores of Lago di Garda and the spritz-fuelled bars of Padua, Venice and Milan, Paula has been contributing to Lonely Planet's Italian guides for over 10 years, including guides to Milan, the Italian Lakes, Venice & the Veneto, Puglia, Sicily and Sardinia. When she's not scooting around the *bel paese*, she writes for a variety of travel publications and websites. You can find her tweeting from lakes, islands and mountains @paula6hardy.

VIRGINIA MAXWELL

Florence & Tuscany Based in Australia, Virginia spends part of every year in Italy indulging her passions for history, art, architecture, food and wine. She is the coordinating author of Lonely Planet's *Florence & Tuscany* and *Florence Encounter*, and has covered both Tuscany and other parts of the country for the *Western Europe* guide and for previous editions of this title. Though reticent to nominate her favourite Italian destinations (arguing that they're all wonderful), she usually nominates Florence and Rome if pressed.

BRENDAN SAINSBURY

Liguria, Piedmont & the Italian Riviera, Bologna Born and bred in Hampshire, England, but now resident in Vancouver, Canada, Brendan first tackled Italy with a famed Inter-rail pass in the 1980s. He has been back innumerable times since as a travel guide, cyclist and – very occasionally – a tourist. This is his fourth Italy-related guidebook (he also wrote Lonely Planet's *Hiking in Italy*), though he has covered numerous other countries for Lonely Planet, including Angola, Cuba and the USA. His favourite Italian city is Bologna.

HELENA SMITH

Southern Italy Helena has been visiting Italy since she was five. At that time chocolate spread on toast was the main draw – now she goes back for the warmth, the art and the atmosphere. Researching this edition took her from mountain villages in Abruzzo to baroque Lecce and the ancient cave city of Matera.

DONNA WHEELER

The Dolomites Italy's northeastern border regions are Donna's dream assignment: complex histories, mountains, the sea, plus all that spectacular white wine and Viennese cake. Donna has travelled throughout Italy for two decades and lived in Turin's Quadrilatero Romano until 2011. She has also written for Lonely Planet on Milan, southern France, Tunisia and Algeria. An erstwhile editor and producer, she now writes about art, architecture and food for several publications and is a creative consultant specialising in the travel experience.